**Crossing Borders, Making Connections**

# Interdisciplinary Linguistics

Editor
Allison Burkette

**Volume 1**

# Crossing Borders, Making Connections

---

Interdisciplinarity in Linguistics

Edited by
Allison Burkette
Tamara Warhol

ISBN 978-1-5015-2104-1
e-ISBN (PDF) 978-1-5015-1437-1
e-ISBN (EPUB) 978-1-5015-1439-5
ISSN 2626-9228

**Library of Congress Control Number: 2020947135**

**Bibliographic information published by the Deutsche Nationalbibliothek**
The Deutsche Nationalbibliothek lists this publication in the Deutsche Nationalbibliografie;
detailed bibliographic data are available on the Internet at http://dnb.dnb.de.

© 2022 Walter de Gruyter, Inc., Boston/Berlin
This volume is text- and page-identical with the hardback published in 2021.
Cover: Steve Johnson on Unsplash
Typesetting: Integra Software Services Pvt. Ltd.
Printing and binding: CPI books, GmbH, Leck

www.degruyter.com

# Acknowledgments

Undertaking an edited volume is always an adventure, and we have several people to thank for their help and support through this process. First and foremost, we would like to thank the chapter authors for responding so positively to our requests for contributions. We are fortunate to have been able to solicit chapters both from linguists and from scholars in related disciplines. Special thanks go to Natalie Fecher from deGruyter for her help and support with this volume and for her enthusiasm for this new series. Finally, we would like to thank Lamont Antieau for his careful copyediting work.

I would like to add my particular thanks to friends, family, and colleagues whose support remains invaluable: my parents Nancy and Wayne Burkette, my children Anne, Kate and Noah, Thomas Whitley, Susan Tamasi, Betsy Barry, Lamont Antieau, and my Kentucky colleagues (and friends) Jennifer Cramer, Kevin McGowan, and Mark Lauersdorf. –AB

Many thanks to my family and friends, whose support is invaluable: my parents, Michael and Kathryn Warhol, my sister, Larisa, Corina Petrescu, Vivian Ibrahim, Brooke White, Lance Herrington, and my colleagues in the linguistics program at the University of Mississippi. –TW

# Contents

**Acknowledgments** —— V

Allison Burkette
**Chapter 1**
**Introduction: Why interdisciplinarity?** —— 1

Becky Childs
**Chapter 2**
**The value of interdisciplinary and transdisciplinary linguistic research** —— 7

Stephany Brett Dunstan, Sonja Ardoin
**Chapter 3**
**Faculty and student affairs partnerships: Creating inclusive campus environments for students of diverse linguistic backgrounds** —— 23

Jessica A. Grieser
**Chapter 4**
**Critical race theory and the new sociolinguistics** —— 41

Rusty Barrett
**Chapter 5**
**You don't even try to understand!: Interdisciplinarity in language and gender studies** —— 59

Arran Stibbe
**Chapter 6**
**Ecolinguistics as a transdisciplinary movement and a way of life** —— 71

Tamara Warhol
**Chapter 7**
**Ethnography in interdisciplinary research in linguistics** —— 89

Allison Burkette
**Chapter 8**
**Connections and interdisciplinarity: Linguistic Atlas Project data from an assemblage perspective —— 99**

Alastair Pennycook
**Chapter 9**
**Reassembling linguistics: Semiotic and epistemic assemblages —— 111**

Paul V. Kroskrity
**Chapter 10**
**Language ideological assemblages within linguistic anthropology —— 129**

Amy J. Hirshman
**Chapter 11**
**A case of archeological classification —— 143**

Jillian R. Cavanaugh, Shalini Shankar
**Chapter 12**
**Language and materiality in global capitalism —— 169**

Carl Lounsbury
**Chapter 13**
**The language of building in the southern American colonies —— 191**

Mark Richard Lauersdorf
**Chapter 14**
**Historical sociolinguistics and the necessity of interdisciplinary collaboration —— 207**

Jiyoon Lee, Matthew Schreibeis
**Chapter 15**
**Comprehensive review of the effect of using music in second language learning —— 231**

K. Jason Coker
**Chapter 16**
**Trashing the Bible —— 247**

Jason M. Thomas
**Chapter 17**
**Towards a post-structuralist economics —— 259**

Heidi E. Hamilton
**Chapter 18**
**Life as a linguist among clinicians: Learnings from interdisciplinary collaborations on language and health —— 275**

**Index —— 299**

Allison Burkette
# Chapter 1
# Introduction: Why interdisciplinarity?

## 1 Introduction

Cross-disciplinary traffic between sister social sciences is not new: *social network theory* originated in sociology (Bott 1971), *practice theory* in education (Lave and Wenger 1991), and *performativity* in philosophy (Butler 1990). Each discipline has its own conceptual flavor; for instance, the concept of the *community of practice* in archaeology is a more education-focused approach, perhaps adhering closer to Lave and Wenger (1991) and Wenger (1998) than sociolinguists do. For example, archaeologists Cordell and Habicht-Mauche (2012) emphasize the passing on of pottery-making techniques from one generation to the next, focusing on material practices and the associated cultural performances. This focus is subtly different from that of Eckert and McConnell-Ginet (2003), who talk about participants in a community of practice

> develop[ing] ways of doing things together. They develop activities and ways of engaging in those activities, they develop common knowledge and beliefs, ways of relating to each other, ways of talking – in short, practices [. . .] it is at the level of the community of practice that ways of speaking are the most closely coordinated. (p. 57)

While archaeologists focus on the physical practices of pottery-making, linguists Eckert and McConnell-Ginet (understandably) focus on language-related practices that (re)create, negotiate, and maintain a group identity. The idea of the community of practice is so valuable precisely because it can be focused and then refocused within another discipline with success. There are many more bridges between linguistics, sociolinguistics, applied linguistics, and our "familial" disciplines, which include (but are not limited to) linguistic anthropology, anthropology, archaeology, sociology, literary studies, economics, and history.

One such bridge is the use and contemplation of metaphor, discussed briefly below as a point of intersection between multiple fields, provided to set the tone for the description that follows of this volume's chapters.

---

**Allison Burkette,** University of Kentucky, allison.burkette@uky.edu

https://doi.org/10.1515/9781501514371-001

# 2 A metaphorical crossing

Linguists George Lakoff and Mark Johnson published *Metaphors We Live By* in 1980, and since then, their work has served as a landmark in the study of language and culture. The main idea of Lakoff and Johnson's book is that metaphors transcend the literary, and that human cognition depends on the ability to see one thing in terms of another. Though now considered almost gospel in linguistics, Lakoff and Johnson's suggestion that "metaphor is pervasive in everyday life, not just in language but in thought and action" was groundbreaking when it was published (1980: 3). That our everyday, non-literary language use is replete with metaphor evidences the internal mechanisms with which we understand the world around us. We deal with difficult and/or abstract concepts by mapping onto them the ideas and characteristics from unrelated, often more concrete, areas that are easier to conceptualize (e.g. TIME IS MONEY or LOVE IS A JOURNEY). These conceptual systems are pervasive and layered such that there are often layers of metaphor hidden within most of our everyday statements. Since Lakoff and Johnson (1980), the study of metaphor has blossomed in linguistics, to include many productive discussions of metaphor and embodiment Gibbs (1999), metaphor as a conceptual blend Fauconnier and Turner (2002), and so on.

A little over two decades after the publication of *Metaphors We Live By*, archaeologist Christopher Tilley built on linguists' ideas in his essay "Metaphor, materiality and interpretation," describing metaphor as "a primary way in which persons and cultures make sense of the world. When we link things metaphorically we recognize similarity in difference, we think one thing in terms of the attributes of another" (2002: 23). Tilley's definition is similar to that of Lakoff and Johnson, and, like the linguists that preceded him, he also explains metaphor as the product of our "embodied experience" of the world (2002: 24). Interestingly, Tilley points out that language itself is often used as a metaphor in archaeology and material culture studies; being able to talk about what artifacts *mean* or what they *symbolize* is an important part of the study of material culture. In these disciplines, the language metaphor allows one to discuss "things as communicating meaning like a language, silent 'grammars' of artefact forms such as sequences of designs on calabashes, pots, or bark cloth" (2002: 23). While this aspect of the language metaphor is part of the larger "textual turn" that takes place in archaeology and material culture studies in the 1980s (see Hodder 1982; Shanks and Tilley 1987; and then Buchli 2000, for a dissenting view), the view that objects can themselves serve as metaphors widens the scope of conceptual metaphor considerably past language.

Tilley (2002) suggests that metaphor is not limited to language or thought; material artifacts are also sites where one thing can be mapped onto another. He explains that, when people create artifacts, they make "both themselves and their social relations" (2002: 25). Physical objects are thus "regarded as texts, structured sign systems whose relationships with each other and the social world is to be decoded" (p. 23). Tilley explains that language and things can serve similar social roles, and yes, that objects can serve as physical metaphors and as such have "communicative agency" (p. 25). Tilley uses the example of the canoes of the Wala Islanders, which he discusses at length in his 1999 work *Metaphor and Material Culture*.[1] These canoes function as material metaphors, physical articulations of social relationships, that play a role in the "creation of social identities and intertwined male and female essences" (1999: 52).

That an object can reflect, capture, express, or shape thought in much the same way as language leads me to ask: How different is language from material culture? I ask this question knowing that Tilley has argued that that "words and things, discourses and material practices, are fundamentally different" (2002: 23), and this, this is the conversation I want to have. I want to talk about language and materiality, about how the concepts of agency and discursivity run through both disciplines – we make objects and objects also make us (e.g. Miller 2005) just like we use language to enact an identity and then language creates that identity for us. I want to talk about intentionality and authenticity, the reality of "subject" and "object", about fetish and stereotype. This kind of discussion has been taking place in linguistic anthropology for some time (see *Language and Communication*, vol. 23, issues 3–4; see also Chapter 10 this volume), but we can talk more, incorporate more, and learn more if cross-disciplinary discussions occurred with greater regularity and if (truly) interdisciplinary research in linguistics became the norm instead of the exception.

## 3 In this volume

The impetus for a book on Interdisciplinary Linguistics was to present a collection of chapters that reflect, encourage, and inspire cutting-edge linguistic research that falls outside the traditional bounds of "sociolinguistics" or "applied linguistics." My co-editor, Tamara Warhol, and I feel that an interdisciplinary approach to the study of language has the potential to do more than traditional

---

[1] A canoe seems a particularly apt carrier of metaphorical meaning, as it is a physical manifestation of a corollary of Lakoff and Johnson's example: LINGUISTIC EXPRESSIONS ARE CONTAINERS FOR MEANINGS, which entails that MEANINGS ARE OBJECTS, which is how you can "give" someone an idea or "get ideas across" to someone else (or have a canoe "carry metaphorical meaning").

labels allow. As a term, "interdisciplinary linguistics" covers topics that deal with language, culture, and communication defined broadly, in a way that promotes inter- and cross-disciplinary dialogue. This volume celebrates the scope of interdisciplinary linguistics and includes voices from scholars in different disciplines within the social sciences and humanities, as well as different subdisciplines within linguistics. The chapters are divided into three general categories: Perspectives, Connections, and Applications.

Chapters in the Perspectives section lay the groundwork for the volume, discussing the definition(s) of and the value of multi-, trans-, and inter-disciplinary work. These chapters address in what areas and for what purposes there is a need for work that crosses disciplinary boundaries; they also address both the challenges and opportunities inherent therein. In Chapter 2, Becky Childs provides an account of the inter/multi/transdisciplinary nature of contemporary linguistics work through an examination of several studies that have utilized these approaches. For Chapter 3, the focus is on higher education, as Stephany Dunstan and Sonja Ardoin discuss how addressing issues of language diversity can act as an entry point to addressing critical issues like race and draw together interdisciplinary partners across campuses. Jessica Grieser authors Chapter 4, in which she draws on the allied fields of sociology, education, and law in order to inform Critical Race Theory, challenging sociolinguistics' assumptions about racism and the power structures that perpetuate it. In Chapter 5, Rusty Barrett tackles a very specific kind of challenge to interdisciplinary study: research gone wrong. Barret examines three specific studies from fields unrelated to linguistics that promote basic language myths about gender and language that are demonstrably wrong and, in fact, only further mistaken assumptions about language and often further negative stereotypes about women. Chapter 6, authored by Arran Stibbe, introduces the field of ecolinguistics, a field that at first glance sits at the intersection of linguistics and ecology, and yet in actuality reaches far beyond these fields to include influences from economics, political science, literary studies, film studies, and religious studies. Stibbe describes for us an interdisciplinary endeavor that uses "linguistic analysis to critically examine the stories that our unequal and unsustainable industrial civilisation is built on" and points towards new ones. This section is rounded out by Chapter 7, written by Tamara Warhol, uses the specific example of educational interactions within a divinity school classroom to illustrate the benefits of ethnography in interdisciplinary investigation.

The Connections section takes a bit of a detour, highlighting scholars from and concepts of different disciplines, presented as fodder for future linguistic work. This section is introduced in Chapter 8, my own contribution, which is an application of the archaeological concept of the *assemblage* to data from the Linguistic Atlas Project. The discussion of assemblage within subfields of linguistics continues in the two following chapters. Chapter 9, written by Alastair Pennycook, discusses the development of the *semiotic assemblage*, a concept that provides alternative ways of thinking about the ways in which particular assemblages of objects, linguistic resources and places come together. Paul Kroskrity's Chapter 10 presents the concept of the *language ideological assemblage* as a resource for dealing with the "complexity of people using and thinking about their languages in social worlds." In Chapter 11, archaeologist Amy Hirschman discusses the challenges of developing and employing a typology for ceramic artifacts – offering linguists insights as to how the language and practices of classification emerge within the archeological context. Chapter 12 continues the discussion of the material, as Jillian Cavanaugh and Shalini Shankar discuss *language materiality* and demonstrate its usefulness in understanding the "relationship between language and dynamics of inequality and political economy, as well as the study of technologically mediated communication." Finally, Chapter 13 looks at the language of houses, as architectural historian Carl Lounsbury discusses the tension within the language of colonial American vernacular builders. Alongside the "transformation of English into a distinctly American English," Lounsbury outlines the "emergence of regional dialects and expressions appears in the common spellings and names attached to architectural features, building types, and construction practices." Here we move from the practiced perspectives from across the disciplines to perspectives that put into practice of "doing" interdisciplinarity.

The chapters included in the Applications section were all framed as sample answers to a not-so-simple question: What does interdisciplinarity look like? The section begins with a call to arms for interdisciplinary research written by Mark Lauersdorf, who outlines in Chapter 14 the multi-disciplined foundations of historical sociolinguistics. Chapter 15, contributed by Jiyoon Lee and Matthew Schreibeis, reviews the application of music to teaching and learning a second language, the result of collaboration between an applied linguist (Lee) and a composer and music educator (Schreibeis). Jason Coker presents a detailed example of what interdisciplinarity looks like at the intersection of Critical White Studies and Biblical Studies in Chapter 16 as an example of how scholars can engage in antiracist biblical studies. In Chapter 17, Jason Thomas explains how textual and narrative analyses in economics have opened new doors "for quantitative researchers looking to enrich existing models of asset prices and macroeconomic dynamics." Finally, Heidi Hamilton's Chapter 18 presents concrete ideas for linguists who wish to contribute to "interdisciplinary team efforts focused centrally on the work of improving health communication and associated health-related issues."

In bringing together these chapters, these voices, and these ideas, we hope to encourage our academic readers to wander into the offices of their not-so-distant disciplinary relatives and strike up conversations about theories and ideas.

Ask questions. Share that new article that made you think. Bring a case study. Take pictures. Collaborate.

## References

Bott, Elizabeth. 1971. *Family and social network*. London: Tavistock.
Buchli, Victor. 2000. Interpreting material culture: The trouble with text. In J. Thomas (ed.), *Interpretive archaeology: A reader*, 363–376. Leicester: Leicester University Press.
Butler, Judith. 1990. *Gender trouble*. London: Routledge.
Cordell, Linda & Judith Habicht-Mauche (eds.). 2012. *Potters and communities of practice*. Tucson: U of Arizona Press.
Eckert, Penny & Sally McConnell-Ginet. 2003. *Language and gender*. Cambridge: Cambridge University Press.
Fauconnier, Giles & Mark Turner. 2002. *The way we think*. New York: Basic Books.
Gibbs, Raymond W., Jr. 1999. Taking metaphor out of our heads and putting it into the cultural world. In Raymond Gibbs & Gerard Steen (eds.), *Metaphor in cognitive linguistics*, 125–144. Amsterdam: John Benjamins.
Hodder, Ian. 1982. *Symbols in action*. Cambridge: Cambridge University Press.
Lakoff, George & Mark Johnson. 1980. *Metaphors we live by*. Chicago: University of Chicago Press.
Lave, Jean & Etienne Wenger. 1991. *Situated learning: Legitimate peripheral participation*. Cambridge: University of Cambridge Press.
Miller, Daniel. 2005. *Materiality*. Durham: Duke University Press.
Shanks, M. & C. Tilley. 1987. *Social theory and archaeology*. Cambridge: Polity Press.
Tilley, Christopher. 2002. Metaphor, materiality and interpretation. In Victor Buchli (ed.), *Material culture Reader*, 23–56. Oxford: Berg.
Wenger, Etienne. 1998. *Communities of practice: Learning, meaning and identity*. Cambridge: Cambridge University Press.

Becky Childs
# Chapter 2
# The value of interdisciplinary and transdisciplinary linguistic research

## 1 Introduction

With connections in the humanities, social sciences, biological sciences, mathematics, and education, linguistics has always been a field that has embraced, utilized, and integrated multiple fields of study. Over time, the multidisciplinary approaches of early linguistic research evolved as the field moved to interdisciplinary research models. This shift has become quite common in the field and across academia more widely, and these moves toward interdisciplinarity in linguistic research have broadened research applications and methodological approaches, and have created new partnerships that have led linguistics more recently toward a transdisciplinary research enterprise. It is in this newer transdisciplinary research approach that we find linguists addressing and answering the question of "So, why does this information about language matter?" It is this question that makes language research important and useful for the general public and for those working in other academic spaces. In these newer interdisciplinary and transdisciplinary approaches, the disciplinary boundaries have faded and are purposefully blended as linguists, or more accurately language researchers, work alongside and with scholars and stakeholders from different disciplines and communities beyond the academy to create research projects, programs, and products that respond directly to contemporary questions and concerns about the role, impact, and function of language in society.

It seems obvious that linguistic research has much to say about the ways that humans interact with one another. From the ways in which our education system has developed and applies theories about language learning to our understanding of the ways that technology has impacted human language behavior, as well as the ways in which public policies, including legal matters, are made and interpreted, we see the reach of linguistics in our day-to-day lives. If we begin to look around not only at the field of linguistics, but expand our gaze more broadly to the pressing questions and concerns in academia and, more importantly, in the public sphere, it is clear that linguistics and, especially, interdisciplinary and

**Becky Childs,** Coastal Carolina University, rchilds@coastal.edu

https://doi.org/10.1515/9781501514371-002

transdisciplinary approaches in linguistic research are necessary to provide information and insight that concern contemporary society.

It is these broader applications of research that keep linguists expanding their studies and broadening their methodologies and the application of their findings to communities beyond the academy. This broadening allows for collaboration with other scholars across academia as well for collaboration with communities and groups outside of academia. Doing so is not without challenges, though: as we work to expand the reach and explanatory nature of linguistic work, we must also expand our methods, research, understanding of other fields, and networks of collaboration and dissemination, all of which takes an investment in moving beyond our traditional academic training and audiences. This chapter provides an account of the interdisciplinary and transdisciplinary nature of contemporary linguistics work through an examination of exemplar language studies that have utilized these approaches in their methodologies or applications. Additionally, the chapter provides narrative excerpts from researchers involved in those studies to help contextualize the experience of conducting this type of work, including the challenges and rewards of undertaking such research.

## 2 What is multidisciplinarity, interdisciplinarity, and transdisciplinarity?

Before beginning a discussion of the importance of integrating and cultivating work from and across multiple disciplines, we must first begin with an understanding of the terms used to describe the various collaborative and integrative methods and frameworks of research presented in this chapter. Often there is confusion when discussing multidisciplinary, interdisciplinary, and transdisciplinary approaches to research (Gozzer 1982). In fact, in some cases the various approaches are viewed as being similar, though, in reality the approaches are quite distinct. When examined together, though, the differences in the focus of each approach become clear.

In multidisciplinary research frameworks, researchers from different disciplines work together on a common question, each drawing on their own disciplinary knowledge, but researchers in this framework stay within their disciplinary boundaries and do not blend or intersect in approaches and dissemination of information. Often in multidisciplinary research projects, the research questions are designed in such a way that each researcher is addressing a particular part of the question directly and contributing knowledge from their field to answer that concern, but there is no integration such that methodologies and general approaches stay discipline-specific and disciplinary boundaries are not pushed or extended.

Interdisciplinary research differs from multidisciplinary research in that this approach integrates knowledge and methods from various disciplines and, rather than staying strictly within disciplinary confines, utilizes a model that is driven to answering the research question as well as possible (Klein 1990). In *Facilitating interdisciplinary research* (2005), interdisciplinary research is described as "a mode of research by teams or individuals that integrates information, data, techniques, tools, perspectives, concepts, and/or theories from two or more disciplines or bodies of specialized knowledge to advance fundamental understanding or to solve problems whose solutions are beyond the scope of a single discipline or field of research practice" (p. 26). The outcomes of interdisciplinary research are a melding of disciplines that push disciplinary boundaries; often the outcomes of such research are new disciplines or changed frameworks within current disciplines.

Transdisciplinary research has a collaborative framework, like interdisciplinary and multidisciplinary research, but it moves beyond the academic sphere. One of the key aspects that makes its approach different than other approaches is that it promotes interfacing and collaborating with communities. This move makes the research more action-based (Stokol 2006) and allows for it to be disseminated and applied to multiple communities where application and potential change from collaborative work can be realized by those outside the walls of the academy (Klein 2004).

## 3 Interdisciplinary research in linguistics

Linguistics has a long history of integrating methodological and theoretical frameworks to address persisting questions about the role (including the production and perception) of language as used by people in the world. Linguistics, as a field, has enjoyed the broader academic moves from strict disciplinary explorations to wider, comprehensive interdisciplinary explorations. As these moves have been made, the scope of the work and the boundaries of the field of linguistics have broadened, and more importantly the audiences that the work reaches and impacts have widened. The following sections examine some examples of methodological and applicational interdisciplinarity and transdisciplinarity.

## 3.1 Methodological interdisciplinarity

One of the areas where there has been significant interdisciplinarity is in the methodologies that linguists have and continue to use in research. From data collection to data analysis, linguists have consistently pushed disciplinary boundaries, implementing and integrating practices from other areas to create research methods that can appropriately and comprehensively address research questions.

Many of the earliest dialectological studies are examples of the early pattern of linguists integrating methods from other fields. For example, early works by Wenker in 1876 (Lameli et al. 2020), which utilized a mail-based questionnaire sent to schools, and Gilliéron and Edmont (1902–1910), which used trained fieldworkers to collect data for analysis, showcase the adaptation of methods from other fields such as anthropology, sociology, and geography. This early work laid a strong foundation for interdisciplinary collaborative methodologies in dialect study, as seen in contemporary dialectology. Over time, dialectology has delved more deeply into interdisciplinary methodologies to answer questions about the social and perceptual questions surrounding dialects. Looking to work in perceptual dialectology, which integrates methods from linguistics, psychology, and geography, among other fields, we see studies, such as those by Preston (1993, 1999) and Campbell-Kibler (2007), using their methods to address broader and more widely sweeping questions about the ways in which dialects are perceived by the public.

More recent work in dialectology, specifically work on modern dialect atlases, illustrates the methodological innovations that are occurring not only within this area but within linguistics more widely. Within modern dialect atlas work, one of the pressing concerns currently is preservation and accessibility of early work (Burkette 2020a). These concerns involve collaborative and integrative methodologies drawing from the digital humanities, material culture, and archeological theory being used to preserve and expand existing corpora and to make the corpora publicly accessible and relevant. Current work on atlas projects must consider not only the ways that contemporary digital innovations can make the mapping of dialects more interactive or easier to visualize, but it must, as Allison Burkette, editor of the Linguistic Atlas Project, notes, "present that linguistic data in a way that responds to and attracts audiences from outside of linguistics" (2020b). Beyond this, Burkette notes that those working on atlas projects must consistently consider what the data they have can tell us about history, literature, anthropology, material culture studies, and other social sciences, and then show the ways that this is relevant for other fields while making those relevant connections accessible. Thus, the modern dialect atlas project is one in which the researcher or research team overseeing the project must be concerned with and consider not only the linguistic viewpoint, but also the ways in which the objects and artifacts that they have been entrusted with can be used by those from other fields. This focus on the broader audience and the innovative melding of methods from numerous fields have moved modern dialectology into a more interdisciplinary methodology.

Similar to the integration of multiple methodological perspectives in the creation and maintenance of linguistic atlas work, modern data preservation and accessibility in fields like endangered language research and sociolinguistics have benefited from the adaptation of methodologies and tools from other linguistic fields and areas outside of linguistics. While similar in some ways, the focus of data preservation and accessibility is different from atlas work in that it works with multiple types of data including audio recordings, documents, and video recordings, among others, often housed across multiple spaces. As the data can take many forms, researchers must consider multiple types of accessibility, portability, and ethical use of the data over time. Further, one of the key factors that drives researchers involved in these research topics is the idea that the data "are valuable and can be of use for a range of investigations unforeseen during the original project for which they are created" (Kendall 2018).

Beginning with the collection of materials and the digitizing of legacy materials, linguists concerned with documentation and preservation have been integrating methods from multiple fields such as computer science and library science when utilizing metadata in the preservation of transcripts, documents, and recordings (both audio and video) to aid in the accessibility of the materials. Portability of data is one topic that language researchers have been innovating with interdisciplinary methods for some time. In their work on portability in language documentation, Bird and Simons (2003) point to many of the concerns with portability of data; specifically they highlight the need for curation plans that account for the consistent technological maintenance of digital archives, thus shifting the focus from being exclusively linguistic in nature to a more robust and wide reaching perspective that integrates multiple disciplinary areas. Further, as issues of ethics, specifically rights for sharing data, have become more pervasive, linguists have been pushed to look outside of the field (to legal expertise) for guidance in developing best practices and procedures.

Corpora building, data maintenance, and accessibility are not the only areas where interdisciplinarity can be seen in linguistic methodologies. Linguistics has a long history of using statistical methods from the social sciences, as well as methods from mathematics and computer science, to create tools and procedures that allow for sophisticated and nuanced analyses of language perception and production. Statistical software such as R (2017), which has widespread usage across the academic and public sector, is used by linguists from various linguistic subdisciplines (Gries 2009; Levshina 2015) to perform analysis of data as well as data visualizations. Within linguistics, multiple tools have been created using empirical methods from other fields for quantitative analysis. The creation of earlier tools such as GoldVarb (Sankoff, Tagliamonte, and Smith 2005), which allowed sociolinguists to perform statistical analysis of linguistic data, as well as research that has led to the development of tools used in phonetic research that normalize vowel data (Adank, Smits, and van Hout 2004), have all taken an interdisciplinary approach in the creation of methodologies and tools for analysis (Kendall and Thomas 2009), as they adapt and adopt expertise and models from other fields to best analyze and interpret linguistic data.

Notable interdisciplinarity within linguistics, though, does not lie only in the "hard" sciences. There are many interdisciplinary methodological perspectives that have roots in other fields, specifically, those that utilize qualitative methods or mixed methods research. Ethnography serves as one of the most obvious examples of an interdisciplinary methodology that has been adopted and adapted by linguists for use in their data collection processes (Blommaert 2007; Levon 2017). While often considered a longstanding component of linguistic methodologies, ethnography does not find its roots in linguistics. In fact, ethnography is a method that has a long history in fields such as anthropology. Linguists, though, have been quick to adopt and adapt ethnography as a methodology because of its focus on culture and community, rather than focusing explicitly on language. Rampton et al. (2004) describe the relationship of ethnography and linguistics as "a matter of degree than of kind" (4). This description points to the connectedness and natural relationship that interdisciplinary methodologies have; moreover, it underscores the importance in recognizing the relatedness of approaches necessary to create truly interdisciplinary research models. (For further discussion of the interdisciplinary nature of linguistics and ethnography, specifically how ethnography can be utilized in various ways across different linguistic research, see Chapter 7.)

The integration of ethnographic perspectives for data collection has led the way for work by many linguists. One of the most well-known studies that utilizes interdisciplinary ethnographic methods is the study of jocks and burnouts that was conducted by Penny Eckert (2000) in a suburban Detroit school. In this study, Eckert utilized an ethnographic method of data collection, participant observation (Levon 2018), to investigate high school social groups and their language use and uncover the ways in which social and linguistic practices are realized in local communities. Through this research method, in which she embedded herself in the community, she uncovered ways in which students aligned themselves with local and extra-local language practices and how that alignment reflected their current social positions and future social aspirations.

In addition to the use of interdisciplinary ethnographic methods of data collection for this work, Eckert also utilized the community of practice framework (Wegner 2000), an interdisciplinary construct that aids in the understanding of the ways in which local and global social and language practices interact, construct, and reinforce one another. It is in this type of interdisciplinary research that we come to understand the ways that utilizing methods and approaches from other disciplines can broaden and reshape our explorations of language practices, as we push the applications beyond linguistics and into other domains inside and outside of academia. Eckert's interdisciplinary research methods have reach within linguistics, anthropology, and sociology. Likewise, the extensions of her research can be relevant and of interest to researchers in psychology and education. Within linguistics, these interdisciplinary approaches often open up and propel researchers in new directions – stretching the field, as in the case of the previously mentioned work, which helps to begin discussions that have moved sociolinguistics into its third wave of research. Third wave sociolinguistic research has moved the field from stricter disciplinary research methods and questions that were typically answered by correlations of linguistic and social variables to considerations of the ways in which language users create social meaning and identity through their language practices (Eckert 2012).

The outcomes of interdisciplinary linguistic research methodologies are leading researchers to discover language truths that bring value to linguistics and other disciplines. Further, these interdisciplinary methods are promoting an academic culture of engaged research that addresses and considers questions and concerns from across academia and society, utilizing approaches that are novel and grounded in proven practices. As linguists continue to innovate, consider, and reconsider the role and place of language in the larger framework of the world, we are sure to see even more valuable interdisciplinary methodologies emerge.

# 4 Moving from interdisciplinary to transdisciplinarity

The application of interdisciplinary perspectives in linguistics is one of the most exciting and fruitful areas in contemporary linguistic research. In discussing the application of research by linguists, I am considering the ways in which linguistic research and the products of linguistic-oriented research go beyond one academic domain. The interdisciplinary research and application and practices detailed in this section examine the ways in which linguists, often working in collaborative teams, are addressing the concerns of multiple audiences. The examples of this type of research that are discussed have often utilized methods and theories from multiple fields and brought them together in nuanced ways to uncover and disseminate information about language through multiple avenues and mediums and across communities in ways that are relevant to each community. These moves to interact and partner with communities outside of the academy to address their questions are one of the ways in which we see linguists taking the next step from interdisciplinary research toward transdisciplinary research and applications.

Perhaps one of the most obvious places where linguists have a fairly extensive history of working in a broader capacity is in addressing educational questions and concerns (Heath 1984). One of the more wide-sweeping early impacts of interdisciplinary work in linguistics that linked it to education and highlighted the conversations and intersecting interests and concerns of linguists and educators revolved around situations of inequality in educational practices and procedures. From the early work of linguists such as Geneva Smitherman (1977), William Labov (1970, 1972b), and Walt Wolfram (1969), the field of linguistics was systematically investigating the ways that dialects, such as African American English, patterned, and they were explaining the rule-governed principled characteristics of these dialects. More importantly, linguists were also explaining the ways in which dialects function as significant social and cultural markers. In this way, we see the beginnings of intersectional work in linguistics, with an increasing concern about the ways that the connected nature of social categories, as reflected in language use, lead to disadvantage or discrimination.

The Students' Rights to Their Own Language document, which was adopted by the College Committee on Composition in 1974 (National Council of Teachers of English 1974), is an example of interdisciplinary work that involved linguists like Geneva Smitherman in the creation of a seminal resolution that has informed a great deal of practice and policy in higher education. Smitherman worked with a wide variety of educators, most of whom were not linguists by training but who had an interest in language and in promoting an inclusive linguistic framework for student learning. This work, addressed by a collaborative team, was done to answer a pressing question in education: How do we address the discrimination that dialect speakers face in the classroom and recognize systematically that dialects are equal? The outcome of this statement, the lasting impact of its legacy, has had long-term impacts in linguistics, education, and in policy-making. However, the process, as with most interdisciplinary and transdisciplinary work, was not without difficulty, as Smitherman (1995) notes. She recalls that "the *Cause* was just if the methods awkward. The Enlightened were, after all, attempting to effectuate change WITHIN THE SYSTEM" (p. 22).

Interdisciplinary applications of linguistic research in education were becoming increasingly important and necessary in the American educational system.

Coming soon after the resolution of Students' Rights to Their Own Language was another educational situation that needed an interdisciplinary approach involving linguists and educators, as well as legal experts, to understand and solve a persisting educational crisis: the Black-White achievement gap (Ansell 2011). The 1979 Ann Arbor Decision was a landmark court case that brought a court ruling which stated that education systems must account for students' home languages or dialects, in this case African American English, in providing education (Michigan Law Review 1980). It is here in this case that we again see the value of interdisciplinary research in linguistics. We see the ways that linguistic work can be applied across and within many situations, especially those situations outside of academic communities and in local and global communities. Moreover, we see the move of linguistic research applications from being interdisciplinary in focus to becoming more transdisciplinary in scope, as the focus of the research and applications are driven more broadly and provide products or outcomes that are seated most appropriately in broader society.

In 1996 another educational situation arose, the Oakland Ebonics Controversy, which would require linguistic expertise, but more importantly, interdisciplinary research applications and partnerships, to again provide answers to questions about education and African American English. Linguists like John Rickford worked alongside educators and educational policy-makers, as they developed a plan to address the public concerns over the proposed education policy and to educate the public about African American English (Rickford 1999). In this situation the interdisciplinary work of linguists was seen in multiple ways, first in the ways in which linguists spent time addressing and answering media inquiries and working to provide an accurate representation of the issues for the general public.

This focus on dissemination of information to the public moved linguists into interdisciplinary and transdisciplinary research applications. Additionally, the collaboration in the revision of educational policies with the Oakland School Board showcases the interdisciplinary scope of the work.

While the previous examples of interdisciplinary research applications have focused on linguists' work that arose in response to a current issue, much recent transdisciplinary linguistic work that engages with educational concerns has taken a more proactive approach. This is due in many ways to a fact that Wolfram (1998) noted, in regard to language and education: "at the grass-roots level, we have not made nearly as much progress as we imagine with respect to dialect and education" (p. 108). As a result, linguists are thinking about and working alongside educators to create products and programs that can be used inside K-12 classrooms and drawing attention to policies and practices in higher education. Through teacher training (Reaser, Adger, Wolfram, and Christian 2017; Charity Hudley and Mallinson 2011, 2014) and the creation of classroom materials (Reaser 2010), linguists are reshaping the scope of linguistics, bringing about a model that is focused on outreach and social responsibility, that is moving to a transdisciplinary research enterprise. Another avenue that is being actively pursued and that also highlights the breadth of interdisciplinarity and outreach of linguistic research applications can be seen in discussions about the makeup of higher education and policies related to higher education (Charity Hudley and Mallinson 2018). For many researchers working in these interdisciplinary avenues, the reasons for broad-based application are important and are directly related to questions in society writ large, as Charity Hudley (2019) notes: "I really think about my work as addressing societal challenges and issues rather than being rooted in a discipline."

Education, while occupying a large part of the applications of linguistic research, is not the only area where we can see the reach of interdisciplinarity in linguistics, as well as the move to transdisciplinary approaches. Interdisciplinary research that has utilized critical race theory has been quite robust for some time (Charity Hudley 2017). Certainly, earlier and contemporary work on education has engaged critical race theory quite vigorously, but more recently, work in linguistics has been engaging structural social inequality, especially as it relates to the legal system (Rickford and King 2016; Voight et al. 2017). In these transdisciplinary research applications, we can see the ways in which language researchers can use collaborative methods, applications, and forms of dissemination to answer public questions about current events. Rickford and King (2016) engaged these topics in their work on the Rachel Jeantel courtroom testimony during the Trayvon Martin court case. In their work, they revealed "how the setting contributed to our perception of her speech and the social and political consequences of producing such stigmatized speech in that space" (King 2020). The outcomes of this research provided critical insight for those involved in the law field and important answers about perception and reception of speakers for the general public, while also providing important information for linguists and about our roles and obligations as interdisciplinary researchers. In fact, King notes (pers. comm. 2020), "This broader approach of looking beyond linguistics taught us and other linguists more about how we could lend our expertise to preventing and/or reducing such bias in the courtroom and beyond" reaffirming the commitment and need for linguists to consider the broad applications of their research for social equality.

Similar to this, research by Voight et al. (2017) has also looked at social concerns that arise at the intersections of language, the law, and critical race theory. In his work on police body camera footage, Voight examines the ways that particular models of discourse or discourse strategies are utilized by police officers, their interpretation by those they interact with, and the ways that these interactions may play out in the procedural justice system. Voight takes an applicational approach to the outcomes of his research and poses possibilities for improved police community interactions. The application of research that addresses contemporary social issues provides practices that can improve the social justice system. These research approaches, like the work of (Voight et al. 2017) and Rickford and King (2016), highlight the value of transdisciplinary linguistic research.

Applications of research on language, gender, and sexuality have provided important information about the ways in which language practices are interpreted in society. (See Chapter 5 by Barrett in this volume for a more comprehensive discussion of the interdisciplinary nature of work on language gender and sexuality.) The applications of such work have provided broader understanding of how social practices through day-to-day interactions can be improved to provide safer and more inclusive environments for all. Zimman (2017) serves as an example of research that focuses on transdisciplinary applications. In his work on trans language, Zimman looks at the ways in which language practices can become trans-inclusive and gender-affirming, providing practices for language reform. Zimman's approach is one that addresses a larger social issue outside of academia, transphobic violence and the delegitimization of trans identities, but he reminds us that the reason linguists must be involved in these discussions is because it is one that is "fundamentally grounded in language" (p. 101). Perhaps most importantly, Zimman reminds all researchers of the widespread value of utilizing transdisciplinary applications, when he says, "Thanks to these efforts, discussions of language and trans inclusion are increasingly found in more mainstream news outlets, radio programs and fictional genres" (p. 101).

The role of technology in communication, and more importantly its impact on language, is a topic that has occupied much recent media coverage. This public interest has provided linguists with opportunities to engage in transdisciplinary research applications. Newly and constantly evolving communication methods such as email, text messaging, and social media have created concern among the public, who fear that these innovations may be irreparably damaging language. As linguists have long known, language change is natural, and, more importantly, it is not bad (Labov 1972a). However, prior to the technology boom, this information was mostly kept within linguistic academic circles because public interest was much more limited. In response to recent public concerns, there has been a proliferation of transdisciplinary applications of research on language in contemporary wired (and now wireless) society. Linguists like Gretchen McCulloch (2019) are doing engaged outreach focused on disseminating information to the public about how language works and the impacts of technology on communication. Of interest in this application of research is its multiple forms of dissemination, via traditional routes such as books, but also the presence of a thriving contemporary focus in the modes of outreach with "pop books", podcasts, and lending expertise to popular websites to engage a broader audience. This research focus on a social concern that does not lie within a disciplinary boundary and that has engagement as a key component clearly illustrates the move to transdisciplinary research applications seen in contemporary linguistics.

# 5 Conclusion

Over time, linguistics has been moving its methods and applications toward a more interdisciplinary focus. While linguists have long known that language carries both content and social information, the connections of that to broader society through methods and application were not as robust as they could be. Because of innovations in methodologies, many of which are adopted and adapted processes and procedures of other fields, linguists have become better able to create research programs that address broader questions about the role and place of language in society more directly and appropriately. The development of these interdisciplinary methods has allowed for collaborations outside of linguistics and has, at times, led to new theoretical models for research as well as pushed the focus of linguistic subfields in new directions.

The value of interdisciplinarity and transdisciplinarity in linguistics can also be seen in the applications and processes researchers are creating. With an eye towards answering questions that do not lie within strict disciplinary lines and with a commitment to interfacing with the broader public, there is a clear trajectory for the continuing transdisciplinary focus of contemporary applications of linguistic research. These transdisciplinary research collaborations have had a great impact on linguistics and have brought more visibility to the importance of recognizing the role of language within the broader social framework. Through reconsiderations of modes of dissemination and engaged research collaboration, transdisciplinary research has brought linguists to interface with the public in meaningful ways, ways that promote social justice and inclusivity and can promote civil social dialogue. In addition, another significant value brought about by this work are reconsiderations of models and methods of dissemination of research and the obligations that researchers have to distribute their research.

The moves away from strict disciplinarity have not been seamless, though, and they are often difficult, as they require much effort. For those engaged in interdisciplinary and transdisciplinary work, there are a number of challenges associated with learning about other disciplines and establishing new networks of collaboration and dissemination. However, the rewards of methodological and applicational innovation are significant and interact with each other in meaningful ways as we create new models and methods for explaining the roles of language in our world.

# References

Adank, Patti, Roel Smits & Roeland van Hout. 2004. A comparison of vowel normalization procedures for language variation research. *Journal of the Acoustical Society of America* 116. 3099–3107.
Ansell, Susan. 2011. Achievement gap. *Education Week*. Retrieved Feb 10 2020 from http://www.edweek.org/ew/issues/achievement-gap/.
Bird, Steven & Gary Bird. 2003. Seven dimensions of portability for language documentation and description. *Language* 79 (3). 557–582.
Blommaert, Jan. 2007. On scope and depth in linguistic ethnography. *Journal of Sociolinguistics* 11. 682–688.
Burkette, Allison. 2020a. Dialect notes, 2020: Linguistic Atlas Project update. Paper presented at the American Dialect Society, New Orleans, LA, January 3.
Burkette, Allison. 2020b. Personal communication. February 3, 2020.
Campbell-Kibler, Kathryn. 2007. Accent, (ING) and the social logic of listener perceptions. *American Speech* 82. 32–64.
Charity Hudley, Anne. 2017. Language and racialization. In Ofelia Garcia, Nelson Flores, & Massimiliano Spotti (eds.), *The Oxford handbook of language and society*. 381–402. Oxford: Oxford University Press.
Charity Hudley, Anne. 2019. Personal communication. October 23, 2019.
Charity Hudley, Anne H. & Christine Mallinson. 2011. *Understanding English language variation in U.S. schools*. New York: Teachers College Press.
Charity Hudley, Anne H. & Christine Mallinson. 2014. *We do language: English language variation in the secondary English classroom*. New York: Teachers College Press.
Charity Hudley, Anne H. & Christine Mallinson. 2018. Dismantling "The Master's Tools": Moving students' right to their own language freedom theory to practice. *American Speech*. 93. 513–537.
Eckert, Penelope. 2012. Three waves of variation study: The emergence of meaning in the study of sociolinguistic variation. *Annual Review Anthropology* 41: 87–100.
Eckert, Penelope. 2000. *Linguistic variation as social practice*. Oxford: Blackwell.
Heath, Shirley Brice. 1984. Linguistics and education. In B. Siegel (ed.), *Annual Review of Anthropology*, 251–274. Palo Alto, CA: Annual Reviews, Inc.
Gilliéron, Jules, and Edmont, Edmont. 1902–1910. *Atlas Linguistique de la France*. Paris: Champion.
Gozzer, Giovanni. 1982. Interdisciplinarity a concept still unclear. *Prospects* 12 (3). 281–292.
Gries, Stefan Th. 2009. *Statistics for linguistics with R*. Mouton de Gruyter.

Institute of Medicine. 2005. *Facilitating interdisciplinary research*. Washington, DC: The National Academies Press.

Kendall, T. 2018. Data preservation and access. In Christine Mallinson, Becky Childs & Gerard Van Herk (eds.), *Data collection in sociolinguistics: Methods and applications*, 195–205. New York: Routledge.

Kendall, Tyler & Erik R. Thomas. 2009. Vowels: Vowel manipulation, normalization, and plotting in R. R package, version 1. 0–3.

King, Sharese. 2020. Personal communication. February 2, 2020.

Klein, Julie T. 1990. *Interdisciplinarity: History, theory and practice*. Detroit: Wayne State University Press.

Klein, Julie T. 2004. Prospects for transdisciplinarity. *Futures* 36. 515–536.

Labov, William. 1970. *The study of nonstandard English*. Urbana, IL: NCTE.

Labov, William. 1972a. *Sociolinguistic patterns*. Philadelphia: University of Pennsylvania Press.

Labov, William. 1972b. *Language in the Inner City*. Philadelphia: University of Pennsylvania Press.

Lameli, A., E. Glaser & P. Stöckle. 2020. Drawing areal information from a corpus of noisy dialect data. *Journal of Linguistic Geography* 8 (1). 31–48.

Levshina, Natalia. 2015. *How to do linguistics with R: Data exploration and statistical analysis*. Amsterdam: John Benjamins.

Levon, Erez. 2017. Ethnographic fieldwork. In Christine Mallinson, Becky Childs & Gerard Van Herk (eds.), *Data collection in sociolinguistics: Methods and applications*, 85–106. New York: Routledge.

Levon, Erez. 2018. Ethnographic Fieldwork. In Christine Mallinson, Becky Childs & Gerard Van Herk (eds.), *Data collection in sociolinguistics: Methods and applications*, 71–79. New York: Routledge.

McCulloch, Gretchen. 2019. *Because Internet: Understanding the new rules of language*. New York: Riverhead Books.

Michigan Law Review. 1980. Black English and equal educational opportunity. *Michigan Law Review* 79 (2). 279–298.

National Council of Teachers of English. 1974. *NCTE Resolution #74.2* Urbana, IL. NCTE.

Preston, Dennis. 1993. *American dialect research, 100th anniversary of the ADS*. Amsterdam: Benjamins.

Preston, Dennis (ed.). 1999. *Handbook of perceptual dialectology*. Vol. 1. Amsterdam: John Benjamins.

R Core Team. 2017. R: A language and environment for statistical computing. R Foundation for Statistical Computing, Vienna, Austria. URL https://www.R-project.org/.

Rampton, Ben, Karen Trusting, Janet Maybin & Richard Barwell. 2004. UK linguistic ethnography: A discussion paper. Retrieved fromhttp://www.lancaster.ac.uk/fss/organisations/lingethn/documents/discussion_paper_jan_05.pdf.

Reaser, Jeffrey. 2010. Using media to teach about language. *Language and Linguistic Compass* 4. 782–792.

Reaser, Jeffrey, Carolyn Temple Adger, Donna Christian & Walt Wolfram. April 2017. *Dialects at school: Educating linguistically diverse students*. New York: Routledge.

Rickford, John R. 1999. The Ebonics controversy in my backyard: A sociolinguist's experiences and reflections. *Journal of Sociolinguistics* 3 (2). 267–276.

Rickford, John R. & Sharese King. 2016. Language and linguistics on trial: Hearing Rachel Jeantel (and other vernacular speakers) in the courtroom and beyond. *Language*. 92 (4). 948–988.

Sankoff, David, Sali Tagliamonte & Eric Smith. 2005. Goldvarb X: A variable rule application for Macintosh and Windows.

Smitherman, Geneva. 1977. *Talkin and testifyin: The language of Black America*. Boston: Houghton Mifflin.

Smitherman, Geneva. 1995. Students' right to their own language: A retrospective. *The English Journal* 84 (1). 21–27. National Council of Teachers of English.

Stokol, Daniel. 2006. Toward a science of transdisciplinary action research. *American Journal of Community Psychology* 38. 63–77.

Voight, Rob, Nicholas P. Camp, Vinodkumar Prabhakaran, William L. Hamilton, Rebecca C. Hetey, Camilla M. Griffiths, David Jurgens, Dan Jurafsky & Jennifer L. Eberhardt. 2017. Language from police body camera footage shows racial disparities in officer respect. Proceedings of the National Academy of Sciences 114 (25). 6521–6526.

Wenger, Etienne. 2000. *Communities of practice*. New York: Cambridge University Press.

Wolfram, Walt. 1969. *A linguistic description of Detroit Negro speech*. Washington, DC: Center for Applied Linguistics.

Wolfram, Walt. 1998. Language ideology and dialect: Understanding the Oakland Ebonics controversy. *Journal of English Linguistics* 26 (2). 108–121.

Zimman, Lal. 2017. Transgender language reform: Some challenges and strategies for promoting trans-affirming, gender-inclusive language. *Journal of Language and Discrimination* 1 (1). 84–105.

Stephany Brett Dunstan, Sonja Ardoin

# Chapter 3
# Faculty and student affairs partnerships: Creating inclusive campus environments for students of diverse linguistic backgrounds

## 1 Introduction

Higher education in the United States is becoming increasingly diverse (National Center for Education Statistics 2019), and more college campuses and university systems have explicit missions to increase the enrollment and augment the success of students from diverse and historically underrepresented backgrounds. This is heightened by predictions of "enrollment crashes" of majority populations, which adds a business imperative to increase recruitment and retention of minoritized populations (Bockenstedt 2019; Conley 2019; Grawe 2019). Notably, in recent years, discussions of diversity in higher education have become more intentional in addressing intersectionality and acknowledging invisible dimensions of identity, such as socioeconomic status/social class (Ardoin and martinez 2019), first-generation college student status (Whitley, Benson, and Wesaw 2018), or geographic origin, notably along rural/urban divides (Koricich, Chen, and Hughes 2018). However, discussions of language diversity remain largely absent across higher education in general, and specifically among student affairs and social justice professionals, who often spearhead diversity and inclusion efforts on campus and who are very often the first and most frequent points of contact for our students. Similarly, in the sociolinguistics community, there are few examples of systematic and sustained collaborations between linguists and student affairs professionals. This represents a notable gap in our efforts to create wholly inclusive and supportive campus environments for our students. Recognition of and attention to language diversity is essential in encouraging equitable student engagement inside and outside the classroom, from encouragement to participate in academic course discussions to connecting with people and making friends (Dunstan and Jaeger 2015, 2016, 2020). Discussions of language as a form of diversity also serve as an entrée to broader discussions of ideologies and discrimination, and often serve as a productive springboard for

---

**Stephany Brett Dunstan,** North Carolina State University, sbdunsta@ncsu.edu
**Sonja Ardoin,** Appalachian State University, ardoins@appstate.edu

https://doi.org/10.1515/9781501514371-003

students to begin to think about complexities of intersectionality and identity, and of their view of their own roles on campus and in society. This chapter serves as a call to action for collaboration between linguists and student affairs practitioners and provides concrete examples for working together to leverage respective expertise and to empower each other as colleagues to more fully support our students. Together, scholar-practitioners can work toward addressing this critical diversity gap, which can only serve to more fully support facilitation of meaningful, equity-based programming and outcomes on our campuses.

Today's American college campuses are arguably more diverse than ever before (National Center for Education Statistics 2019; Espinosa, Turk, Taylor, and Chessman 2019). This diversity occurs along a number of dimensions, some of which are visible, such as race, ethnicity, gender, and sometimes disability and age, and others that are less visible, such as sexuality, religion, and social class. Some of the latter, some would argue, have historically received less attention than those more "visible" forms of diversity, such as gender or race. In recent years, however, there have been notable efforts to increase awareness of some of the more invisible forms of diversity in higher education, particularly with an increasing focus on intersectionality (Crenshaw 1989; Museus and Griffin 2011; Mitchell, Simmons, and Greyerbiehl 2014; Strayhorn 2017) and an understanding of the way that these many elements of lived experiences and selves shape identity and college success. As a result, there has been more programming on college campuses on the part of faculty and student affairs practitioners to address invisible elements of diversity. For example, a number of institutions are focusing on basic needs (e.g., food, clothing, emergency funds) support (Goldrick-Rab, Baker-Smith, Coca, and Looker 2019); celebrating first-generation college student status (Whitley, Benson, and Wesaw 2018); and creating specific offices to serve undocumented students (see Brown University, DePauw University, Sierra College, and University of California at Davis as examples). However, there are few examples nationally of linguistic diversity being addressed specifically as an element of campus diversity. Looking at conference programs from major national student affairs professionals' organizations in the US from the past five years (e.g., NASPA, ACPA) and higher education research (e.g., Association for the Study of Higher Education), there is scant mention of language diversity in higher education. Similarly, looking at major linguistics conferences (New Ways of Analyzing Variation, Linguistic Society of America) over the past five years, there has been a small (but growing) number of presentations that specifically address issues of language diversity on college campuses, but few that specifically involve partners across campuses.

## 2 Why should language diversity be addressed on college campuses?

Charity Hudley (2018: 200) notes that for linguists, "it is crucial for us to think about our collective and individual roles in higher education and to be reflective of the ways that, in addition to how we see ourselves formulating our research, we also formulate our political, social, and intellectual agendas." There has been a significant amount of research on linguistic diversity in K-12 scholarship and its importance (Godley, Sweetland, Wheeler, Minnici, and Carpenter 2006; Godley and Minnici 2008; Mallinson and Charity Hudley 2010; Wheeler 2010; Charity Hudley and Mallinson 2014; Sweetland and Wheeler 2014; Godley, Reaser, and Moore 2015; Charity Hudley and Mallinson 2017), but there has been less research on the role of language diversity on college campuses. However, there is a growing body of work suggesting that issues of language diversity play an important role in shaping campus climates and how students, faculty, and staff see themselves situated in campus communities.

Educational institutions have been noted to reinforce the linguistic norms and preferences of dominant classes (Bourdieu 1991), and for much of the history of higher education in the US, access to postsecondary learning has been limited for members of minoritized groups, particularly racial and ethnic minorities, women, non-Christian religions, and students from low socioeconomic backgrounds (Boyer 2013). Although in recent years college-going trends for students from these oft-intersecting groups has improved, students from historically underrepresented groups in many cases will continue to find themselves minoritized on college campuses. When underrepresented students do enter higher education, they might find themselves entering a world that seems unfamiliar in many ways, including in regard to explicit and implicit codes of power (Delpit 2006) required for participation in the academic discourse community, which has historically privileged the language norms of White, middle and upper-middle classes (Bourdieu 1991; White 2005; White and Lowenthal 2011; White and Ali-Khan 2013; Yosso 2005). For example, linguistic microaggressions are, unfortunately, not uncommon for minoritized student populations. We hear this on our campuses (and across the country) when we hear students of color and/or poor and working-class rural students complimented for being *articulate* when they use linguistic conventions that accommodate the "standard" (based on White middle-class preferences).

One of the most influential factors for college student success outcomes, such as persistence and graduation, is *sense of belonging* (Hausmann, Schofield, and Woods 2007; Hoffman, Richmond, Morrow, and Salomone 2002; Hurtado and

Carter 1997; Locks, Hurtado, Bowman and Oseguera 2008; Strayhorn 2018). Sense of belonging has been conceptualized as "students' perceived social support on campus, a feeling or sensation of connectedness, and the experience of mattering or feeling cared about, accepted, respected, valued by, and important to the campus community or others on campus such as faculty, staff, and peers" (Strayhorn 2018: 4). Students who lack a sense of belonging are more likely to feel marginalized or isolated on campus, and are therefore less likely to engage in the campus environment, persist, and be successful academically.

A strong contributing factor of sense of belonging is the concept in higher education research of *validation* (Rendón 1994). Rendón conceptualizes validation as "an enabling, confirming, and supportive process initiated by in- and out-of-class agents that fosters academic and interpersonal development" (1994: 16). She notes that validation from faculty and staff is critical in making students feel that they belong in college and can succeed academically and socially in college. Validation can take the form of academic validation and interpersonal validation. Academic validation often occurs in the classroom and includes a number of efforts from instructors to increase students' confidence and academic self-efficacy beliefs (e.g. encouraging words from instructors, creation of an inclusive and equitable classroom learning environment, individual attention and feedback, etc.). Interpersonal validation can occur in or outside of the classroom and can be understood more broadly to include "actions that promote the personal and social adjustment both within the curricular and cocurricular contexts of an institutions" (Hurtado, Cuellar, and Guillermo-Wann 2011: 55), for example, mentoring or coaching.

On the topic of the importance of validation for college students, Hurtado et al. (2011) tested the validity of two scales on the Diverse Learning Environments survey (Hurtado 2013) related to 1) academic validation and 2) interpersonal validation using data collected from college students attending community college and four-year institutions who completed the survey between December 2009 and May 2010 (N=4,472). Among their findings, the authors note that "students of color report lower levels of validation that White students, with a more stark difference in academic validation in the classroom" (p. 67) and indicate that item-level analysis suggests that the role of faculty was particularly strong for students of color in making them feel empowered to learn, which contributes to feelings of both academic and interpersonal validation.

So why do validation and sense of belonging matter for language diversity and higher education? Language can be critical in how college students make friends, choose activities, interact with peers, advisors, and faculty, and how they view themselves and others (Caldwell 2015; Dunstan and Jaeger 2016). These activities contribute strongly to a student's sense of belonging in micro- and macro-environments on campus. Students who speak dialects that carry social stigma may be less likely to speak up in class, which can impact how they feel they fit in the classroom and, subsequently, can influence their academic performance (Eliason and Turalba 2019; Dunstan and Jaeger 2015). What's more, the concept of validation comes into play given the preference of students and faculty for standard language ideology and linguistic hegemony on campus, resulting in an ideation of what it means to "sound like a scholar" (Dunstan 2013; Dunstan and Jaeger 2015; Myrick 2019). We posit that a critical aspect of both academic and interpersonal validation is for faculty and staff to validate students' linguistic capital and the value that it brings to campus (Yosso 2005). Hurtado, Alvarado and Guillermo-Wann (2011) state that "the more students witness acts of discrimination or hear disparaging remarks from faculty, staff, or fellow students, the less validated they are likely to feel, and consequently, the lower their sense of belonging on campus" (p. 72), but they also note that intentional acts of validation can mitigate these effects. In conversations in classroom buildings, in residence halls, in our student centers, and across the campus, we have overheard disparaging comments such as "She sounds like such an ignorant hick" or "They talk so ghetto." We will likely continue to hear these types of statements if we do not continue to develop and sustain systematic and widespread education on linguistic diversity for the entire campus community. Educational experiences and partnerships across campus will not only provide learning opportunities but will also provide validating experiences for campus community members. For members of the campus community, particularly students, these validating experiences may aid in increasing their confidence in their ability to succeed as part of the academic community and contribute to their sense of belonging on campus.

Many readers will be able to recall a time that they overheard disparaging remarks about language on their campuses and perhaps even in their classrooms. In the linguistics community, this is a clear and known issue, but nationally there is not yet widespread work being done on it on college campuses in collaboration with student affairs units. There is scant student affairs or social justice programming that specifically addresses issues of linguistic diversity, and there is little engagement among sociolinguists (to the authors' knowledge) with student affairs practitioners to make systematic efforts to address these issues. There are several notable examples of linguists partnering with other academics to support student learning (e.g. an innovative, collaborative effort between linguists and the first-year writing program at Coastal Carolina University; Childs 2018), but few examples of student affairs partnerships. On many college campuses there is, unfortunately, a de facto divide between academic and student affairs. In her discussion of the development and implementation of a successful student affairs initiative on undergraduate research at the College of William & Mary, Charity Hudley (2018) addresses this perceptual divide, noting that she formerly saw her faculty role in linguistics and her student affairs role as the director of the William & Mary Scholars Program as distinct. However, she reflects that foundational to the success of the initiative's goal of increasing inclusivity is the reconciliation of the dual roles of academic and student affairs: "I then realized that developing and directing WMSURE was central to everything I do as a linguist as it was a direct way to contribute to inclusiveness in linguistics both by preparing individual students for graduate school and by creating a model of practice for linguistics faculty who teach undergraduate" (2018: 204). To fully serve the whole student, support from both academic and student affairs perspectives and practices is necessary. However, not all faculty may have the opportunity to engage in dual roles on campus, and many faculty may sometimes feel siloed in their respective fields, facing many competing demands of scholarship, teaching, and service. At the same time, while student affairs professionals are often keenly aware of the importance of tying co-curricular programming to issues of social justice, they too face a number of competing demands, and in some areas, like teaching linguistic diversity, may feel a lack of expertise or empowerment to engage in this type of work, being told implicitly or explicitly that it is outside of their purview. Despite these challenges, we posit that collaborations between linguists and student affairs professionals can perhaps be among the most effective methods to address not only issues of linguistic diversity but provide an entrée for students to engage in broader challenging discussions of inequities facing the campus community and society.

## 3 Why partner with student affairs professionals?

First and foremost, perhaps we should clarify what it is exactly that student affairs practitioners do, and what we mean by "co-curricular" experiences and learning. ACPA-College Student Educators International (ACPA), one of the largest student affairs organizations in the US, states, "At its broadest definition, student affairs could be said to consist of any advising, counseling, management, or administrative function at a college or university that exists outside the classroom" (Love 2003). The scope of student affairs offices is quite broad. ACPA suggests that the varied units across college campuses that are often considered to be in the realm of student affairs include:

> residence life, commuter services, graduate student services, admissions, new student orientation, financial aid, counseling centers, advising centers, leadership development, Greek affairs, student activities, student unions, leadership development, community service, service learning, career planning and placement, discipline and judicial affairs, alumni relations and development, services for students with disabilities, developmental

learning services, and advocacy and support programs (e.g., for students of color, lesbian, bisexual, gay, and transgender students, veterans, women, international students, adults). (Love 2003)

These units on campus help facilitate co-curricular experiences and learning. But what does "co-curricular" mean? Suskie (2015) comically observes that "People of a certain age may recall the days when out-of-classroom experiences were called extracurricular activities, 'extra' meaning outside the curriculum" (p. 5), but notes that presently on college campuses we see more of an integration of learning inside and outside the classroom, given the important role that out-of-class experiences play in reinforcing learning – what we now refer to as "co-curricular" experiences and learning. Suskie suggests that these experiences are not facilitated solely by student affairs practitioners, nor by faculty alone, but through collaboration (2015: 9). Examples of co-curricular learning include student organizations and clubs, community engagement and service learning, study abroad, diversity and social justice education, leadership development, and health and wellness opportunities.

On many college campuses, student affairs practitioners are the first point of contact with students, and sometimes one of their most frequent points of contact (Long 2012). For example, in their first weeks on campus, students often have significant interactions with professional and student employees in student affairs through new student orientation, residence halls, and student organizations, to name a few. As a student progresses through college, they will interact frequently with many other types of student affairs professionals. For example, many students who participate in leadership or civic engagement efforts will work with student affairs staff. Students who visit the career center or the tutorial center are working with student affairs professionals. A student participating in a multicultural student organization or fraternity or sorority will work with student affairs staff on campus. When students seek proactive or reactive wellness measures, they will work with student affairs practitioners in the health promotions office, recreation center, student health center, and counseling center. There are countless times in the average college student's career that they will work with or be guided by student affairs professionals in a number of influential and meaningful ways. These interactions most often occur outside of the academic classroom environment, and these interactions are critical for developing a sense of belonging, receiving validation, reinforcing learning that occurs in the classroom, and developing students in non-cognitive ways as well.

In the field of higher education research, an important and widely used reference book is a text called *How college affects students* (Pascarella and Terenzini 1991, 2005; Mayhew, Rockenbach, Bowman, Seifert, and Wolniak 2016). Now in its third edition, this reference book, originally published in 1991, synthesizes higher education research on a broad range of topics that influence student success from development of critical thinking to the impact of living in on-campus housing. Key, over the years, has been the integration of academic learning and co-curricular experiences for students' academic and psychosocial success. Given the importance of student development inside and outside the classroom, the most recent (2016) version again highlights the importance of co-curricular engagement and the role student affairs practitioners play in supporting the development of the whole student. The authors note that, given the nature of their work, student affairs practitioners work very closely with students and are often tuned into student needs, challenges, and concerns. Student affairs practitioners often have specific training stemming from student development and learning theories to support students' development outside of the classroom (McEwen 2003). For these reasons, Mayhew, Rockenbach, Bowman, Seifert, and Wolniak (2016) suggest that student affairs professionals "harness their knowledge of college students' aspirations, transitions, and experiences, and partner with centers for teaching and learning in co-constructing development workshops for anyone who teaches students" (p. 599).

In the case of developing programming about language diversity for college campuses to create inclusive environments and educate future leaders and citizens, partnerships with student affairs professionals are practical; as Mayhew et al. (2016) additionally note, "co-curricular educators are often at the center of development for students' notions of citizenship through conversations about community expectations in the residence halls and among student organizations . . ." (p. 600). The authors underscore that student affairs professionals are poised to help lead efforts concerning developing students as ethical, responsible citizens, given the nature of their roles and the connectedness of student affairs professionals on campus. Further, Kuh Cruce, Shoup, Kinzie, and Gonyea (2008: 557) encourage faculty to partner with student affairs professionals to leverage their expertise student engagement and "culture-building" in order to "fashion a rich, engaging classroom experience that complements the institution's academic values and students' preferred learning styles." However, again we note that the traditional classroom cannot be the sole location in which this learning and culture building takes place. Indeed, as Long (2012: 1) notes, "student learning takes place in a classroom, but the college or university itself is the classroom. There is no doubt that college is a transformative experience for students. Student learning is, therefore, also about student development."

To support this development, language diversity and tolerance should certainly be core university values and part of the diversity canon. However, linguists cannot be solely responsible for leading this charge. Banta and Kuh (1998: 41) offer that "a faculty cannot by itself accomplish the college's objectives for students' intellectual and personal development; it needs the cooperation of others who work with students where students spend the majority of their time-in employment settings, playing fields, living quarters, and so on." Student affairs practitioners are in a unique position to communicate values of language diversity to new and returning students and to work closely with faculty to buttress learning experiences in the classroom with co-curricular learning experiences. Student affairs professionals often hold master's and doctoral degrees in higher education administration, student personnel, student affairs, etc., for which they receive training in student development theory (e.g., Astin's Theory of Involvement; Bronfenbrenner's Ecological Systems Theory; Chickering's Seven Vectors; Scholssberg's Theory of Mattering Belonging and Theory of Transition), and identity development and critical social theories (e.g., Crenshaw's Intersectionality; Critical Social Theory; Theory of Oppression). Student affairs professionals hold a significant amount of knowledge and expertise related to student learning, development, and creating substantive programming for students to support their growth (Banta and Kuh 1998; Long 2012). However, it is likely to be rare to find a student affairs professional who has training as a linguist. Linguists can partner with student affairs practitioners to offer insights on language and how to incorporate it in the equity and justice conversations on campus. In the next section, we describe examples of how linguists and student affairs practitioners can work together to leverage their respective strengths to advance shared issues around language and social justice.

# 4 Examples of student affairs partnerships that can educate broadly and offer validating experiences

In this section, we offer examples of partnerships between faculty and student affairs professionals on our campuses that have been used to create experiences that will educate students about linguistic diversity. At North Carolina State University, for example, we developed a language diversity education program called "Educating the Educated" (Dunstan, Wolfram, Jaeger, and Crandall 2015), which has a goal of educating campus community members about the value of language as a form of diversity. At the core of the program, a group of faculty, staff, and students (an officially recognized student group called the Language Diversity Ambassadors) partners with faculty and staff across campus to offer training, workshops, and engagement events (e.g. Language and Life Project documentary screenings, panel discussions with visiting scholars). These collaborative efforts advance numerous goals, including: 1) to educate the campus community about the value of linguistic diversity, and 2) to provide validating experiences for linguistically diverse campus community members, particularly minoritized student populations.

Our first example from the Educating the Educated (EtE) program and partnerships with student affairs professionals is one that takes place early in students' academic careers, a time when such interventions and experiences are noted to be important (Rendón 1994; Kuh et al. 2008). The EtE program has partnered with Housing, an integral part of campus life (Pascarella and Terenzini 1991, 2005; Mayhew et al. 2016) by reaching out to residence directors in University Housing to offer to facilitate language diversity workshops during residence advisor (RA) training over the summer. During these training sessions, residence hall advisors were trained on a number of topics related to their jobs, from dealing with facilities issues and handling student crises to planning developmental programming for residents. Our workshop goals were tied to the latter. We offered a "train the trainer" model for talking to students living in residence halls about dialects of North Carolina and the value of linguistic diversity on campus. During the workshops we provided RAs with access to digital resources (e.g., documentaries, video vignettes, audio clips, PowerPoints, maps, etc.) that they could use for programs in their residence halls. We also offered program personnel as a resource – a member of the EtE team could come to a specific residence hall and give a presentation or co-present with an RA. We received helpful feedback from Housing staff about content delivery in the context of Housing programming/presentations that allowed us to better tailor our workshop offerings to be as engaging as possible while still meeting our desired learning outcomes.

An example of an ongoing partnership stemming from our RA training workshops is our partnership with the Women in Science and Engineering (WISE) Village. The housing "villages" at North Carolina State are based on the high impact practice of *learning communities* (Kuh and Schneider 2008). Learning communities have a purpose of creating community among college students to encourage them to interact with each other, faculty, and staff around common academic topics, and to provide sources of social support and personal development (Paige, Wall, Marren, Dubenion, and Rockwell 2017). The WISE Village has partnered with EtE for the past several years to offer a workshop at the beginning of each year for their new residents. It is part of a series of workshops offered to village residents throughout the year to aid in college student success. We talked with the director of the WISE Village about topics of relevance for their students, and one that rose to the surface was student anxiety regarding their being exposed for the first time to diverse dialects, particularly when their instructors spoke a dialect of English unfamiliar to them. Many of our students come from rural backgrounds and may have been exposed to less linguistic diversity prior to arriving on campus (Dunstan 2013). Thus, we created a workshop for the WISE village on this topic centering on the concept of "shared communicative burden" (Lippi-Green 2011). As part of this workshop, we explore biases we might have, for example, as noted by Lippi Green (2011: 73), that we are often more likely to make more of an effort to share the communicative burden when we hear certain "accents" as opposed to others (e.g. American students of European descent may be more willing to make an effort to understand a native French speaker speaking English than a native Chinese speaker speaking English). We discuss the implications for what this means about our feelings, not just with regard to the "accent" but to the person (or group of people) who speaks in such a way. We then talk about practical strategies for sharing communicative burden and successful interactions. In case of difficulties understanding an instructor, we discuss strategies such as using the note-taking outlines many instructors provide to follow lectures, looking for organization cues such as "signposts," strategies for asking clarifying questions, tips for "tuning your ear" to speech patterns, going to office hours to establish rapport and develop relationships with instructors or teaching assistants, etc. The Village Director interacts frequently with students in the village and is able to remind students of these strategies (and many others they have learned in other village workshops) to reinforce their usefulness when students are facing challenges.

A second example of student affairs partnerships is our Alternative Service Break trip. Alternative Service Break trips have a goal of combining leadership, service learning, and outreach to foster personal development and community development (Rhoads and Neururer 1998). On our campus, these trips are facilitated by the Office of Leadership and Civic Engagement, and most trips occur during the week of Spring Break. Trip missions are diverse, from addressing healthcare issues in rural areas to exploring challenges for environmentally sustainable tourism. Staff in the Office of Leadership and Civic Engagement provide the infrastructure for each trip, which includes processes for program application, collecting payment, handling student insurance and medical protocols, issuing purchasing cards, etc. Importantly, they provide leadership training for the staff or faculty member sponsoring the trip and students organizing the efforts. The Office of Leadership and Civic Engagement provides a semester-long course for student trip leaders to participate in pre-departure learning regarding a wide variety of topics, including conflict management, budgeting, and strategies for engaging the group in reflective learning tied to student development theories. On our trip, we travel to the mountains of North Carolina and spend a week teaching the Voices of North Carolina curriculum (Young et al. 2008) to middle and high school students. In addition to teaching this curriculum, college students on the trip also engage in other service activities for the middle and high schools, such as serving on panels about college-going experiences. Our students are prepared to answer questions that middle and high school students have about anything: from how they chose their college to going potluck with a college roommate to what it means to fill out a FAFSA. This trip is parallel to the trip that the North Carolina State University sociolinguistics program has been taking to Ocracoke Island, North Carolina, for the past 25 years (Hazen 2018). EtE also developed a semester-long course that students participating in the trip take pre-departure so that they can learn the Voices of North Carolina curriculum and use it to develop the lessons they want to teach to the middle and high school students in the community we visit during the trip. The student trip leader also participates in this course and contributes information that is being learned in the pre-trip leadership class, particularly with regard to engaging in thoughtful reflection, critical thinking on social justice issues, strategies for advocacy, and communicating the value of public service and civic engagement. Altogether, this partnership results in our students having the opportunity to do language diversity outreach as well as to enhance efforts regarding K-12 to college pipelines. This particular Alternative Service Break trip has partnered with middle and high schools in areas with limited college matriculation rates. Interacting with current college students and learning the Voices of North Carolina curriculum is part of an effort to provide validating experiences for K-12 students to see that, should they aspire to go, they belong in college. The college students are then able to learn by teaching, engage in reflection, and develop leadership skills. In this example, partnering with a key student affairs unit multiplies our reach tremendously and allows us to maintain a program that would be very difficult for an academic department to facilitate as seamlessly. From student affairs colleagues, our students learn leadership skills and development, program facilitation, and strategies for community outreach, and we benefit from their extensive reach in the state and expertise with engaging our students in service learning.

## 5 Concluding thoughts: Broader benefits of diversity work in higher education

Education on issues of linguistic diversity is critical, as they have an impact on the entire campus community, including students (Dunstan and Jaeger 2015, 2016) and faculty (Myrick 2019). If we want to truly diversify higher education and the field of linguistics, we have to be able to attract and retain students from diverse backgrounds, and addressing issues of language diversity may be central to this mission. Addressing issues of language diversity can also be an entry point to addressing critical issues like racial injustice. It is impossible to talk about issues of language diversity without, on some level, thinking about the people who speak those diverse languages and dialects. In this sense, talking about "language" provides an opportunity to open the door for discussions of race, which are often difficult for members of non-minoritized communities, who often need to participate in these discussions the most (DiAngelo 2018.) For example, educational researcher Ty-Ron Douglas (2013) discusses how his Bermudian accent provides an entrée for discussions of identity, race, and stereotyping with his students, as he and his students discuss the assumptions people make about him because of his accent or apparent shifts in their assumptions about him after hearing his accent. Due to what he describes as the privileging of Bermudian English, given its perceived ties by Americans to dialects of British English, he notes that upon hearing his dialect, some individuals with whom he interacts essentially "position me differently than if I had been read as *just* an African-American man" (2013: 62). By sharing his experiences framed around dialects, he opens the door for deeper discussions with his students about race and other crucial topics, including judgments they make about others tied to language. Douglas (2013: 62) notes that "Ultimately, these confessions and discussions give students opportunities to interrogate *who* is perceived as intelligent, who are the insiders, who are the marginalized, and what/whose *standards* or *norms* are used to make these determinations. It is often at this point that my students begin to become ideological border crossers."

Opening this door for students to become "ideological border crossers" is instrumental in being able to think critically about challenging equity and social justice issues. These discussions certainly happen in many linguistics classrooms, but discussions cannot stop there or be limited to only those students who elect to take those courses. Linguists hold critical knowledge and expertise, but they must not be the gatekeepers of this knowledge. One of the most effective ways of reaching the broadest audience on campus may be involving student affairs professionals and units. The coalescing of linguistics and student development theory, paired with creative forms of engagement and practice, holds much promise. Student affairs professionals are also often looking for new ways of communicating ideas about diversity with students and creating validating experiences. They offer significant and diverse perspectives on engaging with and teaching students, and often have large, campus-wide networks for sharing further information and increasing the scope of student outreach. As linguists seek allies, advocates, and partners on campus to advance missions of social justice in higher education, perhaps they need look no further than their scholar-practitioner colleagues next door.

# References

Ardoin, Sonja & becky martinez. 2019. *Straddling class in the academy: 26 stories of students, administrators, and faculty from poor and working-class backgrounds and their compelling lessons for higher education policy and practice*. Sterling, VA: Stylus.

Banta, Trudy W. & George D. Kuh. 1998. A missing link in assessment: Collaboration between academic and student affairs professionals. *Change: The Magazine of Higher Learning* 30 (2). 40–46.

Bourdieu, Pierre. 1991. *Language and symbolic power*. New Haven: Harvard University Press.

Boyer, Patricia G. 2013. Introduction. In Patricia G. Boyer & Dannielle Joy Davis (eds.), *Social justice issues and racism in the college classroom: Perspectives from different voices*, 3–12. International Perspective on Higher Education Research, Volume 8. Bingley, UK: Emerald Group Publishing Limited.

Caldwell, Ebony. 2015. *"Do you understand the words that are coming out of my mouth?" The African American student experience with academic discourse in a community college*. Rochester, NY: St. John Fisher College dissertation.

Charity Hudley, Anne H. 2018. Engaging and supporting underrepresented undergraduate students in linguistic research and across the university. *Journal of English Linguistics* 46 (3). 199–214.

Charity Hudley, Anne H. & Christine Mallinson. 2014. *We do language: English language variation in the secondary English classroom*. New York: Teachers College Press.

Charity Hudley, Anne H. & Christine Mallinson. 2017. It's worth our time: A model of culturally and linguistically supportive professional development for K-12 STEM educators. *Cultural Studies in Science Education* 12 (3). 637–60.

Childs, Becky. 2018. Student voice and linguistic identity: Digital badging as a tool for retention of first year and first generation undergraduates. *Journal of English Linguistics* 46 (3). 186–198.

Conley, B. 2019. The great enrollment crash: Students aren't showing up. And it's only going to get worse. *The Chronicle of Higher Education*. Retrieved from https://www-chronicle-com.proxy006.nclive.org/interactives/20190906-Conley.

Crenshaw, Kimberly W. 1989. Demarginalizing the intersection of race and sex: A Black feminist critique of antidiscrimination doctrine, feminist theory, and antiracist politics. *University of Chicago Legal Forum* 1. 139–167.

Delpit, Lisa D. 2006. Lessons from teachers. *Journal of Teacher Education* 57 (3). 220–231.

DiAngelo, Robin. 2018. *White fragility: Why it's so hard for white people to talk about racism*. Boston: Beacon Press.

Douglas, Ty-Ron M.O. 2013. Confessions of a border-crossing brotha-scholar. In Patricia G. Boyer & Dannielle Joy Davis (eds.), *Social justice issues and racism in the college classroom: Perspectives from different voices*, 55–67. Bingley, UK: Emerald Group Publishing Limited.

Dunstan, Stephany B. & Audrey J. Jaeger. 2015. Dialect and influences on the academic experiences of college students. *Journal of Higher Education* 86 (5). 777–803.

Dunstan, Stephany B. & Audrey J. Jaeger. 2016. The role of language in interactions with others on campus for rural Appalachian college students. *Journal of College Student Development* 57 (1). 47–64.

Dunstan, Stephany B., Walt Wolfram, Audrey J. Jaeger & Rebecca E. Crandall. 2015. Educating the educated: Language diversity in the university backyard. *American Speech* 90 (2). 266–280.

Eliason, Michele J. & Ruby Turalba. 2019. Recognizing oppression: College students' perceptions of identity and its impact on class participation. *The Review of Higher Education* 42 (3). 1257–1281.

Espinosa, Lorelle L., Jonathan M. Turk, Morgan Taylor & Hollie M. Chessman. 2019. Race and ethnicity in higher education: A status report. *The American Council on Education*. https://1xfsu31b52d33idlp13twtos-wpengine.netdna-ssl.com/wpcontent/uploads/2019/02/REHE-Exec-Summary-FINAL.pdf

Godley, Amanda J. & Angela Minnici. 2008. Critical language pedagogy in an urban high school English class. *Urban Education* 43 (3). 319–346.

Godley, Amanda J., Jeffrey Reaser & Kaylan G. Moore. 2015. Pre-service English language arts teachers' development of critical language awareness for teaching. *Linguistics and Education* 32. 41–54.

Godley, Amanda J., Julie Sweetland, Rebecca S. Wheeler, Angela Minnici & Brian D. Carpenter. 2006. Preparing teachers for dialectally diverse classrooms. *Educational Researcher* 35 (8). 30–37.

Goldrick-Rab, S., C. Baker-Smith, V. Coca & E. Looker. 2019. *Guide to assessing basic needs insecurity in higher education*. Philadelphia, PA: The Hope Center for College, Community, and Justice.

Grawe, N. D. 2019. The enrollment crash goes deeper than demographics: Colleges can't stop what's coming, but they can be better prepared. *The Chronicle of Higher Education*. Retrieved from https://www-chronicle-com.proxy006.nclive.org/interactives/20191101-Grawe.

Hausmann, Leslie R. M., Janet Ward Schofield & Rochelle L. Woods. 2007. Sense of belonging as a predictor of intentions to persist among African American and white first-year college students. *Research in Higher Education* 48 (7). 803–839.

Hazen, Kirk. 2018. Sociolinguistic outreach for the New South. *Language variety in the new South: Contemporary perspectives on change and variation*. 321–343. Chapel Hill: University of North Carolina Press.

Hoffman, Marybeth, Jayne Richmond, Jennifer Morrow & Kandice Salomone. 2002. Investigating "sense of belonging" in first-year college students. *Journal of College Student Retention* 4 (3). 227–256

Hurtado, Sylvia. 2013. Diverse learning environments: Assessing and creating conditions for student success. *Final Report to The Ford Foundation*. Los Angeles: Higher Education Research Institute.

Hurtado, Sylvia & Deborah Faye Carter. 1997. Effects of college transition and perceptions of the campus racial climate on Latino college students' sense of belonging. *Sociology of Education* 70 (4). 324–345.

Hurtado, Sylvia, Marcela Cuellar & Chelsea Guillermo-Wann. 2011. Quantitative measures of students' sense of validation: Advancing the study of diverse learning environments. *Enrollment Management Journal* 5(2). 53–71.

Hurtado, Sylvia, Adriana Ruiz Alvarado, and Chelsea Guillermo-Wann. 2015. Creating inclusive environments: The mediating effect of faculty and staff validation on the relationship of discrimination/bias to students' sense of belonging. *JCSCORE* 1(1). 59–81.

Koricich, Andrew, Xi Chen & Rodney P. Hughes. 2018. Understanding the effects of rurality and socioeconomic status on college attendance and institutional choice in the United States. *The Review of Higher Education* 41 (2). 281–305.

Kuh, George D., Ty M. Cruce, Rick Shoup, Jillian Kinzie & Robert M. Gonyea. 2008. Unmasking the effects of student engagement on first-year college grades and persistence. *The Journal of Higher Education* 79 (5). 540–563.

Locks, A. M., Hurtado, S., Bowman, N. A., & Oseguera, L. 2008. Extending notions of campus climate and diversity to students' transition to college. *Review of Higher Education: Journal of the Association for the Study of Higher Education* 31 (3). 257–285.

Lippi-Green, Rosina. 2011. *English with an Accent*, 2nd edition. London: Routledge.

Long, Dallas. 2012. The foundations of student affairs: A guide to the profession. In L. J. Hinchliffe & M. A. Wong (eds.), *Environments for student growth and development: Librarians and student affairs in collaboration*, 1–39. Chicago: Association of College and Research Libraries, a division of the American Library Association.

Love, Patrick. 2003. Considering a career in student affairs. ACPA. https://www.myacpa.org/considering-career-student-affairs.

Mallinson, Christine & Anne H. Charity Hudley. 2010. Communicating about communication: Multidisciplinary approaches to educating educators about language variation. *Language and Linguistics Compass* 44. 245–257.

Mayhew, Matthew, Alyssa Rockenbach, Nicholas Bowman, Trisha Seifert & Gregory Wolniak. 2016. *How college affects students: 21st century evidence that higher education works*. Hoboken, NJ: John Wiley and Sons.

McEwen, Marylu K. 2003. The nature and uses of theory. In Susan R. Komives, D. B. Woodard Jr. & Associates (eds.), *Student services: A handbook for the profession*. 4th ed., 153–178. San Francisco: Jossey-Bass.

Mitchell, Donald Jr., Charlana Y. Simmons & Lindsay A. Greyerbiehl. 2014. *Intersectionality and higher education*. New York, NY: Peter Lang.

Museus, Samuel D. & Kimberly A. Griffin. 2011. Mapping the margins in higher education: On the promise of intersectionality frameworks in research and discourse. *New Directions for Institutional Research* 151. 5–13.

Myrick, Caroline Marie. 2019. *Language and gender ideologies in higher education: An examination of faculty discourses*. Raleigh: North Carolina State University dissertation.

National Center for Education Statistics. 2019. Status and trends in the education of racial and ethnic groups. https://nces.ed.gov/programs/raceindicators/index.asp

Paige, Susan Mary, Amitra A. Wall, Joseph J. Marren, Brian Dubenion & Amy Rockwell. 2017. *The learning community experience in higher education: High-impact practice for student retention*. Abingden, UK: Routledge.

Pascarella, E. T. & P. T. Terenzini. 1991. *How college affects students: Findings and insights from twenty years of research*. San Francisco, CA: Jossey-Bass.

Pascarella, E. T. & P. T. Terenzini. 2005. *How college affects students: A third decade of research*. San Francisco, CA: Jossey-Bass.

Rendón, L. I. (1994). Validating culturally diverse students: Toward a new model of learning and student development. *Innovative Higher Education*, 19(1), 33–51. https://doi.org/10.1007/BF01191156

Rhoads, Robert A. & Julie Neururer. 1998. Alternative spring break: Learning through community service. *NASPA Journal* 35 (2). 100–118.

Strayhorn, Terrell L. 2018. *College students' sense of belonging: A key to educational success for all students*. London: Routledge.
Strayhorn, Terrell L. 2017. Using intersectionality in student affairs research. *New Directions for Student Services* 157. 57–67.
Suskie, Linda. 2015. Introduction to measuring co-curricular learning. *New Directions for Institutional Research* 164. 5–13.
Sweetland, Julie & Rebecca Wheeler. 2014. Addressing dialect variation in US K–12 schools. In *The Routledge handbook of educational linguistics*, ed. Martha Bigelow, Johanna Ennser-Kananen 468–480. Abingdon, UK: Routledge.
Wheeler, Rebecca. 2010. Fostering linguistic habits of mind: Engaging teachers' knowledge and attitudes toward African American Vernacular English. *Language and Linguistics Compass* 4 (10). 954–971.
White, John Wesley. 2005. Sociolinguistic challenges to minority collegiate success: Entering the discourse community of the college. *Journal of College Student Retention: Research, Theory & Practice* 6 (4). 369–393
White, John W. & Carolyne Ali-Khan. 2013. The role of academic discourse in minority students' academic assimilation. *American Secondary Education* 42 (1). 24–42.
White, John W. & Patrick R. Lowenthal. 2011. Academic discourse and the formation of an academic identity: Minority college students and the hidden curriculum. *Higher Education* 34 (2). 1–47.
Whitley, Sarah E., Grace Benson & Alexis Wesaw. 2018. First-generation student success: A landscape analysis of programs and services at four-year institutions. *NASPA – Student Affairs Administrators in Higher Education*. https://firstgen.naspa.org/2018-landscape-analysis.
Yosso, T. J. (2005). Whose Culture Has Capital? A Critical Race Theory Discussion of Community Cultural Wealth. Race, Ethnicity and Education, 8(1), 69–91.
Young, Carl, John Lee, Carol Pope, Candy Beal, Walt Wolfram, Jeff Reaser & Sheryl Long. 2008. The Voices of North Carolina Professional Development Initiative: A new literacies approach to teaching language effectively in the middle grades. In *Society for Information Technology and Teacher Education International Conference*, 4672–4678. Waynesville, NC: Association for the Advancement of Computing in Education (AACE).

Jessica A. Grieser
# Chapter 4
# Critical race theory and the new sociolinguistics

## 1 Introduction

Sociolinguistics has a long history of thinking about language from the perspective of race, especially Black race in the U.S. social context. Yet, as our allied fields of sociology and ethnic studies have moved toward increasingly more complex and confronting conceptions of race, the field of sociolinguistics has been somewhat slower to adopt them. While the seeds of the shift toward adopting the work of allied fields can be seen in very recent work, for example, in the response to the Linguistic Society of America's statement on race (Charity Hudley and Mallinson 2019), we still have some distance to travel to adopt the same approaches that challenge the notion of the social construct of race, acknowledge the root of that construct in racism, and seek to change the structures of power that perpetuate racism. These approaches, part of critical race theory (CRT), have their roots in the legal responses to the Civil Rights Era and have been widely adopted in our allied fields of sociology, education, and law.

This chapter considers what a sociolinguistics informed by the tenets of critical race theory might look like. It takes as a case study the variationist tradition of sociolinguistic study of African American Language (AAL) in the U.S. context, in part, because this variety is the richest source to date of sociolinguistic information about a variety not associated with mainstream, privileged white speakers, and also because it is my own area of expertise. Nevertheless, the discussion here is applicable to the ways we think about all varieties used by minoritized speakers, and I draw on work about the language of other minoritized groups as well. I review the basic tenets and assumptions of critical race theory, then look at the history of sociolinguistic study in the U.S. through the lens of CRT. I discuss some of the reasons why power dynamics and structural racism have gone

---

**Note:** This work was presented at the University of Tennessee's symposium on critical race theory in April 2019 and at the Annual Meeting of the Linguistic Society of America in January 2020. I thank audiences at both for their valuable feedback.

---

**Jessica A. Grieser,** University of Tennessee, jgrieser@utk.edu underexplored in sociolinguistic discussion but set this against some early studies informed by CRT tenets, even if their authors did not explicitly invoke this theory. Finally, I point to recent studies that have implicitly or directly used CRT-based approaches and provide a framework for what a CRT-informed sociolinguistics might look like in practice.

## 2 Why critical race theory?

Critical race theory is rooted in the work of legal scholars and activists reacting to the Civil Rights movement, who recognized during the 1970s that many of the advances gained during the previous decade were stalling and even being rolled back. The next decade called for new theories and new strategies to counter the subtler forms of racism and racial control that were the hallmark of the post-Civil Rights era, and in 1989 the first meeting of "crits," as critical race theorists came to be called, was held in Madison, Wisconsin (Delgado and Stefancic 2017). Its foundations on the insights of critical legal studies and radical feminism helped allow critical race theory to be quickly recognized outside the realm of legal scholarship, and it has been incorporated into the work of other disciplines, especially education, sociology, and American studies. Central to CRT is application: it has an overt activist dimension that challenges scholars to use CRT-informed approaches to better the situation of the people who are being studied.

CRT is useful because it problematizes existing ways of thinking about race. Race is not perceived as categorical, but instead as constructed, and constructed in ways designed to create and maintain power for privileged groups of speakers. CRT-informed work centers the intersections of race and power to expose how aspects of society that might be more often thought of as being differences due to race are, at their core, due to this overlap. It centers the lived, racialized experience of minoritized groups, rather than assuming that the experiences of people from the same group are similar.

Delgado and Stefancic, in their foundational work, point out five central beliefs of CRT. The first is that racism is ordinary, not aberrational. Racism is the paradigm through which the American society is set up to operate, and because of this, racism itself is difficult to address. This is a concept that Bonilla-Silva delves into in much greater depth in another foundational CRT text, *Racism Without Racists* (2018), which shows how racism in the post-civil rights era is usually defined by dominant white groups as being individual, overt prejudicial action from dominant to minoritized groups. This kind of definition neatly elides the recognition of the system of white dominance by making racism about individual bad actors, making the entire concept of racism slipperier to identify and easier for white Americans to ignore.

The second belief is that the system of white over color ascendancy serves important purposes. In his work, CRT scholar Derrick Bell (2004) made the logical, but highly controversial connection that the decision in the landmark supreme court case, *Brown v. Board of Education,* which abolished the legal standing for segregated schools and, in turn, racially segregated public spaces, was not due to a change in the racial order or a newfound lack of societal acceptability for segregation, but rather because desegregation served white interests at the time. This system of *interest convergence* means that the gains of minoritized groups are achievable only within the overarching system of structural racism, and are not countercultural, and, as such, large segments of society have relatively little incentive to eradicate the underlying system.

A third tenet of CRT is that race and races are products of social thought and relations. Consider, for example, the "one-drop" rule, which, during the Reconstruction and its immediate aftermath, legally mandated that all U.S. people with even a single African ancestor be categorized as "Black" and were therefore subject to codes that restricted the legal movement of Blacks. This meant that many people who might be phenotypically classified as white were classified as Black (unless they kept a secret of their ancestry, which no small number did). People living in racist structures, CRT holds, generally ignore scientific truths in favor of creating categories that allow for the identification of to-be-minoritized populations. These depictions have of course changed over time; the concept of a "mixed race" person did not exist until such time as some societal power was granted to the minoritized group that made up the non-white portion of that mixed-race person's ancestry. As Coates puts it succinctly in *Between the world and me,* "Race is the child of racism, not the father" (2015: 7): We socially construct the idea of race in order to draw the lines necessary to support the structural racism inherent in society.

The idea that race is an identity that is created feeds into the fourth tenet, which is that no person has a single, easily stated, unitary identity. Each aspect of who a person is has different material effects on their movement through a society built to marginalize populations in different ways. Like CRT more generally, the specific tenet of *intersectionality* has its roots in the scholarship of law. In the foundational work, Crenshaw (1991) argues that because marginalizations are multiplicative, certain kinds of redress that are aimed at one marginalized identity can skip over redressing the problems of those who have more than one such identity. For example, if a Black woman experiences workplace discrimination, but her boss can show that Black men and white men are treated equally in this work environment, then she cannot seek redress for discrimination based on race. And if she seeks redress based on gender, and her boss can show that white men and white women are treated equally in the same work environment, then she cannot seek redress for discrimination based on gender. The problem she experiences is due to the intersection of her race and her gender, resulting in a unique marginalization that escapes easy classification under existing statutes. CRT holds that these intersections are crucial to understand, and that these non-singular, non-unitary identities must be considered and privileged in the understanding of the impact of race on shared society.

Finally, CRT has a unique voice of color. While white crits exist and are important to the endeavor, CRT holds that, while it is crucial to de-essentialize the experiences of people of color via the considerations of intersectionality, the lived experiences that Black, Indigenous, Asian, and Latinx writers and thinkers experience make them uniquely situated to communicate to their white counterparts, exposing operations of the system which the white counterparts, no matter how well-meaning, are unlikely to know or notice. This is particularly seen in the legal storytelling movement, which calls on people of color to surface their experiences of race and racism in the legal context, applying their unique perspectives to reassess the master narratives of law.

These five tenets make CRT a powerful tool for understanding the ways that people of color use language. Critically, sociolinguistics already holds many of these same assumptions in parallel, but without always surfacing their specific connections to people of color. For example, the wave theory of the development of sociolinguistics (Eckert 2012; see also Tagliamonte 2015) chronicles a movement from the linkage of language use to speakers' membership in broad social categories (first wave), to the attribution of social agency to speakers' use of most locally differentiated (vernacular) features[1] (second wave), to the understanding that meaning is not an "incidental fallout" from socially inscribed language use, but rather is the main purpose of that language use (third wave). That language is socially inscribed sits at the core of the sociolinguistic endeavor, and what critical race theory offers is a way of better exposing the workings of the society in which our speakers' language is inscribed.

# 3 From NORMs to crits: Five early studies

The application of critical race theory-informed approaches has been a somewhat uphill battle. Sociolinguistics has its root in the dialectological studies of the

---

[1] I borrow this definition of vernacular as the most "locally differentiated" variety from Eckert (2001: 19).

early and mid-20th century. Concerned mostly with documenting the existence of features that were maximally divergent across regions, these studies focused on those who were most likely to diverge: speakers who were Nonmobile, Older, Rural, and Male (Chambers and Trudgill 1998). These NORMs, who were also usually white in the U.S. context, served as the foundation for decades of dialectological research because their social situation meant that the influence of other varieties on their speech was negligible. This first-wave approach treated the location of the speakers as the common explanation for their talk, grouping them in an essentialist manner, which, while doing the important work of making visible linguistic variation across space, obscured the socially embedded micro-operations of language practice.

Due in part to this context, the earliest studies of minoritized U.S. speakers took a similar, circumscribing approach to the study of the relationship between language and ethnoracial identity. In the same way that dialect surveys sought to systematically document language variation, which was attributable to region, these early studies sought to systematically document variation that was attributable to race. Like the dialect surveys, these studies collapsed smaller distinctions and privileged the gathering of data from speakers whose speech was maximally divergent from white speech in their area.

Three early foundational studies of African American Language exhibit these difficulties, even as they do the crucial work of surfacing the important differences of the speech of Black communities. Wolfram's work in Detroit (1969), Labov's work in New York City (1972), and Fasold's work in Washington, D.C. (1972) were together among the first to document the patterned ways in which the speech of African Americans differed from privileged white varieties in the same region. Documenting both morphosyntactic and phonological features, they established a shared understanding of the rule-governed structure of African American Language phonology and morphosyntax.

The focus of these early studies on maximal divergence meant that the populations skewed toward young, male, working-class African Americans. While all the early work on AAL included participants who were middle class, women, and speakers of various ages, the young, male, working-class speakers in whose speech the most number of features clustered were the ones who were overrepresented in the data. In this way, they formed a cohort of a new type of NORM, circumscribing many of the ways the variety has been talked about in the intervening decades.

Three decades later, Bucholtz (2003) would go on to argue that this work overly emphasized these speakers in part because of what she terms "strategic essentialism" – that because it was done in the immediate aftermath of the Civil Rights era, the documentation of and defense of AAL as a patterned linguistic variety did important work with regard to advocating for racial justice and for pushing back against educational systems that would categorize its speakers as deficient. This essentialism, however strategic, is nevertheless an essentialism, and Wolfram (2007, 2015) points out that these roots led to several ideological myths within the sociolinguistic imagination about AAL specifically: that the variety is internally homogenous and has a uniform trajectory of either divergence or convergence with white varieties; that it is aregional; and that it is mostly the language of the working class. These myths persisted in structuring the kinds of questions asked in sociolinguistics about AAL and about other ethnoracially affiliated varieties.

Yet even as these early studies were setting up this mythology, within a decade the first generation of prominent African American linguists were changing the landscape of AAL study. Baugh's (1983) work used his own extensive networks in Philadelphia to explore the ways that the variety was implicated in style shifting and as a part of Black agency. In particular, Baugh engaged directly with the issue of Black Street Speech as a product of Black people needing to make headway in, and exist in, a society dominated by whites. His careful tracing of the contexts in which Black Street Speech surfaces lends an important dimension that pushes back on the static portrayal of the variety given ten years earlier. Like those slightly earlier works, Baugh provides a careful documentation of the variety at phonological and morphosyntactic levels, but he importantly inscribes the use of the variety within the framework of response to a society created by white racial ideologies.

A second early study which resisted and upended classic ideas that circumscribed Black speakers is Rickford's (1987) study of his homeland of Guyana.[2] In studying the continuum of acrolectal, mesolectal, and basilectal features among the people of Cane Walk, Rickford found that the best explanation for variation of morphological features was social class. Estate Class (EC) speakers, those who were field workers and farm workers, favored basilectal features, while Non-Estate Class (NEC) speakers favored mesolectal features. Further, speakers' style shifting across the features revealed their extensive communicative competence (à la Hymes 1972) across the continuum, which suggested that language use among the EC allowed them to resist the power structures imposed upon them by the NEC.

---

[2] Rickford's study is not of the variety we now call African American English. However, his findings with respect to the ways that Black speakers respond to power structures are nevertheless relevant here, as they implicate the ideas that Black language does not conform to the expectations of higher status (in the U.S., usually white) speakers, and is frequently employed as a form of resistance.

A principal way in which these two early studies by Black linguists differ from those done slightly earlier by white linguists is in their direct grappling with the implications of intra-community power structures and racism on the use of language. Both studies provide rich quantitative data about the Black varieties with which they engage – AAL in Baugh's case, and Guyanese Creole in Rickford's – and situate language use within an understanding of the ways these varieties are created, maintained, and used within power structures. Both provide different, richer explanations for language use beyond race, gender, and social class, pointing to speaker agency, resistance, and sociolinguistic competence as the richest explanatory models.

These studies are contemporaneous with the roots of critical race theory, and certainly pre-date CRT's wide adoption outside the realm of legal scholarship. Yet they provide a compelling argument that the same questions which drive CRT are broadly applicable to the field of sociolinguistics: that when we study the language of marginalized populations, especially African Americans, explorations that decenter differences between groups in the pursuit of documenting features and instead privilege the understanding of the ways systemic injustices and differentiated power structures have contributed to language use provides a fuller explanation for linguistic variation.

# 4 Putting power and race together

Throughout the remainder of the 20th century, the picture of African Americans and their language became more nuanced and complex. Work on African Americans and their English has diversified to include questions of uniquely African American approaches to literacy (Lanehart 2010), style shifting (Rickford and McNair-Knox 1994), gender (e.g. Kirkland 2015; Lanehart 2009a; Morgan 2002), acquisition (Green 2010), and class (Weldon 2020; Spears 1998, 2015). The work of linguists, especially Black sociolinguists, complicated the picture of African Americans and their language, and also began to engage directly with questions of power. Lippi-Green's (2012 [1997]) groundbreaking book situated language variation, including a long discussion of Black English varieties, within the ways that language varieties are subordinated, not due to their linguistic qualities, but rather due to the power structures between speakers.

Most sociolinguistic interventions directly addressing the intersections between language, racism, and power have occurred in the realm of education. In *King v. Ann Arbor,* many experts in sociolinguistics joined together to testify on behalf of 15 Black students at Martin Luther King Jr. Elementary School, an elementary school in predominantly white Ann Arbor, Michigan. The plaintiffs asserted that the language variety spoken by the students, and their teachers' lack of ability to recognize that variety, resulted in the students being sidelined into speech pathology and learning disability programs that did not apply to them. This, they argued, constituted educational malpractice: psychologists and speech pathologists and specialists who evaluated the students found them to be no less capable of learning than any of their white peers. Instead, AAL presented a language barrier that the teachers were refusing to overcome in teaching them.

Professionals from multiple allied fields, including education, speech pathology, and linguistics, principally assembled by linguist Geneva Smitherman, testified on behalf of the students (see Smitherman 1981). In 1979, Judge Charles Joiner found in favor of the plaintiffs, finding that the school had failed to take into account the students' language in their education and therefore was in violation of the Equal Education Opportunity Act. In doing so, Joiner effectively wrote into law the validity of AAL as a language variety.

From a critical race perspective, the *King* case cannot be understood without thinking about the role played by white racial power. The curriculum in this mostly white school district was set by speakers of a white variety of English, and the school setting, where standard language ideology is the order of the day, provides downward pressure that tends to suppress language variation under the guise of teaching varieties of English deemed as "professional" or "school," or otherwise seen as superior. The harm done was not merely the fact that the students lacked access to their language variety, but also the ways in which the school wielded its power to sideline them based on their status as nonnative speakers of the privileged white variety spoken by their teachers.

One might think that this lesson need only be learned once, but almost precisely two decades later this same race/language/power struggle played out again 2,000 miles away in Oakland, California. In 1996, the Oakland Unified School District passed a resolution regarding the language in use by a large number of its African American students as "not a dialect of English" and documenting its existence as a variety with "systematic, rule-governed, and predictable patterns" in its grammar (Board of Education 1996). This was done in order to proactively earmark state and federal funding for the development of educational programs designed to acknowledge the gap between AAL and standardized white varieties in the schools and to provide means for that gap to be bridged in ways which supported the students' academic success.

The resolution was met with uproar from Black and white Americans alike. AAL was maligned by news outlets, ridiculed in political cartoons, and openly denounced by prominent Black personalities like Jesse Jackson and Oprah.[3] By the time the news cycle died down, many of those personalities would end up agreeing with what had mostly been misunderstandings about what the resolution said and what its aims were,[4] but the damage had been done, leaving linguists once again at the beginning of the 21st century to re-make the case for AAL against the power structures of the American educational system.

Because of the unique struggle between AAL and other minoritized varieties against privileged, mostly white varieties of the school setting, it is not surprising that it is in the realm of educational linguistics where scholarship that explicitly acknowledges issues of power and racism is most common. Alim (2004) chronicles the experiences of Black youth in a high school in a working class suburb in California, explaining both the language-internal and social constraints of the students' style shifting using African American Language styles, and showing the effects of gender and hip-hop nation affiliation on the language these youth employ. Thirty-five years after Baugh, Alim's work similarly highlights the critical importance of documenting agentive style-shifting in the quest to understand the ways in which language use is inscribed in the speech community, and the ways in which it serves to press back against hegemonically white school identities privileged in the educational setting.

Paris's (2011) educational ethnography similarly explores the role of AAL in the school setting and shows how it is co-opted by students of other ethnicities as a means of constructing identities of "difference." While they are understood by their classmates as not Black, AAL borrowing allows Latinx and Pacific Islander students in the school to index nonwhite identities, with implications for the ways their identities are addressed in the school setting as well as for multicultural literacies more generally.

These studies are rooted in the understandings of the relationship between minoritized populations and systems of power. They also take into account the multiplicity of identities, and the ways in which, for example, nonwhite identity is layered with youth identity or specific racial identities in the kinds of linguistic expressions that manifest those identities. Lanehart (2009b) has explicitly discussed the role which intersectionality theory could play in sociolinguistics.

---

[3] The controversy has been written about at length by many scholars of AAL; Baugh (2000) and Rickford and Rickford (2000) provide particularly accessible accounts of the controversy and its aftermath.
[4] A particular stumbling block in the resolution was the use of the linguistics domain word "genetically-based" to describe AAL in the resolution; this meant that AAL descended structurally from other languages, but was read by many naive readers as meaning that African Americans spoke the language as a consequence of their genetics.

Drawing on Tabouret-Keller (1997, cited in Lanehart 2009b), she argues that intersectionality offers a way in with respect to thinking about reconceptualizing the singular, etic identities of race, sexuality, ability, and the like into thinking of them as coalitions between various types of identities, challenging the concept of group identities, which are in reality "centered on the intersectional identities of a few" (p. 6), for example, that our conceptions of Black language have been centered on language of Black, cisgender, heterosexual, working-class men. When we consider instead a subject with a maximally different intersectional identity, perhaps a middle-class, Black, lesbian woman, the ways in which she uses African American Language will no doubt be different and will change the ways we encounter and think about AAL more generally.[5]

The 2010s have seen a shift toward studies that privilege increasingly complex thinking about the relationships between language and race as well as language and power. Some of this has also come in the realm of educational linguistics. Charity Hudley and Mallinson (2010, 2014) have argued extensively for the importance of educators understanding language variation and rejecting standard language ideology (Lippi-Green 2012), and situate these understandings within the concept of the institutional power wielded by teachers in the school setting. The concept of *raciolinguistics* (see Flora and Rosa 2015; Alim, Rickford, and Ball [eds.] 2016) has acknowledged that the "co-naturalization of language and race is a key feature of modern governance, such that languages are perceived as racially embodied and race is perceived as linguistically intelligible" (Rosa 2019: 2). Race is transcribed through language, and language is inscribed upon racialized bodies. It therefore ought to be unsurprising that racism is also transcribed through the ways in which we respond to language, and that language is shaped in response to racism. Surfacing these connections changes the way we understand and study language used by minoritized speakers, and as the 2010s have moved forward, increasingly more scholars have used this tension explicitly in their work.

## 5 Language, race, and activism

The most recent decade of scholarship has pushed hard on the connections between the societal inscription of racist ideologies and the material effects of

---

[5] Lanehart points out that this was a particular study subject she sought for her conference and subsequent edited volume on African American women's speech, and that she could not find such a study.

those connections on language. As mentioned above, this is particularly evident in the adoption of the raciolinguistic approach to language study, which considers explicitly the ways in which language is raced and race is languaged. Pioneers in this particular approach include Jonathan Rosa and Nelson Flores (2017), whose work principally aims to decouple the links between race and language that often are taken for granted. Also working from the framework of linguistics and education, they have argued that even while education as a whole has generally moved in the direction of accepting as valid the language practices of minoritized speakers, this is often done in the service of teaching students how to shift into a standardized, privileged variety when it is "appropriate" to do so. These discourses of appropriateness dominating the educational landscape have had the effect of rendering these minoritized speakers' language practices as deficient. Rosa and Flores argue that, instead, the ways in which linguistic diversity is talked about in education need to break down the entire paradigm of standard language practices, challenging the entire notion of identifiable standardized language.

In his work on "inverted Spanglish," Rosa (2016, 2019) shows how Latina/o youth in a Chicago public high school co-opt the white language practice of Mock Spanish (Hill 2007). Rosa shows how the youth he studies subvert the ideological connections between people racialized as Latinas/os and Mock Spanish and turn them on their head, coupling phrases common in Mock Spanish with hyper-anglicized pronunciations to stereotype not Latina/o speakers, but the white speakers who use this kind of mock language in their own speech. This turns the covert racist discourse of Mock Spanish into another covert discourse, but this time, one which pushes back on whiteness and on the demands placed on the speakers by the ideologies of bilingualism and monolingualism with which they are otherwise surrounded in the school setting.

Raciolinguistic approaches also allow insight into the ways in which minoritized speakers use language to resist power structures placed on them by hegemonic white society. In my own work in Washington, D.C. (Grieser 2013, 2018, fc.), I have found that while the traditional, more etic categories of gender and social class findings hold as explanations for African Americans' use of AAL, its stylistic variation is equally rooted in its use as a means to resist pressures for urban renewal that would take a city once dubbed "Chocolate City" for its immense African American population and change its demographics. AAL becomes a linguistic resource to resist the pushing out of a Black population that traces its roots to the 1600s.

A second sphere where CRT-motivated work has become increasingly apparent is in the realm of studies of linguistic discrimination and especially of AAL as it intersects with the legal system. Drawing on his 2016 Presidential Address to the Linguistic Society of America, John Rickford with Sharese King (2016) highlights several ways in which Black speakers are misheard in legal settings. Centering on the speech of Rachel Jeantel, the principal witness for the prosecution in the trial of George Zimmerman, the man who shot and killed Trayvon Martin in Florida and who would go on to be acquitted in the killing based on Florida's "stand your ground" statute, they show how Jeantel's Haitian Creole-influenced African American Language led to her testimony being both accidentally and willfully misheard and therefore, dismissed, by the jury. They trace these mishearings of vernacular speakers, finding mishearings of testimony offered by speakers of Jamaican Creole and AAL. They conclude by calling for an explicit intervention by linguists, who are best situated to apply our extensive knowledge of language theory to the real-world problems encountered by minoritized speakers in legal settings.

John Baugh, long a pioneer in exposing the workings of linguistic discrimination (Purnell, Idsardi, and Baugh 1999; Baugh 2005), explores the relationship between minoritized people's language, especially African Americans, and systemic injustices in the U.S. legal system in his (2018) book. Tracing the intersections of language and the justice system through the field of forensic linguistics, linguistic injustice, linguistic profiling, and the problems inherent in earwitness testimony, the book interleaves its findings about the specific (in)justices speakers experience as a result of systemic racism stemming back to the African slave trade and its perpetual aftermath in the United States. It traces the history of linguistic interventions in the pursuit of a more just society, and like Rickford and King, makes an explicit call for linguists to use our unique skills to intervene.

While on the whole work that uses linguistics to intervene in legal settings does not tend to explicitly invoke CRT, many of CRT's tenets are inherent in the tendency of this work to begin from an assumption of a system that privileges white voices and white ways of understanding against which minoritized speakers are (mis)heard. They further take into account issues of intersectionality, such as Rickford and King's explication of the combination of racism, colorism, sexism, and ableism that combined to cause Jeantel's speech to be "pilloried" by naive hearers of dark-skinned, heavyset Jeantel (2016: 956–957). Importantly, they carry the tenet of activism of CRT: that a core task of researchers is not only to understand, but also to use that knowledge to make changes in ways that promote justice and equality.

One final emerging body of scholarship is important to note in thinking about the ways in which CRT-informed scholarship is already becoming extant in sociolinguistic literature. CRT, as discussed in the introduction, holds that race is not an immutable category, but rather that it is the product of social thought and the structures within which that thought is inscribed. This suggests that within linguistics, we need to take a more nuanced look at how we think about the entire concept of race. This has so far been exemplified in the work of Nicole Holliday, whose studies of a population of Black/White biracial men has complicated straightforward hypotheses about the relationships between language and racial identity. In an experimental design where she predicted effects of a white or Black co-interlocutor (2016, 2019), Holliday instead found that the best predictor for variation in the AAL intonational patterns she observed is the kind of multiracial identity (see Roquemore and Brunsma 2008) ascribed to by the speaker. This quite literally complicates the entire idea of race as being a single category that a speaker statically inhabits, suggesting that linguistic studies of racial identity and language need to take into effect a much larger range of such identities, and also consider carefully the ways in which racial identity intersects with other kinds of marginalized identities as we seek explanations for our language observations.

## 6 Critical raciolinguistics

We can see that CRT makes its inroads into contemporary sociolinguistic thought simply by virtue of the kinds of thinking sociolinguists find themselves turning to in the 21st century. As our understanding of race becomes more nuanced, as we confront structures of power in educational systems, and as we create means for linguistic understanding and advocacy in the legal system, aspects of critical race thinking are bound to find their way into sociolinguistic scholarship. Yet, even in many studies which rest on the foundations of studying the intersection between race and power, the tenets of CRT are not explicitly written about. What, then, might a sociolinguistics informed by critical race theory look like?

A CRT-informed sociolinguistics centers power dynamics and takes racism as a given in its explanations for linguistic variation. Wolfram, in his sociolinguistic myth explanation for the homogenous ways linguists have explored AAL (2007, 2015), talks about the myth of aregionality: that, due to the discipline's roots in dialectology, finding a variety that seemed to be rooted in something other than the speakers' physical location was seen as so novel that inherent regional differences were underplayed for a long period of the scholarship.[6] Another way to

---

[6] Allowing linguists easy access to data to counter this myth through scholarship is one of the driving factors in the creation of the Corpus of Regional African American Language (Kendall and Farrington 2018).

approach the regional similarity is neither to overemphasize it nor to ignore it, but instead to center explorations into the ways in which racist processes such as Jim Crow laws in the south and redlining in the north contributed to the maintenance of a distinct African American speech community in the Reconstruction era and beyond. Such explanations would in turn better unearth the role of AAL and other minoritized language varieties as the "tool[s] for ordering the chaos" (Smitherman 2006: 96) of experience of racial minorities, and the ways in which the language practices of these groups are means of resistance and subsistence in a society which is actively built against us.

A CRT-informed sociolinguistics calls for humanizing the research subjects and the researchers. In privileging the "unique voice of color," it calls for linguists to listen carefully to our subjects and drive our explanations for our data with the speakers' local explanations instead of dominant narratives about race and power. It calls for us to listen to the students at Rosa's school not as appropriating Mock Spanish but asks us to listen to the ways they recycle a racist framework to do their own distinct racial work. In addition, it calls for more linguists who represent the varied racial experiences in the nations where they reside, and for senior scholars to do the work of training those scholars and then elevating their voices.

A CRT-informed sociolinguistics incorporates work from allied fields. Of course, this includes critical race theory itself, as well as associated theories such as intersectionality theory, but also other social theories from psychology, sociology, and education. This has been done, for example, in the adoption of community of practice theory in the 1990s (Eckert and McConnell-Ginet 1992; Bucholtz 1999), and these theories often provide new nuances to sociolinguistic knowledge, enabling sociolinguists to build on existing ways of knowing and talk back to our sister social sciences. Importantly, it welcomes as linguists those whose work is principally driven by theories from those allied fields, and recognizes as valid those approaches to language study and the knowledge they have to offer.

Finally, a CRT-informed sociolinguistics takes care to consider intersection, and not to privilege any one intersection as being representative of a given style. It considers the roles which each identity a speaker brings to the table plays in the varieties they use, in the discourses they create, and the ways those contribute to that speakers' positioning in the world. It takes as the norm not the NORMs but rather the multiplicity of the ways in which we all use language to situate ourselves in a world with particular biases, and power dynamics, and finds the specific ways in which our language enables us to press back against them.

# References

Alim, H. Samy. 2004. *You know my steez: An ethnographic and sociolinguistic study of styleshifting in a Black American speech community.* Durham, NC: Duke University Press Books.
Alim, H. Samy, John R. Rickford & Arnetha F. Ball (eds.). 2016. *Raciolinguistics: How language shapes our ideas about race.* New York: Oxford University Press.
Baugh, John. 1983. *Black Street Speech: Its history, structure, and survival.* Austin, TX: University of Texas Press.
Baugh, John. 2000. *Beyond Ebonics: Linguistic pride and racial prejudice.* Oxford: Oxford University Press.
Baugh, John. 2005. Linguistic profiling. In Sinfree Makoni, Geneva Smitherman, Arnetha Ball & Arthur K. Spears (eds.), *Black linguistics: Language, society, and politics in Africa and the Americas*, New York: Routledge. 155–168.
Baugh, John. 2018. *Linguistics in pursuit of justice.* Cambridge: Cambridge University Press.
Bell, Derrick. 2004. *Silent Covenants: Brown v. Board of Education and the Unfulfilled Hopes for Racial Reform.* Oxford: Oxford University Press.
Board of Education of Oakland Unified School District. 1996. Resolution of the Board of Education adopting the report and recommendations of the African-American Task Force; A policy statement and directing the superintendent of schools to devise a program to improve the English language acquisition and application skills of African-American Students. Oakland, CA.
Bonilla-Silva, Eduardo. 2018. *Racism without racists: Color-blind racism and the persistence of racial inequality in the United States*, 5th edn. Lanham, MD: Rowman & Littlefield Publishers.
Bucholtz, Mary. 1999. "Why be normal?": Language and identity practices in a community of nerd girls. *Language in Society* 28 (2). 203–223.
Bucholtz, Mary. 2003. Sociolinguistic nostalgia and the authentication of identity. *Journal of Sociolinguistics* 7 (3). 398–416.
Chambers, Jack K. & Peter Trudgill. 1998. *Dialectology.* Cambridge: Cambridge University Press.
Charity Hudley, Anne H. & Christine Mallinson. 2010. *Understanding English language variation in U.S. schools. Multicultural Education Series.* New York: Teachers College Press.
Charity-Hudley, Anne H. & Christine Mallinson. 2014. *We do language: English language variation in the secondary English classroom.* New York: Teachers College Press.
Charity Hudley, Anne H. & Christine Mallinson. 2019. LSA Statement on Race. https://www.linguisticsociety.org/content/lsa-statement-race <Accessed 2020>.
Coates, Ta-Nehisi. 2015. *Between the world and me.* New York: Spiegel & Grau.
Crenshaw, Kimberle. 1991. Mapping the margins: Intersectionality, identity politics, and violence against women of color. *Stanford Law Review* 43 (6). 1241–1299.
Delgado, Richard & Jean Stefancic. 2017. *Critical race theory: An introduction.* New York: NYU Press.
Eckert, Penelope. 2001. Style and social meaning. In John R. Rickford & Penelope Eckert (eds.), *Style and sociolinguistic variation*, 119–26. Cambridge: Cambridge University Press.

Eckert, Penelope. 2012. Three waves of variation study: The emergence of meaning in the study of sociolinguistic variation. *Annual Review of Anthropology* 41. 87–100.

Eckert, Penelope & Sally McConell-Ginet. 1992. Communities of practice: Where language, gender, and power all live. *Locating power: Proceedings of the 1992 Berkeley Women and Language Conference*, 89–99. Berkeley: Berkeley Women and Language Group.

Eckert, Penelope. 2001. Style and Social Meaning. In John R Rickford & Penelope Eckert (eds.), *Style and sociolinguistic variation*, 119–26. Cambridge: Cambridge University Press.

Fasold, Ralph W. 1972. *Tense marking in Black English: A linguistic and social analysis*. San Diego, CA: Harcourt College Pub.

Flores, Nelson & Jonathan Rosa. 2015. Undoing appropriateness: Raciolinguistic ideologies and language diversity in education. *Harvard Educational Review* 85 (2). 149–171.

Green, Lisa J. 2010. *Language and the African American child*. Cambridge: Cambridge University Press.

Grieser, Jessica. 2013. Locating style: Style-shifting to characterize community at the border of Washington, D.C. *University of Pennsylvania Working Papers in Linguistics* 19 (2).

Grieser, Jessica. 2018. Talking shop and talking cop: Topic-based variation in African American English and discursive positioning. Paper presented at Annual Meeting of the Linguistic Society of America, Salt Lake City, UT.

Grieser, Jessica. Forthcoming. *The Black side of the river: African Americans and the linguistic practices of place*. Washington, DC: Georgetown University Press.

Hill, Jane H. 2007. Mock Spanish: A site for the indexical reproduction of racism in American English. In Joseph F. Healey & Eileen O'Brien (eds.), *Race, ethnicity, and gender: Selected readings*, 270–285. Los Angeles: Sage.

Holliday, Nicole. 2016. *Intonational variation, linguistic style and the Black/Biracial experience*. New York: New York University dissertation.

Holliday, Nicole R. 2019. Multiracial identity and racial complexity in sociolinguistic variation. *Language and Linguistics Compass*. 13 (8).

Hymes, Dell. 1972. On communicative competence. In J. B. Pride & Janet Holmes (ed.), *Sociolinguistics. Selected readings*, 269–293. Harmondsworth: Penguin.

Kendall, Tyler & Charlie Farrington. 2018. The Corpus of Regional African American Language. Version 2018.04.06. Eugene, OR: The Online Resources for African American Language Project.

Kirkland, David. 2015. Black masculine language. In Sonja Lanehart (ed.), *The Oxford handbook of African American language*, 834–849. Oxford: Oxford University Press.

Labov, William. 1972. *Language in the inner city*. Philadelphia: University of Pennsylvania Press.

Lanehart, Sonja L. 2009a. *African American Women's language: Discourse, education, and identity*. Newcastle: Cambridge Scholars Publishing.

Lanehart, Sonja L. 2009b. Diversity and intersectionality. Paper presented at Texas Linguistic Forum.

Lanehart, Sonja L. 2010. *Sista, speak!: Black women kinfolk talk about language and literacy*. Austin: University of Texas Press.

Lippi-Green, Rosina. 2012[1997]. *English with an accent*, 2nd ed. New York: Routledge.

Morgan, Marcyliena. 2002. *Language, discourse and power in African American culture*, vol. 20. Cambridge: Cambridge University Press.

Paris, Django. 2011. *Language across difference: Ethnicity, communication, and youth identities in changing urban schools*. Cambridge: Cambridge University Press.

Purnell, Thomas, William Idsardi & John Baugh. 1999. Perceptual and phonetic experiments on American English dialect identification. *Journal of Language and Social Psychology* 18. 10–30.

Rickford, John R. 1987. *Dimensions of a Creole continuum: History, texts & linguistic analysis of Guyanese Creole*. Palo Alto, CA: Stanford University Press.

Rickford, John & Faye McNair-Knox. 1994. Addressee-and topic-influenced style shift: A quantitative sociolinguistic study. In Douglas Biber & Edward Finegan (eds.), *Sociolinguistic perspectives on register*, 235–276. Oxford: Oxford University Press.

Rickford, John R. & Sharese King. 2016. Language and linguistics on trial: Hearing Rachel Jeantel (and other vernacular speakers) in the courtroom and beyond. *Language* 92 (4). 948–988.

Rickford, John & Russell Rickford. 2000. *Spoken soul: The story of Black English*. Hoboken, NJ: Wiley.

Rockquemore, K., D. L. Brunsma & J. R. Feagin. 2008. *Beyond Black: Biracial identity in America*. Lanham, MD: Rowman & Littlefield Publishers.

Rosa, Jonathan. 2016. From Mock Spanish to inverted Spanglish. In H. Samy Alim, John R. Rickford & Arnetha F. Ball (eds.), *Raciolinguistics: How language shapes our ideas about race*, 65–80. Oxford: Oxford University Press.

Rosa, Jonathan. 2019. *Looking like a language, sounding like a race*. Oxford: Oxford Studies in Anthropology.

Rosa, Jonathan & Nelson Flores. 2017. Unsettling race and language: Toward a raciolinguistic perspective. *Language in Society* 46 (5). 621–647.

Smitherman, Geneva. 1981. "What go round come round": King in perspective. *Harvard Educational Review* 51 (1). 40–56.

Smitherman, Geneva. 2006. *Word from the mother: Language and African Americans*. New York: Routledge.

Spears, Arthur K. 1998. African-American language use: Ideology and so-called obscenity. In Salikoko S. Mufwene, Guy Bailey, John Baugh & John R. Rickford (eds.), *African-American English: Structure, history, and use*, 226–250. London/New York: Routledge.

Spears, Arthur K. 2015. African American Standard English. In Sonja Lanehart (ed.), *The Oxford handbook of African American language*, 786–799. Oxford: Oxford University Press.

Tabouret-Keller, Andrée. 1997. Language and identity. In Florian Coulmas (ed.), *The handbook of sociolinguistics*, 315–326. Oxford: Blackwell.

Tagliamonte, Sali A. 2015. *Making waves: The story of variationist sociolinguistics*. Hoboken, NJ: John Wiley & Sons.

Weldon, Tracey. 2020. *Middle class African American English*. Cambridge: Cambridge University Press.

Wolfram, Walt. 1969. *A sociolinguistic description of Detroit Negro speech*. Washington, DC: Center for Applied Linguistics.

Wolfram, Walt. 2007. Sociolinguistic myths in the study of African American English. *Language and Linguistics Compass* 2. 292–313.

Wolfram, Walt. 2015. The sociolinguistic construction of African American language. In Sonja Lanehart (ed.), *The Oxford handbook of African American language*, 338–352. Oxford: Oxford University Press.

Rusty Barrett
# Chapter 5
# You don't even try to understand!: Interdisciplinarity in language and gender studies

## 1 Introduction

While the study of language and gender is inherently interdisciplinary, the field is deeply rooted in linguistics and, until fairly recently, linguists have conducted the overwhelming majority of research in this area. However, it is becoming more and more common to see (often really bad) research on language and gender emerge from scholars working in fields other than linguistics or gender studies. In studies that often gain widespread media attention, scholars in economics and business and some other unrelated fields have begun to promote research on language and gender that ignores research from linguists and gender scholars. Often, such studies promote language ideologies that contribute to gender inequality by placing (especially young) women's speech under unnecessary scrutiny. The conclusions of such research are often basic language myths that are demonstrably wrong. In this paper, I examine three such studies of language and gender, focusing on the ways in which they reproduce mistaken assumptions about language and/or gender and propagate negative stereotypes.

As scholarly disciplines, both gender studies and linguistics face the problem of *self-avowed authority syndrome*, a disorder in which non-specialists assume that because they have some sort of personal experience of the object of some field of study, they are natural experts. People with no training whatsoever in linguistics are often perfectly happy to pontificate about the proper placement of prepositions and stop complete strangers to warn them about the inherent evils of words like *unsweet* or *inflammable*. In the same way, those with no knowledge of research on gender often have no problem making incredibly ignorant claims about sex and gender (especially if those claims support cisheteropatriarchal ideologies and oppress women and/or gender-nonconforming and transgender individuals). The problem seems to arise from the misconception that speaking a language makes one an expert in language or that having genitals somehow makes one an expert on gender and sexuality. The occurrence of this "self-avowed authority syndrome"

**Rusty Barrett,** University of Kentucky, erbarr2@email.uky.edu is much less common in other disciplines. Apart from rare examples like Donald Trump claiming to have a "natural knack" for epidemiology, those distraught by psychics or biology are likely to attribute their opinions to God (rather than to their own natural brilliance). Unfortunately, academics are not immune to this disorder, and it is particularly common to see horrible ideas surface in research on language and gender conducted by scholars in disciplines related to neither language nor to gender. Here, I examine the implications of self-avowed authority syndrome in language and gender research. These studies often reproduce "common sense" (i.e. ignorant) understandings of gender and language, in turn, giving false scientific validation to sexist stereotypes that oppress women and LGBTQ+ people. Sadly, these "interdisciplinary" studies typically overlook research in both linguistics and gender studies.

## 2 English speakers make the best feminists

A paper by psychologists (Prewitt-Freilino et al. 2012) finds that degrees of gender equality correlate with gendered patterns in language. They find what is basically a hierarchy of how much social equality is afforded by different gendered forms of grammar, with the most egalitarian social structures corresponding to the grammars of languages like English (surprise!). Based on the work of other social psychologists, they place the world's languages into three basic categories:
- gendered languages: grammatical gender on nouns and pronouns, categories = masc/fem
- natural gender language: gender usually unmarked on nouns, but gender marked on pronouns
- genderless languages: no gender marking (even on pronouns) or grammatical gender ≠ masc/fem

These categories are not generally used by scholars in linguistics, but are not uncommon among psychologists. Linguists do not use these categories because the reality of gender and grammar across languages is more complex than these categories would suggest. So, for example, it is usually the case that "natural gender languages" (like English) have a number of gendered nouns (primarily nouns for humans). So, English has pairs like actor/actress, waiter/waitress, grandmother/grandfather, and so on, although some such pairs have fallen out of common usage through the activism of feminist linguists (e.g. waiter/ess > server). Similarly, many "gendered languages" have non-gendered words (such as the neuter category in Russian or German). And, of course, "genderless" languages have nouns for humans that are gendered (mother, girl, etc). From a linguistic perspective, these categories are far from ideal. They represent a basic lack of understanding with regard to grammatical gender and how it works in different languages. Similarly, the binary treatment of gender as based on biological sex is inaccurate. Research in gender studies has made it clear that gender is not binary, and sex assigned at birth does not always correspond to gender identity (although the erasure on non-binary identities is common in large-scale studies where gender details are unavailable). So, there are basic problems with the categories the authors use to divide languages into groups.

There are also problems with the explanation of the social outcomes that Prewitt-Freilino et al. (2012) claim one should suspect with each language type. They claim that "genderless" languages are closer to encoding chauvinism compared to "natural gender" languages. Their explanation for this claim is that because genderless languages do not have gendered pronouns, speakers presume that nouns refer to men (rather than women) whenever they occur. In contrast, they claim, using gendered pronouns affords women opportunities by linking gender to nouns through anaphora (e.g. "She is a doctor"). Languages with extensive patterns of grammatical gender are claimed to be the worst offenders because the masculine forms are used as a default, masking cases where the individual is female. The lack of gender pronouns supposedly amplifies this effect as the ungendered third singular pronouns is always assumed to be male. These ideas are just plain silly, and the evidence they provide does not support the claims they make. For example, Prewitt-Freilino et al. (2012) discuss a study finding that the use of *he or she* is less likely to trigger the image of a woman compared to singular *they*. In other words, psychological chauvinism is more likely to be triggered with gendered pronouns compared to a non-gendered third person pronoun (like singular *they*). Of course, genderless languages have non-gendered pronouns (like singular *they*), which should mean that speakers are *less* likely to presume maleness when hearing a noun. Naturally, this is exactly the opposite of what the authors actually argue. Their attempts to explain why "natural gender" languages are the least sexist come across like a fixed game with English chosen as the winner before the game begins.

The place of gender in grammar can change over time, particularly when dominant understandings of gender are also changing. In particular, forms that reflect gender bias tend to fall out of usage either through active campaigns against sexist language or by simply becoming irrelevant over time (like Lakoff's (2004 [1975]) example of *lady doctor*). From *Miss* to *Ms.* to *Mx.*, the way that we represent gender in English has been undergoing change for quite some time. Similar proposals have been made for Spanish, where some speakers now use – *e* as a gender-neutral ending (to account for non-binary individuals who are erased in masculine/feminine pairs like *trabajador/trabajadora*). The theoretical framework proposed here would predict that a case like *trabajador/trabajadora* giving way to *trabajadore* would correlate with an increase in gender equality, while we would expect equality to decrease with the introduction of an unmarked pronoun, like *ele* in place of *él/ella*. The assumption Prewitt-Freilino et al. (2012) might be working under is the idea that languages don't show variation or change, which any linguistic would immediately recognize as wrong.

These are not, however, the most egregious errors in the Prewitt-Freilino et al. (2012) paper. That prize goes to the way they categorize countries according to a single language type. First, each nation must correspond to a single language. Thus, a multilingual country like Guatemala (where half of the population speaks a genderless Mayan language) is categorized according to the colonial language (Spanish), erasing indigenous languages from their study. The authors count colonial languages in a number of countries where the majority speaks a local language, like Gambia (categorized as English) and Burkina Faso (categorized as French). In addition, they omit all Creole languages on the basis that the place of gender in their grammars cannot be determined. This, despite the fact that Creoles should be no more difficult than any other language in terms of determining how gender is used. Creoles generally follow the pattern of their lexifier languages, but a number of English-based Creoles do not maintain gender distinctions in pronouns, so that these Creoles are readily classified as "genderless" languages. This is the case for Western Jamaican Patwa (i.e. on the west side of the island), where there is no distinction between *hi* and *shi*. Patwa is classified as "natural gender" because of the eastern dialect, but this misrepresents the actual patterns in the language. In addition to cutting out all contact varieties, Prewitt-Freilino et al. (2012) make very bizarre choices. For example, Ireland (where the overwhelming number of speakers speak English) is categorized as "genderless," presumably on the basis of Gaelic (although Gaelic is structurally a "natural gender" language just like English). Similar, Zimbabwe is categorized as a "natural gender" country (perhaps based on English), although the vast majority of citizens in Zimbabwe speak Shona, a genderless language. In contrast, South Africa is categorized as a "genderless" country, erasing the speakers of English and Afrikaans (both "natural gender" languages). Although they take their languages from the CIA Factbooks, at times it seems like the authors simply guessed at what language is spoken where. For example, the main language of Belize is English ("natural gender") with a number of "genderless" indigenous languages (Yukatek Maya, Mopan Maya, Q'eqchi Maya, and Garifuna). Yet, Prewitt-Freilino et al. (2012) categorize Belize as speaking a "gendered" language – the one pattern *not* found in the country. One cannot help but wonder if the authors looked at a map and guessed that everyone between the US and Brazil probably speaks English. In the article, we see the authors create dubious language categories and then haphazardly throw countries into those categories without regarding the actual linguistic complexity found in those countries.

The ultimate result is that Prewitt-Freilino et al. (2012) have created a "language-based" categorization of nation states that basically shows that economic equality falls along clear lines according to patterns of colonization. Nations colonized by the British ("natural gender languages") are less sexist than nations colonized by France, Spain, or Portugal. Nations colonized by Romance speakers are less sexist than those who maintain local languages in the face of colonization. This last group includes a number of African nations where indigenous languages have been made official. So, basically, Prewitt-Freilino et al. (2012) have created a model demonstrating that white people are less sexist than Brown people who are less sexist than Black people. The paper ends up being a perfect example of going to great lengths to demonstrate that racist stereotypes are somehow based on empirical evidence. It tells us nothing about language and nothing about gender, but it definitely concludes that English is among the most progressive languages in terms of sexism. There is no interdisciplinarity here as the authors assume that grammar is not particularly complicated and linguistics isn't needed. So, all of the world's languages can fit easily into three fixed categories created by social psychologists who probably "couldn't parse their way out of a paper bag" (to quote Nora England).

## 3 Vocal fry will ruin your life

The next example of self-appointed authority syndrome comes from biologist Rindy Anderson and her colleagues' (2014) paper, "Vocal fry may undermine the success of young women in the labor market." This paper gained media attention and played a central role in the ongoing moral panic over women's use of creaky voice. Again, we see a paper that simply perpetuates pre-existing stereotypes and doesn't tell us anything new about language or gender. In this research, creaky voice (or vocal fry) was explained to male and female subjects who were then asked to make a recording imitating creaky voice. Of course, no linguist would use imitations of language features as the basis for a study unless they were actually studying imitation itself (as in Preston 1992). Listeners were asked to judge a series of voices, including regular speech and the imitations of creak. The results found that women's speech was judged more harshly when they were imitating creaky voice. Of course, they could have asked the subjects to imitate Charlie Brown's teacher and the men's voices would have better judgments. We live in a sexist world. We are told that creaky voice makes women sound insecure and uncertain. In other words, when imitating a pronunciation that isn't their own, men are less likely to be perceived negatively than women are. To fully appreciate the atrociousness of this paper, a little background on creaky voice is warranted.

First, creaky voice is a totally normal means of phonation used in many different languages. In English, it has traditionally been associated with the speech of cisgender heterosexual men. The use of creaky voice, particularly towards the end of an utterance, has long been a feature of men's speech, evoking masculinity and authority. No one ever complained about men's use of creaky voice, even though they use it much more than women do. The anxiety over women's use of creak is part of a long tradition of denigrating the language of young women on the basis of features that are found in men's speech. These exact critiques have been made about, like, the use of *like* in, like, the 1980s and the use of uptalk (rising intonation at the end of a declarative utterance). These features were (and are) common in the speech of men, but only spark criticism when they are used by women. Young women tend to be leaders in patterns of language change, so they may use innovative forms more frequently than men. Even so, the unwillingness to see the same forms in the speech of men is remarkable and consistent. Young women are told that they apologize too much in the workplace and that it makes them sound insecure and uncertain. Of course, apologies by men go largely unnoticed (unless they are public apologies for misconduct). For example, the majority of emails I write begin with the words, "Sorry to just be getting back to you." I have never been told that this makes me sound insecure or uncertain.

While the speech of young women may not actually index insecurity, the scrutiny focused on their language is all about instilling insecurity. It is a standard form of sexism that simply creates one more obstacle for young women in the workplace. Women are scrutinized for their clothing, their shoes, their hair, their makeup, how often they go to the bathroom, and so on. Language is just one more example. Research like that of Anderson et al. (2014) is not helpful. It is not helpful to science because it uses a flawed methodology. It is not helpful to women, for whom the paper simply provides one more aspect of their behavior to be examined and criticized. It is only helpful to the institutionalized sexism that depends on placing women in precarious situations.

## 4 Gossipmongers always get the best husbands

The final example I would like to consider is "Women's gossip as an intrasexual competition strategy: An evolutionary approach to sex and discrimination" from the *Oxford handbook of gossip and reputation* (Davis et al. 2019). In the disciplinary triage, evolutionary psychology has the most urgent need for help from linguists (other than Steven Pinker, who has already helped quite enough). In terms of producing research that simply reproduces gender stereotypes, evolutionary psychology is among the worst offenders. It is, after all, the academic approach that pedophile rapist Jeffrey Epstein adored (Walling 2019), as well as the basis for Pinker's (2002) defense of the idea that rape was a "natural" result of human evolution.

Evolutionary psychology attempts to find the evolutionary forces that might have resulted in current patterns of human psychology. Evolutionary psychology takes an essentialist approach to gender, assuming that gender differences in behavior are the natural result of evolution. One of the widely discussed examples is the finding that women prefer the color pink (over blue) because of evolutionary adaptation. Within this proposal, women's "natural" preference for pink over blue results from adaptation related to the need of gathering foods. The preference for pink evolved because it makes it easier to find berries (berries only came in pink back then). Since women were gatherers (and men were hunters), this meant that the adaptation only occurred as a female biological trait (Hulbert and Ling 2007, see also Alexander 2003). It turns out that the "pink for girls, blue for boys" distinction is not at all universal. Indeed, even in the United States (where the pink/blue idea has the strongest adherents), the pattern was inconsistent up until the 1940s when a clear pink/female-blue/male distinction solidified (see Del Giudice 2017). The value of a female pink preference for making it easier to find berries is pretty dubious (even if we were to assume that all berries were pink back in the day). This pink berry hypothesis is just one more case of scholars validating justifications for gender inequality rather than actually studying the social and systemic factors that allow gender inequality to persist.

This is also the case in *Women's gossip as an intrasexual competition strategy: An evolutionary approach to sex and discrimination* (Davis et al. 2019). Here, we discover that women's tendency to gossip results from natural selection by which women who gossip more obtain "better" male partners. The theory basically boils down to "she who talks shit about other women the most gets the man." Of course, there is no actual evidence behind the idea that women gossip more than men do. Rather, the entire idea of "gossip" is a means of denigrating, sanctioning, and dismissing women's language use. In other words, gossip is not something women do; rather, it is a label placed on women's language in order to trivialize their ideas and concerns. This is largely why the concept of "gossip" is slippery and difficult to define. The term is not descriptive; it is pejorative.

The authors behind the "intrasexual competition strategy" theory recognize that it is necessary to define "gossip" before making claims about it. Their definition of gossip is the *transmitting or receiving of socially relevant information about the new, deviant, and/or prosocial behavior of other people* (Davis et al. 2019: 304). This definition could probably apply to the majority of human interactions: reading a newspaper article about some Florida man, listening to a history lecture, reading the stats for your fantasy football team, browsing through selfies on Instagram, most cases of mansplaining, and so on. If this is your definition of gossip, men gossip more than women do simply because men talk more and often find ways of silencing women's voices. Despite this very open-ended definition, the authors quickly move to a much more specific "conventional understanding" that gossip is "a wicked, sneaky, and malicious form of information" (Davis et al. 2019: 304). They then discuss two basic types of gossip: *strategy learning gossip* and *reputation gossip*. The first type is spreading information that is relevant to genetic fitness. Information like "Jessica is allergic to peanuts" would be this type of gossip, providing the listener with non-judgmental information about Jessica's potential for producing good offspring. The other type, reputation gossip, is intended to convey how others see a specific person (like, a potential rival for a man). It is reputation gossip that women supposedly cannot help but produce both when talking with male partners and female friends. Thus, saying *Emily has sex with a lot of men* (one of their actual examples) conveys the idea that offspring from Emily might be fathered by just about anybody, so the odds of the baby being yours are pretty low. This utterance, in turn, increases the gossiper's chances for producing offspring with "better" male partners while reducing those chances for Emily.

So, the story is that loving to spread gossip evolved as a natural product of women's competition for potential sexual partners. Of course, there are actual studies on patterns of "slut shaming" that do not support the idea that it is a universal feature of women's psychology. In a study of slut shaming on college campuses, Elizabeth Armstrong and her colleagues (2014) found that middle-class women were much more likely than working-class women to gossip about the reputation of others. Working-class women were much more likely to be the subject of slut shaming (despite the fact that the working-class women actually had fewer sexual partners compared to the middle-class women). Reputation gossip is not uniform across social classes and seems to be used mostly by middle-class women to discourage working-class women from gaining access to middle-class men as potential mates. This suggests that reputation gossip is more likely about maintaining class privilege (and that it is a technique that is not available to all women).

## 5 Who needs linguists?

Each of these three studies reproduces sexist, misogynistic, and even racial stereotypes. Thus, we see broad claims that would probably be avoided if they were not framed as being about language. In this sense, these are rather ordinary cases of *symbolic revalorization* (Woolard and Schieffelin 1994) in which attention to language comes to discursively stand in for other (sanctioned) forms of discrimination. It is no surprise that a study would reproduce the stereotype that life is best for women in English-speaking countries and worst for women in Spanish-speaking countries. It is always much easier to learn new things if you already believe them to be true. The claim about grammatical gender is, perhaps, not particularly different from saying that white men are better to women compared to Latinos, particularly when examined in terms of white assumptions equating quality of life with level of income. Making the issue a question of language simply makes a prejudicial claim more palatable.

Telling women that they will be judged negatively for their speech solely on the basis of people *imitating* creaky voice does little more than contribute to the broader discourses that serve to produce the very insecurity they warn against. There is a regular cycle beginning with a modicum of public attention to some feature quickly followed by researchers discovering that this aspect of women's speech makes them sound insecure, unassertive, and so on. The media then picks up on the idea, and women are warned about the dangers of using the feature under scrutiny, fueling both actual insecurities of women in the workplace and the insecurities imagined by listeners. Of course, telling women that they "sound" insecure in the workplace makes their unequal treatment somehow their own fault – she uses too much creak, she lets her intonation rise at the end of sentences too frequently, and so on. Studies that primarily point out some flaw in women's language tell us very little about language or gender. They only demonstrate that misogyny is so deeply rooted that researchers can simply reproduce misogynist ideas and fail to recognize them for what they are simply because they are about how women speak rather than about how women are treated.

Similarly, we do not need a study to explain why women are unable to control their innate desire to gossip about potential rivals in order to gain advantage in the competition for good potential fathers. It would probably be more useful to have a study examining why anyone with a PhD would simply assume that such an ignorant sexist idea could possibly be true (without the need to even consider the possibility that there might be empirical evidence showing otherwise). A common problem with self-appointed authority syndrome is the tendency of victims to conduct research that proves ideas they already hold. This not only perpetuates bad (harmful) ideas, but actually gives those ideas scholarly validation. Such research does not enlighten our understanding of humanity and the world we live in – it simply helps uphold and maintain systemic forms of inequality.

At the beginning of this ~~rant~~ paper, I claimed that self-appointed authority syndrome was common when it comes to the study of language because people assume that speaking a language means that you understand how it works. However, the problem is exacerbated by the fact that many highly educated people have almost no understanding of linguistics as an academic discipline. Because linguistics is a comparatively small academic field, scholars in other fields often overlook the potential for interdisciplinary research with linguists. Beyond the *how many languages do you speak* annoyances from the public, academics in other disciplines (and administrators in particular) simply do not know what linguists do. In my academic career, I have repeatedly encountered scholars (and deans) who operated under a false assumption that they understood what linguistics was all about. Linguists all study the decipherment of ancient texts or they all research how to help people learn a new language or they all document Indigenous languages. Linguistics is all about helping people learn to write good, or (my favorite) linguistics is like history but a lot easier because you only study language and don't have to worry about actual people. If one has an extremely narrow idea of what linguistics actually entails, then there is no reason to learn about linguistics in order to study language and gender (because all linguists study speech pathology or whatever it may be). Until we, as linguists, can get other scholars to recognize what we do and why it matters, we will continue to see bad research on language conducted by those suffering from self-appointed authority syndrome.

In language and gender studies, the biggest issue regarding interdisciplinarity is the lack of it. All too often, the ubiquity of our disciplinary focus allows people to presume that the study of language is already covered by other disciplines. It is true that linguists study aspects of language relevant to archaeology, cultural anthropology, history, psychology, sociology, gender studies, ethnic studies, political science, education, geography, literature, philosophy, and so on. The fact that we are everywhere can make us hard to see; we are the proverbial trees in the unseen forest. We need to work so that other disciplines will recognize that regardless of what aspect of language one considers, linguists have the toolkit to examine it systematically. If those in other disciplines recognized the value of our field, perhaps we would have fewer business professors terrifying young women with horror stories of poor girls whose lives were ruined because they succumbed to the perilous temptation of creaky voice.

# References

Alexander, Gerianne M. 2003. An evolutionary perspective of sex-typed toy preferences: Pink, blue, and the brain. *Archives of Sexual Behavior* 32 (1). 7–14.

Anderson R. C., C. A. Klofstad, W. J. Mayew & M. Venkatachalam. 2014. Vocal fry may undermine the success of young women in the labor market. *PLoS ONE* 9 (5). e97506. doi:10.1371/journal.pone.0097506

Armstrong, Elizabeth A., Laura T. Hamilton, Elizabeth M. Armstrong & J. Lotus Seely. 2014. "Good girls": Gender, social class, and slut discourse on campus. *Social Psychology Quarterly* 77 (2). 100–122.

Davis, Adam, Tracy Vaillancourt, Steven Arnocky & Robert Doyel. 2019. Women's gossip as an intrasexual competition strategy: An evolutionary approach to sex and discrimination. In Francesca Giardini & Rafael Wittek (eds.), *The Oxford handbook of gossip and reputation*, 303–321. New York: Oxford University Press.

Del Giudice, Marco. 2017. Pink, blue, and gender: An update. *Archives of Sexual Behavior* 46. 1555–1563.

Hurlbert, A. C. & Y. Ling. 2007. Biological components of sex differences in color preference. *Current Biology* 17. R623–R625. doi:10.1016/j.cub.2007.06.022.

Lakoff, Robin. 2004 [1975]. *Language and woman's place: Text and commentaries* (Ed. by Mary Bucholtz). New York: Oxford University Press.

Pinker, Steven. 2002. *The blank slate: The modern denial of human nature*. New York: Penguin Books.

Preston, Dennis R. 1992. Talking black and talking white: A study in variety imitation. In Joan H. Hall, Nick Doane & Dick Ringler (eds.), *Old English and new: Studies in language and linguistics in honor of Frederic G. Cassidy*, 327–354. New York: Garland.

Prewitt-Freilino, Jennifer L., T. Andrew Caswell & Emmi K. Laakso. 2012. The gendering of language: A comparison of gender equality in countries with gendered, natural gender, and genderless languages. *Sex Roles* 66. 268–281.

Walling, Alexandra. 2019. Why Jeffrey Epstein loved evolutionary psychology: And why evolutionary psychologists loved him right back? *The Outline*. September 19. https://theoutline.com/post/7956/jeffrey-epstein-evolutionary-psychology?

Woolard, Kathryn A. & Bambi B. Schieffelin. 1994. Language ideology. *Annual Review of Anthropology* 23. 55–58.

Arran Stibbe
# Chapter 6
# Ecolinguistics as a transdisciplinary movement and a way of life

## 1 Introduction

I've noticed a "story" that appears sometimes within humanities disciplines: that writing needs to be objective, impersonal, disengaged, dispassionate and disinterested. That it's necessary to mimic the writing style of natural science in order to appear credible. Calling something a "story" does not imply that it's true or false, right or wrong, helpful or unhelpful. It does, however, imply that it is only one perspective among other possible perspectives, one account of the world among other possible accounts. For me, the essence of "transdisciplinary" is an awareness of disciplinary stories, and a willingness to move beyond them in pursuit of a wider vision. Trans, for me, means "transcend" – transcending the restrictions, limitations and worldviews of any academic discipline, not for the sake of it, but because the broader vision necessitates it.

My goal for this chapter is to describe ecolinguistics as a transdisciplinary movement, and I've chosen not to follow the disciplinary story that academic writing needs to be objective and disengaged by writing the chapter as a personal narrative. And I'm doing so not for the sake of it but because a transdisciplinary movement necessarily jumps out of the confines of academic space and into personal space, into community space, into nature. It refuses to be confined within the walls of libraries, classrooms, theories or third-person writing.

## 2 From linguist to ecolinguist

My personal narrative begins in a dilapidated beach café in Japan, with the owner explaining why she doesn't kill the cockroaches that occasionally scurry across the floor. "A cockroach is a manifestation of life," she says, "just like a cat is a manifestation of life, just like a monkey is a manifestation of life, and just like a person is a manifestation of life." In many hours of conversation with elders in Japan, I came to appreciate their deep respect for life and how they used

**Arran Stibbe,** University of Gloucestershire, astibbe@glos.ac.uk

https://doi.org/10.1515/9781501514371-006

language in inspiring ways to communicate that respect. There was the saying of *itadakimasu* before eating to express gratitude to the plants and animals that died for the meal; the concept of *mottainai* to express regret for waste; and *wabi*, an aesthetic appreciation of imperfection and transience. There was *haiku*, with its ability to place ordinary animals and plants in what van Leeuwen (2008: 51) calls the "activated roles" of agent, senser, sayer, as beings leading their own lives for their own purposes and deserving of respect for that. And much more – a traditional culture rich in appreciation of the natural world and linguistic techniques to express that appreciation.

At that time, I was a linguistics lecturer teaching writing, reading and conversation in a Buddhist university in the mountains of northern Kyushu. Even in the mountains modernist forces were edging in, with an ideology of cutting down, flattening and concreting over nature. So, I started using environmental EFL textbooks to raise students' awareness of issues that were crucial to their future and the future of life on Earth. These textbooks were written by authors far away in the UK and USA, but I soon discovered that they were full of harmful ideology. Instead of respect and care for plants, animals and the natural world, the textbooks treated them as resources, for example: "Much of what humans do with their biological resources – including . . . species harvested from natural populations – depends on our having an accurate inventory of life on Earth" (environmental textbook in Stibbe 2012: 129). It's the pronoun "their" in "their biological resources" which stands out for me – that all animals and plants are presupposed to be human possessions. And, of course, "inventory" uses a business frame to turn all life into stocks of resources to be deployed at will.

Instead of discouraging consumerism by encouraging students to find joy in nature, the textbooks seemed to promote a love of material products: "Simply stated, cars offer fun and freedom. When we get behind the wheel and get on the road, we can flee the monotony of daily life . . . even if we are forced to spend most of our time sitting in traffic jams, the allure of the automobile is its promise of escape" (environmental textbook in Stibbe 2012: 126). This echoes the style of car advertisements by framing daily life as a prison, and the car a means of escaping it and finding freedom. I became deeply interested in the messages and ideologies behind these "environmental" textbooks and ended up analysing 26 of them (Stibbe 2012: 121–144).

I found that textbooks were uninspiring because they didn't challenge the underlying worldviews that led to ecological destruction in the first place, and often used language in ways that entrenched and promoted those worldviews. We could speculate this is because of the role that TEFL has traditionally played in linguistic imperialism and in deliberately spreading consumerism around the world to open up new markets for western goods: "Corporate consumerism and US lifestyle are thus wedded to the learning of English" (Phillipson 2010: 111).

The linguistic patterns I found, with their underlying ideologies, ran through the textbooks and formed a particular *discourse*. Critical Discourse Analysis (Fairclough 2014) therefore seemed like an ideal tool to reveal and resist them. Except that at that time Critical Discourse Analysis was almost entirely focused on the liberation of groups of humans oppressed by other humans (e.g., racism and sexism), even though it's exactly these groups that are most vulnerable to ecological destruction.

I had come across ecocriticism, ecopsychology and ecofeminism, and one morning I woke up and thought it would be wonderful if there was an *ecolinguistics*, too. That we need an ecolinguistics. So, I Googled "ecolinguistics" and found, inevitably, that it already existed. And equally inevitably I found there was a bizarre range of studies which labelled themselves as "ecolinguistic". There were studies of road signs that were "ecolinguistic" because their texts were outside. There were TEFL studies of the kinds of English that learners experience in their lives, which were ecolinguistic because learners interacted with a "learning environment". There were "language ecology" studies that examined linguistic interaction using a metaphor that described languages in terms of biological species – what Pennycook (2017: 134) calls "precarious analogies between languages and species".

Closer to actual ecological issues were studies that critiqued the language of environmentalism (Harré *et al.* 1999) or examined how the grammar of the English language itself constrained the environmental imagination (Goatly 2001; Halliday 2001). Halliday (2001: 193), for instance, described how "There is a syndrome of grammatical features which conspire . . . to construe reality in a certain way; and it is a way that is no longer good for our health as a species".

While I was pleased that ecolinguistics had been established, I longed for the simplicity of all the other ecological humanities. The prefix eco- in ecopsychology, ecocriticism, ecofeminism and the others quite simply means a consideration of not only humans but the wider ecological world of animals, plants, forests, rivers, soil, rain and the ecosystems that life depends on. And the prefix also implies an action orientation – action towards social justice for humans through countering ecological destruction (which threatens us all, but vulnerable populations most), and care for the countless other species with which we share the Earth. The latest ecological humanities subject is "marine humanities", which Vincent Ooi (2017: 83) describes simply as such: "Marine humanities is a very recent term to characterize an interdisciplinary field that examines the continuing narrative and construal of underwater and ocean environments, with the ultimate goal of understanding and preserving these environments".

I felt that if ecolinguistics was to become a credible ecological humanities subject like the others, then it needed to take ecology seriously rather than using it as a metaphor to mean "outdoors", "environment" in a general sense, or "interaction". It needed to go beyond "linguistics" to become fully transdisciplinary, combining linguistics with a rich conception of ecology and an action orientation.

At a personal level, I also needed to transcend my academic background in linguistics and develop myself as a transdisciplinary researcher. I therefore left Japan and headed to Scotland to undertake a unique and challenging MSc in Human Ecology at the Centre for Human Ecology in Edinburgh. This was a truly transdisciplinary course. At its heart was activism, and it aimed to provide the intellectual, emotional and practical skills to be an effective activist. The modules covered scientific ecology, psychology, economics, spirituality, social change, pedagogy, feminism, anti-racism, action research and community development. It did all this within a human ecology framework that considered the interactions of humans, animals, plants, forests, rivers and the wider ecosystems that life depends on.

The Centre for Human Ecology has a chequered history. It used to be part of the University of Edinburgh, but was quite unique in its transdisciplinary combination of academia and activism. Among many other things, it campaigned against a superquarry on the island of Harris, bringing over a Native American chief to give evidence in a public enquiry to determine the future of the quarry; and it worked with residents of the isle of Eigg to enable a community buyout of the island. In 1996, the University of Edinburgh axed it, for controversial reasons. The University was accused of being embarrassed about the radical approach of the Centre, which it denied (Wynne-Jones 1996). Monbiot (2013: 281) describes how the work of the Centre was controversial but its standards widely acknowledged to be high, quoting an external examiner who wrote that the centre had "developed an intellectually innovate, creative and exacting approach to issues of mounting public significance, in important respects helping blaze a trail". He concludes that "Many observers felt that the centre had been closed because its radicalism was incompatible with the ethics of a university receiving an increasing proportion of its income from corporations" (Monbiot 2013: 282). When I studied there, the centre had re-established itself as an independent college, free to explore a radically transdisciplinary approach to its fullest.

I graduated from the Centre for Human Ecology ready to become a very different kind of academic, one still based in linguistics but with an approach transcending the confines of the discipline, and the confines of language, to engage in wider concerns that are central to the future of life. I was ready to become a transdisciplinary academic. Luckily, I was offered a post as a lecturer in English Language at the University of Gloucestershire, a university which at the time had a radical strategy based on "diversity, social justice, and sustainability". At the time of writing, Gloucestershire is no. 1 in the UK for sustainability, according to the People & Planet University League (2019). If anywhere was going to support transdisciplinary approaches, it was Gloucestershire.

The Centre for Human Ecology taught me that it's essential to be "engaged" in the world, not just in order to make a practical difference and benefit society, but also because without engagement academic work is liable to detach from reality and float around in a world of abstractions. With ecological humanities, the engagement quite literally "grounds" the academic work in the reality of communities and the Earth. I created an Edible Garden on campus, where staff, students and the local community could learn from experts in permaculture and grow vegetables and friendships together. The police started bringing young offenders to the garden to build bridges through growing vegetables together. I became a Parish Councillor and joined the steering groups of community organisations, working towards environmental justice and protection of green space. I worked with Greenpeace on their campaign strategy, with the United Nations Environmental Program on the National Ecosystem Assessment, and with local companies on aligning action with values. I attended environmental protests such as Climate Camp and put my name to the original letter that launched an Extinction Rebellion. And I developed my own personal connection with community and nature by running in all weathers, through photography, food growing and community projects.

Some of this work had an obvious linguistic element to it. On the UNEP humanities working group, I argued that the discourse of ecosystem assessments erases animals and plants by continuously referring to them in abstractions: *mammal, flora, fauna, organisms, assemblages of species, biotic components, biomass*; or by framing them as human resources: *timber, fishery species, biological resources, natural capital assets, stocks of ecosystem resources* (Stibbe 2014: 583). And with Greenpeace, I conducted detailed linguistic research into how the meat and dairy industry frames the consumption of environmentally damaging animal products to help them design a strategy to oppose this framing.

However, sometimes there wasn't an obvious linguistic element to my engagement – it was engagement aligned with the "eco" side of "ecolinguistics" but not, at least at first glance, with the "linguistic". I was, however, gaining a holistic understanding of the world, which was vital for my ecolinguistics work – it helped answer why I was doing what I was doing and to build the philosophical basis of my academic practice. And often, even when the linguistic angle wasn't immediately obvious it would later emerge. For example, the discourse of permaculture shaped and guided the community gardening, and I later came to see it as a beneficial discourse which provides new stories to live by.

My work with the Parish Council and local community organisations to protect a valuable area of countryside that was threatened with development seemed remote from linguistics at first. I was engaging the community in reflection on the value of green space in their lives and turning the responses into documents and oral testimony seeking legal protection for the land. But as I was writing the documents, I found I was able to apply ecolinguistic techniques to represent nature saliently, vividly, as something which needed to be respected, valued and protected. My photographs, which were designed to capture the value of the threatened land, also formed part of the documents making our case. And these were based on a grammar of visual design that paralleled the linguistic grammar of haiku (Stibbe 2005).

Although I'm a linguist, I never could be constrained by the linguistic. My PhD was about metaphors of illness and described how in language we tend to talk of illness as a fight. But I saw the same metaphor visually, for example, an advertisement represented the medicine it was selling as a suit of armour protecting the vulnerable patient. This was exactly the same metaphor, but in visual form. I realised then how artificial it would be to draw a line around language and not include other modes of expression.

Likewise, my research on the representations of nature in haiku started with language but ended up transcending it to analyse photographs and films. I started by arguing that the concrete, vivid and direct ways that ordinary plants and animals are so carefully and authentically depicted in haiku display a level of attention and care that is absent from the abstractions of environmental discourse. When Matsuo Basho wrote his famous haiku *Furuike ya / Kawazu tobikomu / Mizu no oto,* he was describing a moment of connection he felt at an ancient pond as a frog jumped in and he heard the sound of the water, with the sound connecting him as hearer with the activities of a frog who was actively engaged in leading his own life for his own purposes (Ancient pond / A frog jumps in / Sound of the water). Not that I was promoting the reading of haiku, but rather the use of the linguistic devices used in haiku: featuring ordinary animals and plants, using basic level categories (i.e., the most concrete an imaginable forms such as *frog* instead of *fauna),* the avoidance of metaphor, animals and plants in activated positions as actors, sensers and sayers, and various linguistic ways of establishing identity and empathy with animals and plants (Stibbe 2012: 145–166). If ecosystem assessment reports could have even a sprinkling of these features, they could much more powerfully stir people's imaginations and encourage them to care about the immediate victims of ecological destruction rather than "species assemblages".

With the linguistic features of haiku in my mind I soon started noticing something akin to haiku appearing in Japanese animation. In the film *Tonari no*

*Totoro* ('my neighbour Totoro'), there are short cutaway scenes lasting just a few seconds quite unrelated to the main plot where ordinary nature is featured: a snail slides up a pumpkin flower; a leaf floats down a stream; butterflies flit; clouds pass over the moon; a frog walks in the rain before letting out an enormous croak. And I noticed my photography changing as I read more haiku – the landscapes gave way to close-up depictions of the ordinary birds, insects, flowers and plants that I encountered on my barefoot walks in the mountains. When I noticed this I developed a visual grammar of haiku, using Kress and van Leeuwen's (2006) framework, showing how certain camera angles, placing of subject, lighting, background, shot size and perspective conveyed the same salience and care as the linguistic features of haiku (Stibbe 2005).

Of course, ecolinguistics is centrally interested in language but if corresponding grammatical and semantic patterns are found in images, films, music or even garden design, then it does not make sense to artificially draw a disciplinary line around language. And the object of study goes beyond language in another way because what we are often dealing with are cognitive structures that lie in the minds of individuals rather than existing in particular texts. Michael Halliday (2001: 192), in a speech which is often cited as founding ecolinguistics, stated that:

> countless texts repeated daily all around the world contain a simple message: growth is good. Many is better than few, more is better than less, big is better than small, grow is better than shrink, up is better than down. Gross National Products must go up, standards of living must rise, productivity must increase. But we know that these things can't happen. We are using up . . . the fresh water and the agricultural soils that we can't live without . . . We are destroying many of the other species who form part of the planetary cycle.

And it's true – when reporters or politicians are describing an increase in economic growth, even in the richest countries, they tend to use positive language, as if it's obviously something to celebrate. It would be extraordinary to think that each time they write or speak about economic growth they weigh up the pros and cons of a growing economy (e.g., more jobs or more ecologically damaging products sold) and conclude that economic growth is, indeed, good. No, the story that "economic growth is good" is something which is embedded in their minds and manifests itself in the positive vocabulary. And this story is not an original one they thought up themselves – it exists across the minds of individuals in a society in what van Dijk (2009: 19) calls "social cognition". So, from language we soon start heading in the direction of cognition, psychology and sociology.

But we need to head in the direction of philosophy, too, in order to provide criteria for critical analysis. Ecolinguistics involves critical analysis of language to reveal whether particular combinations of linguistic features (i.e., discourses) are conveying ecologically destructive or beneficial stories. In all critical research there is judging going on – certain discourses are exposed for conveying racist, sexist, homophobic or anti-immigrant ideologies, for the purpose of resisting those ideologies and working towards the creation of a more equal society. Usually the framework used to judge the stories against remains implicit – the reader will obviously agree that racism is wrong, and the features identified by the analyst can be categorised as promoting racism.

In ecolinguistics, things are more complicated, however, since in addition to oppressed groups of humans, there are animals, plants, forests, rivers and ecosystems to be concerned about. And it isn't just the current generation of humans and other species to be concerned about, but future generations, too. I realised that it's essential for ecolinguists to reflect on the philosophical foundations of their criticism and establish a clear ecological philosophy (or *ecosophy*) to judge discourses against. *Ecosophy* is Arne Naess's term to describe an explicit enumeration of values and assumptions about what matters, who matters, what facts about the world are to be assumed and what we should do (Naess 1995: 8). An ecosophy necessarily, by definition, includes consideration of not only humans but other species and the physical environment. Of course, anyone analysing texts with an ecological sensibility will have their own ecological philosophy, but I suggest that it's important to reflect on it, make it explicit, and to develop it over time as we read more, analyse more data, and have more direct experience of the world.

My own ecosophy can be described in one word as *Living!*, with the explanation mark being normative, in the sense that living is something to be celebrated and respected. I further elaborate that:

- *Living!* applies to all species, and future as well as current generations;
- *wellbeing*, not just survival, is important;
- living is only possible if we respect environmental limits;
- this inevitably means a reduction in consumption,
- reduction in consumption must come from the rich while the poor increase their consumption to allow all to live with high wellbeing. (Stibbe 2015: 14)

So, when I'm judging discourses, I can ask whether the speakers value the lives and wellbeing of all species, whether they encourage people to reduce consumption, whether they promote redistribution, etc. Another analyst could use a completely different ecosophy, and the results of analysis will always depend on what ecosophy is used. Some people say, "surely they have to have a good ecosophy for the results to be valid", but I am not sure exactly who can be the adjudicator between two different ecosophies. I just believe that in aggregate it will be beneficial for the world if linguists at least *consider* future generations, other species and the ecosystems that life depends on in their analyses.

That is why I founded the *International Ecolinguistics Association* (IEA; 2019), an organisation of 800 ecolinguists from across the world who share research ideas. I never push my own ecosophy on the group, but over the years I've been subtly encouraging members to include consideration not only of the human world but also other species and the physical environment in their analyses (yes, this is necessary even in a group of people calling themselves "ecolinguists", for reasons mentioned above).

Armed with an ecosophy and a toolkit for analysing language to reveal underlying stories (what is now referred to internationally as a "bucket of tools" after I jokingly referred to it like that in a keynote speech), I have been exploring a wide range of discourses. I have analysed the discourse of neoclassical economics; agricultural industries; weather forecasting; men's health magazines; Japanese haiku; new nature writing; ecosystem assessment; sustainable development; Native American writing and more. The task is always the same: analysing the language to reveal underlying stories, judging them as destructive or beneficial using my ecosophy, promoting discourses which convey beneficial stories, and resisting discourses which convey destructive stories.

My promotion of positive discourses and resisting of negative discourses has an applied and practical dimension which has led to some small and modest results. A few examples: Firstly, my work with the Parish Council resulted in permanent legal protection for a large area of countryside, against all odds. Councillor Flo Clucas, OBE, testified that the linguistic techniques used in my documents played a vital role in persuading the government inspector and council to grant that protection. Secondly, I sent a critical analysis of the Millennium Ecosystem Assessment to its director, who praised it and declared that future assessments should better balance the needs of appealing to policymakers with representing the intrinsic value of nature (described in Stibbe 2012: 101). Thirdly, my analysis of the discourses of the meat and dairy industries for Greenpeace informed a major international campaign to encourage people to reduce consumption of animal products (Greenpeace 2019). And fourthly, the industry journal *Poultry* published an article which drew extensively from my research and concluded that:

> Transparency of contemporary animal production practices and a real ethic of care and respect for animals must be embodied not just in our practices but also in the internal and external discourse of animal agriculture.   (Croney and Reynnells 2008: 390)

The importance of this last example is the pronoun in the call for "*our* [i.e., the poultry industry] practices" to change, written by someone within the industry itself.

I've been asked to publish papers or chapters in business books, environmental communication books, sustainability education books, and economics and ecology journals. I've been invited to give talks to all kinds of audiences: artists, veterinary scientists, business school academics, TEFL teachers, environmental scientists, classicists, media and cultural studies academics, and business people in local companies. All are interested in how the stories they are conveying in their communication align with their deep value system (i.e., values that go beyond immediate financial gain towards building a better world). In giving these talks and writing these publications I'm often reaching the producers of the discourses that I'm critiquing (or praising), which is one of the ways that ecolinguistics has the potential to contribute to change.

A key question arises. I'm applying ecolinguistics to a great range of areas of academic and professional practice, but how can I have the expertise in all these areas to be able to critique them in such detail? The answer is that I don't have that expertise, but in a way that is an advantage because the stories that a discipline is based on may be so ingrained within that discipline that they go unnoticed. There's the idea of "threshold concepts" (Meyer and Land 2005), which are permanent, irreversible changes in how we see the world when we "get" particular concepts. Getting a threshold concept can even be accompanied by a shift in identity (e.g., a transition to becoming an "economist", or "agribusiness executive"). Sometimes it's useful for discourses to be analysed by those who have not crossed the threshold. That's not to say that I'm entirely ignorant. When I was analysing the discourse of neoclassical economics, I spent a great deal of effort in reading economics textbooks that are used widely around the world, seeking out critical accounts of neoclassical economics, and attending events and courses on a range of approaches to economics.

Actually, I didn't just "read" the economics textbooks, I analysed their linguistic features to reveal the underlying stories that they conveyed. The key story that leapt out for me was that humans are fundamentally selfish, always wanting more goods, and only wanting only to maximise their own profits, utility or power (Stibbe 2015: 35–44). I think we have based our economic system and society on that story, with advertising and our cultural models of "success" actively shaping people in the shadow of the economic theory (rather than what the neoclassical economists claim, which is that they are just objectively describing reality). As a counterbalance, I also investigated the language of alternative economic approaches such as Ecological Economics and New Economics (e.g., NEF 2019). I wanted to discover other possible stories of what our economic system is and what it could become if we saw humans as altruistic and caring, and worked to re-shape people according to this model rather than the selfish one. There is a lot more to say about this, but I will just make the point that while I was learning about neoclassical economics I was simultaneously analysing and critically judging the stories behind the discipline I was studying. Perhaps this is the way that we should always approach learning new disciplines.

The same applies for agribusiness. I have read most of the Pork Industry Handbook, which is more than 1000 pages, and learned much about the techniques for raising pigs from birth to slaughter. And needless to say, while I was reading it, I was critically analysing the language and the stories it conveyed – that pigs were objects, machines, or resources only of interest in terms of their financial contribution to the pork-production enterprise (Stibbe 2012: 19–34). This I described as a negative discourse because it went against my ecosophy of *Living!* by distracting attention away from the lives and wellbeing of pigs and perpetuating an inhumane and ecologically destructive way of producing food. And I've analysed many other agribusiness documents which represent cows, chickens, fish and other animals in similar and even worse ways.

I find the discourses of neoclassical economics and agribusiness disturbing because of what they have to say about what it means to be human and what it means to be an animal. Although it's unpleasant analysing them, it's essential for two reasons. The first is an obvious one, because these discourses influence billions of people's lives and trillions of animals' lives and need to be analysed carefully and rigorously to reveal and resist underlying destructive stories. The second reason is because understanding the stories that underpin our unequal and unsustainable civilisation is essential in the search for new stories to live by – it helps us realise what kind of stories we lack and what kind of stories we need.

And this is the positive part of ecolinguistics – the search for new stories to live by. Against a backdrop of the destructive stories of industrial civilisation I have been enjoying analysing beneficial discourses – discourses which are based on completely different stories and highlight paths towards kinder, more sustainable forms of civilisation. I have analysed the discourses of Japanese haiku and animation for their sensitivity towards animals and plants, new economics for promoting stories of altruism and compassion, New Nature Writing, Native American writing, permaculture, lyrical science, ecopoetry, the discourse of ecological NGOs, ecofeminist discourse, and the slow food movement. In analysing these inspiring discourses, I am doing what Martin (1999: 51–52) calls *Positive Discourse Analysis*:

> If discourse analysts are serious about wanting to use their work to enact social change, then they will have to broaden their coverage to include . . . discourse that inspires, encourages, heartens; discourse we like, that cheers us along.

These positive discourses encourage us to value other people and the natural world, and to find paths towards wellbeing which do not rely on consumerism: time spent with family, time in nature, learning and giving to the community. They promote compassion for all humans and widen the circle of compassion to animals, plants, forests, rivers and the ecosystems that life depends on. And at a deeper level then encourage us to rethink what it means to be human within an interconnected world where the ecosystems that support life are unravelling.

In analysing these positive discourses, I am not acting as a disengaged, objective observer, looking for intellectually interesting linguistic features to catalogue. No, I am looking for meaning, for ways to rethink who I am and my place on the Earth. And I'm doing that because I realise that many of the stories I've subconsciously adopted from the society around me work against my own wellbeing and that of other people and the wider community of life. As I analyse positive discourses I reveal beneficial new stories to live by. These positive stories have an impact on my personal life: they influence how I live my life down to the smallest details: what I eat, what I buy, what kind of exercise I do, what I notice as I walk to work, where I invest money, and how I think about myself, other people, animals and nature. Ecolinguistics, for me, is a way of life.

I'll just give one final example – the best one I think in illustrating ecolinguistics as a transdisciplinary movement. Some years ago, I analysed the discourse of the UK travel industry and found an appraisal pattern (Martin and White 2005) which represented British weather negatively, for example "Fed up with wet summers and ice-cold winters?", "Winter in the UK can be a depressing experience; freezing temperatures, grey skies and sleet" (Stibbe 2019: 72). The travel discourse framed holidays as an "escape", for example "escape to the sun and leave the rain behind", or "are you looking to escape the gloomy British weather" (Stibbe 2019: 73). This framing renders life under the UK skies a prison, and the holiday a means to find freedom. And I found the same appraisal pattern in UK weather forecasts, which used words with negative prosody for every kind of weather with even a hint of moisture. Mist, clouds and rain were described using negative appraisal items such as *outbreak, plague, nuisance, disappointing, threat, dreary, murky* and *invasion*. On the other hand, hot, sunny, bright and dry days were described as *fine, pleasant, nice, lovely, beautiful, fantastic, glorious, perfect, glorious* and *cracking* (Stibbe 2019: 74). These patterns, I claimed, are destructive since they turn us away from finding wellbeing in the natural world around us and instead encourage us to stay indoors being entrained by gadgets, go shopping in a covered mall, or fly off to the sun.

I undertook an unusual kind of research. I read Japanese haiku and UK New Nature Writing, which conveyed entirely different stories about the weather: finding beauty in the morning mist or the sound of rain dripping from glossy leaves. And each morning, at 6am, I went running in the weather world, allowing the new stories to influence my reaction to the changing patterns of weather that I experienced. I discovered the beauty that the poets and writers described so eloquently, and even though the plan was to spend a year running in the weather world, I am still reading and running years later and finding wellbeing and a sense of my place within a wider community of life. It's not just about myself and my own wellbeing, of course; ecolinguistics is about wider changes. So I made teaching materials based on the research which have been translated into Slovenian, Italian, and Turkish and have been used by thousands of teachers and students (Stibbe 2017). Teachers who used the research in their practice describe how it helps learners question the stories told by their culture, become aware of alternative stories, become more active in working towards transformation, and find reconnection with nature. It's a very simple exercise, but I've found listening to the voices of nature writers and going outside to enjoy the natural world on misty or rainy days is a way of resisting the capitalist stories which tell us to stay indoors, get in the car, shop or fly to the sun instead.

## 3 Conclusion

I've described my personal story, of starting out as a linguist, being inspired by the discourses I came across in Japan, and ending up an *ecolinguist*. I described how as an ecolinguist I critique and resist discourses such as neoclassical economics and agribusiness, which I see as underpinning our unequal and ecologically destructive society. I described how I search for new stories to live by analysing inspirational texts; and how this exercise informs my own thinking about my place in the world and the practical day to day decisions I make in my life. And I described the modest ways I've tried to be active in using the research to make a difference in the world. The best word I can think of for this approach to research is *transdisciplinary*.

I'll conclude with some ideas about what *transdisciplinary linguistics* means, which are actually, of course, ideas about what transdisciplinary linguistics *should* mean, given that there are many different ways of interpreting the term and no ultimate judge to determine which is the correct one.

Firstly, I would say that transdisciplinary linguistics shares the same goals as ordinary linguistics – conducting rigorous research to uncover original knowledge about language. It's not transdisciplinary in the sense of having no connection whatsoever with a specialised focus on an area of study. And a combination such as "eco" and "linguistics" still needs a central core to avoid the prefix "eco" branching off in random directions (like being a synonym for "outdoors", "interaction" or "environment"). I tend to express this core as "Ecolinguistics explores the role of language in the life-sustaining relationships of humans, other species and the physical environment", but any expression is fine if it includes language, humans, other species and the future of life in some way.

I would also say that transdisciplinary linguistics necessarily engages with the real world and therefore has an ethical and practical dimension. Academics live within a society that is unequal, unsustainable and on a path towards ecological collapse, and have the social status and power to exert an influence on that society. Once linguists have transcended the limitations of disciplinary concerns, then they can conduct research aimed at transforming society, and can put that research into practice to create actual change. As Trampe (2017: 326) writes, "An ecological perspective of language developed using a 'transdisciplinary' approach opens up new perspectives of both a theoretical and a practical nature".

Exactly what kind of changes a transdisciplinary researcher seeks depends on their philosophy and what it says about ethics and the kind of society that's worth working towards. I would argue that *all* transdisciplinary research should be conducted within an *ecosophy*, that is a philosophy which considers not just humans but also animals, plants and the ecosystems that life depends on. Given what we now know about the human influence on those ecosystems, a philosophy that failed to consider anything beyond the confines of human society seems severely lacking. That's not to say that every piece of linguistic research needs to be explicitly about social justice and protecting the future of life, but that avoiding these issues needs to be a deliberate act that is carefully reflected on, rather than just unconsciously following a narrow discipline that predominately ignores them.

The higher goal of transdisciplinary research is, I would say, to contribute to transforming or benefiting society and the ecosystems that life depends on, with the generation of subject-specific knowledge a lower goal. This means that research activities may start with a linguistic focus but can go well beyond linguistics to connect with other areas of knowledge, enquiry and practical action. There comes a point when staying within the boundaries of linguistics is

## Chapter 6 Ecolinguistics as a transdisciplinary movement and a way of life

artificial and unhelpful to the wider goals – for example when it becomes obvious that the phenomenon being analysed exists equally in visual as well as linguistic modes, or that factors which aren't specifically linguistic are paying an important role. As Hildo Honório do Couto (2017: 159) writes:

> Traditional [linguistic] theories have been compared to windows through which we can see a limited portion of the object of study. Precisely because their view is limited, investigators can describe its finest details . . . Unfortunately, this is only a tiny part of language. In order to use an ecological methodology, the investigator would have to go to the roof of the house, from where they would have a general view of the object of investigation.

It could be argued that linguistics always has to be at least interdisciplinary, since language is always "about" something, and to analyse it you have to understand that "something". When I was analysing the language of neoclassical economics, I needed to understand economics. However, economics itself cannot be understood in isolation from psychology, from political systems, or from the natural world that (reluctantly) supplies the raw materials for production. Everything is connected to everything else, so transdisciplinary enquiry needs a holistic, systems perspective (Alexander 2017: 197). It therefore becomes essential for transdisciplinary researchers to be involved in learning and activities far beyond language, understanding context, building bridges to other areas, gaining flashes of insight and ideas for new paths to follow, and building an ecological philosophy.

In terms of expression, transdisciplinary research need not be bound by the formal conventions of academic writing – after all, these are part of the "stories" of the discipline that are subject to critical analysis. I disseminated my weather-world research through a photography collection that detailed my haiku-inspired appreciation of the changing faces of nature through the seasons; through a web diary that described my personal bodily experience in comparison to the day's weather forecast and my reading of nature writing; through teaching materials, and through an academic book chapter written as a first person narrative (as this one is). And that's how it works with transdisciplinary research – you get drawn into all kinds of activities and forms of expression that you just couldn't experience if you stayed within the narrow confines of linguistic research.

I mentioned the Centre of Human Ecology because there's a danger that transdisciplinary research is not seen as "proper" research, particularly when the research is challenging powerful forces in society. I want to argue that transdisciplinary research is, absolutely, "proper" research. Firstly, because it discards feigned objectivity for upfront and critically reflective subjectivity: the vision and goals are open to see, and awareness of how they shape the research process is built into the research. Secondly, because the world does not come neatly divided into separate areas – language is not separate from the minds and psychology of humans, humans are not separate from society, and societies are not separate from the ecosystems that life depends on. Any attempt to draw a circle around an area is artificial and inaccurate. Thirdly, because the choice to direct research towards the end of transforming our unequal and unsustainable society is just as much a political choice as to conduct abstract research which perpetuates current society by leaving its foundations unchallenged.

I would say that transdisciplinary linguistics, if done well, is every bit as "proper" as disciplinary linguistics and can potentially be more accurate and scientific rather than less. There are academics, such as Peter Finke (2017: 407), who go so far as to call for the discipline of linguistics and, indeed, the whole university system, to move towards a transdisciplinary approach:

> we have – partly without noticing it – entered the first steps to an age of transdisciplinarity. We therefore need to rapidly abandon the plethora of discipline-specific worldviews, and with them the ways of organizing our universities. From this point of view, our institutional bureaucracy lags far behind our awareness of the real demands. In consequence, linguistics as we knew it is approaching its end.

Finke sees linguistics playing a leading role in a transdisciplinary research alliance of scientists and scholars of many fields, coming together to repair the damage our society has inflicted on the planet. I would also like to see, and be part of, a great coming together of transdisciplinary researchers to question the stories of an unequal and unsustainable civilisation and contribute to the search for new stories to live by.

## References

Alexander, Richard. 2017. Investigating texts about environmental degradation using critical discourse analysis and corpus linguistic techniques. In Alwin Fill & Hermine Penz (eds.), *The Routledge handbook of ecolinguistics*, 196–210. New York: Routledge.
Croney, Candace & Richard Reynnells. 2008. The ethics of semantics: Do we clarify or obfuscate reality to influence perceptions of farm animal production? *Poultry Science* 87 (2). 387–391.
van Dijk, Teun. 2009. *Society and discourse: How social contexts influence text and talk*. Cambridge: Cambridge University Press.
Fairclough, Norman. 2014. *Language and power*, 3rd edn. London: Routledge.
Finke, Peter. 2017. Transdisciplinary ecolinguistics. In Alwin Fill & Hermine Pen (eds.), *The Routledge handbook of ecolinguistics*, 406–419. New York: Routledge.

Goatly, Andrew. 2001. Green grammar and grammatical metaphor, or language and myth of power, or metaphors we die by. In Alwin Fill & Peter Mühlhäusler (eds.), *The ecolinguistics reader: Language, ecology, and environment*, 203–225. London: Continuum.

Greenpeace. 2019. *Reduce meat and dairy and save the planet!* Available from: https://lessismore.greenpeace.org/ [Accessed 28 Dec 2019].

Halliday, Michael. 2001. New ways of meaning: The challenge to applied linguistics. In Alwin Fill & Peter Mühlhäusler (eds.), *The ecolinguistics reader: Language, ecology, and environment*, 175–202. London: Continuum.

Harré, Rom, Jens Brockmeier & Peter Mühlhäuser. 1999. *Greenspeak: A study of environmental discourse*. London: Sage.

Honório do Couto, Hildo. 2017. Ecosystemic linguistics. In Alwin Fill & Hermine Penz (eds.), *The Routledge handbook of ecolinguistics*, 149–162. New York, NY: Routledge.

IEA. 2019. *The International Ecolinguistics Association*. Available from: http://ecolinguistics-association.org [Accessed 29 Dec 2019].

Kress, Gunther & Theo Van Leeuwen. 2006. *Reading images: The grammar of visual design*, 2nd edn. London: Routledge.

van Leeuwen, Theo 2008. *Discourse and practice*. Oxford: Oxford University Press.

Martin, James Robert. 1999. Grace: The logogenesis of freedom. *Discourse Studies* 1 (1). 29–56.

Martin, James Robert & Peter White. 2005. *The language of evaluation: Appraisal in English*. New York: Palgrave Macmillan.

Meyer, Jan & Ray Land. 2005. Threshold concepts and troublesome knowledge (2): Epistemological considerations and a conceptual framework for teaching and learning. *Higher Education* 49 (3). 373–388.

Monbiot, George. 2013. *Captive state: The corporate takeover of Britain*. London: Pan Macmillan.

Naess, Arne. 1995. The shallow and the long range, deep ecology movement. In Alan Drengson & Yuichi Inoue (eds.), *The deep ecology movement: An introductory anthology*, 3–10. Berkeley: North Atlantic Books.

NEF. 2019. New Economics Foundation [online]. *New Economics Foundation*. Available from: https://neweconomics.org/ [Accessed 28 Dec 2019].

Ooi, Vincent. 2017. A corpus-based linguistics profile of marine humanities discourse. *Journal of global and area studies* 1 (2). 93–109.

Pennycook, Alastair. 2017. *Posthumanist applied linguistics*. London: Routledge.

People & Planet University League. 2019. People & Planet University League [online]. *People & Planet*. Available from: https://peopleandplanet.org/university-league [Accessed 27 Dec 2019].

Phillipson, Robert. 2010. *Linguistic imperialism continued*, 1st edn. New York: Routledge.

Stibbe, Arran. 2005. Chance encounters: Ecology and haiku-inspired photography [online]. *Language and ecology*. Available from: http://ecolinguistics-association.org/visual [Accessed 28 Dec 2019].

Stibbe, Arran. 2012. *Animals erased: Discourse, ecology, and reconnection with the natural world*. Middletown, CT: Wesleyan University Press.

Stibbe, Arran. 2014. Ecolinguistics and erasure: Restoring the natural world to consciousness. In C. Hart & P. Cap (eds.), *Contemporary critical discourse studies*, 538–602. London: Bloomsbury Academic.

Stibbe, Arran. 2015. *Ecolinguistics: Language, ecology and the stories we live by*. London: Routledge.

Stibbe, Arran. 2017. Living in the weather-world: Reconnection as a path to sustainability. [online]. Available from: https://intheweatherworld.wordpress.com/publications/.

Stibbe, Arran. 2019. Discovering the weatherworld: Combining ecolinguistics, ecocriticism and lived experience. In S. Slovic, S. Rangarajan & V. Sarveswaran (eds.), *Routledge handbook of ecocriticism and environmental communication*, 71–83. Abingdon, Oxon/New York: Routledge.

Trampe, Wilehelm. 2017. Euphemisms for killing animals and for other forms of their use. In Alwin Fill & Hermine Penz (eds.), *The Routledge handbook of ecolinguistics*, 325–341. New York: Routledge.

Wynne-Jones, Ros. 1996. University suspends its 'gadfly' ecologists. *The Independent*, 28 Apr.

Tamara Warhol
# Chapter 7
# Ethnography in interdisciplinary research in linguistics

## 1 Introduction

As a graduate student in educational linguistics, my colleagues and I used to ask one another "are you more education-y or more linguistic-y" due to the interdisciplinary nature of the sub-discipline (Hornberger 2001; Hornberger and Hult 2006; Spolsky 1990). This question exemplifies "Mode 1 interdisciplinarity" – borrowing concepts and methods from one discipline and applying them to another to offer new insights about a research problem (Gibbons et al. 1994). "Mode 2 interdisciplinarity" – a newer paradigm – is conceptualized as drawing on theories and methods from multiple disciplines to address common research questions (Gibbons et al. 1994). If a "Mode 2" stance is taken, the question "are you more education-y or more linguistic-y" reveals a tension plaguing interdisciplinary research in educational linguistics. Without taking adequate care, the dialectic between the two disciplines may be eclipsed by the needs of one. This question by novice educational linguists by no means presents an accurate portrait of current interdisciplinary research in the field. This volume alone, while not specifically about "Mode 2 interdisciplinarity" between education and linguistics, describes the interdisciplinary relationships between linguistics and fields such as education, but also archaeology, critical race theory, economics, gender studies, music, and religion, to name just a few. However, the question does raise the specter of how to conduct "Mode 2" interdisciplinary research using theories and methods from linguistics as well as from another field. One way in which linguistics has worked with other disciplines to answer common research questions is through ethnography. Drawing on an example from a study of language in a divinity school seminar, this study illustrates how combining educational and linguistic analyses through ethnography can illuminate academic language socialization.

**Tamara Warhol,** University of Mississippi, twarhol@olemiss.edu

## 2 Ethnography

Literally, writing culture, ethnography (Mitchell 2007) is both the process and product of authorship and an approach to the study of social processes in different contexts (Duranti 1997). Describing the details of the approach – and whether it is a comprehensive approach, with attendant ontological and epistemological stances, or merely a research strategy – is hotly contested (Blommaert and Jie 2010; Hammersley 2018; Rampton, Maybin and Roberts 2015). Attempting to present a unified definition, a sociologist, Hammersley (2018: 4), synthesizes several definitions of ethnography and suggests that they have the following elements in common:
– Emphasizes relatively long-term data collection process,
– takes place in naturally occurring settings,
– relies on participant observation, or personal engagement more generally,
– employs a range of types of data,
– aims to document what actually goes on,
– emphasizes the significance of meanings people give to objects, including themselves, in the course of their activities, in other words culture, and holistic in focus.

This list extracts commonalities across different definitions of ethnography, but each of the items on the list may be, and have been, questioned: "What does 'long-term mean?'" "Which sources of data are combined and how?" "Is it ever possible to document 'what is actually goes on,' even through participant observation?" etc. (Hammersley 2018: 5; cf. Clifford, 1988). Yet, while not unproblematic, Hammersley's list does present a "thin definition" of ethnography, not explicitly including ontological or epistemological claims, instead focusing on the research strategies used (Hammersley 2018: 7).

Although a self-admitted "thin definition," Hammersley's (2018) list enumerates many of the same aspects of ethnography found in definitions by sociolinguists (e.g., Johnstone 2000), linguistic anthropologists (e.g., Duranti 1997; Hymes 1980), and linguistic ethnographers (e.g., Rampton, Maybin and Roberts 2015): an emphasis on long-term data collection, participant observation, documenting practices and beliefs, and relating an insider's perspective. What the list omits, which sociolinguists, linguistic anthropologists, and linguistic ethnographers include, is researcher reflexivity, the emic-etic dialectic, and the centrality of language. Rampton, Maybin and Roberts (2015) write:

> Ethnography recognises the ineradicable role that the researcher's personal subjectivity plays throughout the research process. It looks to systematic field strategies and to accountable analytic procedures to constrain self-indulgent idiosyncrasy, and expects researchers

to face up to the partiality of their interpretations (Hymes [1978] 1996: 13). But the researcher's own cultural and interpretive capacities are crucial in making sense of the complex intricacies of situated everyday activity among the people being studied, and tuning into these takes time and close involvement. (p. 16)

Researchers must recognize how their own beliefs affect their interpretation. On the one hand, they must acknowledge their own biases and how these biases can skew their findings. On the other hand, these beliefs provide the researcher with contrastive insight, which allows them to contextualize insider knowledge in social theory. They engage in an emic (insider viewpoint) – etic (outsider viewpoint) dialectic. Hammersley (2018) unsurprisingly omits these items from his list. His goal is synthetic; he writes to find some common ground – despite the disagreements – in which people across disciplines can do ethnography. Questions of subjectivity and dialectic are ontological and epistemological questions usually emerging from the field of study in which it is used.

Ethnography has its origins in anthropology, and Blommaert and Jie (2010) argue that ethnography necessarily carries the ontological and epistemological assumptions of the field, including those about language. To do ethnography is not merely to perform a series of actions; rather, to do ethnography means taking a stance about the object of study – culture – and through what means it can be understood – language. Anthropology places culture at the forefront its analyses; however, culture is not seen as a static entity but rather something that is done (Heath and Street 2008). Language, in turn, is considered a resource, which is deployed to construct identities, institutions, practices, and social relations, that is to say, culture. As such it is never "context-less"; rather, "language is context" (Blommaert and Jie 2010: 7; Duranti 2003). Thus, the attendant ontological and epistemological assumptions of anthropology actually place language at the heart of ethnographic inquiry.

# 3 Ethnography and linguistics

With language at the heart of anthropological inquiry, interdisciplinary research drawing on linguistics and anthropology has been conducted since the early 20th century. Tracing the trajectory of the notion of language as culture in U.S. anthropology, Duranti (2003) notes that the study of language in order to understand culture emerged in the early 20th century with the study of native American languages by anthropological linguists such as Boas and Sapir. Through their study and description of native American languages, these anthropologists challenged the notion of culture as biologically inherited and argued that it was instead learned. Moreover, they suggested that different cultural and thus linguistic practices are understandable when viewed within their own contexts, introducing the notions of cultural and linguistic relativity. Yet, these researchers relied more on the elicitation of word lists and grammatical patterns than on ethnography for data collection.

Ethnography came to the forefront of such interdisciplinary research with the introduction of the ethnography of speaking – eventually the ethnography of communication – in the 1960s. Reacting to the linguistics program advocated by Chomsky, which focused on deriving grammatical rules from native intuitions, Hymes, an anthropologist, and Gumperz, a linguist, proposed an alternate paradigm. In *The ethnography of communication* (1964) and *Directions in sociolinguistics: The ethnography of communication* (1972), Gumperz and Hymes suggested the study of language-in-use rather than just the study of linguistic forms. Hymes (1974: 32) characterizes the ethnography of communication as a "method of describing the interaction of language and social life (usually at the societal level/speech community) using practices from the discipline of anthropology and linguistics." Primarily through participant observation, ethnographers of communication are interested in capturing the context in which speech occurs and how diversity is organized. In addition to the chapters in Gumperz and Hymes's 1972 edited collection, their call generated a number of other edited collections (e.g., Bauman and Sherzer 1974) as well as full-length ethnographies of communication/speaking (e.g., Basso 1988; Haviland 1977; Heath 1982; Philips 1983; Sherzer 1983) in the following decades.

The ethnography of communication changed the focus of study of language from an abstract concept to "a social and cultural object" (Blommaert 2018), and ethnography became an essential method within sociolinguistics and linguistic anthropology of understanding language's role in social processes. At the microlevel, interactional sociolinguists (e.g., Gumperz 1972; Zentella 1982) and microethnographers (e.g., Erickson and Schultz 1982; McDermott 1977) exploited ethnography to study how language and other forms of communication – prosody, eye gaze, gesture, etc. – interact to create social meaning, particularly in intercultural communication. Collecting audio and/or video recordings alongside of doing participant observation, these researchers studied the linguistic and social construction of face-to-face interaction. Through their research, they came to recognize the importance of contextualization and contextualization cues in achieving mutual understanding of the interaction (Gumperz 1982). Likewise, variationist sociolinguists (e.g., Eckert 1989; Rickford 1986) also began to combine ethnographic methods with quantitative methods. Rather than rely on pre-determined demographic categories, these sociolinguists sought to discover variation among local, participant-designed categories and configurations.

Ethnography continues to be a valuable tool in the study of communicative practices; however, now rather than study language "as a social and cultural object," researchers are studying how language constructs context and is in turn constructed by context (Blommaert 2018). Furthermore, researchers outside of linguistic anthropology and sociolinguistics have adopted the methodology. In the United Kingdom, linguistic ethnographers utilize the method to explore how different contexts – education, health care, the legal system, etc. – are discursively constructed (Snell, Shaw & Copland 2015). The example below demonstrates how ethnography can be used to explain academic language socialization – the purview of both education and linguistics.

## 4 Ethnography of a divinity school seminar

Ethnography has helped me in my own work to understand how students and teachers co-construct the meaning of authoritative texts through their interactions (e.g., Warhol 2007, 2011). Only through long-term participant observation of classroom interactions, coupled with analysis of transcripts from audio and/or video recordings, have I been able to discern and document how participants engage in text interpretation. The example below comes from a study of a biblical interpretation seminar at a divinity school and demonstrates how only through ethnographic data collection was I able to make sense of the interaction.

Participants in religious studies courses form unique communities in that the participants are actively engaged in the study of the religion. Within religious studies courses, the interactions of course participants offer overt examples of negotiations about the meaning of religious texts. One spring semester, I observed and audio-taped a New Testament interpretation seminar at the divinity school. The course was neither an introductory exegesis nor an advanced Greek exegesis course. Rather, student participants were expected to be familiar with methods of Biblical interpretation; however, they were only required to read the English translation of the Biblical texts. Members of the seminar included the professor, four doctoral students, and six Master's students. The professor specialized in New Testament studies with an emphasis on the Pauline corpus. The majority of the students could and did read the Greek version of the Bible in addition to a text in English or their mother-tongue, but at least two of the Master's students relied on an English text alone. Because of the class size, the professor used a variety of teaching strategies including lecture and class discussion. The small class size and teaching strategies employed in the course permitted close analysis of interactions.

Several data collection methods were used during this study. First, as noted above, classes were observed throughout the entirety of the spring semester. After each class, ethnographic field notes were written detailing class activities and interactions. Second, every class period was audio-taped in its entirety. Logs of activity sequences were made of each tape and relevant stretches of talk from the tapes were transcribed using commonly accepted transcription notations from conversation analysis (Schegloff 2007). Finally, the course literature was read after the class for which it was assigned was observed and audio-taped. Although, as in biblical interpretation, preconceived ideas cannot be totally divorced from ethnographic research, such preconceptions may be limited if the researcher does not read or reread the texts prior to class and attend class with an opinion on them. Collectively, these data collection methods allowed the research to be triangulated and the findings validated as emerging from more than one source. Ethnographically informed discourse analysis of tape transcripts was performed to investigate how participants came to interpret the text.

Ironically, slang and vulgarity, rather than religious or academic language, pervaded classroom discourse in the divinity school seminar. Almost every class, some form of slang or vulgarity was used as the participants talked about the text. For example, one class in which the participants were discussing *gnosis* (knowledge) as a prophylactic, the professor compared having knowledge to wearing a giant condom over one's head. Although shocked at first, I eventually came to see that slang or vulgar language served as a scaffold to more academic religious discourse. As in the condom example, sometimes the professor would proffer vulgarity or slang herself. Other times, the professor would build on student language, repeating slang terms to affirm the content of student answers. In both cases, the professor used the slang terms to demonstrate the meaning and usage of more formal academic discourse. The following analysis provides an illustrative example of how slang routinely was used as a scaffold.

In the excerpt below, the class participants discuss how the apostle Paul portrays himself in Galatians 1:11–2:14, which is the beginning portion of an autobiographical narrative that Paul uses in a letter "to the churches of Galatia" in response to a "different gospel" than the one he had initially preached to them (Gal. 1:1–6). Prior to Paul's evangelical activities among them, the Galatians were probably polytheists; Paul then preached his gospel and formed the churches in Galatia, but he did not designate adherence to Jewish law as requisite for church membership. However, following Paul's departure from Galatia, another group came and preached a "different gospel." Adherence to Jewish law figured prominently in this different gospel, and some Galatians did begin to follow Jewish law, including the practice of circumcision (Gal. 6:1). When Paul hears about the activities of this rival group and the Galatians' acceptance of their ideas, he writes to the

Galatians in response. Paul draws on his own story to persuade the Galatians of the legitimacy of his gospel. During the class analyzed here, the professor reads Galatians 1:11–2:14 aloud, translating from the Greek into English. When she finishes her reading, the professor asks the class: "What is going on here?"

```
1    P:    we'll stop there and then we'll go on. What do you
            see going on?

2    S1:   he's really pissed off because

3    P:    (laughter) he's really pissed off

4    S1:   because the others went to Galatia and were trying to
5           convince the Galatians that they should circumcised
6           (inaudible) Paul (inaudible) and show that his
7           customs are legitimate and that the Jerusalem
8           Church agreed. this is a nice (.2) uh a very good
9           epistle why do you not like it?

10   Class: (laughter)

11   P:    we'll talk about my personal feelings in a minute.
12          let's would anyone like to build on this point or add
13          another one (.1) or respond to it. (2.0) T your
14          mouth is open. (laughter) it looked like you were
15          about to speak.

16   S2:   [[You've known me long enough to know that my mouth
17          is usually open.(laughter)

18   P:    so she S1 says S1 says he is pissed off and
19          he's responding to another way of approaching (.2)
20          life in Christ (.3) judaizing (.3) he doesn't LIKE
21          (.2) it he's reacting to it. others of you what do
22          you see?
```

In the excerpt, the professor (P) and student 1 (S1) discuss Paul's anger about the behavior of the Galatians. Responding to the professor's question, "What do you see going on here?" S1 says, "he's really pissed off" (lines 1–2). The personal deictic, "he" presumably refers to Paul, as the student is answering a question about Paul's autobiographical text, and "pissed off" suggests that she wants to emphasize Paul's anger. As a colloquial or slang phrase, "pissed off" may seem inappropriate language for religious settings as described by anthropologists of religion (e.g., Keane 2004), and the professor's initial laughter does suggest that the phrase is not the expected response. Yet, the professor neither ignores the student's answer nor chastises her for her language. Instead, she reiterates the student's answer in the following line. Her first repetition of phrase prompts the student to continue (line 4) and her second repetition sets up an invitation for other students to participate in the interaction (lines 21–22). Thus, the professor first uses slang to encourage the student to continue her exegesis of the passage, and then she reiterates the phrase to provide similar language with which other students could contribute.

In this excerpt, however, the professor does not only appropriate and employ the student's terminology to interpret the text, she also utilizes a more formal academic register. The professor first quotes the student saying: "S1 says he is pissed off" (line 18). This indirect quotation serves to acknowledge the student's contribution as well as attribute the particular phrase to the student. The professor then recontextualizes the student's voice by re-accentuating it with the voices of modern Biblical commentators. The professor says, "so she S1 says S1 says he is pissed off and he's responding to another way of approaching (.2) life in Christ (.3) judaizing (.3) he doesn't LIKE (.2) it he's reacting to it" (lines 20–21). The professor links the student's phrase "pissed off" with a coordinating conjunction and adds language from modern Galatian commentators interested in Paul's stance on Judaism (e.g., Nanos 2002). The entire phrase "another way to approaching (.2) life in Christ (.3) judaizing" uses lexis and syntax characteristic of the field of religious studies. The phrase "life in Christ" is an idiomatic phrase for the more common phrase "being Christian," and the term "judaizing" is a gerund that collectively describes adherence to the religious practices from the Torah. These terms offer unique vocabulary for describing the causes for Paul's anger, and the professor's grammar functions as a vehicle for relating slang terms to the language of biblical exegesis.

The analysis above relied not just on linguistic analysis of the transcript, but also insider knowledge from participant observation. Only knowing that slang and vulgarity was routinely used could I interpret the professor's laughter and repetition as affirming and a scaffold. Without such knowledge, I might have interpreted her responses as nervous or chastising. Thus, ethnography helped me put the pieces together.

## 5 Conclusion

Although it has its roots in anthropology, ethnography has emerged as a powerful method across disciplines for interdisciplinary research of communicative practices. Moreover, since the inception of the ethnography of communication, it has been used for "Mode 2 interdisciplinarity" – drawing on theories and methods from multiple disciplines (even if it is just anthropology and linguistics) to address common research questions (Gibbons et al. 1994). As an illustrative example, this chapter demonstrated how ethnography could be used to answer a question about academic language socialization, a topic for both education specialists and linguists.

## References

Basso, Keith H. 1988. Speaking with names: Language and landscape among the western Apache. *Cultural Anthropology* 3 (2). 99–130.
Bauman, Richard & Joel Sherzer. 1974. *Explorations in the ethnography of speaking*. Cambridge: Cambridge University Press.
Blommaert, Jan. 2018. *Dialogues with ethnography: Notes on classics, and how I read them*. Bristol, UK: Multilingual Matters.
Blommaert, Jan & Dong Jie. 2010. *Ethnographic fieldwork: A beginner's guide*. Bristol, UK: Multilingual Matters.
Clifford, James. 1988. *The predicament of culture: Twentieth-century ethnography, literature, and art*. Cambridge, MA: Harvard University Press.
Duranti, Alessandro. 1997. *Linguistic anthropology*. Cambridge: Cambridge University Press.
Duranti, Alessandro. 2003. Language as culture in U.S. anthropology: Three paradigms. *Current Anthropology* 44 (3). 323–335.
Eckert, Penelope. 1989. *Jocks and burnouts: Social categories and identity in the high school*. New York: Teachers College Press.
Erickson, Fred & Jeffrey Schultz. 1982. *The counselor as gatekeeper*. New York: Academic Press.
Gibbons, M., C. Limoges, H. Nowotny, S. Schwartzman, P. Scott & M. Trow 1994. *The new production of knowledge: The Dynamics of science and research in contemporary societies*. London: Sage.
Gumperz, John J. 1972. Verbal strategies in multilingual communication. In R. Abrahams & R.C. Troike (eds.), *Language and cultural diversity in American Education*, Englewood Cliffs, NJ: Prentice Hall.
Gumperz, John J. 1982. *Discourse strategies*. Cambridge: Cambridge University Press.
Gumperz, John J. & Dell Hymes (eds.). 1964. The ethnography of communication. *American Anthropologist* 66 (6). pt. 2.
Gumperz, John J. & Dell Hymes (eds.). 1972. *Directions in sociolinguistics: The ethnography of communication*. New York: Holt, Rinehart and Winston.
Hammersley, Martyn. 2018. What is ethnography? Can it survive? Should it? *Ethnography and Education* 13 (1). 1–17.
Haviland, John B. 1977. *Gossip, reputation, and knowledge in Zinacantan*. Chicago: University of Chicago Press.

Heath, Shirley Brice. 1982. *Ways with words: Language, life, and work in communities and classrooms*. Cambridge: Cambridge University Press.
Heath, Shirley Brice and Brian V. Street. 2008. *Ethnography: Approaches to language and literacy research*. New York: Teachers College Press.
Hornberger, Nancy H. 2001. Educational linguistics as a field: A view from Penn's program on the occasion of its 25$^{th}$ anniversary. *Working Papers in Educational Linguistics* 17 (1–2). 1–26.
Hornberger, Nancy H. & Francis M. Hult. 2006. Educational linguistics. In Keith Brown (ed.), *The handbook of educational linguistics*, 2$^{nd}$ edn., 76–81. Oxford: Elsevier.
Hymes, Dell. 1974. Studying the interaction of language and social life. In Dell Hymes (ed.), *Foundations in sociolinguistics: An ethnographic approach*, 29–66 Philadelphia: University of Pennsylvania Press.
Hymes, Dell. 1980. *Language in education: Ethnolinguistic essays*. Washington, DC: Center for Applied Linguistics.
Hymes, Dell. 1996. Ethnography, linguistics, narrative inequality: Toward an understanding of voice. London: Taylor and Francis.
Johnstone, Barbara. 2000. Qualitative methods in sociolinguistics. Oxford: Oxford University Press.
Keane, Webb. 2004. Language and religion. In Alessandro Durant (ed.), *A Companion to Linguistic Anthropology*, 431–448. Malden, MA: Blackwell Publishing.
McDermott, Ray P. 1977. School reactions as contexts for learning in school. *Harvard Educational Review* 47. 298–313.
Mitchell, Jon P. 2007. Ethnography. In W. Outhwaite & S. Turner (eds.), *The Sage handbook of social science methodology*, 55–66. Los Angeles, CA: Sage.
Nanos, Mark D. 2002. *The irony of Galatians: Paul's letter in first-century context*. Minneapolis, MN: Fortress Press.
Philips, Susan U. 1983. *The invisible culture: Communication in classroom and community of the Warm Springs Indian reservation*. Prospect Heights, IL: Waveland Press.
Rampton, Ben, Janet Maybin & Celia Roberts. (2015). Theory and method in linguistic ethnography. In Julia Snell, Sara Shaw & Fiona Copland (eds.), *Linguistic ethnography: Interdisciplinary explorations*, 14–50. London: Palgrave Macmillan.
Rickford, John. 1986. The need for new approaches to class analysis in sociolinguistics. *Language and Communication* 6. 215–221.
Schegloff, Emmanuel A. 2007. *Sequence organization in interaction: A primer in conversation analysis*. New York: Cambridge University Press.
Sherzer, Joel. 1983. *Kuna ways of speaking: An ethnographic perspective*. Austin: University of Texas Press.
Snell, Julia, Sara Shaw & Fiona Copland (eds.). 2015. *Linguistic ethnography: Interdisciplinary explorations*. London: Palgrave Macmillan.
Spolsky, Bernard. 1990. Educational linguistics: Definitions, progress, problems. *Journal of Applied Linguistics* 6. 75–85.
Warhol, Tamara. 2007. Gender constructions and Biblical exegesis: Lessons from a divinity school seminar. In Allyson Jule (ed.), *Language and religious identity: Women in discourse*, 50=72. Hampshire, England: Palgrave MacMillan.
Warhol, Tamara. 2011. *How novice language teachers talk about teaching writing*. (Publicly accessible Penn Dissertations. Paper 337.) Available at http://repository.upenn.edu/edissertations/337.
Zentella, Ana Celia. 1982. Spanish and English in contact in the United States: the Puerto Rican experience. *Word* 33(1–2): 41–57.

Allison Burkette
# Chapter 8
# Connections and interdisciplinarity: Linguistic Atlas Project data from an assemblage perspective

## 1 Introduction

In writing this, my goal is to braid together two strands of inquiry – in a manner that will hopefully not be too ungainly – into a single discussion of the benefits of interdisciplinary thinking. Being able to engage with a theory from outside of one's own discipline and then bring that engagement to bear on new kinds of data and ideas can be rewarding on a number of levels. The connections we make between our own research and that being undertaken in other disciplines – whether they be sister disciplines, disciplinary cousins, or fields completely unrelated to our own – can offer support and validation for claims we wish to make. These connections can offer a path forward, suggesting new ways of thinking and new avenues of exploration. When you find something that makes sense in a way that transcends disciplinary context, it might help you make sense of an issue or question you've been grappling with in your own research. If nothing else, cross-disciplinary support can reassure you that (at the risk of sounding like an alien enthusiast) you are not alone.

I personally have an affinity for theories from archaeology and material culture studies (e.g. Burkette 2015, 2018). (You'll notice that this volume contains a few chapters from scholars within those fields as well.) Ideas from these fields about artifacts, "thingness", and materiality have influenced the way that I approach my own research and have prompted me to think more deeply about the relationship between language and other cultural behaviors. It seems to me that many concepts apply equally well to both linguistic and archaeological data; thus, this chapter will consider the application of the archaeological concept of the assemblage to materials from the Linguistic Atlas Project (LAP) and will jointly consider the merits of cross-disciplinary cooperation in the process of creating a new digital home for LAP materials.

**Allison Burkette,** University of Kentucky, allison.burkette@uky.edu

## 2 Assemblage

In archaeology, artifacts that are found near each other can be referred to as an *assemblage*, a group of artifacts that are often treated as a whole, which means they are typed, defined, and categorized together (Knappet 2011: 7). An example of an assemblage of Anglo-Saxon artifacts is included as Figure 8.1. The idea of the assemblage has been popular in archaeology since the 1950s, starting as a literal grouping of objects near each other and developing into a more dynamic and abstract concept in the early 2000s (Hamilakis and Jones 2017). Joyce and Pollard (2012) provide the canonical contemporary definition of an assemblage as being

> a collection of artefacts or ecofacts (animal bones, or seeds, etc.) recovered from a specific archaeological context – a site, an area within a site, a stratified deposit, or a specific feature such as a ditch, tomb, or house. So, an assemblage is a collection of material related through contextual proximity. (p. 291–292)

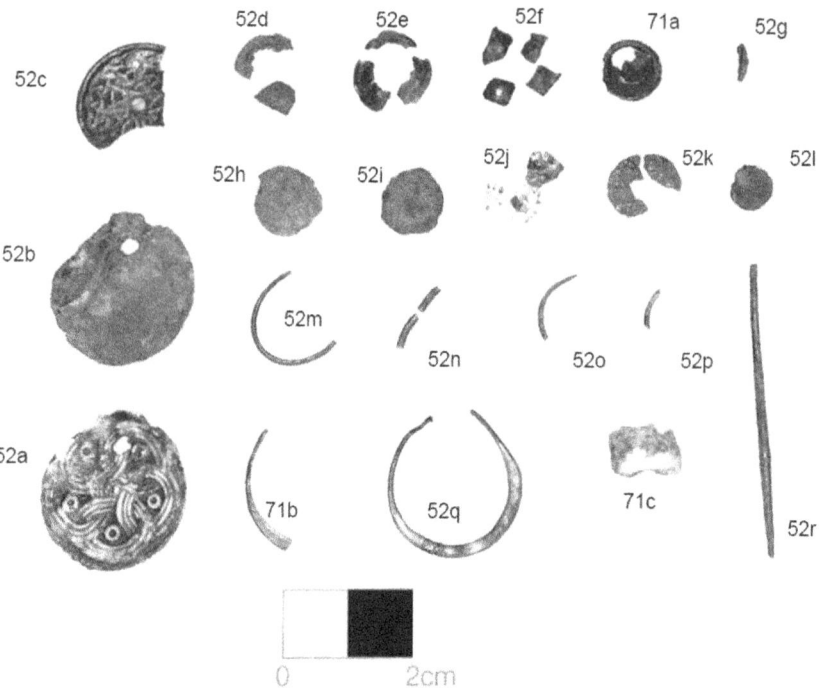

**Figure 8.1:** Assemblage of artifacts from an Anglo-Saxon grave. (Image from The Portable Antiquities Scheme/ The Trustees of the British Museum / CC BY-SA (https://creativecommons.org/licenses/by-sa/2.0)).

Items in an archaeological assemblage are interpreted as being in use during the same time (if not formed at the same time) and as potentially having been used for related social purposes and/or processes. Joyce and Pollard also note that assemblage items may be assigned to a single date, "although the contents of an assemblage may include material of an earlier date recognized as having been curated, recycled, or otherwise moved through time" (2012: 291–292). All elements of an assemblage, then, may not have originated at the same time or in the same place; the point is that they ended up in the same place. An assemblage is more than the sum of its parts. Even a single artifact can be viewed as an assemblage, a collection of uses, functions, forms, and ideas that are all part of the life cycle of one object (Knappet 2011: 168); put another way, an assemblage can function as a big picture encapsulated within a small object. Edgeworth (2012) explains that the idea of assemblage has broadened "to describe groupings of vibrant materials, flows, forces and agencies of all kinds, both human and non-human, material and cognitive" (p. 86; also see Rathje, Shanks, and Whitmore 2013: 363).

The concept of an assemblage is similar to anthropologist Webb Keane's use of "bundling" to talk about how objects are inhabited by their own histories. Keane suggests that "qualities bundled together in any object will shift in their relative salience, value, utility, and relevance across contexts," which means that the social and historical meaning(s) of any object are fluid, flexible, and additive, changing as the context changes (2005: 188–189). Objects, then, are bundled as social objects with their histories and with all of their potential meanings, which are then continually revealed against a backdrop of changing contexts.

The concept of an assemblage has been related directly to language, though perhaps not for an audience of linguists, by Deleuze and Guattari (1980) and Delanda (2016). This concept also resonates within critical applied linguistics (see Pennycook's Chapter 8, this volume) and within linguistic anthropology (see Kroskrity's Chapter 9, this volume). This chapter hopes to demonstrate how the concept of an assemblage can be used to both conceptualize and contextualize linguistic data, specifically that of the Linguistic Atlas Project (LAP), which, as we shall see, is especially well-suited for such an application.

## 3 Connections and interdisciplinarities

The Linguistic Atlas Project (LAP) was founded in 1929 at the behest of the American Dialect Society and remains the most thorough and expansive study of American English undertaken to date. The LAP consists of several sub-projects, divided by geographical region, each of which represents a collection of linguistic data (vocabulary, grammar, and pronunciation) in the form of dialect interviews during which people were asked a series of targeted questions, such as "What do you call the piece of furniture that has drawers for you to keep your clothes in?" (*Bureau*, *dresser*, and *chest of drawers* were common answers in the 1930s and '40s). Only a handful of the earliest interviews were recorded via phonograph, which meant that fieldworkers relied on spontaneously written International Phonetic Alphabet (IPA) to capture pronunciation, in addition to vocabulary. Even after technology developed such that interviews could be more easily recorded, much of the regional survey data was still also entered as IPA onto worksheet pages in the field (sometimes to be "proofread" later and a new paper record created). The most recent LAP interviews have been more sociolinguistic in nature; they have become more like directed conversations than targeted Q & A, have been digitally recorded, and have been transcribed in full. In addition, many of the older field pages (e.g. those from the Linguistic Atlas of New England and the Linguistic Atlas of the Middle and South Atlantic States) have been transcribed into normal English orthography and entered into spreadsheets. The result is an enormous amount of data that exists in various formats: handwritten text, typed text, .csv files, images, and an array of audio recordings.

When the Linguistic Atlas Project moved its physical holdings from the University of Georgia to the University of Kentucky, it afforded us the opportunity to look through 400+ acid-free boxes that had been stored at the UGA Library Repository. Feeling not unlike archaeologists, the Kentucky team has been digging through boxes and trying to sort out the chaff (like blank graph paper) from the treasure (such as a letter of encouragement from Hans Kurath to Lee Pederson, reassuring him that, although distilling Atlas data can be time-consuming, he was "doing something of fundamental importance"). We found Raven McDavid's field workbook (filled with handwritten notes, suggestions, and cross-references), cassette tapes of interviews that have since been digitized, term papers from the 1960s, and twelve boxes of notebooks filled with two sets of proto-Excel spreadsheet pages containing responses to questions asked of the Linguistic Atlas of the Gulf States speakers, one set organized by workbook page and line number, and another set organized alphabetically. The process may not be the literal sieving that one does at an archaeological site, but it is a physical, time-intensive, and frequently dusty undertaking.

LAP materials provide a particularly interesting site for the application of the concept of assemblage since the field notebook pages are both linguistic data and physical artifacts – the pages from the atlases of New England (LANE) and of the Middle and South Atlantic States (LAMSAS) are between 70 and 90 years old. The current Atlas staff has been working with archivists in our university's Special Collections Research Center (SCRC) to create an online platform for the LAP materials, a collaboration that entails linguists thinking like archivists and considering the high-resolution scans of Atlas materials not just as "data" but as digital objects. Likewise, the special collections archivists have had to consider what researchers within linguistics would want from a "digital LAP", how linguists would wish to use the material as data, and how an online platform could facilitate the access and manipulation of the material as data. Part of the success of an interdisciplinary endeavor such as this one is mutual respect. I asked the SCRC archivists about opportunities and challenges that, from their perspective, are particular to the digitization and online mounting of LAP materials and received the following response:

> The Atlas is an incredible set of data, both in the sense of the rich information it holds but also in its structure. Those who worked on the LAP took a wonderfully systematic approach to gathering and recording the information. (I'm sure there are some inconsistencies and errors, but when you think about the size of the data and the length of time it was gathered, it's impressive there's not more.) So the challenge is taking this structure, which for the most part is recorded on paper, and migrating it into a digital environment. It's not simply just scanning the physical material, but transcribing the data and using the original structure to inform a new schema that allows the data to be sorted, filtered, and searched in a digital library (a.k.a. online database) environment. It's thrilling to think about how the careful work that was done before the age of the internet actually makes it possible for the LAP to easily transition to an online environment, thus exponentially increasing access. (Dorpinghaus, pers. comm.)

The archivists accept the challenge of translating LAP "structures" to the SCRC structures already in place as part of their existing digital collections. From the other side, colluding with archivists necessitates my having to think about metadata in a different way as well, a "library way" in which one considers data structure as well as materials for public consumption in addition to academic interest. Trying to get LAP materials online also causes one to think about organization in a different way, since digitized objects aren't tethered to each other the same way that physical pages in a folder are. How do you connect, for example, the audio of an entire interview with a single field notebook page from that interview? What points of connection run through the materials such that they can be gathered together? Informant numbers and target items are certainly places to start, but what other nodes and edges can we identify? These are the kinds of data structure issues that are part and parcel of the digital humanities, and conceptualizing data-as-digital-object as an assemblage helps to identify additional potential links.

## 4 LAP as an assemblage

Where, then, is the connection to the archaeological concept of the assemblage? In addition to the LAP folders forming their own kind of strata within cardboard boxes, folders and their pages are treated similarly to an archaeological assemblage in a physical sense. Archaeological artifacts found in the same place/layer are cleaned, cataloged, arranged, and placed on display so that one can see each piece individually and in relation to the other items (as seen in Figure 8.1). Similarly, working with physical Atlas materials often entails reordering and reorganizing pages, folders, boxes. There are two main ways of organizing LAP interview materials: by the page number of the field notebook (which means, say, "page 9" of every survey informant would be foldered together) or by informant (with all field notebook pages of a single informant housed within a single folder). The transcription of the field pages IPA is easier (especially for student transcribers) if the pages are collected in folders by page number. Trying to divine the intent of hurriedly scrawled IPA can be time-consuming, but it gets easier as one grows accustomed to the topic(s) represented by each target, and as one gets a feel for what's possible as a response to each question. At any rate, just as decisions are made in framing archaeological objects as an assemblage, so too are decisions made about how to order and approach LAP materials. It seems germane to point out that archaeology, too, is digitizing collections for the benefit of both the public and the academic researcher. (Figure 8.1 is again a good example.)

Let us now turn to a specific example in order to explore how this "assemblage thing" might work as applied to LAP data: Figure 8.2 is an image of a LANE field notebook page (pg. 9) from the interview with informant #152. For anyone familiar with LANE (or LAMSAS) field notebook pages, several aspects of the page reproduced as Figure 8.2 mark it as unusual. The neat handwriting, for instance, is wildly uncharacteristic of most field pages with on-the-spot transcription of IPA, most of which has a cursive-like quality that can make it difficult to read. Visually, also, the page looks sparse; this informant gave single responses to most of the questions, and there is little fieldworker commentary on the responses that were given. The commentary that is there indicates that informant #152 said that chest of drawers "= bureau" which was then noted as being a piece that she "never called 'dresser.'" Both the terms *bedroom* and *chamber* were given in response to the "room where you sleep" question; the comment on the right noting that the latter refers only to a room on the second floor (not uncommon for New England speakers). We also see that she responded to the question about paper shades first with *curtain* (not unusual for the time), but then later in conversation referred to them as (a) *shade*. Most

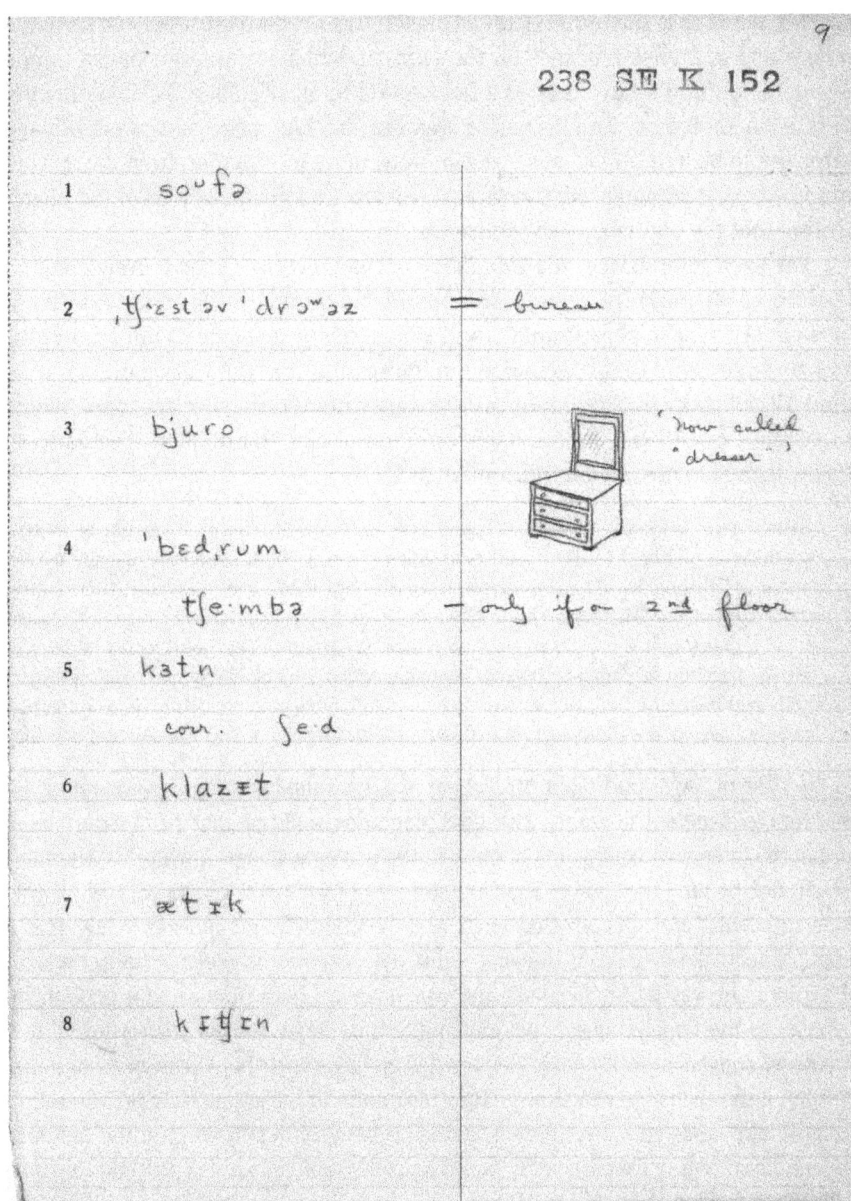

**Figure 8.2:** Linguistic Atlas of New England field notebook page: Page 9 from the interview with informant number 152, in community number 238 (South Egremont), as indicated by the stamped codes in the top right corner of the page.

striking perhaps is the rather detailed sketch that accompanies the response *bureau* (there are reflection lines on the mirror!), which is cause for pause as one wonders how you'd have time as a fieldworker to make such a detailed drawing during an interview. This is where treating the LAP page as an assemblage turns out to be helpful, because we can draw more information from the myriad of sources that comment on the same interview interaction as part of the bigger picture that the digitized page represents.

For each interviewee, the *Handbook of the Linguistic Atlas of New England* (Kurath et al. 1939) includes an informant biography. Each of the informant bios contains basic demographic (and sometimes genealogical) information as well as statements that summarize the impression that the informant made on the LAP fieldworker. These impressions vary from rather objective assessments to harsh evaluations, to (perhaps unintentionally) humorous observations. Below is the bio included for informant #152:

> Retired farm worker (woman), 89. Lived here until age 51, except for a year of school-teaching in Sheffield (c. 5 m. southeast) when she was 20. After middle age she moved about to Southfield (c. 12 m. southeast, town of Sandisfield), to Mill River (c. 10 m. southeast, town of New Marlborough), to Newark, NJ, and Stottville, NY. Has lived in Pittsfield (c. 22 m. north) for the last 6 years. F born here, she thinks, of old local family. M born in Mt. Washington (c. 5 m. southwest). Grammar school and academy here. Failing physically and mentally. Hard to interview because of clouded memory. Expressions often had to be suggested. B 74. (56 pages in first part of record by J.) (Kurath et al. 1939: 200)

In the case of LANE informant #152, there is a less-than-flattering assessment of the 89-year-old's mental acumen. The final notations indicate that "J" (Martin Joos) began the interview (completing about half the worksheet pages), while "B" (Bernard Bloch) finished it. (The "74" indicates that it was Bloch's 74th interview of 87.) It was Joos, then, who drew the bureau sketch, and the informant bio hints as to how it was possible to make a detailed drawing while also making on-the-spot-transcriptions: the informant was failing mentally and was having a hard time coming up with responses to the targeted questions. Joos might then have had more time during this interview conversation to make a detailed sketch; perhaps he was in need of a distraction if the exchange was slow-going. This informant's responses are an interesting mix of "old" and "new," as she distinguishes between a bedroom on the first and second floor, noting that the latter would be called a *chamber*, a distinction that was a little old-fashioned (even for the time), but gives more modern responses to other questions, such as *attic* (*garret* would definitely have been a viable option for an 89-year-old New Englander) and *closet* (as opposed to *clothes closet*). Certainly, every speaker's vocabulary is a mix of old and new, but given the bio statement above, one wonders if some of the newer terms were suggested by the fieldworker, and that one of the suggestions, that of *dresser*, was roundly dismissed.

An assemblage perspective turns the digital object represented in Figure 8.2 into the locus of a kind of narrative, a small story about two people, their interaction, and its physical setting. The sketches on these pages are of actual physical objects (one assumes), preserved at the time on paper, and now digitized – a circle of being and transferring through different mediums: the physical, a drawn representation, and now a digital object that transcends the material. The now-digitized sketches that we find scattered throughout the LAP field notebooks are points where the material, digital, and immaterial coalesce.

If assemblages can be characterized as "bundles of people and artifacts, materials, features, potentials, affordances, values" (Rathje, Shanks, and Witmore 2013: 363), then we are called to consider as part of the larger picture all of the connected ideas, conversations, and objects that radiate out from this digitized page, this one

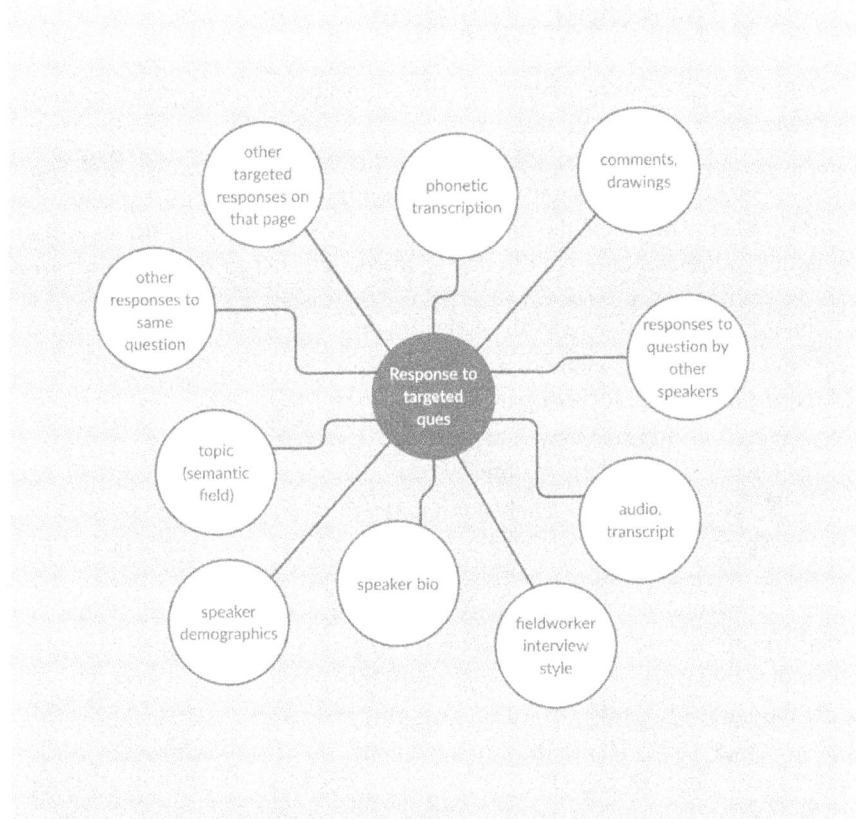

**Figure 8.3:** A simplified sketch of an LAP response assemblage.

set of responses. In this case, the larger picture includes the other 15 Joos interviews, the other LANE sketches, and the other field pages included in informant #152's file, all of which represent a building-out of another part of the assemblage, from different points of departure. Figure 8.3 contains an (over)simplified visualization of what the bigger assemblage picture might look like for a single LAP response. The shaded circle in the middle is the (hypothetical) starting point, a single LAP response, from which the related lines stretch; the lighter circles that surround that response represent related pieces of information that, together, form an assemblage, which could then be expanded to include the nodes and edges connected to other responses. What you choose to include in the assemblage that you organize in front of you depends on what questions you would like to ask, what directions you wish to go, or what explorations you are undertaking.

## 5 Tying the strands together

Finally, how do these two strands – the application of assemblage theory to LAP data and the interdisciplinary partnership between the LAP and the special collections archives – come together? Assemblage theory suggests that single pieces of data are not isolated – not only do they have grammatical and discourse contexts, but there are other kinds of connections that could take an inquiry in a number of different directions. It would be fair to ask, though, how is this different from the usual way that Atlas data is examined?

Consider briefly how we (ok, "I") normally treat LAP data, especially the older data collected in interviews for which there are not full transcripts. Take an individual informant's response to the "bureau" question from LANE; let's use *chest of drawers* as an example. That individual utterance of *chest of drawers* is one of 290 *chest of drawers* responses, which make up 26% of data for the "bureau" questions. The response is counted only as part of a larger list, presented as one among a number occurrences, that are then discussed as something of social and/or historical value, perhaps as a regionally associated feature, and maybe a dot on a map. None of this is wrong; none of this is a "bad" way to present LAP data. These are valid and interesting (!) ways to think about the words given as responses during the LAP targeted interviews. If, however, the *chest of drawers* in question is the one uttered by LANE informant #152 and recorded by Martin Joos, then you miss the whole picture (not to mention the pretty little picture).

Let me be clear, there is nothing wrong with response lists and percentages or any kind of table or chart whose job it is to display data and their distribution.

But it's not the whole picture. Lists, percentages, tables, and charts don't give you the answers to all the questions. What if I wanted to look at every instance of a-prefixing written down by the fieldworkers, or every past tense verb, both of which were recorded many times outside of the page/line number designated for their elicitation? What if I wanted to collect all the sketches of dressers (to think about mid-century material culture) or wanted to look closer at the times that fieldworkers transcribed what onlookers or auxiliary informants said? (Like the time one informant's wife said about her husband's response of *chifforobe* to the "bureau" question, "he doesn't say that".) What if I wanted every mention of a specific place, or wildflowers, or a World War? Or what if I wanted to look at the house-related vocabulary from every informant whose bio noted that they were born in the house in which they were currently living?[1] To address "what ifs?" such as these with the ease and speed to which we in the digital age have become accustomed, I would need a system that allowed me to move through the data in a manner not bounded by the "usual way" of approaching LAP data. Conceptualizing LAP data as an assemblage helps broaden one's field of vision and that helps us ensure that visitors to the SCRC-generated website are also able to access information from a multitude of connection points, because the data structure that we collaborated on allows for it.

I'm going to conclude with another observation from archaeology, this one from Edgeworth (2012): "It is the character of archaeological work that one thing always leads on to another, and new avenues of research continually open up, leading in particular directions, giving rise always to further questions as investigation of things and materials proceeds" (p. 86). I think this is a really hopeful place to be, a place where there are always further questions and investigations. I also think that this is a really hopeful time in linguistics, precisely because we *are* listening and sharing across disciplinary boundaries.

# References

Burkette, Allison. 2015. *Language and material culture*. Amsterdam: John Benjamins.
Burkette, Allison 2018. *Language and classification: Negotiating meaning-making in the classification and categorization of ceramics*. New York: Routledge.
DeLanda, Manuel. 2016. *Assemblage theory*. Edinburgh: Edinburgh University Press.
Deleuze, Gilles & Felix Guattari. 1980. *A thousand plateaus: Capitalism and schizophrenia*. Minneapolis: University of Minnesota Press.
Dorpinghaus, Sarah. Personal email correspondence. 8/21/2020.

---

[1] Dibs. Totally doing this next.

Edgeworth, Matt. 2012. Follow the cut, follow the rhythm, follow the material. *Norwegian Archaeological Review* 45 (1). 76–92.

Hamilakis, Yannis & Andrew Meirion Jones. 2017. Archaeology and assemblage. *Cambridge Archaeological Journal* 27 (01). 77–84.

Joyce, Rosemary & Joshua Pollard. 2012. Archaeological assemblages and practices of deposition. In Mary C. Beaudry & Dan Hicks (eds.), *The Oxford handbook of material culture studies*, 291–312. Oxford: Oxford University Press.

Keane, Webb. 2005. Signs are not the garb of meaning: On the social analysis of material things. In D. Miller (ed.), *Materiality*, 182–205. Durham, NC: Duke University Press.

Knappet, Carl. 2011. *An archaeology of interaction*. Oxford: Oxford University Press.

Kurath, Hans. 1939. *Handbook of the linguistic geography of New England*. Providence: Brown University, for ACLS. [2nd ed., rev., New York: AMS Press, 1973.]

Rathje, William, Michael Shanks & Christopher Witmore. 2013. *Archaeology in the making: Conversations through a discipline*. London: Routledge.

Alastair Pennycook
# Chapter 9
# Reassembling linguistics:
# Semiotic and epistemic assemblages

## 1 Introduction

This paper makes two arguments in relation to linguistics and assemblages. The first concerns a framing of social semiotics that eschews assumptions about languages as structural entities, and focuses instead on the spatial gathering of linguistic resources and other material elements. A focus on semiotic assemblages reconfigures what counts as language and how social, spatial and material worlds interact. This understanding of assemblages as entangled groupings of different elements allows for an appreciation of the ways in which different trajectories of people, semiotic resources and objects meet at particular moments and places. The notion of semiotic assemblages opens up alternative ways of thinking that focus not so much on language use in particular contexts – as if languages preexist their instantiation in particular places – but rather on the ways in which particular assemblages of objects, linguistic resources and places come together.

To enable this kind of rethinking, we need an approach to language other than that provided by conventional linguistic disciplines. The second focus on assemblages is therefore concerned with questions of disciplinary knowledge. Rather than looking at linguistics or socio- and applied linguistics[1] in interdisciplinary or transdisciplinary terms (which retain some aspects of disciplinary constraints), it is more productive to view them as temporary assemblages of thought and action that come together at particular moments when language-related concerns need to be addressed. This flexible account of (applied) linguistic practices focuses on epistemic assemblages as a conjunction of language-oriented projects (research where language, broadly understood, is a central concern), epistemes

---

**1** I focus in this paper mainly on socio- and applied linguistics (or applied sociolinguistics), but I see this discussion as applying generally across the domains of linguistics, sociolinguistics and applied linguistics, a field that has been unhelpfully broken up into these overlapping subfields.

---

**Alastair Pennycook,** University of Technology Sydney, Alastair.Pennycook@uts.edu.au (comprehensive concepts that cut across the humanities and social sciences) and matters of concern (things that matter socially and politically). Put together, these two forms of assemblage-related thinking create a space for reassembling linguistics as a field open to wide-ranging epistemological approaches to a variety of ontological dispositions on language.

## 2 Rethinking the scope of language

A number of recent approaches to socio- and applied linguistics have taken up, in various forms and with various terminologies (Pennycook 2016), the notion of translinguistic practices (e.g., Li Wei 2018), which as Canagarajah (2013: 6) explains, implies an understanding not only that "communication transcends individual languages" (we use repertoires of linguistic resources without necessary recourse to the notions of languages), but also that "communication transcends words and involves diverse semiotic resources and ecological affordances" (we draw on a wide set of possible resources to achieve communication). Here, then, we have two contemporary challenges to more conventional approaches to language: one questioning the status of languages, as identifiable and separable systems; the other questioning the status of language, as an identifiable and stable set of linguistic resources.

The tensions that this reorientation produces can be seen across many fields of linguistic analysis, a good example being the emergent field of linguistic landscape research, where studies may vary from statistical analysis of identifiable languages in the public space to qualitative studies of spatial semiotics with no mention of languages at all. Some studies continue to pursue the original focus on the first term – linguistic – concerning themselves mainly with signage containing written text. From this perspective, the "linguistic" refers principally to named languages (languages that can be identified as distinct from others), as well as language varieties and aspects of style (scripts, fonts, design), while the "landscape" is the public space in which these signs occur. While the first aspect of a translinguistic perspective (beyond individual languages) has also influenced this research focus on identifiable languages written on signs – suggesting the need for "a holistic view that goes beyond the analysis of individual signs as monolingual or multilingual" (Gorter and Cenoz 2015: 63) – the key interest in many of these studies remains "the presence, representation, meanings and interpretation of languages displayed in public places" (Shohamy and Ben-Rafael 2015: 1). Although translingual questions may be raised about the extent to which languages can be easily distinguished (and especially the extent to which language items can be convincingly counted or their relative salience can be represented numerically), the idea of "language" remains more or less stable.

A second, emergent trajectory, however, takes up the other aspect of the translinguistic focus (beyond language), making the landscape the primary focus and asking how such material spaces can be viewed in semiotic terms. The distinction rests in part on what we take to comprise a text, or, more broadly, language. An expansive semiotic perspective might include sensory landscapes such as smellscapes (Pennycook and Otsuji 2015b), pointing to the role that smell may play in the interpretation of place – particularly in its interpellative and associational capacities – without drawing any potential relations between smells and languages. A focus on bikescapes (Pennycook 2019) draws attention to the role of bikes within urban semiotics, as material discourse markers and sites of struggle over the regulation of public and private space. Reversing the priorities of the first framework, this perspective focuses on the landscape itself (urban transport, for example), making the interpretive act rather than intentionality central (how we read rather than how we write the landscape), and potentially eschewing any reference to named languages (focusing on semiotic resources, such as tattoos, graffiti, bikes and smells; Karlander 2018; Peck and Stroud 2015; Pennycook 2010).

This second focus, then, with its interest in space and semiotics, is concerned with the landscape as a set of signs, where landscape is foreground rather than background, signs are semiotic items rather than forms of public signage, and the term "language," if it is used, may be an umbrella term for social semiotics rather than referring to particular linguistic varieties. For some, this focus on semiotic texts can still be contained within a notion of linguistic landscapes (LL), which may include "images, photos, sounds (soundscapes), movements, music, smells (smellscapes), graffiti, clothes, food, buildings, history, as well as people who are immersed and absorbed in spaces by interacting with LL in different ways" (Shohamy 2015: 153–154). For others, by contrast, it may be more useful to consider such broad approaches in terms of semiotic landscapes (Jaworski and Thurlow 2010), leaving the notion of linguistic for a more select set of written texts that can be more easily described as language.

This uncertainty over the scope of linguistic landscapes is a product of the current push to reconfigure what counts as language and how social, spatial and material worlds interact. A range of related terms – conjunctural analysis (Varis 2017), entanglements (Toohey et al. 2015; Kerfoot and Hyltenstam 2017) or assemblages (Canagarajah 2018; Pennycook 2017) – have been taken up to account for the ways that multiple material and semiotic elements combine at particular moments. The notion of assemblages as "ad hoc groupings of diverse elements, of vibrant materials of all sorts" (Bennett 2010: 23) allows for an understanding of how people, semiotic resources and objects on different trajectories coalesce at particular conjunctures. Just as the social semiotic approach to linguistic landscapes reverses the focus of research, an assemblage approach shifts attention away from language use in particular contexts – as if languages are already-given systems that can be deployed in different places – in favour of an approach to the ways in which particular assemblages of objects, linguistic resources and places come together.

## 3 Semiotic assemblages

In a series of studies of Bangladeshi-owned corner shops in Tokyo and Sydney (Pennycook and Otsuji 2017, 2019), we have developed the idea of semiotic assemblages to account for the complexity of interacting factors. This gives us a way to address the intricacy of things that conjoin in the vibrant exchanges of everyday urban life. Asking the question "Where is language?" – a question that may make little sense to the mainstream of language studies – Finnegan (2015) suggests that the "cognitive language-centred model of the nature and destiny of humanity" with its focus on language in the mind misses so much that matters, including not only many other cultural modes such as music, dance and drama, but also "the gestural, pictorial, sculptural, sonic, tactile, bodily, affective and artefactual dimensions of human life" (p. 18). To arrive at a better understanding of the multilingual, multimodal and multisensorial interactions in these shops, it has been useful to think of language not as something residing in the head, but as a set of distributed resources that come together in particular and momentary constellations.

The related notion of spatial repertoires (Canagarajah 2018; Pennycook and Otsuji 2015a) pushes language outside the head, not merely as a social resource but also as a spatial and artefactual one. From this perspective, the material surrounds are understood not only as a context in which we interact, but rather as part of an interactive whole that includes people, objects and space through a focus on "how the composite ecology of human and nonhuman interactions in public space works on sociality and political orientation" (Amin 2015: 239). From this point of view, there is a strong focus on both practices – those repeated social and material acts that have gained sufficient stability over time to reproduce themselves – and on "the vast spillage of things" which are given equal weight to other actors and become "part of hybrid assemblages: concretions, settings and flows" (Thrift 2007: 9). Thinking along these lines, "the human is not approached as an autonomous agent, but is located within an extensive system of relations" (Ferrando 2013: 32). Thrift (2007: 8) talks of a "material schematism in which the world is made up of all kinds of things brought into relation with one another by many and various spaces though a continuous and largely involuntary process of encounter."

Bennett (2010: 6) is likewise interested in thing-power: "the curious ability of inanimate things to animate, to act, to produce effects dramatic and subtle," and the ways these things come together in assemblages. The idea is developed from the work of Deleuze and Guattari (1987), who focus on an "assemblage of bodies, of actions and passions, an intermingling of bodies reacting to one another" as well as a "collective assemblage of enunciation, of acts and statements of incorporeal transformations attributed to bodies" (1987: 88). For Deleuze and Guattari, the notion of assemblages addresses the need to combine qualities of both stasis and change together in any understanding of the properties of a thing. Their concern was to develop an understanding of assemblages as "concrete collections of heterogeneous materials that display tendencies towards both stability and change" (Adkins 2015: 14). Although their work is often seen as emphasizing change – ideas such as "becoming" have been widely taken up – it is important to see that this was part of an argument against an overemphasis on the stability of things and, indeed, of languages as systems. Notions of fixity and fluidity have to be taken together, therefore: We may appear from some perspectives to live in a world of fixity, yet fluidity is always at play; or from other perspectives we may appear to be surrounded by fluidity though this is always in relation to forms of fixity (Otsuji and Pennycook 2010).

In our studies of Bangladeshi corner shops, we focused therefore not only on the diverse linguistic resources that were inevitably at play – in the Tokyo store, it was common to use Bangla, English, Japanese, Hindi and Urdu among other languages (French, Uzbek and Moroccan Arabic turned up recently; Pennycook and Otsuji 2019, in press) – but also on what we came to call "assembling artefacts." These were typically items such as imported riverine fish, spice and rice, or locally grown (and slightly different) vegetables (onions and bitter melon), as well as items such as mobile phones and SIM cards. When these objects encounter the variable affordances of these different shops, they enter into new and momentary sets of relationships within semiotic assemblages. Such objects need to be taken very seriously as part of the action. Assembling artefacts such as fish draw the attention of customers to the freezers where they are stored, and to discussions of bones, taste, size and "cleanliness" (whether they have been gutted and scaled). Central to our studies has been the way objects such as fish and phone cards are part of assemblages of material and semiotic resources as customers, goods and languages assemble and disassemble at particular moments. This has implications for how we understand the role of objects in social semiotics as part of a critical sociolinguistics of diversity.

Assemblages describe the way things are brought together and function in new ways, and provide a way of thinking about "distributive agency" (Bennett 2010: 21), which links usefully to the notions of distributed language and cognition: Neither agency nor language nor cognition is best understood as a property of the individual, as something located in the human mind or tied to personal action; rather it is a distributed effect of a range of interacting objects, people and places. Assemblages can therefore be seen as "temporary arrangements of many kinds of monads, actants, molecules, and other dynamic 'dividuals' in an endless, nonhierarchical array of shifting associations of varying degrees of durability" (Appadurai 2015: 221). This turns the focus towards "the effects of relational interactions and assemblages, in various kinds of more-than-human networks entangled with one another, that may be messy and incoherent, spread across time and space" (Fenwick and Edwards 2011: 712). With their "uneven topographies" (Bennett 2010: 24), assemblages are not centrally governed by one material or event: "The effects generated by an assemblage are, rather, emergent properties, emergent in that their ability to make something happen (a newly inflected materialism, a blackout, a hurricane, a war on terror) is distinct from the sum of the vital force of each materiality considered alone." Assemblages describe the way things are brought together and function in new ways, and provide a way of thinking about how agency, cognition, identity and language can all be understood as distributed beyond any supposed human centre.

This is important not just for the sake of accomplishing better and more complete linguistic ethnographies but also to redress an historical imbalance that has placed language and cognition in the head, while relegating the body and the senses to the physical. Recent shifts to encompass an understanding of the body, senses and things have brought much greater attention to "touches, sights, smells, movements, material artefacts" and "shared experiences, dynamic interactions and bodily engagements" to go beyond the narrow story of cognition and language in the head (Finnegan 2015: 19). Although sociolinguistics has been better than its logocentric linguistic cousin in acknowledging various roles for the body – studies of nonverbal communication, for example – the body has often been conceived as "secondary to language rather than as the sine qua non of language" (Bucholtz and Hall 2016: 174). In their call for "an embodied sociocultural linguistics" (2016: 174), Bucholtz and Hall argue not only for making more salient bodily aspects of communication commonly acknowledged but often peripheralized, such as voice ("the embodied heart of spoken language" [2016: 178]) or style (where clothing, posture and attitude may do a lot of the work of enregisterment), but also for understanding how the body is discursively constructed, and how recent thinking has sought to understand how the body is "imbricated in complex arrangements that include nonhuman as well as human participants, whether animals, epidemics, objects, or technologies" (2016: 186). It is to describe these "complex arrangements" (or entanglements) that the idea of semiotic assemblages has proved useful.

The notions of distributed language, cognition, agency and identity (Pennycook and Otsuji in press) allow us to see how these are produced in material webs of human and nonhuman assemblages. Looking at language in these terms helps us see that meaning emerges from interaction. Rather than considering linguistic repertoires as internalised individual competence or as the property of an imagined community, the notion of a semiotic assemblage expands the semiotic inventory and relocates repertoires in the dynamic relations among objects, places and linguistic resources, an emergent property deriving from the interactions between people, artefacts and space. Extending the notion of a nexus of practice as a "semiotic ecosystem" (Scollon and Scollon 2004: 89) – where "historical trajectories of people, places, discourse, ideas, and objects come together" (p. 159) and the focus is on "moments of action rather than on abstractable structures such as cultures and languages" (Scollon and Scollon 2007: 620) – it is possible to start to think about how all these items come together in any one moment. This focus on the moment – on "moments of action" (Scollon and Scollon 2007: 620), on "spontaneous, impromptu, and momentary actions and performances" (Li Wei 2011: 1224), on "temporary arrangements" (Appadurai 2015: 221) – emphasizes the transitory nature of assemblages.

The notion of semiotic assemblages thus allows for an understanding of how different trajectories of people, semiotic resources and objects meet at particular moments and places. In addition to the understanding of the vibrancy of matter, the importance of things (particularly, the products bought and sold in the shops we studied) and the significance of place as more than just the geographical context in which language happens, we can start to see how linguistic resources are part of the action, part of the material, social and economic processes involved in an assemblage. The interest here is not so much in the identification of an assemblage (to give a name to a particular assemblage) but in an understanding of the momentary material and semiotic resources that intersect at a given place and time. Akin to Li Wei's (2011: 1224) moment analysis, the focus here is not so much on establishing patterns of linguistic use (genres, stages of interaction, and so on) but on understanding the relation between social practices in place and the constellations of objects, people and linguistic resources that come to matter at a particular moment.

## 4 Beyond interdisciplinary linguistics

Although applied linguistics has been subjected to the same kind of disciplinary mechanisms as many other disciplines – handbooks, introductory texts, symposia, and the like, all trying hard to make the case for disciplinary cohesion – there has never been a compelling case to consider it a discipline. It has always been difficult to nail down what applied linguistics really is. For some, it is a field of practice informed by real-world language problems, so applied linguists are "practical people working as a community, and it is their modes of practice and communicating with one another, as much as anything, which define them as a professional group" (McCarthy 2001: 118). For others, applied linguistics is better understood as a theory of the practice, suggesting that applied linguistics is "the practice of language study itself, and the theory that could be drawn from that practice" (Kramsch 2015: 455). For others, it is an "interdisciplinary area of inquiry" where research on language-related issues meets wider public concerns (Rampton 1997: 11).

A lot of work has nonetheless been done over the years to consolidate applied linguistics as a discipline, perhaps suggesting a field desperately trying to convince itself and others of its disciplinary status. A revealing part of this process has been not only what is placed within the fold of applied linguistics – from early concerns with language teaching (and particularly of English) to a wider smorgasbord of interests such as translation, speech pathology, multilingual families, language policies, language maintenance, language in professional contexts, and more – but also what is kept out. In his preface to *The Oxford handbook of applied linguistics*, for example, Kaplan (2002) explains how critical applied linguistics (Pennycook 2001) was not included because of its supposed rejection of theories of language, scepticism towards metanarratives, and critique of traditional applied linguistic claims to neutrality. Davies' (1999: 145) *An introduction to applied linguistics* likewise warns of the threat of critical applied linguistics as "a judgemental approach by some applied linguists to 'normal' applied linguistics on the grounds that it is not concerned with the transformation of society." Above all, however, it is not this supposedly judgemental attitude or this desire to change society that is at stake here, but rather the threat to "normal" applied linguistics, and the ways in which critical applied linguistics is "dismissive totally of the attempt since the 1950s to develop a coherent applied linguistics" (Davies 1999: 141).

Although this applied linguistic gatekeeping might be interpreted as centrally concerned with the political advocacy entrenched in critical applied linguistics, it is really the disciplinary boundaries that are at stake here. The opposition to critical work that has been a feature of such handbooks and

## Chapter 9 Reassembling linguistics: Semiotic and epistemic assemblages

introductions has been based more on a concern that some approaches to critical applied linguistics undermine applied linguistics as a discipline than because of its political focus, that a transgressive approach to applied linguistics (Pennycook 2006) is as much a challenge to its epistemological security as to its political neutrality. But how well do the claims to disciplinarity that is being so assiduously guarded stack up? There are several reasons to suggest that despite the desperate handbooking of applied linguistics, its disciplinary status is weak. As another who tried his hand at writing an introduction to the field observed, applied linguistics has a "lack of unitary theory and of clear disciplinary boundaries" (McCarthy 2001: 21). This, he suggested, might be seen as a form of disciplinary strength, with "its very openness to outside influences being its strongest and most enduring quality."

There are other reasons – more political than epistemological – to reject disciplinary claims. The hierarchical organization of knowledge in disciplines through processes of classification and framing plays a significant role in the regulation of access to knowledge (Bernstein 2000). As May (2014: 15) suggests, this helps us to see how and why disciplines "are so often defined (and confined) by a narrowly derived set of research assumptions, approaches, and related models of teaching and learning." Within a broader North/South politics of knowledge (Pennycook and Makoni 2020), these disciplining effects have an even greater negative impact. Applied linguistics has been narrowly constructed around particular Western or Northern frames of knowledge and language. Indeed, the attempt to ascertain the origins of applied linguistics as a discipline frequently falls into the Anglocentric trap of assuming its first use must have been in English, and to have emerged somewhere in the USA just after WWII (McCarthy 2001). As Oda and Takada (2005) make clear, however, the term 応用言語学 (Ouyou gengo gaku: applied linguistics) was in use in the 1930s in Japan, and we could doubtless trace alternative lineages through other languages and traditions.

Levon's (2017: 280) review of Coupland's (2016) edited book on sociolinguistic debates points to "the geopolitical positioning of the various contributions" being almost exclusively in the North: The effects of the overwhelming majority of contributors being located in the global North (and primarily in North America and Western Europe), he suggests, are twofold: on the one hand, "it makes it seem as if sociolinguistics does not take place outside of North America and Western Europe, whereas this is clearly not the case." It is unfortunate and limiting that sociolinguists from elsewhere – Africa, South America, or South and East Asia – are not included. On the other hand, this absence perpetuates "a particular geopolitics of knowledge that privileges Northern perspectives and prevents Southern scholars from contributing a differently positioned interpretation of events and practices that concern them . . . " (Levon 2017: 280–281). This critique thus points to two kinds of omission: First, scholars from outside Europe and North America are not included, which means generally that these contexts of research are also not included; and second, alternative epistemologies that might derive from these southern contexts (southern epistemologies) are not as a result given any space (Pennycook and Makoni 2020).

There remains in socio- and applied linguistics a deplorable blindness towards contexts and ideas outside the Global North. Under claims of commonality – humanity, language, disciplinarity – classed, raced and locality-based understandings of language use are assumed to be applicable to the majority world. An inequitable knowledge hierarchy ensures that certain assumptions about language, diversity and education are given precedence over other possibilities elsewhere. When the northern gaze does fall on its southern neighbours, such assumptions continue in ways of thinking about multilingualism, mother tongue education, language preservation, research and so on. As Ndhlovu (2018: 118) explains, "although the high-sounding metaphors of human rights, anti-imperialism and biodiversity resonate with contemporary international conversations around social justice and equity issues, passionate appeals to them have not done much good because the standard language ideology remains ensconced as the only valid and legitimate conceptual framework that informs mainstream understandings of what is meant by 'language'."

It is often assumed that southern multilingualism must be concerned with language endangerment or diversity. This is more about the northern rush to worry about saving languages for the good of humanity or to marvel at the complexity of language resources in southern contexts than an engagement with southern matters of concern (Mufwene 2016). To assume that the South is diverse or that languages are endangered is to continue to gaze from northern perspectives. This is not to say that many southern contexts are not places of great diversity, nor that many languages may cease to be used. Rather, it is to challenge the assumptions both that such concerns are essentially what matter in the South and that the notions of diversity or endangerment make sense in such contexts. We need to raise more important questions than mother tongue education or language endangerment, not so much because they don't matter, but rather because they are ill-framed. As long as "colonial definitions, categories, and methods are imposed onto Indigenous language work" (Leonard 2017: 32), language projects will continue to be unsuccessful – in terms of not providing either expected linguistic or broader social, cultural and economic outcomes – and to be viewed with suspicion by local communities. In order to develop more successful language reclamation projects, Leonard (2017: 32) argues, we need to decolonise language.

For de Souza (2017: 206), the problem is that "the posture of some mainstream social scientists who claim to be pro-indigenous, and in favour of the preservation of indigenous languages and epistemologies" remains all too often "trapped within the bounds of their own Enlightenment epistemologies." When these researchers "claim to listen to the indigenous other, they apparently only hear their own voices and values" unable to escape from the "bounds of lazy thinking, and thus liable to waste the wealth of experience of the ecology of knowledges that surrounds them but remains invisible to their eyes." De Souza (2017) is here taking up Santos' (2012) notion of "lazy reason" ('razão indolente') – the critique that dominant modes of thinking cannot understand or engage with alternative modes of thought. This "lingering inheritance of coloniality and its unequal distribution of knowledges, bodies, and languages" persists and may be something that applied linguistics, in its focus on education, needs to be aware of in order to "avoid, albeit unwittingly, continuing the legacy of coloniality" (de Souza 2017: 206).

Orthodox applied linguistics has long been content to accept definitions of language provided by linguistics and to focus instead on the application of such models. It has been common to assume that one is dealing with "determinate rule-based systems called 'languages'" (Harris 1990: 49), rather than asking the more useful question as to how our language ideologies are derived. The challenge, as de Korne and Leonard (2017: 7) remark, is how to avoid these "narrow perspectives on language use and knowledge that are potentially harmful to speech communities" and how to support the "promotion of minoritised languages by ground-level participants [as] fundamentally a political act through which participants negotiate control over linguistic authority, knowledge production, and self-definition through their linguistic practices." Albury's (2016: 306) studies of folk linguistic attitudes toward te reo Māori in Aotearoa/New Zealand points to the problem of "universal language revitalisation theories that draw on Western European perspectives on language but assume universal relevance" and shows instead how many assumptions about standardisation, literacy and corpus planning are questioned from Māori perspectives. From this point of view, "folk linguistic research methods can contribute to the decolonization of sociolinguistic theory and method by understanding, voicing, legitimising, and ultimately applying more ontologies and epistemologies of language than those that generally premise current scholarship" (Albury 2017: 37).

In order to redress these deep-seated concerns about the coloniality of linguistics, we need not merely to encourage a more inclusive applied sociolinguistics that opens the doors to southern voices and encourages more research in southern contexts; we need to open up to a much wider range of ways of thinking. The challenge, therefore, is about more than an agenda of southern inclusion but rather about expanding epistemological repertoires (Di Carlo 2018), of opening up to the obligation to understand that inquiries into applied linguistic concerns elsewhere in the world must also be inquiries into other ways of thinking that offer possibilities of disciplinary renewal. This is why the emphasis on decolonizing linguistics has been so important: It is about challenging the ways in which language studies have been tied to broader colonialities, while seeking both different epistemologies and ontologies of language (Pennycook 2020b). Interdisciplinarity will not be enough for such a project since disciplines are both problematic in themselves and limited in their capacity to open up new ways (or waves; Ingersoll 2016) of knowing: We need to think instead of how language studies can be more widely informed.

# 5 Towards epistemic assemblages

The notion of interdisciplinarity on the one hand problematically keeps the notions of disciplines in place, while on the other hand it misses the point that it would be better to talk in terms of epistemes rather than disciplines. When we draw on other domains of work (geography, philosophy, sociology, anthropology, gender studies, cultural studies and so on), we do so most often because these fields have also been subject to related epistemological shifts (social, discursive, somatic, sensorial, spatial, practice and other so-called "turns"). When we borrow from other fields or disciplines, therefore, it is often precisely because those fields are drawing on related schools of thought. Interest in space, practice or ecology, for example, is not a result of a newfound concern with geography, sociology or biology, but rather with the epistemic effects of these areas putting ideas into play across the humanities and social sciences.

By talking in terms of epistemes, I am drawing in part on Foucault's (1966) notion of the episteme as a system of thought that provides the conditions of possibility for discourse, thought and action in different epochs (Pennycook 2018b). To develop recent work in posthumanist applied linguistics (Pennycook 2018a), for example, I drew on geography, philosophy, religion, cognitive science, biology, sociology, political science and so on, but largely to the extent that writers in these fields were taking up questions related to posthumanism (new materialism, speculative realism, distributed cognition, sensory landscapes, spatial activism and so on). From proclamations about the death of "Man" to investigations into enhanced forms of being, from the advent of the Anthropocene to new materialist ways of thinking about distributed cognition, the posthumanist episteme raises significant questions for applied linguistics in terms of rethinking the relation between humans and all that is deemed non-human (objects, contexts, the environment, animals and so on).

The engagement with these various areas of study implies not so much a commitment to or even a borrowing from other disciplines as an exploration of an emerging posthumanist episteme. When I took up Bogost's question "What's it like to be a thing?" (2012: 10; Pennycook 2018a), for example, or Godfrey-Smith's (2017: 77) related question "What does it feel like to be an octopus?" I wasn't engaged in transdisciplinary work with digital media (Bogost's background) or the history and philosophy of science (Godfrey-Smith's background) but with questions of object-oriented ontologies (Bogost's interest) or the evolution of intelligent life (Godfrey-Smith's interest) as part of an exploration of the posthumanist episteme. The similarity of their questions is not coincidental: They are both posing challenges to anthropocentric claims about being and consciousness. So to draw on spatial, sensorial, affective, posthumanist or other ways of thinking is not so much an inter- or trans-disciplinary issue as it is an epistemic question.

There are several lessons to be learned from the reimagining of language within socio- and applied linguistics discussed earlier. The translinguistic focus on repertoires of semiotic resources suggests a way of thinking about applied linguistic theory in terms of epistemological resources that we draw on in order to engage in certain language-related concerns. Interdisciplinarity is not the solution to overcoming disciplinary straightjacketing, not only because it has clearly been co-opted by various academic regimes (funding bodies and other institutions now require us to make inter- or transdisciplinary genuflections), or because the idea has rarely offered more than a superficial sense of plurality, but also because engagement across domains is more often an engagement across epistemes, and because the real questions applied linguistics needs to face are those of its applicability and responsibility to a wider set of contexts and ideas than has been the case up to now. Rather than thinking of applied linguistics as an inter- or transdisciplinary endeavour, therefore, it is more useful to think of it in terms of an epistemic assemblage.

# 6 Conclusion: Refreshing epistemological repertoires

By analogy with the perspective on semiotic assemblages, we might start to think of applied linguistics less in disciplinary or inter- or transdisciplinary terms, and more as temporary assemblages of thought and action that come together at particular moments when language-related concerns need to be addressed. This flexible account of applied linguistic practice takes us not only beyond concerns about its disciplinary status but also beyond the idea of an inter/transdisciplinary applied linguistics. It also helps us see how applied linguistic practices, which may appear diverse, confused or undisciplined, are instead the conjoining of different language-oriented projects, epistemes and matters of concern (Latour 2004). Such an understanding makes it possible to see how work that apparently draws on other disciplines is really engaged in emerging epistemes that cut across areas of the social sciences and humanities. It opens up applied linguistics to an ethical engagement with alternative ways of thinking about language and context from the Global South, so that renewal of applied linguistics comes not via other disciplines but rather through alternative forms of knowledge.

Disciplines are held in place by a range of factors, external and internal. The former – conferences, handbooks, departments and so on – seek to frame the area and its work. Disciplines, like standard languages, have always been exclusionary: on the upside, they help consolidate ideas, enhance collaboration, bring solidity to a field; on the downside, they narrow the area of interest, its ideas and methods, and they exclude so much that does not fit. Disciplines are hegemonic knowledge structures. While challenges to applied linguistics as a discipline may bring a downside of insecurity, instability and incoherence, they also bring many benefits of flexibility, innovation and breadth. Like language standardization, while there may be gains to be made by such processes or normalization, this history of consolidation and exclusion has also rendered applied linguistics unhelpfully narrow in its epistemologies, politics and methods. There are a number of reasons to reject claims to disciplinary status for applied linguistics, including a more persuasive argument that a field of applied study is ordered not so much by a core disciplinary focus but rather by the questions it asks and the fields it engages with – language policy, language in the professions, language in education and so on – and that the understandings of language, the matters of concern, and the research tools to engage with them change accordingly.

Internal disciplinary factors are more concerned with the object of knowledge at its heart. Questioning the notions of language and languages within applied linguistics has several effects. It opens up applied linguistics to a wider set of possibilities about what matters: As Toohey (2019: 953) suggests, ideas born of new forms of materialism, such as assemblages or entanglements (Pennycook 2020a), have major implications for applied linguistic pedagogy and research, encouraging us "to ask new questions, and be alert to innovate, experiment, and learn new ways of teaching, researching, and being." With changes to the ways linguistics and socio- and applied linguistics fit together – linguistics is losing its status as the intellectual centre to which social and applied effects are added – these shifts in the ways we think about semiotic and epistemic assemblages open up possibilities of starting the long overdue process of reassembling linguistics beyond its structuralist dreams of identifiable languages separated from each other and an identifiable conception of language separable from its surrounds. Applied linguistics as a constellation of shifting interests around language in the world provides some hope of renewal for linguistics as the study of language matters.

# References

Adkins, Brent. 2015. *Deleuze and Guattari's A Thousand Plateaus: A critical introduction and guide*. Edinburgh: Edinburgh University Press.
Albury, Nathan John. 2016. Defining Māori language revitalisation: A project in folk linguistics. *Journal of Sociolinguistics* 20. 287–311. doi:10.1111/josl.12183
Albury, Nathan John. 2017. How folk linguistic methods can support critical sociolinguistics. *Lingua* 199. 36–49.
Amin, Ash. 2015. Animated space. *Public Culture* 27 (2). 239–258.
Appadurai, Arjun. 2015. Mediants, materiality, normativity. *Public Culture* 27 (2). 221–237.
Bernstein, Basil. 2000. *Pedagogy, symbolic control and identity: Theory, research, critique* (Revised edition). London: Taylor & Francis.
Bennett, Jane. 2010. *Vibrant matter: A political ecology of things*. Durham, NC: Duke University Press.
Bogost, Ian. 2012. *Alien phenomenology, or what it's like to be a thing*. Minneapolis: University of Minnesota Press.
Bucholtz, Mary & Kira Hall. 2016. Embodied sociolinguistics. In N. Coupland (ed.), *Sociolinguistics: Theoretical debates*, 173–197. Cambridge: Cambridge University Press.
Canagarajah, Suresh. 2013. *Translingual practice: Global Englishes and cosmopolitan relations*. New York: Routledge.
Canagarajah, Suresh. 2018. Translingual practice as spatial repertoires: Expanding the paradigm beyond structuralist orientations. *Applied Linguistics* 39 (1). 31–54. doi: doi:10.1093/applin/amx041
Coupland, Nikolas. (ed.). 2016. *Sociolinguistics: Theoretical debates*. Cambridge: Cambridge University Press.
Davies, Alan. 1999. *An introduction to applied linguistics: From theory to practice*. Edinburgh: Edinburgh University Press.
De Korne, Haley & Wesley Leonard. 2017. Reclaiming languages: Contesting and decolonising 'language endangerment' from the ground up. In Wesley Leonard & Haley Korne (eds.), *Language documentation and description*, 5–14. London: EL Publishing.
Deleuze, Gilles & Félix Guattari. 1987. *A thousand plateaus: Capitalism and schizophrenia*. (Trans. B. Massumi). Minneapolis: University of Minnesota Press.
De Souza, Lynn Mario 2017. Epistemic diversity, lazy reason, and ethical translation in postcolonial contexts. The case of Indigenous educational policy in Brazil. In C. Kerfoot & K. Hyltenstam (eds.), *Entangled discourses: South-north orders of visibility*, 189–208. New York: Routledge.
Di Carlo, Pierpaolo. 2018. Towards an understanding of African endogenous multilingualism: Ethnography, language ideologies, and the supernatural. *International Journal of the Sociology of Language* 254. 139–163.

Fenwick, Tara & Richard Edwards. 2011. Considering materiality in educational policy: messy objects and multiple reals. *Educational Theory* 61 (6). 709–726.
Ferrando, Francesca. 2013. Posthumanism, transhumanism, antihumanism, metahumanism, and new materialisms: Differences and relations. *Existenz* 8 (2). 26–32.
Finnegan, Ruth. 2015. *Where is language? An anthropologist's questions on language, literature and performance*. London: Bloomsbury.
Foucault, Michel. 1966. *Les mots et les choses: Une archéologie des sciences humaines*. Paris: Éditions Gallimard.
Godfrey-Smith, Peter. 2017. *Other minds: The octopus and the evolution of intelligent life*. London: William Collins.
Gorter, Durk & Jasone Cenoz. 2015. Translanguaging and linguistic landscapes. *Linguistic Landscape* 1 (1/2). 54–74
Harris, Roy. 1990. On redefining linguistics. In H. Davis & T. Taylor (eds.), *Redefining linguistics*, 18–52. London: Routledge.
Ingersoll, Karin. 2016. *Waves of knowing: A seascape epistemology*. Durham, CT: Duke University Press.
Jaworski, Adam & Crispin Thurlow (eds.). 2010. *Semiotic landscapes: Language, image, space*. London: Continuum.
Kaplan, Robert. 2002. Preface. In Robert Kaplan (ed.), *The Oxford handbook of applied linguistics*. Oxford: Oxford University Press.
Karlander, David. 2018: Backjumps: Writing, watching, erasing train graffiti. *Social Semiotics* 28 (1). 41–59.
Kerfoot, Caroline & Kenneth Hyltenstam. 2017. Introduction: Entanglement and orders of visibility. In Caroline Kerfoot & Kenneth Hyltenstam (eds.), *Entangled discourses: South-North orders of visibility*, 1–15. New York: Routledge.
Kramsch, Claire. 2015. Applied linguistics: A theory of the practice. *Applied Linguistics* 36 (4). 454–465.
Latour, Bruno. 2004. Why has critique run out of steam? From matters of fact to matters of concern. *Critical Inquiry* 30 (2). 225–248.
Leonard, Wesley. 2017. Producing language reclamation by decolonising 'language'. In W. Leonard & H. De Korne (eds.), Language documentation and description, 15–36. London: EL Publishing.
Levon, Erez. 2017. Situating sociolinguistics: Coupland – Theoretical debates. *Journal of Sociolinguistics* 21 (2). 272–288. doi:10.1111/josl.12233
Li, Wei. 2011. Moment analysis and translanguaging space: Discursive construction of identities by multilingual Chinese youth in Britain. *Journal of Pragmatics* 43. 1222–1235.
Li, Wei. 2018. Translanguaging as a practical theory of language. *Applied Linguistics* 39 (1). 9–30.
May, Stephen. 2014. Disciplinary divides, knowledge construction, and the multilingual turn. In Stephen May (ed.), *The multilingual turn: Implications for SLA, TESOL and bilingual education*, 7–31. London: Routledge.
McCarthy, Michael. 2001. *Issues in applied linguistics*. Cambridge: Cambridge University Press.
Mufwene, Salikoko. 2016. A cost-and-benefit approach to language loss. In L. Filipović & M. Pütz (eds.), *Endangered languages and languages in danger: Issues of documentation, policy, and language rights*, 115–143. Amsterdam: John Benjamins.

Ndhlovu, Finex. 2018. *Language, vernacular discourse and nationalisms: Uncovering the myths of transnational worlds*. Cham: Palgrave Macmillan.
Oda, Masaki & T. Takada. 2005. English language teaching in Japan. In G. Braine (ed.), *Teaching English to the world: History, curriculum and practice*, 93–101. New York: Lawrence Erlbaum Associates.
Otsuji, Emi & Alastair Pennycook. 2010. Metrolingualism: Fixity, fluidity and language in flux. *International Journal of Multilingualism* 7 (3). 240–254.
Peck, Amiena & Christopher Stroud. 2015. Skinscapes. *Linguistic Landscape* 1 (1/2). 133–151.
Pennycook, Alastair. 2001. *Critical applied linguistics: A critical introduction*. Mahwah, NJ: Lawrence Erlbaum.
Pennycook, Alastair. 2006. Uma lingüística aplicada transgressiva. In L. P. Moita Lopes (Org.), Por uma lingüística aplicada indisciplinar, 67–84. São Paulo: Parabola.
Pennycook, Alastair. 2010. Spatial narrations: Graffscapes and city souls. In A. Jaworski & C. Thurlow (eds.), *Semiotic landscapes: Language, image, space*, 137–150. London: Continuum.
Pennycook, Alastair. 2016. Mobile times, mobile terms: The trans-super-poly-metro movement. In N. Coupland (ed.), *Sociolinguistics: Theoretical debates*, 201–206. Cambridge: Cambridge University Press.
Pennycook, Alastair. 2017. Translanguaging and semiotic assemblages. *International Journal of Multilingualism* 14 (3). 269–282.
Pennycook, Alastair. 2018a. *Posthumanist applied linguistics*. London: Routledge.
Pennycook, Alasatair. 2018b. Applied linguistics as epistemic assemblage. *AILA Review* 31. 113–134.
Pennycook, Alastair. 2019. The landscape returns the gaze: Bikescapes and the new economies. *Linguistic Landscape* 5 (3). 217–247.
Pennycook, Alastair. 2020a. Translingual entanglements of English. *World Englishes* 39 (2). 222–235.
Pennycook, Alastair. 2020b. Pushing the ontological boundaries of English. In C. J. Hall & R. Wicaksono (eds.), *Ontologies of English. Reconceptualising the language for learning, teaching, and assessment*, 355–367. Cambridge: Cambridge University Press.
Pennycook, Alastair & Sinfree Makoni. 2020. *Innovations and challenges in applied linguistics from the Global South*. London: Routledge.
Pennycook, Alastair & Emi Otsuji. 2015a. *Metrolingualism: Language in the city*. London: Routledge.
Pennycook, Alastair & Emi Otsuji. 2015b. Making scents of the landscape. *Linguistic Landscape* 1 (3). 191–212.
Pennycook, Alastair & Emi Otsuji. 2017. Fish, phone cards and semiotic assemblages in two Bangladeshi shops in Sydney and Tokyo. *Social Semiotics* 27 (4). 434–450.
Pennycook, Alastair & Emi Otsuji. 2019. Mundane metrolingualism. *International Journal of Multilingualism* 16 (2). 175–186
Pennycook, Alastair & Emi Otsuji. In press. Metrolingual practices and distributed identities: People, places, things and languages. In W. Ayres-Bennett & L. Fisher (eds.), *Multilingualism and identity: Interdisciplinary perspectives*. Cambridge: Cambridge University Press.
Rampton, Ben. 1997. Retuning in applied linguistics. *International Journal of Applied Linguistics* 7. 3–25.

Santos, Boaventura de Sousa. 2012. Public sphere and epistemologies of the south. *Africa Development* 37 (1). 43–67.
Scollon, Ron & Suzie Wong Scollon. 2004. *Nexus analysis: Discourse and the emerging internet*. London: Routledge.
Scollon, Ron & Suzie Wong Scollon. 2007. Nexus analysis: Refocusing ethnography on action. *Journal of Sociolinguistics* 11 (5). 608–625.
Shohamy, Elana. 2015. LL research as expanding language and language policy. *Linguistic Landscape* 1(1/2). 152–171.
Shohamy, Elana. & Eliezer Ben-Rafael. 2015. Introduction: Linguistic landscape, a new journal. *Linguistic Landscape* 1(1/2). 1–5.
Thrift, Nigel. 2007. *Non-representational theory: Space/ politics/ affect*. London: Routledge.
Toohey, Kelleen. 2019. The onto-epistemologies of new materialism: Implications for applied linguistics pedagogies and research. *Applied Linguistics* 40 (6). 937–956.
Toohey, Kelleen, Diane Dagenais, Andreea Fodor, Linda Hof, Omar Nuñez & Angelpreet Singh. 2015. 'That sounds so cooool': Entanglements of children, digital tools, and literacy practices. *TESOL Quarterly* 49 (3). 461–485.
Varis, Piia. 2017. Superdiverse times and places: Media, mobility, conjunctures and structures of feeling. In Karel Arnaut, Martha Sif Karrebaek, Massimiliano Spotti & Jan Blommaert (eds.), *Engaging superdiversity: Recombining spaces, times and language practices*, 25–46. Bristol: Multilingual Matters.

Paul V. Kroskrity
# Chapter 10
# Language ideological assemblages within linguistic anthropology

## 1 Introduction

This chapter traces the recent emergence of the concept of *language ideological assemblages* within contemporary linguistic anthropology. While the concept of assemblage has a significantly longer history in archeology (Joyce and Pollard 2010) and cultural anthropology (Ong and Collier 2005; Tsing 2015), the first mention in linguistic anthropology is traceable to a conference paper by me in 2016 on the topic of indigenous multilingualisms. Language ideological theory (Schieffelin, Woolard and Kroskrity 1998; Kroskrity 2000a) had already been established as an especially useful tool for analyzing complex language contact data especially in contexts of sociopolitical marginalization and counterhegemonic resistance. Although well established in the study of language dynamics, language ideologies[1] – "the beliefs, feelings, and conceptions about language structure and use that index ... political economic interests ..." (Kroskrity 2010:192) – seemed to require further intensification and a magnification of scope and scale (Blommaert 2007; Carr and Lempert 2016). Based on analogous efforts and directed toward these goals of greater expansion and inclusion, the emerging concept assumed a preliminary form and was named language ideological assemblages (LIA) (Kroskrity 2016, 2018). Like most theories, this one provides a metaphor designed to encourage language scientists and scholars to reconceptualize what counts as data and what should be regarded as an appropriate manner of analysis (Blommaert 2007: 1–2). In the late 20th century heyday of Chomsky's transformational-generative grammar, linguists in the US were likely to talk about such matters using categories of "descriptive" and "explanatory" adequacy (Chomsky 1965). But that project was another

---

[1] I am following the theoretically motivated practice of using a default plural for denoting the language beliefs, practices, and conceptions that are the focal phenomena. I have used this manner of designation since my overview chapter in *Regimes of language* (Kroskrity 2000b). This approach encourages users to expect that language ideologies are most beneficially analyzed as a multiplicity.

---

**Paul V. Kroskrity,** University of California, Los Angeles, Paulvk@anthro.ucla.edu

https://doi.org/10.1515/9781501514371-010

exercise in purification designed to extract "pure" languages from their speakers and further remove those speakers from their unruly and disparate social worlds (Latour 1993).² The linguistic anthropological goal motivating language ideological assemblages is much the opposite of that linguistic fiction with its imagined "ideal speakers" and "completely homogenous speech communities." Today, linguistic anthropologists need conceptual resources for confronting the complexity of people using and thinking about their languages in social worlds profoundly shaped by political economic disparities and by juxtapositions of cultural contact but also by those speakers' own desires to belong – to nations, clans, tribes, global movements – and to use their linguistic resources to create and/or authenticate relevant, and often intersectional, identities.

## 2 Why assemblages?

Historically, my initial professional encounters with the concept of "assemblage" dated back to my early anthropological training as a graduate student at Indiana University taking required courses in archeology as part of the traditional four-subfield approach. Reading archeological debates of that period (1971–1976) and having written a term paper on Pueblo Bonito, I became aware of archeological assemblages and initiated my own intellectual understanding of assemblage as a bit of professional metalanguage. I drew from the conventional archeological notion of a collection of disparate artifacts that came from a particular site (Joyce and Pollard 2010). I liked the idea of looking at things that somehow come together. This was, for me, a call for making a heterogeneous collection of data in which the objects were somehow related to each other. For archeology these objects are conventionally limited to artifacts and objects actually found at a particular site but for much linguistic anthropology – given the portability of most language forms and ideas about language(s) – the initial appeal of the heterogeneous assemblage would also later suggest the possibility of apprehending connections between such disparate objects as language ideologies, language contact products (loanwords, grammatical diffusion) and processes (compartmentalization, convergence), the political economic basis of structural violence, culturally appropriate speech practices, speech norms, cultural protocols involving

---

**2** Latour (1993) is not, of course, critiquing Chomskyan linguistics; I am. This amounts to a recontextualization of his theme of purification to new territories. Viewing Chomsky's purifying practices as, at least in part. motivated by his goal of creating a modern, scientific linguistics does provide a useful understanding.

the circulation and concealment of linguistic knowledge (Debenport 2015), language policies of the state and its hegemonic institutions (McCarty 2016) and globalized language ideologies related to language endangerment (Hill 2002; Whiteley 2003).

But while the notion of archeological assemblage suggested applicability and relevance to linguistic anthropology, it was for me more of a starting point in this conceptual quest than an ending one. Further curiosity about the potential of assemblage and related notions led me to consider earlier sources in social theory, and later, more temporally proximate ones within cultural anthropology. My first encounter in social theory outside of archeology prompted me to consider European scholarship where some precedents had been established. One of the first sources that I encountered was Latour's (2007) *Reassembling the social*. This introduction to Actor-Network theory and to assemblages that included people, technologies, and other objects suggested the applicability of the assemblage approach to understanding social phenomena and processes. But soon after, I located a key intellectual source that I would later recognize as one more widely acknowledged as a very influential and informing source. In the social philosophy of Deleuze and Guattari (1987: 88) and their concern with linking both an "assemblage of bodies, of actions and passions, an intermingling of bodies reacting to one another" with "a collective assemblage of enunciation, of acts and statements," the concept of assemblage had clearly taken on new forms of social relevance and inclusion. Their book, *A thousand plateaus: Capitalism and schizophrenia,* represented what I still regard as an unusual and inspiring collaboration of a philosopher and post-Marxist psychoanalyst. In it, and other works by these authors, I found the extension of assemblage to very disparate social and personal phenomena including but not limited to cultural artifacts, political economic systems, and personal worlds. I was struck by the dynamic admixture and juxtaposition of political economic systems and intensely personal projects of individual social actors. For DeLeuze and Guattari, it was not sufficient to observe the existence of assemblage-like configurations, but rather to make that observation of connection into a preparatory space that might allow us to better view the practices and structures through which these configurations were constantly being constructed, de-constructed, and reconstructed in the desires and actions of actual people. What I found particularly useful here as a linguistic anthropologist was the potential for a more dynamic view of people using their languages within constellations of facilitation and constraint. Instead of the reifications of languages, and language ideologies for that matter, as thing-like objects, this approach promised a restoration of a more dynamic view of languages as continuously being restructured by their speakers.

This emphasis on *becoming* (Delueze and Guattari 1987: 305; Biehl and Locke 2010: 337) is not only theoretically liberating in undoing the fixity of linguistic categories but also in its rebellion against a strict Marxian determinism of individual action. For them the subjective *milieus* of individual people are the locus of potentially destabilizing desires that have the potential to maintain as well as to disrupt the norms and structures that may seem to constrain them.[3] As they say, "History is made only by those who oppose history (not by those who insert themselves in it, or even reshape it")" (Deleuze and Guattari 1987: 295). As someone seeking to reshape assemblage into something useful for language ideological research, I was struck by two features of their work as especially compatible and promising. One was the dynamic destabilization on a theoretical level of language use in the social worlds of speakers. Many of the early definitions of language ideologies understood them to be dynamic forces in unstable arenas of linguistic practice. For example, the following extract from Michael Silverstein's (1985: 220) "Language and the culture of gender": "The total linguistic fact, the datum for a science of language, is irreducibly dialectic in nature. It is an unstable mutual interaction of meaningful sign forms contextualized to situations of interested human use, mediated by the fact of cultural ideology." In this passage, and the article from which it is extracted, Silverstein injects a new level of analysis – now usually called "language ideologies" – designed to complicate the overly inert and fixed categories of a linguistics without actual speakers who are displaced by its theoretical preoccupation with decontextualized language. For me, assemblages also offered a renewed focus on the dynamic and complicating factors of actual language use, but they also offered the possibility of reintegrating individuals into language ideological analysis. It is no secret that linguistic anthropology was at least two decades behind cultural anthropology in its confrontation with political economy, and while this movement was predicated on the need to emphasize political economic structures and their influence on all language use, my own research in both the Village of Tewa (Kroskrity 1993) and Western Mono Communities of Central California (Kroskrity 2009) balanced attention to collective patterns with an attempt to understand the lingual life histories of specific individuals. For me this was an especially attractive feature of Deleuze and Guattari's assemblage and one that had spoken to me as a call for creating a linguistic anthropological version of language ideological assemblages.

---

3 Though the French *milieu* may be translated as 'surroundings, middle, and medium', it is used in Deleuze and Guattari (1987) most often to represent the subjective worlds of specific individuals.

## 3 Becoming language ideological assemblages

Continuing to trace what Kaplan (1964) would call the "logic-in-use" behind the creation and eventual publication of language ideological assemblages, my next step was to see what cultural anthropologists were doing with the assemblage notion. Since cultural anthropologists interested in issues of social inequality and political economy, more generally, were certainly part of the reading audience I was hoping to speak to, I needed to understand how they were deploying assemblages. Without offering a more complete treatment of the full range of variation, I can summarize my sampling of cultural studies by saying that there was considerable variety. On the one hand, Ong and Collier (2005: 4) used the concept of assemblage to label emergent global configurations including disparate phenomena like "technoscience, circuits of licit and illicit exchange, systems of administration or governance, and regimes of ethics and values." While its emphasis on Foucaultian discursive formations added a significant edge to the concept of assemblage as an inclusive yet emergent configuration, I found little new here to assist my evolving project of language ideological assemblages.

But this soon changed as I became aware of Anna Lowenhaupt Tsing's (2015) more ecologically inspired adaptations of assemblage in *The mushroom at the end of the world: On the possibility of life in capitalist ruins*. As the first linguistic anthropologist to articulate the need for an analogous concept that might redirect theoretical attention to the dynamic juxtaposition of linguistic ideologies, practices, and political-economic structures, and challenge the utility of examining a single linguistic community, I was especially influenced by Tsing's (2015: 23) model:

> Ecologists turned to assemblages to get around the sometimes fixed and bounded connotations of ecological 'community'. The question of how the varied species in a species assemblage influence each other – if at all – is never settled; some thwart (or eat) each other; others work together to make life possible; still others just happen to find themselves in the same place. Assemblages . . . allow us to ask about communal effects without assuming them. They show us potential histories in the making. . . . Assemblages cannot hide from capital and the state; they are sites for watching how political economy works . . . we need to see what comes together not just by prefabrication, but also by juxtaposition.

As I was struggling with language ideological assemblages, I was writing a professional paper in which I was attempting to compare and contrast changing regimes of multilingualism in two very different Native American communities. It became clear that I needed to understand the complex interactions of indigenous language ideologies in connection with the flows of those emanating from the nation-state and its hegemonic institutions (Kroskrity 2018). I found several features of Tsing's polyphonic version of assemblages and the ecological imagery she used to be especially useful in re-theorizing my project in accord with an analogously fortified understanding of language ideological assemblages.[4] One was the erasure of conventional boundaries between communities. Many studies of the language and communication of specific indigenous groups attempt to focus strictly on their Indigenous and pre-contact features or they represent the colonization (Dozier 1956) or the hegemonic institutions of the state as utterly determining language contact outcomes, including the life and death of Indigenous languages, and therefore the only factor that needed attention. But certainly, language policies of a nation-state may have an impact on its Indigenous and minority language communities. While this is likely to fit the pattern of scornful suppression described by Nancy Dorian (1998) as the *ideology of contempt*, it is possible in this nominally post-colonial world that some policy changes may assist Indigenous projects of revalorization and revitalization of Indigenous languages (Field and Kroskrity 2009). Another reason to erase analytic boundaries between language communities, and between national boundaries as well, is the existence of globalized discourses such as UNESCO's declarations of the language rights of Indigenous people (Whiteley 2003). Indeed, there are also situations involving creolization and translanguaging that call into question the very boundaries, usually taken for granted, between languages in contact (e.g. Migge and Léglise 2013; Pennycook 2017).

A second feature that is especially relevant here is the juxtaposition of the various elements of language ideological assemblages. Contiguous elements have come together, but only through the participant-observation of ethnography can we begin to read the directionality and intensity of influence. Do Indigenous language users have cultural means of naturalizing and perhaps resisting the various forms of linguistic inequality (Kroskrity 2000c) or do they experience the jagged contact of nation-state and First Nations languages and cultures more often as one of juxtaposition (as in the groundbreaking monograph on the Kaska [Meek 2010])?

---

[4] Tsing (2015: 23–4) describes her type of assemblages as polyphonic and goes on to explicitly use a musical analogy. "Polyphony is music in which autonomous melodies intertwine" (Tsing 2015: 23). She contrasts the polyphony of baroque music, with its moments of harmony and dissonance, to classical music in which we hear music "from a single perspective" (Tsing 2015: 24).

A third attribute is the omnipresent influence of capital and state power. These forces may not be directly visible in all ethnographic moments, but they are always responsible for structuring the very assemblages we concoct in order to explore the worlds of all language users and the imposed and intrinsic interests that guide their worldly actions. Just as global capitalism has had an impact on almost every part of the natural world, its impact on languages, speakers, and linguistic diversity has been as variegated as it has been pervasive. Tsing's (2015) model of polyphonic assemblages and its consistent emphasis on political economic forces thus serves as an especially useful model benchmark for a related and emergent notion of language ideological assemblages. This is especially true for linguistic anthropology as a subfield within anthropology that often draws a sharp analytical focus on the micro-phenomena of linguistic structures, interpersonal interaction, and details of the communicative setting. These are of course still very important – they are the evidence of ongoing efforts of becoming – but they must be balanced with a much larger understanding of context that includes the various political economic forces that have brought particular people, languages, and places together.

# 4 LIA as an extension of language ideological theory

Though I have so far presented the emergence of language ideological assemblages as a collection of various desirable and necessary conceptual features of preexisting scholarship, it is appropriate to consider the role of theory-internal considerations in shaping my own assessments of what might be most valuable and useful. This would be a good time to state that I was not looking for a precise definitive concept but rather one that would fit into sociological notions of a "sensitizing concept" (Blumer 1986). These are concepts that encourage new lines of inquiry and new ways of understanding complex social phenomena. In my view, some fortification and intensification of language ideological theory was desirable for several reasons. One of these related to its own history of success going from the status of a re-opening of presumably closed questions in linguistic theory (Silverstein 1979), combining with a movement emphasizing the need to bring language back into the material world through a reintegration of language data with political economic theory (e.g. Hill 1985; Gal 1979; Irvine 1989; Woolard 1985). While the success of that movement is sometimes described as an ascent to paradigmatic domination, whatever success the approach enjoyed soon became a presupposed background rather than an explicitly discussed and debated intellectual project (Cody 2010; Kroskrity 2015). If use of the phrase "language ideologies" and some sprinkling of associated metalanguage from its collective literature (e.g. fractal recursivity, erasure [Irvine and Gal 2000]; sites of ideological production [Silverstein 1998; Philips 2000], indexical orders [Silverstein 2003]) count as expressions of its dominance, then I would concede it is indeed in that category. But as an intellectual worker who would like see it actually encourage and guide research along more productive lines, I viewed language ideological assemblages as a much-needed resource to reach beyond the mere identification of specific ideologies (such as standardization, and linguistic purism) in order to produce a wider frame in which to explore and better understand complex communicative events, language contact and change, and such processes as language shift, multilingual adaptations, language ideological change, and forms of language revitalization.

In earlier formulations (Kroskrity 2000b, 2010) I have described language ideologies as a cluster concept consisting of multiple dimensions. Several of these in my view are routinely neglected in much of the work that can be self-described as influenced by language ideological approaches. Within a language ideological assemblage approach, I sought a model that would double-down on several key dimensions. One is the need for more attention to pervasive but often indirectly observed forces conventionally viewed as resulting from positionalities within political economic structures of varying scale. Another is the attention to speakers' awareness, ranging from practical to discursive consciousness and very much related to their own experience of socialization – as either the result of explicit instruction or implicit pattern – to those language ideologies (Kroskrity 1998). The final dimension I will discuss involves multiplicity. This has long been recognized (e.g. Kroskrity 2000b) as a key feature of language ideologies – their potential interaction with and/or opposition to other ideologies, not just those that are local or indigenous but all the ideologies that are thrust into the *milieu* of speakers by nation-states and global discourses. In my view the potential benefits of these features of language ideological approaches have not been as routinely realized as I had hoped. Since all three features fit well with the notion of assemblage I thought it an especially appropriate theoretical vehicle for reasserting their importance and rescuing these valuable resources from theoretical inattention. Multiplicity and positionality are obviously key aspects of the assemblages as represented, and I see the emphasis on awareness as related to antecedent and informing understandings of how the subjective milieus of specific persons fit or collide with other elements in the assemblage (Deleuze and Guattari 1987). What the assemblage package adds to each of these is the theoretical guidance and encouragement to understand their relationship to each other and to understand their interactive and emergent role in becoming.

## 5 Ready for prime time: Hailing an academic public

The invitation to participate in a session of the 2016 American Anthropological Association annual meeting devoted to indigenous multilingualisms created an especially appropriate occasion in which to deploy the emerging concept of language ideological assemblages. Ruth Singer and Jill Vaughn were the organizers of the conference and later editors of the special issue of *Language & Communication* (Singer and Vaughan 2018), in which revised versions of the talk-based articles were published. Like several in our session, my paper, and eventual article, treated complex Indigenous communities with long histories of multilingualism that predated either colonial impact or influence from a nation-state. In both the paper and the article, the task of conveying the distinctive array of language ideologies in two very different Native American language communities required much of the time and most of the word count permitted by those academic genres. Accordingly, time and space for defining and unpacking language ideological assemblages was limited. In the opening pages of the article, I wrote (Kroskrity 2018: 134):

> I will demonstrate that divergent Indigenous *language ideological assemblages (LIA)* associated with multilingualisms have shaped distinctive patterns of language shift – a process significantly more totalizing among the Western Mono. By introducing the conceptual framework of LIA, I want to emphasize that the proper appreciation of indigenous multilingualisms is to understand their component language ideologies as part of a larger complex of relevant beliefs and feelings, both Indigenous and externally imposed, that may complement, contest, or otherwise dynamically interact with each other to modify language ideologies and linguistic practices. Frustrated by language ideological research that often looks at a single ideology – say that associated with purism or standardization – I am attempting to redirect attention to the interaction of clusters of ideologies that occur within or across linguistic communities. Though the notion of assemblage exists in Latour's (2007) network theory, I find more of a basis for analogical extension from ecological theory. As represented by the cultural anthropologist Anna Tsing (2015: 22), "Ecologists turned to assemblages to get around the sometimes fixed and bounded connotations of ecological 'community'. . .".

This brief revelation of the concept was itself an abbreviated mix of theory-internal motivations and a selective grafting of some of Tsing's own very cogent but succinct statements about her use of the assemblage model. Later in the article, I concluded by suggesting that language ideological assemblages had proven useful in seeing the different elements in LIAs of the Western Mono and Village of Tewa communities, and had proven consequential to understanding processes of language shift and language revitalization (Kroskrity 2018:134). I was also able to relate differences in what today might look like very similar language ideologies of language and identity to different patterns of shift and revitalization. Though members of both groups might talk about how language is an important expression of their cultural identities, a language ideological assemblage approach revealed important differences in whether the ideologies expressed today had long-term indigenous sources (as for the Village of Tewa) or were more recent reshapings of regional, egalitarian multingualism in which a singular regional identity, involving trilingualism in Indigenous languages, was replaced via fractal recursivity (Irvine and Gal 2000) with an analogous 1:1 linguistic nationalism. Just as English was iconized to national identity on the scale of the nation-state, so Mono would be reideologized as the icon of Mono tribal identity. On the surface, this may seem similar to the language and identity ideologies that exist for the Village of Tewa where that ideology is expressed in the local expression *Naavi hiili, naavi woowatsi na-muu* 'My language is my life'. But the different language ideological assemblages of these communities clearly establish multiple Indigenous discourses of identity for the Tewa that have emblematized their heritage language for centuries longer than the Mono have theirs. This can be advanced as one of the reasons why the Tewa are generally more successfully enduring language shift to English than the Mono communities (Kroskrity 2018:143). Although I have not reproduced here many of the actual details of the language assemblages I represented in that article, I have selectively provided evidence for my sense of the potential value of this approach. Though I feel that language ideological assemblages have served me well as a more inclusive strategy for organizing the disparate kinds of data necessary to better understand the dynamics of complex language use and language change, I feel that my initial effort did not satisfactorily define LIA. I hope to do that more adequately in the following section.

## 6 Concluding by looking forward

As when I attempted to unpack language ideologies as a multidimensional cluster concept (Kroskrity 2000b), I was initially inclined to follow the same strategy as useful here. But there is at least one important difference. When I wrote the introduction to *Regimes of language*, there was already a sizable collective literature that could be described as having a language ideological approach. But that is still not true of language ideological assemblages. Therefore, I instead offer the following provisional, refined, but perhaps continuously in process definition.

Language ideological assemblages are dynamic configurations of human actors and their beliefs, feelings, and conceptions about language(s) and communication as they are produced and expressed within their individual milieus and the intersubjective worlds of mutual influence from institutions, political economic structures, state power, technologies, global systems, and mediated, mediatized, and multimodal forms of expression.[5]

# References

Biehl, João & Peter Locke. 2010. Deleuze and the anthropology of becoming. *Current Anthropology* 51 (3). 317–337.
Blommaert, Jan. 2007. Sociolinguistic scales. *Intercultural Pragmatics* 4 (1). 1–19.
Blumer, Herbert. 1986. *Symbolic interactionism: Perspective and method*. Berkeley: University of California Press.
Carr, E. Summerson & Michael Lempert. 2016. *Scale: Discourse and dimensions of social life*. Berkeley: University of California Press.
Chomsky, Noam. 1965. *Aspects of the theory of syntax*. Cambridge, MA: Massachusetts Institute of Technology Press.
Cody, Francis. 2010. Linguistic anthropology at the end of the naughts: A review of 2009 *American Anthropologist* 112 (2). 200–207.
Debenport, Erin. 2015. *Fixing the books: Secrecy, literacy, and perfectibility in indigenous New Mexico*. Santa Fe, NM: School of Advanced Research Press.
Deleuze, Gilles & Felix Guattari. 1987. *A thousand plateaus: Capitalism and schizophrenia*. Translated by Brian Massumi. Minneapolis: University of Minnesota Press.
Dorian, Nancy. 1998. Western language ideologies and small language prospects. In Lenore A. Grenoble & Lindsay J. Whaley (eds.), *Endangered languages: Current issues and future prospects*, 3–21. Cambridge: Cambridge University Press.

---

[5] Though I label the conceptual framework language ideological assemblages, I certainly see the value of thinking about this as semiotic assemblages (as in the creative and inspiring work of Pennycook [2017], which is similar to my project here). Though the notion of semiotic ideologies has been established, I am not convinced it is necessary here. Why? For the entire history of linguistic ideology (Silverstein 1979), later aka language ideologies, the understanding of language was as a semiotic system. By metonymy, language in this school has always stood for a broader range of signs, and semiotic systems. So unless there is a reason to call special attention to semiotic systems that have very different affordances than those of language, semiotically construed, I do not see a motivation for its unmarked use. But for a well-argued alternative approach to semiotic ideologies, see Keane (2003).

Dozier, Edward P. 1956. Two examples of linguistic acculturation: the Yaqui of Sonora, Arizona, and the Tewa of New Mexico. *Language* 32(1).146–57. [Reprinted in *Language in culture and society*, Dell Hymes (ed.), 509–20. New York: Harper. 1965].

Field, Margaret C. & Paul V. Kroskrity. 2009. Revealing Native American language ideologies. In Paul V. Kroskrity & Margaret C. Field (eds.), *Native American language ideologies*, 3–28. Tucson: University of Arizona Press.

Gal, Susan. 1979. *Language shift: Social determinants of linguistic change in Austria*. San Francisco: Academic Press.

Hill, Jane H. 1985. The grammar of consciousness and the consciousness of grammar. *American Ethnologist* 12 (4). 725–737.

Hill, Jane H. 2002. "Expert rhetorics" in advocacy for endangered languages: Who is listening and what do they hear? *Journal of Linguistic Anthropology* 12 (2). 119–133.

Irvine, Judith. 1989. When talk isn't cheap: Language and political economy. *American Ethnologist* 16 (3). 248–267.

Irvine, Judith & Susan Gal. 2000. Language ideology and linguistic differentiation. In Paul V. Kroskrity (ed.), *Regimes of language*, 35–83. Santa Fe, NM: School of Advanced Research.

Joyce, Rosemary A. & Joshua Pollard. 2010. Archaeological assemblages and practices of deposition. In Dan Hicks & Mary C. Beaudry (eds.), *The Oxford handbook of material culture studies*, 291–311. Oxford: Oxford University Press.

Kaplan, Abraham. 1964. *The conduct of inquiry: Methodology for behavioral science*. San Francisco: Chandler.

Keane, Webb. 2003. Semiotics and the social analysis of material things. *Language & Communication* 23 (3–4). 409–425.

Kroskrity, Paul V. 1993. *Language, history, and identity: Ethnolinguistic studies of the Arizona Tewa*. Tucson: University of Arizona Press.

Kroskrity, Paul V. 1998. Arizona Tewa speech as a manifestation of a dominant language ideology. In Bambi Schieffelin, Kathryn Woolard & Paul V. Kroskrity (eds.), *Language ideologies: Practice and theory*, 103–122. New York: Oxford University Press.

Kroskrity, Paul V. 2000a. *Regimes of language: Ideologies, polities, identities*. Santa Fe, NM: School of Advanced Research.

Kroskrity, Paul V. 2000b. Regimenting languages: Language ideological perspectives. In Paul V. Kroskrity (ed.), *Regimes of language*, 1–34. Santa Fe, NM: School of Advanced Research.

Kroskrity, Paul V. 2000c. Language ideologies in the expression and representation of Arizona Tewa ethnic identity. In Paul V. Kroskrity (ed.), *Regimes of language*, 329–359. Santa Fe, NM: School of Advanced Research.

Kroskrity, Paul V. 2009. Embodying the reversal of language shift: Agency, incorporation, and language ideological change in the Western Mono community of central California. In Paul V. Kroskrity & Margaret C. Field (eds.), *Native American language ideologies*, 190–210. Tucson: University of Arizona Press.

Kroskrity, Paul V. 2010. Language ideologies – Evolving perspectives. In Jurgen Jaspers (ed.), *Language use and society*, 192–211. Amsterdam/Philadelphia: John Benjamins.

Kroskrity, Paul V. 2015. Language ideologies: Emergence, elaboration, application. In Nancy Bonvillain (ed.), *Handbook of linguistic anthropology*, 95–108. New York: Routledge.

Kroskrity, Paul V. 2016. On recognizing persistence in the indigenous language ideologies of multilingualism in two Native American communities. Paper presented at the Annual

Meeting of the American Anthropological Association, Minneapolis, MN. November 17, 2016.

Kroskrity, Paul V. 2018. On recognizing persistence in the indigenous language ideologies of multilingualism in two Native American communities. *Language & Communication* 62 (2). 133–144.

Latour, Bruno. 1993. *We have never been modern*. Cambridge: Harvard University Press. Translated by Catherine Porter.

Latour, Bruno. 2007. *Reassembling the social: An introduction to actor-network theory*. Oxford: Oxford University Press.

McCarty, Teresa. 2016. Policy and politics of language revitalization in the USA and Canada. In Serafin Coronel-Molina & Teresa L. McCarty (eds.), *Indigenous language revitalization in the Americas*, 15–34. New York: Routledge.

Meek, Barbra. 2010. *We are our language: An ethnography of language revitalization in a northern Athabaskan community*. Tucson: University of Arizona Press.

Migge, Bettina & Isabelle Léglise. 2013. *Exploring language in a multilingual context: Variation, interaction, and ideology in language documentation*. Cambridge: Cambridge University Press.

Ong, Aihwa & Stephen Collier (eds.). 2005. *Global assemblages*. Hoboken, NJ: Wiley-Blackwell.

Pennycook, Alastair. 2017. Translanguaging and semiotic assemblages. *International Journal of Multilingualism* 14 (3). 269–282.

Philips, Susan U. 2000. Constructing a Tongan nation state through language ideology in the Courtroom. In Paul V. Kroskrity (ed.), *Regimes of language*, 229–257. Santa Fe: School of Advanced Research.

Schieffelin, Bambi, Kathryn A. Woolard & Paul V. Kroskrity. 1998. *Language ideologies: Practice and theory*. New York: Oxford University Press.

Silverstein, Michael. 1979. Language structure and linguistic ideology. In Paul R. Clyne, William Hanks, & Carol L. Hofbauer (eds.), *The elements: A parasession on units and levels*, 193–247. Chicago: Chicago Linguistics Society.

Silverstein, Michael. 1985. Language and the culture of gender : At the intersection of structure, usage, and ideology. In Elizabeth Mertz & Richard J. Parmentier (eds.), *Semiotic mediation*, 219–259. Orlando, FL: Academic Press.

Silverstein, Michael. 1998. The uses and utilities of ideology: A commentary. In Bambi Schieffelin, Kathryn Woolard, & Paul V. Kroskrity (eds.), *Language ideologies: Practice and theory*, 123–145. New York: Oxford University Press.

Silverstein, Michael. 2003. Indexical order and the dialectics of sociolinguistic life. *Language & Communication* 23 (3–4). 193–229.

Singer, Ruth & Jill Vaughan. 2018. Indigenous multilingualisms. (Special Issue) *Language & Communication* 62 (B). 83–196.

Tsing, Anna Lowenhaupt. 2015. *The mushroom at the end of the world*. Princeton, NJ: Princeton University Press.

Whiteley, Peter. 2003. Do "language rights" serve indigenous interests? Some Hopi and other queries. *American Anthropologist* 105 (4). 712–722.

Woolard, Kathryn. 1985. Language variation and cultural hegemony: Towards an integration of sociolinguistic and social theory. *American Ethnologist* 12 (4). 738–748.

Amy J. Hirshman
# Chapter 11
# A case of archeological classification

## 1 Introduction

Archaeology is an inquiry into human behavior, typically in the past, through the study of the material residue of that behavior. As people act, they leave an imprint behind; archaeologists study that imprint. As you can imagine, given the time depth of human activity, archaeologists have a lot of materials to sort through. A key methodology to wrangling this material, and the information contained within, is through classification of all those artifacts. One key category of artifacts is ceramics, which can come in the form of vessels, tools, figurines, beads, or sculptures, to name just a few forms that this pliable material can take in the hands of creative humans. And once ceramic objects were adopted by people in past cultural contexts, they often became a dominant class of artifacts to be found in archaeological sites. This chapter concerns the classification of ceramic vessels. After a brief discussion of the manufacture, use, and discard of ceramic vessels, I turn to several ways in which archaeologists classify ceramic artifacts. This chapter then describes the ceramic classificatory schema for the Lake Pátzcuaro Basin, Mexico, in order to explicate the processes, attributes, and decisions that contribute to the formation of a classification within archaeology.

The production of any ceramic object is a complex synthetic process, and potters make many decisions during production. What follows is a brief outline of hand-built vessels, though artisanal ceramics can include wheel-thrown vessels, as well as other forms such as figurines, beads, or smoking pipes. Vessels require "paste," a prepared clay and water mixture, from which a pot is made, which is also called a "fabric" after the vessel is fired. Clays, byproducts of erosion, are "fine-grained, naturally occurring materials that become plastic and malleable when wet and hardens with the application of heat" (Rice 2015: 453). While clays are widely available, not all clays are useful for the purposes of making a pot. As such, potters need to prepare the clays by grinding, removing naturally occurring materials by sieving or levigating, and/or by the addition of aplastic materials as a "temper," such as sand crushed rock, organics, or other ground ceramics referred to as "grog." The relationship between clay and the additional materials, essentially a recipe used

**Amy J. Hirshman,** West Virginia University, amy.hirshman@mail.wvu.edu

by the potter, is determined by the potter on the basis of tradition, training, feel, and the intended function of the vessel after fabrication. Variation in pastes can therefore indicate behavioral trends, such as different potting traditions, changes in potting resources or technology over time, or the presence of multiple potters within a region.

Pastes can be formed into a nearly endless variety of forms and sizes based on function and cultural dictates; as such, morphology (shape) has a technical and social dimension. Basic vessel forms can be identified as plate, bowl, vase, or jar; however, within those categories exists near-endless variation within and between cultural traditions. In describing the shape of a vessel, the aspects that are typically described are the general shape, the rim and lip, which together form the border of the orifice of the vessel (the lip being the outermost edge), the body, which is the bulk of the vessel, and the base, or bottom (Figure 11.1). Vessels may also have additional elaborations, such as handles or spouts, as well as supports or other elaborated base structures. The thickness of the vessel base, body wall, or rim/lip can also reflect vessel technology of the vessel, social norms, or both.

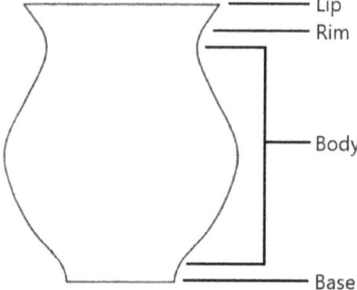

Figure 11.1: Basic parts of a ceramic vessel.

The flexibility of vessel construction also extends to surface decoration, which communicates social messages to users and observers. Surfaces can be incised or adorned with appliques while wet or excised after drying. Vessels are often slipped, which is a thin clay slurry applied to all or part of a vessel. Once nearly dry, with or without a slip, the surface is at least roughly smoothed, but time can be taken to burnish the exposed surfaces; burnishing, which is essentially rubbing the surface with a smooth, hard object, such as a stone, can also bring the surface to a high polish. If additional decoration is needed, paint and/or glaze can also be applied. "Resist" or "negative" is the application of black smudging on the vessel surface in a second firing by using a material, such as wax, that will eventually melt away; it is merely one of a number of post-firing applications that can be added to a vessel. Surface decoration has a technical component, for example, slipping increases water impermeability, but its expression is heavily determined by cultural rules and expectations.

Once dry, vessels can be fired in a controlled context, such as kilns and bonfires, which result in well-fired, but not vitrified, "pottery." Often the firing leads to an incomplete oxidation of the vessel fabric, which is identifiable as a "firing core," or a grey region in the middle of the fabric wall. Pottery can be used in many contexts, such as storing, cooking, serving food or beverages, and display, and can constitute the humblest kitchen tool or bear enormous social prestige as a status-bearing gift. Archaeologically, whole vessels can be found in burials or other caches, and broken fragments abound in the archaeological record. These shards, which in archaeology-speak are called "sherds," are so copiously available in many archaeological settings that we must somehow use them to make sense of the materials we are excavating. Descriptions of pottery production and the organization of potters abound in the anthropological literature; one such English example from Michoacán, Mexico, is by Williams (2017; for a summary of ethnographic Michoacán ceramic studies, see Hirshman 2020).

# 2 Classification of ceramics

The literature on classification is voluminous, and excellent reviews and investigations of classification in archaeology exist elsewhere (e.g. Adams and Adams 1991; Bortolini 2017; Dunnell 1971; Read 2007; Rice 2015; Santacreu, Trias, and Rosselló 2017; see also Burkette 2018 for a linguist's perspective on ceramic classification). Rice presented a tripart discussion about general trends in Americanist ceramic classification. She first highlights folk, or overtly emic, classification schemas, which rely on both the vessel and the makers' and users' perception of shape, size, use and contents (Rice 2015: 224). Two difficulties with this approach are, one, the variation in role and status among makers and users can lead to varying classifications within a cultural context; there is no one classification (e.g. Kempton 1981; Huston and Merkens 2002). Two, many archaeological contexts utilize materials older than or outside of direct informant information or explanatory texts.

A second general trend emphasizes vessel form, or morphology: the basic shapes, contours, sizes, and proportions of vessels, with accompanying ideas regarding function (Rice 2015: 232–244). Additional features, such as handles and supports, further contribute to vessel variation. "This is an exercise in emic classification, as well as in paradigmatic classification: creating equivalent units (e.g., bowl jar, plate) on unordered dimensions (e.g., diameter, rim type, appendages)" (Rice 2015: 232). This classification schema requires a sound set of whole or nearly whole objects, from which to assess form and measure dimensions.

A third classificatory trend identified by Rice is "devised, formal, or scientific classifications, which are created by the analyst" (2015: 229). Within Americanist archaeology, two key trends are analytical classification, which is a paradigmatic inquiry, and formal taxonomic typologies, of which the type-variety system is perhaps the best known (Rice 2015: 229–232). Both focus on attributes within the ceramics, which are singular variables such as raw materials or decorative applications, and are applicable in contexts without direct cultural information or with predominantly fragmentary collections. One criticism of devised classifications is that they require the analyst to decide what is an important attribute, at the expense of others (Rice 2013: 25). However, the number of attributes is potentially limitless, and as such, these methods do guide the analyst's decision-making process in a formal fashion that will enable the comparison of final classifications. Indeed,

> *all* classifications result in loss of information; it is theoretically and practically impossible for any classification to take into consideration all possible attribute states of an entity (see Dunnell 1971: 115, 117). The fundamental issue is to specify initially what information is "important," that importance dictated by the underlying goal or purpose of the classificatory exercise.           (Rice 2013, 25, italics in original)

Both are used in the Tarascan case study in a complementary fashion, though the methodologies do not have the same end goals and need not be used co-jointly.

Analytical classification is rooted in the foundational classificatory work of Rouse (1939, 1960; see also Krause 2016; Read 2007) and is useful for identifying the areal distribution of cultural affiliation and cultural change (Rouse 1960: 320–321). Modal analysis assesses all attributes as equal, and among them seeks modes: "any standard, concept, or custom which governs the behavior of the artisans of a community. . . . such modes will be reflected in the artifacts as attributes which conform to a community's standards, which express its concepts, or which reveal its customary way of manufacturing and using artifacts" (Rouse 1960: 313). Ceramic analysis proceeds from the identification of attributes reflecting raw material and technology of manufacture, to shape and decoration, then function and use, which is the general trajectory of the manufacture and use of a vessel (Rouse 1960: 314–315). Nevertheless, this is not a hierarchical identification; rather the classes form "a single series of classes or subclasses" (Rouse 1960: 316). As such, attribute states can be analyzed in a variety of cross-cutting ways, such as time, technology, color, or decoration. Modal analysis is linked to data- and computer-driven analysis in Americanist archaeology, as it is subsumed within the search for naturally occurring groups within a cultural assemblage. But the analysis can be accomplished without computer assistance and is centered on modes as a nomothetic, not polythetic, attribute state (Rouse 1960).

The type-variety method is a hierarchical classification method widely used in North American and Mesoamerican archaeological studies. Chiefly developed for designating temporal chronologies and dating sites, the system is so widespread that published classifications have become crucial for comparing ceramic complexes between regions as well. The hierarchy is: Ware>group>type>variety. The "ware" is composed of a combination of "paste composition . . . identified through paste texture, kind of temper, paste, hardness (rarely used), porosity, and color [and] surface finish . . . recognized by means of slip or the lack of slip, by smoothness or roughness, by luster . . . and by color" (Sabloff and Smith 1969: 278). "Group" is a lumping mechanism for related types, when the assemblage is too small or too weathered for further subdivisions (Parsons 1967; Sabloff and Smith 1969: 278-279). A "type" is then identified based on details of surface decoration or vessel shape. Within types, a "variety" is a further subdivision based on surface decoration or form. As with modes, the analyst makes decisions regarding the appropriate attributes, especially regarding type and variety identification; however, as noted, the basic paste and surface attributes are identified by the methodological process itself. This method also requires a binomial naming system, of location name and descriptive name (e.g. Wheat, Gifford and Wasley 1958: 57; Smith, Willey and Gifford 1958: 334-336; Willey, Culbert and Adams 1967: 291).

Using these two methodologies of modes and type-variety in tandem is established in Americanist archaeology (e.g. Rice 1976; Rouse 1960: 315; Sabloff and Smith 1969; Smith, Willey and Gifford 1960; Willey, Culbert and Adams 1967). They are both useful in contexts of new research, where modes or salutary attributes are unknown, or with small or fragmentary ceramic assemblages, as the methods direct the analyst toward certain types of attributes, from which dominant cultural patterns may arise. In the Tarascan case, prior research, and the publications of that research, was limited in scope and focused upon a relatively small collection of whole vessels from the ritual center of the Tarascan state. Using a small survey collection from a larger area of the state capital, Helen Pollard conducted both a modal and type-variety analysis and formally named the initial types for the Lake Pátzcuaro Basin, the center of the late Postclassic Tarascan state (1972, 1993). Below is a description of her methodology and the resulting information and its applications.

One problematic aspect of the type-variety system is the definition of ware as dependent upon both paste and surface. Rice (1976: 540) highlighted that not all Mesoamerican applications of the type-variety system started with "paste" as part of the ware category. My impression is that the use of paste has been more extensive in the Gulf Coast region (e.g. Arnold 2003; Ortiz 1975; Stark 1989; Pool 1990, 1995; Venter 2008) and Maya region (e.g. Parsons 1967). Paste was not as extensively used in ceramic classifications by archeologists working in the central Mesoamerican highlands, which included not only the Tarascan culture, but also Teotihuacan and the Aztecs, among others.

The combination of "paste," which deals in raw materials and potting technology, and as previously discussed, requires not one but multiple attributes, and "surface," which reflects the initial surface decoration process of slipping (or not) and the extent of burnishing that the potter gives the surface of the vessel. Rice points out that wares dependent solely upon these surface attributes and not paste "are methodologically more consonant with the hierarchical ordering technique of the type-variety system and with the scope of broad inter-site and intra-regional comparison" (1976: 541). Rice highlights that except in a few cases where the paste and surface are tightly combined, such as in Teotihuacan's "Thin Orange Ware," surface treatments can often occur over a range of paste categories; thus paste effectively "*crosscuts* types and wares" (Rice 1976: 541; italics in original). However, unless paste is part of the definition of the type, it is impossible to separate imported ceramics from local copies without later laboratory testing. For example, Teotihuacan's "Thin Orange Ware" was actually made elsewhere (Rattray and Harbottle 1992).

Paste would be all but hidden from consumers of the ceramics. Though paste may be the starting point for a potter, a consumer is only concerned with whether the vessel meets their applied needs. Such needs, such as the ability to withstand the thermal shock of repeated heating/cooling cycles of a cooking pot, are directly tied to the paste. But the consumer may not care why a vessel can endure such temperature changes – only that it must. Further, a consumer may be interested in the social messaging of a serving bowl much more than how many inclusions occur in the paste fabric, or if it was thoroughly oxidized in the firing process.

Paste is also somewhat "hidden" from the excavator. The attributes for paste in the type-variety system are identifiable in hand specimens but are still easier to identify in the lab on a washed sherd than in the field. Kolb observed that "ideally, the attributes used to identify types are ones that are identifiable with the naked eye, and are found on small fragments of pottery, so that the sorting of potsherds into types is fast and straightforward" (2011: 7–8). Paste is just more time-consuming to identify as part of the initial identification.

Turning to the Tarascan ceramic typology, Pollard used paste in her ware definition. The crosscutting effect Rice identified means that the Tarascan typology is quite complex, more so because of the paste diversity within the Lake Pátzcuaro Basin ceramics. As described below, paste figures prominently in the classification, but the use of both the type-variety system and a modal analysis means the available information is also flexible in its potential applications.

# 3 Case study: Ceramics from the Lake Pátzcuaro Basin

The example detailed here uses a ceramic classification schema implemented with archaeological surveys and excavations in the Lake Pátzcuaro Basin, Michoacán, México (Figure 11.2). Approximately one-ninth the size of the Valley of Mexico, the Lake Pátzcuaro Basin is a highland intra-drainage basin with a spring-fed freshwater lake ringed by volcanic cones. While this research focused primarily on the emergence and development of the Tarascan state (CE

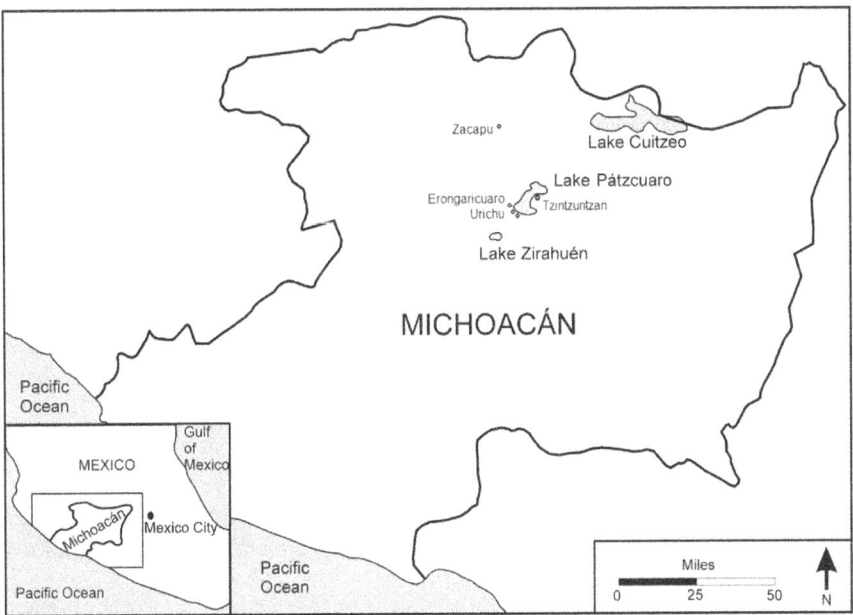

**Figure 11.2:** Map of the Lake Pátzcuaro Basin showing sites mentioned in the text (Used by permission of Hirshman).

1350–1525), the archaeological data indicates the basin was continuously inhabited from at least the Late Preclassic (ca. 50 BCE), to the Tarascan state period (e.g. Pollard 2008), through contact with the Spanish until today. In this study, "Tarascan" refers to the ancient political entity rather than the ethnic identity of most commoners within the state or the descendant population today, who are known as the Purépecha, which is also the name of their language (e.g., Pollard 2008). Ceramic artifacts reflect the entire cultural sequence, with production occurring within the basin throughout this entire time. Figure 11.3 is a cache of Tarascan-era ceramics from the site of Urichu.

**Figure 11.3:** Ceramic sherds and vessels from an excavated cache at Urichu (Used by permission of Pollard).

Archaeological excavations began in the basin in 1937 on the main ceremonial platform at the capital, Tzintzuntzan, and extended over nine field seasons until 1968 (Castro-Leal 1986). Ceramic typologies were constructed from the ceramics from the ceremonial platform at Tzintzuntzan (Moedano 1941, 1946; Noguera 1931, 1965; Rubín de Borbolla 1939, 1948), but they privileged the Tarascan state-era, high-status whole vessels excavated there, and as published were "incomplete" (Castro-Leal 1986: 75).

Within this context, Pollard developed a type-variety ceramic typology. The ceramics for this analysis were collected as part of her dissertation work at

Tzintzuntzan (1970–72; Pollard 1972; see also 1993, Appendix 2). Pollard's survey collection also reflected the state period, but exhibited greater diversity due to the wider range of activities carried out away from the ceremonial center of the state; for example, habitation zones would include some ritual and ceremonial feasting, but also daily food storage, preparation and consumption. This collection was also small as well as fragmentary, so Pollard used Parsons' (1967) type-variety study as a model. Small samples are hard to refine into all the classificatory levels of the type-variety system, so Parsons added "group" as a placeholder when collections were not to be resolved into types and varieties due to insufficient sample size. "In order to derive the maximum information from the collection," Pollard (1993: 200) combined this type-variety analysis with a modal analysis, as will be described below. Pollard explained the typology in her dissertation (1972, Appendix II) and revisited the typology again in her volume on the Tarascan state (1993, Appendix 2).

With the revisions, Pollard also incorporated the work of Castro-Leal (1986) and Moguel Cos (1987). Castro-Leal provided the most thorough discussion of the ceramics from the ceremonial platform, with a focus on the 1962–1964 excavations (1986). Castro-Leal expanded upon the rather basic previous descriptions and followed a modified type-variety analysis that used paste (using the attributes of "Desgrasante, textura, color, cocción": 'inclusions, texture, color, firing'), surface, decoration, and forms. The named types privileged surface treatment, such as "Tipo Domestico con Engobe y Pulido" (domestic type with slip and polish), "Rojo Pulido" (red polish), and "Policromo" (polychrome). Moguel Cos (1987) analyzed a small sample comprising approximately 2,000 sherds collected from hundreds of sites as part of a large regional survey. Drawing upon previous literature and constrained by the expectations of the initial project, Moguel Cos first divided the collection into large categories of monochrome, bichrome, polychrome, incised, bases, supports, figurines, pipes, malacates (fish net weights), colonial, and modern, before subdividing these large groups into smaller types (Moguel Cos 1987: 50). These are not coequal categories; however, the final presentation of types by Moguel Cos describe types based on the large group, then paste, surface, form, and decoration for the types within each large group. Pollard indicates that both Castro-Leal and Moguel Cos's "analyses combine portions of the modal and taxonomic classifications" (Pollard 1993: 201), but also cautioned that there should be no expectation for identical results given the constraints of their respective projects in terms of scale and sample sizes. Where comparable, Pollard cited the overlapping groups from these studies when she completed her descriptions, as will be demonstrated below. Later elaboration by Pollard (2001), after the multi-year project centered upon Urichu in the southeast portion of the basin, was based on a much larger sample and drew upon comparable types from additional research at Tzintzuntzan (e.g. Cabrera Castro 1996), and the Zacapu Basin, to the north, notably for earlier time periods (e.g. Arnauld, Carot, and Fauvet-Berthelot 1993; Michelet, Arnauld, and Fauvet Berthelot 1989).

The Tarascan case is useful for thinking through devised ceramic classifications. The total number of whole vessels from the lake basin is small and from highly specialized cultural contexts, such as high-class burials and ritual vessel caches. A morphological study would be inadequate for discerning larger past cultural patterns; consequently, sherds comprise the basic, if fragmentary, data set for any analysis. Previous classificatory work was careful but was partial and did not employ systematic categories (Castro-Leal 1986; Moguel Cos 1987). Finally, the current classification schema employs both a modal analysis and a type-variety analysis. The type-variety analysis also began with "paste," so the implications of that choice are revealed in the analysis; subsequent research has also illuminated that choice.

Pollard chose to combine the analytical and hierarchical methods "to derive maximum information from the collection" (Pollard 1993: 200). She began with the modal analysis, and following Rouse's "procedure of making artifacts" (1960: 314, Figure 1), she identified attributes related to paste, form, and surface finish and decoration, in that manufacturing order, exhaustively identifying the variation found within the assemblage in regard to the range of rims, handles, and supports, as well as slip and paint combinations (Appendix 1). In doing so she followed Sabloff and Smith's definition of a mode as a "selected attribute or cluster of attributes which display significance in their own right" (1969: 279, quoted by Pollard 1993: 200). Though a modal analysis conceptualizes all attributes as equal, Appendix 1 presents the information in an ordinal form for organizational purposes. This sort of modal analysis enables the isolation and comparison of attributes across the assemblage, since commonalities suggest cultural patterns, either across space or through time.

Pollard describes her modal analysis of "paste" as identical to that which she did for the type-variety system (see Appendix 1). This analysis followed the paste attributes identified in the type-variety literature (e.g. Parsons 1967: 54; Sabloff and Smith 1969; see also Rice 1976). Pollard's paste attributes and descriptors are:

> Color range (based on Munsell Soil Color Chart)
> Texture (percent of inclusions): sparse <15 percent; moderate. 15–30 percent; heavy, >30 percent
> Size of particles: fine, 0.01–0.25mm; medium, 0.26–0.50 mm; coarse, 0.51–1.00 mm
> Hardness (Mohs Scale [a geologic scratch text of mineralogical resistance, here repurposed to indicate hardness of the sherd surface])

Firing (even-uneven [as noted by the absence or presence of a "firing core", an unoxidized portion of the middle of the sherd that did not fire as evenly as the surface of the sherd])
Fracture ([of the broken edge of the sherd] attributed as straight, irregular, friable)
Inclusions: types identified by I. M. Drew (then of the Sackler Laboratory, Columbia University). She concluded that except for sherd materials, all inclusions are natural to the clay. (Pollard 1993: 202)

Pollard tracked each variable on a fresh, clean break on a sherd as a hand specimen; these traits can be identified visually or through low-power (e.g. 10x) magnification and, except for inclusion, require no additional equipment beyond a hand lens. However, some inclusions are large enough for low magnification identification as well.

Pollard identified eleven paste categories at Tzintzuntzan, and four additional paste categories were identified at Urichu (Pollard 2001). In naming the pastes, Pollard basically followed the suggested binomial naming convention for the type-variety system, for example, "Yaguarato cream," with an immediate location name followed by descriptive name (e.g. Wheat and Wasley 1958: 57). Pollard observed that

> Due to the small size of the collection and the fragmentary nature of the sherds, the presence/absence of slip and the color of slip was not sufficient to create new wares, but only to distinguish groups within wares. In this way sherds that have come from the same vessel, only part of which was slipped, or from vessels that had polychrome decoration on only a portion of the surface, would not be separated. (1993: 200)

In other words, it is possible to have a skewed distribution of unslipped or only slipped vessel bottoms without many comparably complete vessel rims, and a similarly skewed distribution of painted rims without enough painted vessel bottoms. Since the bottom of a vessel is not normally exhibited, effort made to paint and otherwise decorate the bottom of a vessel is unnecessary in most common usages of a vessel; therefore, potters or their decorating designees would focus on the visually presented parts of the vessel such as the external rim and body of the vessel, as well as the interior bowl surfaces. Thus, by focusing on "paste" as the initial common variable or attribute in the analysis, Pollard kept together sherds from the same vessel that could be potentially separated from one another if the typology was created first on the basis of decoration. Pollard notes that surface decoration is often repeated across different paste categories, and the pastes also cross-cut categories identified through surface decoration by both Castro-Leal and Moguel Cos (Pollard 1993: 201). Paste descriptions for three common paste categories are:

*Ware:* Tariacuri Brown. Paste: 1. color: 5YR/4/4,6 yellowish red; 7.5YR/4/4 brown; 2. texture: medium compact with medium-fine size inclusions and high percentage of inclusions; 3. hardness: 3–4; 4. inclusions: basalt, quartz; some have a bit of red, which is an iron oxide or sherd material; 5. firing: even firing; thicker pieces tend to have a gray core; some clouding; 6. fracture: straight.

*Ware:* Yaguarato Cream. Paste 1. color: 5YR/6/6, 5 YR/5/6, 2.5 YR/6/6, reddish yellow; 2. texture: fine, compact paste with medium-fine size inclusions, medium-heavy percentage of inclusions; 3. hardness 3–4; 4. Inclusions: basalt, iron oxide, some clear quartz; the basalt is predominant inclusion; 5. firing: some gray cores, several blackened surfaces and firing clouds; 6. fracture: fairly straight.

*Ware:* Querenda White. Paste: 1. color: 7.5YR/7/6, 5 YR/6/6. 7.5 YR/6/4 (yellowish brown); 2. texture: very compact paste; I. M. Drew commented that the example she examined was fired to almost a glassy state; fine size and sparse percentage of inclusions; 3. hardness: 3.5–4; 4. inclusions: iron oxide, possibly some sherd, occasionally basalt; 5. firing: almost glassy in some cases: a large gray-green core is characteristic; 6. fracture: even, straight.

(1993: 209, 211, 215)

While overlap occurs among some of the attributes, such as the size or the type of inclusions, the overall trends vary from paste to paste.

Pollard completed the "ware" class by combining "paste" with "surface," which consists of the following surface finish attributes:

Slip (presence or absence; thickness; condition)
Color range (based on Munsell Soil Color Chart)
Hardness (Moh's scale)
Texture (smooth, rough, grainy)
Polish (matte, lustrous, highly lustrous, none)
(1993: 202)

The descriptions for each ware indicate the range found within that given ware category, as integrated with the paste description. The surface descriptions for the same three wares:

*Ware:* Tariacuri Brown. *Surface* 1. slipped; medium thick and uniform application; often the color of the clay; hardness: 2–4; 3. texture: smooth; many eroded sherds; 4. polish: lustrous to highly lustrous; 5. color; Cream (Santa Ana), red (Cucuchucho), white (Tziranga), unslipped (las Granadas), gray (San Juan), pink (La vinata).

*Ware:* Yaguarato Cream. *Surface* 1. slipped; 2. hardness: 2–3; 3. texture: smooth; 4. polish; lustrous, highly lustrous; 5. color: cream (San Pablo), pink (Cocupao), red (Santa Fé).

*Ware:* Querenda White. *Surface* 1. slipped and slipless, the sherds are heavily eroded; 2. hardness: 3–4; 3. texture: smooth, whether slipped or not; 5. polish: one uneroded is lustrous, the rest unclear; 5. color: red (Ojo de Agua) or slipless.   (Pollard 1993: 209, 211, 215)

The names within parentheses indicate group names within each of the wares. The groups are determined by slip absence or presence/color, form, and decoration. For example, within the ware Tariacuri Brown, six groups occur, along with their descriptions on the basis of slip/color, vessel form, and decoration (Pollard 1993: 209–210). The three most frequently occurring of these groups are:

*Santa Ana Group* The vessels are covered with a uniform application of cream slip (5YR/6/4,6 5YR/5/4 reddish brown).

Vessel forms: 1. bowl (convex wall, outsloping wall, incurved wall, incurved rim, composite silhouette, and miniature); 2. plates; 3. grater; 4. everted rim jars; 5. spouted vessels of all types.

Decoration: 1. red and white on cream; 2. red on cream; 3. negative, red and white on cream; 4. plain cream slip; 5. red and/or white bands, wavy lines, dots, dashes, and circles; 6. double spiral; 7. "Z" band; 8. "X" motif; 9. ripple modeled (mode 3.2.2).

Remarks. Decorative motifs are often in one color paint on top of the paint of another color; they are usually found on the interior and upper exterior of bowls; spouted vessels contain motifs on their entire upper (and sometimes lower) exteriors; red bands are commonly associated with interior and exterior lips of everted rim jars; white bands are often on the necks of everted rim jars; and the double spiral and "Z" bands are on spout handles and solid handles of spouted vessels. Includes types "Blanco y rojo sobre café" and "Policromo" (Castro-Leal 1986: 110–111).

*Cucuchucho Group* The vessels are covered with a uniform application of red slip (2.5 YR/4/6,8).

Vessel forms: 1. bowls (Convex wall, outsloping wall, incurved rim); w. everted rim jars; 3. spouted vessels.

Decoration: 1. white on red; 2. negative on red; 3. white dots, curvilinear lines; 4. excision (almost fluting); 5. ripple modeled.

Remarks. Most sherds have no decoration. Includes "Rojo Pulido" and "Rojo Pulido con decoración negativa" (Castro-Leal 1986: 87–98), and "Policromo Tarasco blanco-negro/rojo" (Moguel Cos 1987)[1].

*Las Granadas* The vessels are unslipped and easily confused with the Santa Ana Group because the body surface color is close to the cream slip.

Vessel forms: 1. everted rim jars; spouted vessels.

Decoration: 1. red and white paint; red, white, and cream paint; 3. white and red bands, dots, parallel lines, curvilinear lines; 4. double spiral; 5. "Z" band; 6. cross-hatching.

Remarks: Includes "Policromo" (Castro-Leal 1986: 111).

*Tziranga Group* The vessels are covered with a thin and unevenly applied white slip (2.5Y/8/2).

Vessel forms: 1. bowls (convex wall, miniature); 2. spouted vessels.

Decoration: 1. red on white; 2. red and white on white; 3. negative on red on white; 4. plain white slip; red and/or white bands, stripes, dots, dashes; 6. double spiral.

---

1 Pollard originally mis-cited this reference as "Cos 1985" but it should be "Cos 1987" as is reflected in this chapter.

> Remarks: The motifs are on the interior and upper exterior of bowls and the bodies of spouted vessels. Includes "Rojo sobre blanco" (Castro-Leal 1986: 109). (Pollard 1993:209–210)

This sort of description continues across all 15 wares currently defined within the type-variety typology (Pollard 1972, 1993). With the additional ceramic materials analyzed from subsequent projects, at Urichu (modern Uricho; Pollard 2001) and Erongaricuaro (Pollard 2005; Pollard and Haskell 2006), this classification now has formal varieties rather than the placeholder of groups for many of the initially classified ceramics (Pollard 2001). This should be expected, for "the type is never an entirely stable entity; it is always in a relative state of flux, being added to or subtracted from as ceramic knowledge increases" (Smith, Willey and Gifford 1960: 334). However, with this typology, archaeologically derived sherds can be described and identified in a formal classification that enables chronology building and regional comparisons.

# 4 Applications of the Tarascan ceramic classification

This is a complex typology. Many of the decorative schemas (slip colors, paint colors and paint combinations) occur within multiple wares (Pollard 1993, 2001; see also Hirshman 2008; Hirshman and Ferguson 2012). Therefore, groups, types and varieties may seem repetitive, even redundant. Rice also noted the tendency for paste to "cross-cut" decorative categories (Rice 1976: 541).

However, recall that Pollard was both following protocols as published at the time and also attempting to limit sherds from the same vessel being placed into different classification categories. She intentionally chose to work with "paste" as part of the ware category in the hierarchical type variety system:

> A common form of ceramic analysis in Mexico uses the paint and slip color as the primary attributes to distinguish wares, with rather larger ranges of paste variation in each one. To make my analysis comparable to other studies, I have indicated, where possible, the equivalent name for the ceramic groups defined by Castro-Leal (1986) . . . and from Moguel Cos (1987) . . . .Their analyses combine portions of the modal and taxonomic classifications used here. However, it means that some of their types, such as "polychrome," cross-cut several different ceramics groups. (Pollard 1993: 201)

Just because we can see these patterns in the pastes does not mean they meant something to the potters; however, the consistency of the paste patterns indicates some behavioral regularity of those in the past. First, the paste categories are reproducible to analysts: Pollard's students can sort ceramics into the same categories

(Haskell 2008; Hirshman 2008; Hirshman and Ferguson 2012; Hirshman and Haskell 2016). Second, the paste categories have relatively distinct chemical signatures. Neutron Activation Analysis (NAA) is a technique that identifies the elemental composition of an object and has been used to develop groupings of compositionally (chemically) similar ceramics within archaeological contexts (Glascock 1992; Neff 1992). Analysis of sherds using NAA from the sites of Tzintzuntzan, Urichu, and Erongaricuaro indicate a general, unequal bifurcation of the samples: samples belonging to or assigned to much smaller compositional groups related to a "main pottery group," composed of Tariacuri Brown, Yaguarato Cream, Tariacuri Coarse and Yaguarato Coarse samples, and a "Pottery Group 1," and chemically related smaller groups dominated by Querenda White and Tecolote Orange samples. Another study found four compositional groups from the site of Angamuco, from the far eastern portion of the lake basin (Cohen, Pierce, and Fisher 2019). Though Cohen did not sample sherds based on paste category, two of her groups align with these two larger compositional groups. Cohen also noted the compositional groups cross-cut decorative treatments. The compositional research further indicates a spatial dispersion of ceramic production throughout the basin (Cohen, Pierce, and Fisher 2019; Hirshman 2008; Hirshman and Ferguson 2012).

Identifying the pattern that similar decorative techniques occur and reoccur over different paste categories has been a significant finding about Tarascan ceramics. We have known all along that there is unusually higher than expected paste diversity in a relatively small lake basin (Hirshman and Ferguson 2012). The diversity in paste recipes and compositional groups both point to a decentralized, and dispersed, potting industry within the basin. This, in turn, has enabled us to gain deeper understanding of the Prehispanic ceramic economy of the lake basin and the relationship of commoners with the Tarascan state (Hirshman 2017; Hirshman and Haskell 2106; Hirshman and Stawski 2013; Pollard 2008).

Pollard's classification forms the basis of several other studies on archaeologically derived ceramics from the Lake Pátzcuaro Basin. Ceramic artifacts, as a significant focus of research, provide insight into temporal and social change within the basin (Pollard and Cahue 1999), the economic system of the basin (Hirshman 2017), and relationships between high elites of the capital and lower elites at the various secondary and tertiary communities within the basin over time (Hirshman and Haskell 2016; Pollard 2017). Studies of the dispersion of different types of vessels and other ceramic artifacts in the basin seem to indicate that very few ceramic artifacts were reserved for the exclusive use of the political elites (Pollard 2017); most ceramics, even those with significant labor input and sociopolitical messaging, could be found in both commoner and elite contexts (Hirshman and Haskell 2016; Pollard 2017; Stawski 2008). Ceramic production appears to occur at a dispersed community level within households (Cohen,

Pierce and Fisher 2019; Hirshman 2008; Hirshman and Ferguson 2012; Hirshman, Lovis and Pollard 2010). As the population in the basin increased, so, too, did the number of potters (Hirshman 2008; Hirshman and Ferguson 2012). Most ceramic vessels moved in a market exchange context (Hirshman and Ferguson 2012; Hirshman 2017); however, at least one form, a highly decorated, spouted, basket-handled beverage serving vessel, seemed to have been used in elite gift-giving (Pollard 2017).

Other studies have leaned heavily on attributes identified in the modal analysis. Hirshman (2008) contrasted changes in the ceramic assemblage from Urichu with larger socioeconomic and political change within the basin as the Tarascan state emerged. A cluster analysis of changing frequencies and relationships among attributes such as general morphology, presence/absence of slip, slip color, paint, and paint color provided the foundation for a study of ceramic productive organization. "Paste" was not utilized in the final analysis of the assemblage, as it became a confounding factor – significant overlap occurred among attributes across paste categories, creating too much complexity within the resultant cluster. Just as Pollard (1993: 200–201) had noted, paste crosscut the distribution of modal attributes within the assemblage. By focusing the analysis on changing attributes other than paste, Hirshman (2008; Hirshman, Lovis and Pollard 2010) determined that ceramic production underwent a change concurrently with the emergence of local political elites but did not fundamentally change again with the emergence of the state. As many of these attributes require additional effort on the part of the potter (e.g. slip takes more time than unslipped, or a second paint color requires greater effort than a single paint color), the additional labor was also tracked over time using attributes (Hirshman 2008). Stawski (2008), moreover, analyzed the occurrence of modes associated with social classes within the Tarascan state using cluster analysis and the spatial distribution of ceramics across the site of Tzintzuntzan to identify "residential zones and/or public zones based on social status" (Stawski 2008: 48).

# 5 Conclusion

There is never a perfect classification schema. Investigators must make choices and find a way forward through the competing interests of the sheer complexity and range of variables in an assemblage, on one hand, and the pressing needs of research questions and time limitations, on the other. The devised classification schema discussed here provides a guide for decision-making, especially in contexts with little prior research and small samples. These criteria are rooted in the technological process of production, so there is a comparability between regions, even if the emphasized attributes vary by culture.

While we would ideally wish to identify the categories used by people in the past, that, too, is often obscured by the number of social roles and statuses that people lived within in their cultural context. Therefore, any system that can make sense of the complexity and then bend itself to an array of questions and yield useful results is a useful research tool.

# 6 Acknowledgements

I want to thank Dr. Allison Burkette and Dr. Tamara Warhol for the invitation to participate in this volume, and the opportunity to explicate Pollard's work. I need to thank Dr. Helen Pollard for her many years of work with Tarascan ceramics, as well as many conversations over the years and her comments on various drafts of this paper. I also wish to thank Dr. Marcie Venter for helping with the ceramic classification literature from the Gulf Coast region. Dr. Sarah Surface-Evans assisted with the map.

# References

Adams, William Y. & Ernest W. Adams. 1991. *Archaeological typology and practical reality: A dialectical approach to artifact classification and sorting*. Cambridge: Cambridge University Press.

Arnauld, Marie Charlotte, Patricia Carot & Marie-France Fauvet-Berthelot. 1993. *Arqueología de las Lomas en la Cuenca lacustre de Zacapu, Michoacán, México*. Cuadernos de Estudios Michoacanos 5, Mexico: Centro de estudios mexicanos y centroamericanos.

Arnold, Phillip J. III. 2003. Early formative pottery from the Tuxtla Mountains and implications for Gulf Olmec origins. *Latin American Antiquity* 14 (1). 29–46.

Bortolini, Eugenio. 2017. Typology and classification. In Alice M. W. Hunt (ed.), *The Oxford handbook of archaeological ceramics*, 651–670. Oxford: Oxford University Press.

Burkette, Allison. 2018. *Language and classification: Meaning-making in the classification and categorization of ceramics*. New York: Routledge.

Cabrera Castro, Rubén. 1996. Ceramic suntuaria de Tzintzuntzan, Michoacán. In Ana Maria Crespo & Carolos Viramontes (eds.), *Tiempo y territorio en arqueología. El centro norte de México*, Colección Científica, 323, 37–58. Mexico: Instituto Nacional de Antropología e Historia.

Castro-Leal, Marcia. 1986. *Tzintzuntzan, capital de los Tarascos*. Morelia, Mexico: Gobierno del Estado de Michoacán.

Cohen, Anna S., Daniel E. Pierce & Christopher T. Fisher. 2019. Geochemical analysis and spatial trends of ceramics and clay from Angamuco, Michoacán. *Journal of Archaeological Science: Reports* 23. 216–230.

Dunnell, Robert C. 1971. *Systematics in prehistory*. New York: The Free Press.
Glascock, Michael D. 1992. Neutron activation analysis. In Hector Neff (ed.), *Chemical characterization of ceramic pastes in archaeology*, Monographs in World Archaeology No. 7, 11–26. Madison: Prehistory Press.
Haskell, David L. 2008. *Tarascan kingship: The production of hierarchy in the prehispanic Pátzcuaro Basin, Mexico*. Gainesville, University of Florida dissertation.
Hirshman, Amy J. 2008. Tarascan ceramic production and implications for ceramic distribution. *Ancient Mesoamerica* 19. 299–310.
Hirshman, Amy J. 2017. Documenting accommodation and change in the Tarascan ceramic economy. In Sandra L. López Varela (ed.), *Innovative approaches and exploration in ceramic case studies*, 41–52. Oxford: Archaeopress Publishing Ltd.
Hirshman, Amy J. 2020. "They too can help": Hidden producers and flexibility in the organization of collaborative labor in pottery-making households in Michoacán, México from the 1940s to 2020. *Ethnoarchaeology* 12 (1). 1–20.
Hirshman, Amy J. & Jeffrey R. Ferguson. 2012. Temper mixture models and assessing ceramic complexity in the emerging Tarascan state. *Journal of Archaeological Science* 39 (10). 3195–3207.
Hirshman, Amy J. & David Haskell. 2016. Evaluating contrasting models of ceramic production in the Tarascan state: Negotiations in clay. In Eduardo Williams & Blanca Maldonado (eds.), *Cultural dynamics and production activities in ancient Western Mexico*, 201–214. Oxford: Archaeopress Publishing Ltd.
Hirshman, Amy J., William A. Lovis & Helen P. Pollard. 2010. Specialization of ceramic production: A sherd assemblage based analytic perspective. *Journal of Anthropological Archaeology* 29 (3). 265–277.
Hirshman, Amy J. & Christopher J. Stawski. 2013. Distribution, transportation, and the persistence of household ceramic production in the Tarascan state. *Ethnoarchaeology* 5 (1). 1–23.
Hutson, Scott R. & Robert Markens. 2002. Rethinking emic pottery classification. *Kroeber Anthropological Society Papers* 88. 8–27.
Kempton, Willett. 1981. *The folk classification of ceramics: A study of cognitive prototypes*. New York: Academic Press.
Kolb, Charles C. 2011. Chaine operatoire and ceramics: Classifications and typology, archaeometry, experimental archaeology, and ethnoarchaeology. In Simona Scarcella (ed.), *Archaeological ceramics: A review of current research*, BAR International Series 2193, 5–19. Oxford: Archaeopress.
Krause, Richard A. 2016. *A universal theory of pottery production: Irving Rouse, Attributes, modes, and ethnography*. Tuscaloosa: The University of Alabama Press.
Michelet, Dominique, Marie Charlotte Arnauld & Marie-France Fauvet-Berthelot. 1989. El Proyecto de CEMCA en Michoacán. Etapa 1: Un balance. *Trace* 16. 70–87.
Moedano, Hugo. 1946. La ceramicao de Zinapécuaro, Michoacán. *Anales del Museo Michoacano* 2. 439–449.
Moedano, Hugo. 1941. Estudio preliminar de la cerámica de Tzintzantzun, Temporada III 1939–1940. *Revista Mexiana de Estudios Antropológicos* 5 (1). 21–42.
Moguel Cos, Ma. Antonieta. 1987. Trabajos de salvamento arqueológico en las cuencas de Cuitzeo, Pátzcuaro, y Zirahuén: Un intent de interpretación cultural. Mexico City, Escuela Nacional de Antropología e Historia (ENAH), INAH, tesis de licenciado en arqueologia.

Neff, Hector. 1992. Introduction. In Hector Neff (ed.), *Chemical characterization of ceramic pastes in archaeology*, Monographs in World Archaeology No. 7, 1–10. Madison, WI: Prehistory Press.
Noguera, Eduardo. 1931. *Exploraciones arqueológicas en las reiones de Zamora y Pátzcuaro, estado de Michoacan*. Anales del Museo Michoacano 4 (7). 88–104.
Noguera, Eduardo 1965. *La cerámica arqueológia de mesoamérica*, Instutito de Investigaciones Historicas 86. Mexico City: Universidad nacional Autónoma de Méxcio.
Ortiz Ceballos, Ponciano. 1975. La cerámica de los Tuxtlas. Jalapa, Mexico, Universidad Veracruzana tesis de licenciatura.
Parsons, Lee A. 1967. *Bilbao, Guatemala: An archaeological study of the Pacific Coast Cotzumalhuapa region, volume 1*. Publications in Anthropology, Volume 1. Milwaukee Public Museum. Milwaukee: Milwaukee Public Museum.
Pollard, Helen Perlstein. 1972. *Prehispanic urbanism at Tzintzuntzan, Michoacan*. New York: Columbia University dissertation.
Pollard, Helen Perlstein. 1993. *Taríacuri's legacy: The prehispanic Tarascan state*. Norman: University of Oklahoma Press.
Pollard, Helen Perlstein. 2001. Informe Final tomo 3 la cerámica. Informe al Consejo de Arqueología, Instituto Nacional de Antropología e Historia.
Pollard, Helen Perlstein. 2005. Proyecto Erongaricuaro. Informe tecnico parcial al Consejo de Arqueologia, Instituto Nacional de Antropología e Historia. Temporada 1 (Campo) 2001, Temporada 2 (Laboratorio) 2002–2004.
Pollard, Helen Perlstein. 2008. A model of the emergence of the Tarascan state. *Ancient Mesoamerica* 19. 17–230.
Pollard, Helen P. « Markets, tribute, and class in Tarascan commodity consumption: the Lake Pátzcuaro Basin », Americae [en ligne] | 2, 2017, mis en ligne le 27 juillet 2017. URL : http://www.mae.parisnanterre.fr/articles-articulos/markets-tribute-and-class-in-ta rascan-commodity-consumption-the-lake-patzcuaro-basin/
Pollard, Helen Perlstein & Laura Cahue. 1999. Mortuary patterns of regional elites in the Lake Pátzcuaro Basin of Western Mexico. *Latin American Antiquity* 10 (3). 259–280.
Pollard, Helen P. & David Haskell. 2006. Proyecto Erongaricuaro. Informe tecnico parcial al Consejo de Arqueologia, Instituto Nacional de Antropología e Historia. Temporada II. May.
Pool, Christopher A. 1990. *Ceramic production, resource procurement, and exchange at Matacapan, Veracruz, Mexico*. New Orleans: Tulane University dissertation.
Pool, Christopher A. 1995. La céramica del Clásico tardio y el Postclássico en la sierra de los Tuxtlas. *Arqueologia* 13–14. 37–48.
Rattray, Evelyn & Garman Harbottle. 1992. Neutron activation analysis and numerical taxonomy of thin Orange ceramics from the manufacturing sites of Rio Carneo, Puebla, Mexico. In Hector Neff (ed.), *Chemical characterization of ceramic pastes in archaeology*, 221–231. Madison, WI: Prehistory Press.
Read, Dwight. W. 2007. *Artifact classification: A conceptual and methodological approach*. Walnut Creek, CA: Left Coast Press.
Rice, Prudence. 1976. Comment: Rethinking the ware concept. *American Antiquity* 41 (4). 538–543.
Rice, Prudence. 2013. Type-variety: What works and what doesn't. In James John Aimers (ed.), *Ancient Maya pottery: Classification, analysis, and interpretation*, 11–28. Gainesville: University Press of Florida.

Rice, Prudence. 2015. *Pottery analysis: A sourcebook*, 2nd edn. Chicago: The University of Chicago Press.

Ross, Virginia L. 1939. Some pottery types of the Highlands of Western Mexico. New Haven, CT, Yale University Master's thesis.

Rouse, Irving. 1960. The classification of artifacts in archaeology. *American Antiquity* 25 (3). 313–323.

Rouse, Irving. 1939. *Prehistory in Haiti: A study in method*, Yale University Publications in Anthropology, No. 21. New Haven: Yale University Press.

Rubín de la Borbolla, Daniel F. 1939. Antropología Tzintzuntzan-Ihuatzio: Temporadas I y II. *Revista Mexicana de Estudios Antropológicas* 3 (2). 99–121.

Rubín de la Borbolla, Daniel F. 1948. Arqueología Tarasca. In El Occidente de México 4a. *Mesa Redonda, Sociedad Mexicana de Estudios Antropológico* 5 (1). 29–33.

Sabloff, Jeremy A. & Robert E. Smith. 1969. The importance of both analytic and taxonomic classification in the type-variety system. *American Antiquity* 34 (3). 278–285.

Santacreu, Daniel Albero, Manuel Calvo Trias & Jaime García Rosselló. 2017. Formal analysis and typological classification in the study of ancient pottery. In Alice M. W. Hunt (ed.), *The Oxford handbook of archaeological ceramics*, 181–199. Oxford: Oxford University Press.

Smith, Robert E. Gordon R. Willey & James C. Gifford. 1960. The type-variety concept as a basis for the analysis of Maya pottery. *American Antiquity* 25 (3). 330–340.

Stark, Barbara L. 1989. *Patarata pottery: Classic period ceramics of the South-Central Gulf Coast, Veracruz, Mexico*, Anthropological Papers of the University of Arizona No. 51. Tucson: The University of Arizona Press.

Stawski, Christopher James. 2008. Residential zoning at prehispanic Tzintzuntzan, Mexico revisited: A quantitative analysis. East Lansing, Michigan State University Master's thesis.

Venter, Marcie L. 2008. Community strategies in the Aztec imperial frontier: Perspectives from Totogal, Veracruz, Mexico. Lexington, University of Kentucky dissertation.

Wheat, Joe Ben, James C. Gifford & William W. Wasley. 1958. Ceramic variety, type cluster, and ceramic system in southwestern pottery analysis. *American Antiquity* 24 (1). 34–47.

Willey, Gordon R., T. Patrick Culbert & Richard E. W. Adams. 1967. Maya Lowland ceramics: A report from the 1965 Guatemala City conference. *American Antiquity* 32 (3). 289–315.

Williams, Eduardo. 2017. *Tarascan pottery production in Michoacán, Mexico: An ethnoarchaeological perspective*. Oxford: Archaeopress Publishing Ltd.

# Appendix 1

## Ceramic modes (after Pollard 1993: 202–208)

1. *Paste composition.* Eleven local wares defined; see description under typological analysis.
2. *Vessel form.*
    2.1 *bowls*
    2.1.1 *convex wall bowls* Have a round/flat base; with/without supports; if with, are usually hollow-tripod supports up to 4.0 cm diameter at juncture

with bowl. One tetrapod example. Rims are direct; lips are rounded, squared, and tapered. Diameters at the lips range from 15 to 45 cm; the 40–45 cm ones have a simple vertical handle or lug. Wall range from 0.4 cm to 1.2 cm thick.

2.1.2 *outsloping wall bowls* Walls are inclined outward in a straight line, probably associated with a flat base. Lips are beveled and tapered with diameters from 30 cm to 35 cm and walls from 0.4 cm to 0.6 cm thick.

2.1.3 *everted rim bowls* Have a pronounced bending out and extension of the rim; bases were probably rounded; lips are tapered or rounded. Diameters 12–25 cm and walls 0.4–0.7 cm thick.

2.1.4 *incurved rim bowls* An extreme form of convex wall bowl with the rim of a *tecomate*. Bases are rounded with/without basket handles. Lips are squared or bolstered (thickened); diameters at the lip are 10–30 cm and walls 0.8–0.9 cm thick.

2.1.5 *composite silhouette bowls* There is a sharp change in the curvature about 1.25 cm from the lip creating a shouldered vessel; with/without basket handles; some with a small convex protrusion between the shoulder and the lip. The bases are rounded; lips are rounded; diameters 10–12 cm and walls 0.2–0.6 cm thick.

2.1.6 *miniature bowls* They are a distinctive feature of the assemblage. They have rounded bases and tripod supports; diameters 3–6 cm, heights 2–3 cm, and walls 0.2–0.6 cm thick.

    2.1.6.1 *everted rim miniature bowls* Includes types A, B, and C of Moedano (1941: 30).
    2.1.6.2 *convex wall miniature bowls* Includes type D of Moedano (1941: 30).
    2.1.6.3 *flange wall miniature bowls* A small protrusion encircling the vessel 1.0 cm below the lip. Includes type E of Moedano (1941: 30).

2.2 *brasero* Possibly an *apaxtle* (Noguera 1965: Fig. 17). A straight-walled or inslanting open vessel. Probably flat-bottomed, with small appliqué pellets on the exterior surface and rim edge. Pellets: 1.0 cm diameter, 0.3 cm thick; vessel is 40+ cm in diameter, with walls 1.2 cm thick.

2.3 *sieve* convex wall vessel with random punctures 1.0–1.5 cm apart. Vessel surface was smoothed on the outside but left with the clay pushed up around the holes on the inside. Walls are 1.2 cm thick, no diameter estimate possible.

2.4 *graters* Shallow convex vessels with punctate depressions in interior. Depressions are 0.3–0.5 cm in diameter, 0.3 cm deep, and > 1.0 cm apart. They are found with/without supports, lips are rounded; 20 cm in diameter with walls 0.6–0.8 cm thick.

*2.5 plates*

*2.5.1 convex wall plates* A slight curvature on round/flat based vessels; no supports; lips are tapered or rounded. Diameters range from 10–12 cm and 15–25 cm, with walls 0.45–0.60 cm thick. These may be large and small plates, which could be distinguished in larger collections.

*2.5.2 flat base plates* Similar to a *comale* or griddle; square or rectangular slabs with supports. Edges are flattened on the sides but not raised above the level of the vessel floor. Noted a slight rise and thickening toward the edge, although one example has a downslope and thinning toward the edge. Slabs are 1.5 cm thick; one is ca. 8 by 8 cm and another is ca. 15 by 15 cm.

*2.6 jars*

*2.6.1 everted rim jar* Often referred to as an *olla*. Several kinds of rim eversion have been recognized, but the small sample size makes classifying difficult. Probable varieties include: even curve with/without stirrup handles; sharp curve, large jar (20–25 cm diameters, Castro-Leal 1986, using material from excavations on the main platform extends this to 17–29 cm); sharp curve, small jar (6 cm diameter); elongated neck, even curve rim; elongated neck, sharply everted rim (almost a bottle, called a *florero*); interior thickening with an even curve.

Bodies are globular or shouldered; lips are rounded, tapered or bolstered; vessels are with/without supports; and diameters range from 6 cm to 35 cm at the lip.

*2.6.2 incurved jars* Often referred to as a *tecomate*. Neckless, round-based jars; lips are squared; diameter at lip is 20–32 cm, and walls are 0.5–0.6 cm thick.

*2.6.3 miniature jar* A small everted rim jar with a spherical body; maximum diameter is 3.5 cm; diameter at orifice is 1.5–2.0 cm; walls are 0.3 cm thick.

*2.6.4 ripple wall jar* A small jar with an undulating wall that forms a series of horizontal bands around the vessel body. Only body sherds represented in this collection. Examples are in the Lumholtz collections (American Museum of Natural History, New York) and illustrated in Ross (1939), and in the INAH collection from excavations at TZ-25 (Tzintzuntzan).

*2.7 spouted vessels* This is a category of closed vessel that takes many forms in the ceramic complex. Listed below are those represented in this collection. Body sherds are often unassignable to a particular shape.

*2.7.1 handled teapot* A solid handle with a separate spout and orifice in the center top. It resembles a modern teapot.

*2.7.2 spout handle* A hollow-handled vessel with an orifice (or two) in a handle. May also have a separate spout. Bodies may be globular, shouldered, or almost flanged. This category was tabulated on the number of spout-handled sherds.

2.7.3 *loop handle* The handle is attached to the lip of an everted rim orifice in the center top. They may be miniature in size.

2.7.4 *animal effigy* Locally called *patojas*. Vessels in the shape of an animal, usually a bird of some kind (not necessarily a duck, however).

2.8 *supports*

2.8.1 *small supports* Supports less than 4.0 cm long and probably associated with miniature bowls.

    2.8.1.1 *spider support*
    2.8.1.2 *conical support*
    2.8.1.3 *flat oblong support*
    2.8.1.4 *foot-claw support*
    2.8.1.5 *flared support*
    2.8.1.6 *hollow cylindrical support*
    2.8.1.7 *solid foot support*

2.8.2 *regular supports* Supports that are generally longer than 4.0 cm

    2.8.2.1 *solid conical support*
    2.8.2.2 *solid spider support*
    2.8.2.3 *hollow rattle cylindrical support*
    2.8.2.4 *hollow rattle wide top support*
    2.8.2.5 *hollow nub support*
    2.8.2.6 *drilled cylinder support*
    2.8.2.7 *large hollow support* attached to a convex bowl
    2.8.2.8 *possible annular base*

3. *Surface finish and decoration*

    3.1 *slip and paint* Colors used refer to:

| | | | |
|---|---|---|---|
| red | 2.5 YR/4/6,8 | 10R/4/4,6,8 | 10R/5/6,8 |
| white | 2.5Y/8/2 | 2.5YR/N2,5/0 | 5YR/8/1,2 |
| | 10YR/7/1 | 10YR/8/1,2,3 | |
| cream | 2.5YR/5/6,8 | 2.5 YR/6/6,8 | 5YR/5/4,6 |
| | 5 YR/6/4,5,6 | | |
| pink | 10YR/5/3 | | |
| black | 10YR/2.5/0 | | |

    3.1.1 *unslipped*

        3.1.1.1 *unpainted*

        3.1.1.2 *painted*

            3.1.1.2.1 *red*

            3.1.1.2.2 *white*

  3.1.1.2.3 *red, white, and cream*
  3.1.1.2.4 *negative on red and white*
 3.1.2 *slipped*
  3.1.2.1 *unpainted*
   3.1.2.1.1 *red*
   3.1.2.1.2 *cream*
   3.1.2.1.3 *pink*
   3.1.2.1.4 *white*
   3.1.2.1.5 *gray*
  3.1.2.2 *painted*
   3.1.2.2.1 *white-on-red slip*
   3.1.2.2.2 *negative-on-red slip*
   3.1.2.2.3 *red-on-white slip*
   3.1.2.2.4 *red-and-white-on-white slip*
   3.1.2.2.5 *negative-on-red-on white slip*
   3.1.2.2.6 *red-on-pink slip*
   3.1.2.2.7 *red-and-white-on-pink slip*
   3.1.2.2.8 *red-on-cream slip*
   3.1.2.2.9 *white-on-cream slip*
   3.1.2.2.10 *red-and-white-on-cream slip*
   3.1.2.2.11 *negative-on-red-and-white-on-cream slip*
   3.1.2.2.12 *negative-on-cream slip*
   3.1.2.2.13 *white-on-all-over-red-on-cream slip* The vessel is slipped and then painted over the entire slip in red.
   3.1.2.2.14 *all-over-red-on-cream* (includes mode .13)
   3.1.2.2.15 *red, white, and black-on-cream*
3.2 decorative technique
3.2.1 *appliqué conical pellets* Called *al fresco* by Moedano (1941:26)
3.2.2 *modeled corrugation* Produces a ripple effect (see 2.6.4)
3.2.3 *excision* A technique by which small areas are gouged out of the vessel surface.
3.2.4 *incision* On interior bottom of bowls. A technique by which a narrow depressed line is cut by means of a sharp instrument. This technique is not common among the sherds but is more frequent on the stems of pipes.
3.2.5 *negative decoration* This includes all sherds with negative irrespective of slip or paint; also called resist. Involves the covering of the vessel with a temporary protective material, followed by a coat of darker color, and the removal of the protective material from selected surfaces. This is a frequent technique on polychromes in this collection.
3.3 Decorative motifs

3.3.1 red and white vertical dashes (interior jar rim or everted rim of a miniature bowl)
3.3.2 red band (1.0–1.5 cm wide, on interior and/or exterior jar or bowl)
3.3.3 "X" motif
3.3.4 "S" band
3.3.5 "Z" band
3.3.6 double spiral on bowl
3.3.7 thin parallel lines, red on white slip
3.3.8 line of white dots
3.3.9 white neck band on everted rim jars
3.3.10 white or red lines on interior rim
3.3.11 hatching, red lines on zoned white paint
3.3.12 checkerboard, red on white
3.3.13 spiral with tick or lines
3.3.14 combination of 1 and 7. Thin lines on vertical dashes, some dashes ending in upward curve.
3.3.15 motifs on handles
    3.3.15.1 1.5 cm wide handle; white dots on a red band
    3.3.15.2 2–3 cm wide handle; double spiral (3.3.6) and/or zoned curvilinear and parallel lines surrounding the spiral.
    3.3.15.3 2–3 cm wide handle; ´band with dots
    3.3.15.4 solid red handle, any size; slip or paint
3.3.16 motifs on small supports (minilegs)
    3.3.16.1 parallel vertical red lines
    3.3.16.2 parallel vertical white lines
    3.3.16.3 parallel horizontal white lines
    3.3.16.4 lower exterior painted red
    3.3.16.5 lower exterior painted white
    3.3.16.6 alternate red and white vertical lines

Jillian R. Cavanaugh, Shalini Shankar
# Chapter 12
# Language and materiality in global capitalism

## 1 Introduction

In this piece, originally published in 2012, we introduced the term "language materiality" and continue to find it useful to understand current directions in scholarship about the relationship between language and dynamics of inequality and political economy, as well as the study of technologically mediated communication.[1] In many communicative contexts, the way people connect with one another has become ever more reliant on how we use our screens and keyboards. Likewise, scholars have increasingly explored the materiality of sound and music in ways that broaden discussions of language materialities to sound and qualia. These directions in scholarship that have followed conditions on the ground, are, in other words, ethnographically-driven (Cavanaugh and Shankar 2014). As we observed in our introduction to an edited volume on language and materiality (Shankar and Cavanaugh 2017: 4), "Language, per force, requires a medium," and as the forms that language takes and the possibilities of its circulation have multiplied and expanded, so has scholarship aimed to capture its multidimensionality. Some of these efforts culminated in an edited volume, *Language and materiality: Ethnographic and theoretical explorations* (Cavanaugh and Shankar 2017), in which we brought together scholars taking up various perspectives on how to approach language materially. From in-depth analyses of "fontroversies" (font controversies), to the transformations of names and naming within particular U.S. Indigenous groups, to por por horns in Ghana, the broader frame for these studies originated in this chapter.

---

[1] This chapter was first published in the *Annual Review of Anthropology* in 2012 (vol. 41, pp. 355–369) as Shankar and Cavanaugh "Language and materiality in global capitalism." (DOI:10.1146/annurev-anthro-092611-145811). That text is reprinted by permission of the authors and with new commentary by the authors in the form of a new introduction, a postscript, and added readings. The footnoted definitions throughout this text originally appeared as marginalia.

---

**Jillian R. Cavanaugh,** City University of New York, Brooklyn, jcavanaugh@brooklyn.cuny.edu
**Shalini Shankar,** Northwestern University, sshankar@northwestern.edu

https://doi.org/10.1515/9781501514371-012

## 2 Language and materiality

Language and materiality have long been considered separate phenomena: the linguistic seen as inherently immaterial, the material as concrete and nondiscursive.[2] Recent studies have featured an intriguing and productive convergence of the two that suggests the illustrative potential of considering language and materiality within the same analytic frame. In this review, we consider points of articulation, convergence, and divergence of language and materiality from a range of ethnographic and theoretical perspectives. Bodies of work on language and political economy and language ideology, as well as on semiotics, intertextuality, and interdiscursivity, for instance, have turned to consider the material alongside the linguistic to address broader questions varying from nationalism and class to religion and cultural production.[3] Taking our cue from linguistic anthropologists and scholars in allied disciplines who have considered the material as mattering in different ways – as a property of language, in combination with language, as exhibiting materialized characteristics of form, or as evidencing commodified values that can circulate in ways previously unseen – our goal is to put scholarship from various academic lineages in conversation with one another. To bring these various, and as yet disparate, works together, we offer "language materiality" as a term to characterize an emerging field of inquiry.[4] The representative but by no means exhaustive works we include overlap, differ, and potentially bridge gaps between conceptions of power, meaning, and value – for instance, between semiotic and political economic approaches in linguistic anthropology. By discussing how these works exemplify an emerging field of scholarship, we consider how a joint focus on language and materiality may address current exigencies of neoliberal projects, global capitalism, and new forms of circulation.[5] Accordingly, we invite scholars of material culture to consider how language is involved in commodification, circulation, and value formation, and also urge linguistic anthropologists

---

2 Materiality is the state or quality of being material, embedded within and taking meaning and value from sociocultural and political economic structures and processes.
3 Semiotics is the study of signs or symbolic systems. Intertextuality refers to culturally constructed, maintained, and interpreted connections among texts. Interdiscursivity refers to culturally constructed, maintained, and interpreted connections among instances of language use (spoken or written).
4 Although we refer to this emerging field of inquiry as "language materiality," throughout the text we purposefully vary the terms by which we characterize the range of scholarly efforts that engage with the linguistic and the material.
5 Global capitalism is the contemporary state of capitalism, characterized by global structures of inequality; flows of capital, goods, and people; and neoliberal governance.

to continue to consider systematically the material dimensions of language in use.[6]

## 3 Bringing language and materiality together

Since at least Herder and Marx, the state or quality of being material, physical, or object-like is claimed in western thought to be different from that of the ideational realm; objects, things, and bodies are opposed to ideas. A growing body of literature, however, overtly or otherwise suggests that this distinction may not be universal or useful and that the state of the material requires greater attention, especially with regard to language. Earlier inquiries in linguistic anthropology, such as the ethnography of speaking approach, attended to relevant contextual features that co-occurred with talk, such as the grog consumed during gossip (Brenneis 1984; see Goffman 1979; Gumperz 1982). Later studies of context focused on how it shapes and is shaped by dynamics of language use (Duranti and Goodwin 1992; see Agha 2007; Irvine 2001; Irvine and Gal 2000; Silverstein 2003), but here too the material dimensions of context were not theorized as such. Arguably, materiality may not have seemed as relevant as it has become in our current era, in which the material can entail facets of linguistic context, and linguistic forms may acquire material qualities when they are pressed into new modes of objectification, circulation, and recontextualization.[7]

We build here from two distinct though often overlapping lines of inquiry: one concerned with the value of language, and the other more focused on meaning. The first emerges out of an interest in how material conditions shape ideologies and uses of language, including political economic approaches to language that understood it as a material form of social practice (Voloshinov 1973; Williams 1977). Work on language and political economy explores important connections to the material conditions that govern the choices speakers make about language (Gal 1989; Irvine 1989; Jaffe 1999a; Woolard 1985). Language as symbolic capital may be interchangeable with material forms of capital under market conditions, and linguistic forms may draw their value from both material and symbolic domains (Bourdieu 1977, 1991). Bringing to the fore how issues of language and power are linked in everyday talk, the paradigm of language ideologies, which act as "a mediating link between

---

**6** Commodification is the transformation of value, meaning, and potentially form of a non-commodity (external to a market) into a commodity (internal to a market).
**7** Objectification is a process by which nonobjects are given object-like qualities, involving the externalization and materialization of meaning and value.

social forms and forms of talk" (Woolard 1998: 3; Kroskrity 2000; Schieffelin, Woolard, and Kroskrity 1998), has been invaluable for linking quotidian language use to evaluative processes of display, judgment, and social category formation. By considering the material conditions of language use rather than materiality itself, studies of language ideology, as well as of language and political economy, have advanced conversations about formations of nationalism, processes of modernity, and inequalities of gender, class, race, and ethnicity, among other topics.

Semiotic approaches more explicitly concerned with meaning-making have tended to consider materiality as a mediating property of social life. For instance, focusing on the medium has been offered as a counterpoint to mentalist approaches to language (Schneider 2006; Wittgenstein 1991), and linguistic signification has been seen as a material process inseparable from other social activity (Coward and Ellis 1977). Semiotic studies may identify ontological characteristics that material social practices exhibit, considering materiality insofar as it is embodied and enacted by individuals or examining the lives and biographies of texts and other linguistic artifacts (Hull 2003). Recent work has developed Peircean semiotics to connect explicitly the material and verbal dimensions of signification (Kockelman 2006; Lee 1997; Manning and Meneley 2008), at times capitalizing on how such an analytic suggests a non-teleological relationship between language and materiality, one in which meaning is mutually constituted (e.g., Daniel 1984; Mertz and Parmentier 1985; Munn 1986; Myers 2001). Keane's (2003, 2007) "semiotic ideology" extended language ideology to consider how meaning is signified through utterances, things, or both together. Keane's work joins others focused on how linguistic form and meaning are reproduced and potentially transformed as they circulate across contexts through processes such as intertextuality and interdiscursivity (Briggs and Bauman 1995; Irvine 2005; Silverstein and Urban 1996). The focus on movement of linguistic forms and meanings also drives the emerging field of mediatization, which considers the circulation of signs through local and mass media (Agha 2011b).

Studies that highlight the political, economic, or semiotic are by no means mutually exclusive; indeed, some of the most dynamic areas emerge in the overlap of these approaches. Efforts to bring processes of meaning making and value formation within the same ethnographic and analytic frame, such as Kockelman's (2006: 78) agenda to "bring together Marx's dialectic and Peirce's semiotic," for instance, offer useful strategies for analyzing what Kockelman calls the modes of semiotic capital that characterize neoliberalism.[8] Indeed,

---

[8] Neoliberalism is an economic ideology of capitalism that valorizes the free market and suggests that all aspects of life have market value.

when inquiries into the linguistic and the material are put in conversation with critical studies of globalization and neoliberalism, scholarship emerges that attends to vital dimensions of materiality in language, as well as the role language plays in making materiality meaningful (e.g., Coupland 2010; Heller 2011). Recent scholarship on global capitalism has illustrated the heightened significance of materiality in an era in which domestic and foreign policy agendas are dominated by capital accumulation and the commodification of culture (Ho 2009; see Comaroff and Comaroff 2009). If, as Harvey (2005: 11) asserts, "the neoliberal project is to disembed capital from [state regulation and ownership] constraints," then the role of language in national and global capitalist agendas must be considered for how linguistic forms are involved in such deregulation and its effects. Related to this are debates to reconsider context in ways that take into account new and emerging forms of linguistic commodification and their circulation (Lee and LiPuma 2002).

In an era of global capitalism when language is subject to novel processes of commodification and circulation, several interconnected concerns emerge that characterize much of the work in this review. In the works we discuss below, language and materiality together play a role in the production of meaning and value at individual, community, society, national, and global levels, beginning with how words and objects work together within semiotic systems and how embodiment, aesthetics, and style illustrate the intersection of the linguistic and the material. We then turn to questions of linguistic objectification and the circulatory possibilities of linguistic forms, followed by a discussion of language commodification in global capitalism. Before concluding with how language and materiality interact to contribute to contemporary anticapitalist projects, we consider the complexity of global capitalist agendas of language commodification and circulation and suggest promising directions for this emerging field.

# 4 Cosignification of material words and symbolic objects

Ethnographic contexts in which the linguistic and material cosignify foreground the synergy between words and objects in creating semiotic representations that either dimension alone may be unable to achieve. One illustrative example includes Basso (1996), in which the symbolic resources of language and land together teach moral values and serve as tools for historical memory, personal reflection, and the strengthening of community (see also Hoffman 2008; Keane

2007; Modan 2007). In Weiner's (1984) account of the Trobriands, when non-kin individuals confront one another with "hard words," such direct confrontation may be rectified only through material redress, in this case, yams, as participants "state the Negative with objects" (p. 174). Jones (2012) shows how magicians' talk or "patter" is just as important as visual presentation in the efficacy of magic tricks in performance, whereas Coupland (2011) theorizes how particular numbers correlate with ways of measuring material and social phenomena. The performance of expertise, which is largely linguistic, "not only determines the value of cultural objects. [I]t also confers value on those who interact with these objects, including the experts so enacted" (Carr 2010: 18).

Seminal work on the social value of commodities (Appadurai 1986; Miller 1998; Myers 2001) has been enhanced by examining their interactions with language use. Agha (2011a) has laid out a schema for examining "commodity registers," which considers how objects are represented through language as well as how they are meaningfully grouped to reflect and activate social differences. Commodities that utilize language can demonstrate an uneasy balance between gift and commodity, as in Jaffe's (1999b) examination of greeting cards, in which the language on the cards is only part of what gives them value. Value is mediated through the words printed on the cards and personalized signs such as handwriting, which create and maintain relationships between sender and receiver and underscore the material significance of this communicative form (see Ahearn 2001; Danet 1997). Words and objects together shape meanings of ethnicity and class in the consumption practices of Silicon Valley Desis (South Asian Americans), such that value is indexed in ways that minimize class disparities within this ethnic community (Shankar 2008). As Bourdieu (1984, 1991) has argued, language and objects may be integrated into hierarchies of taste and distinction that contribute to social formations of ethnicity, race, and class. In Shandler's (2006) investigation of the significance of Yiddish to contemporary Jews who may not speak it, objects bearing Yiddish, including mugs with humorous phrases, dreidels, and dictionaries, enable this language to be consumed, even fetishized. In a different context, Hill (2008) documents the appearance of a register she calls "mock Spanish" on such objects as greeting cards, coffee mugs, and outdoor advertisements such as billboards and bus shelters; these objects' mass production and circulation create racialized representations of Spanish speakers.

Focusing on the linguistic and the material together offers insight into various processes of capitalist value formation. Message, vital to politics as well as advertising, pairs language with materialized forms of affect and emotion in ways that foster identification. Hill (2000: 264; see Silverstein 2011) builds on Jakobson's notion of the poetic function to consider how the duality of message is composed of a complex interplay of signs – including words, comportment, gesture, lighting, bodily movements, etc. – brought together in performance. In advertising, message pairs select values with a commodity or service in ways that foster consumer identification (Goffman 1979; Manning 2010; Shankar 2012; Silverstein 2005). Brand names and trademarks are forms of intellectual property based on social alterity (Coombe 1998) and can come to stand for particular types of social authenticity (Manning 2010; Meneley 2007; Parmentier 1994). In some cases, the successful integration of the linguistic and the material into a brand identity ultimately contributes to its dilution and downfall, such as those that are defeated by their own success through "genericide," which renders brands indistinguishable from their imitators (Moore 2003). These different, yet overlapping, instances of cosignification can be considered together to reveal processes of local meaning-making, value formation, and the construction and maintenance of social hierarchy.

# 5 Embodiment, aesthetics, and style

Some studies of language use identify the body, and the voice in particular, as especially significant. As a powerful analytic and ethnographic concept that has also been used to explore distribution of access to power (Gal 1991), "voice" refers to the linguistic and material assemblage of how someone sounds and the relative social value of that assemblage within a system of other voices (see Bakhtin 1981). Fox (2004) argues that the act of voicing is a material and symbolic process at the heart of Texas working-class culture. Voice as phonation originating in the mouth and vocal tract and taking the form of speech and song is "the central locus in the production of social and cultural being" (Feld et al. 2006: 333–334). Indeed, how the voice sounds is part of what it means and does in particular social and cultural contexts; for instance, "for Ilongots, true verbal art has social force" (Rosaldo 1984: 140). As a material presence, voice is located in time and space, in what Bakhtin (1981) and others who have developed his idea might call a "chronotope," and is expressed through various face-to-face and mediated forms of language (Taylor 2009; Weidman 2010), including saying place names (Basso 1996), telling stories connected to places or describing routes through meaningful landscapes (Feld 1990; Feld and Basso 1996), and singing with twang or without (Feld et al. 2006). In these and other ways, embodiment links "the materiality of sound to the sociality of vocal practice" (Feld et al. 2006: 340; see also Jakobson 1960; Weiner 1991). In this view, talk is inseparable from the material speaking context, grounded in the mouths and bodies that produce it and otherwise experience it sensuously, shaped by the social and cultural contexts in which it occurs (Geurts 2002; Zimman and Hall 2010). Bourdieu (1977: 660; 1989) contends that "linguistic capital is embodied capital," and embodied language and linguistic competence are dimensions of bodily "hexis" through which the speaking subject's relation to the social world is expressed and achieved. Agha (2007) portrays enregisterment as similarly producing personae marked by embodied dispositions, comportment, and other nonlinguistic features that contribute to the formation of social stereotypes. Likewise, Fader (2009) presents "embodied signs" in analyses of Hasidic gendered socialization practices such as socially significant vowels or items of clothing to show how language use, material culture, and beliefs about the body intersect.

Inoue (2011) charts the creation of gendered subjects of modernity among nineteenth- century Japanese stenographers and how the decline of this profession shifted the mediation of meaning from the embodied materiality of the stenographer to "dematerialized signifiers encoded in the text" (p. 189). Embodiment of language, for instance during language shift, may join time and place with feeling and evaluation in ways that create meaning and value simultaneously (Cavanaugh 2009). Looking at embodiment and aesthetics from a different perspective, "style" integrates linguistic and material elements with a focus on the meanings and values such performance engenders. Irvine (2001) contends that material and linguistic differentiation are crucial to style, especially insofar as they enable juxtaposition of social categories in a political economic system. Early studies from the Birmingham School's Centre for Contemporary Cultural Studies offered class-based analyses of how individuals and groups strive to create differentiation through their use of signs (Hebdige 1979), as well as gender-based critiques of accounts that marginalized the cultural practices of girls (McRobbie 1991). Styles are socially recognizable and typifiable, linking ways of speaking and material practices such as dressing to categories that position individuals and shape the reproduction of class status and social dispositions (Bourdieu 1984; Eckert 2000; Willis 1981). Along with bodily adornment and comportment, language variation including phonological features such as vowel elongation and shortening and lexical appropriation from other speech communities indexes style and forms the basis of social evaluation regarding race, ethnicity, and gender (Mendoza-Denton 2008; Rampton 2006; Reyes 2007; Woolard 2008). Such pairings of distinct linguistic features with commodities can extend beyond the local to consider the relevance of mass-produced, global material and linguistic forms in local productions of style and, thus, complicate dynamics of power and political economy in new and interesting ways (e.g., Alim et al. 2008; McElhinny 2007; Shankar 2011).

## 6 Objectification, circulation, and communicative technologies

Since Malinowski's (1984) study focusing on the Kula, anthropologists have illustrated how objects gain value as they circulate, whether they are involved in systems of exchange (Weiner 1992) or in other types of flows and scapes (Appadurai 1996). Numerous scholars have astutely complicated Bourdieu's (1991) portrayal of the linguistic marketplace and characterization of language as symbolic capital (e.g., Irvine 1989; Swigart 2001; Woolard 1985), but his basic insight that language is embedded and circulates within systems of political, economic, social, and cultural distinction has been foundational to investigations of language's role in the production of value. Whether the context of circulation is immediate and face-to-face or mediated in some way – as in reported speech and other intertextual and interdiscursive events – the material remains critical for the linguistic to make sense (see Hull 2012 and Faudree 2012). For example, in Bergamo, Italy, while everyday use of the local vernacular decreases, it is increasingly objectified through entextualization (into dictionaries, volumes of poetry, etc.) and via its performance in certain valued contexts, such as plays, which transform the vernacular from a communicative medium to one of acquisition and display (J. Cavanaugh and S. Shankar in process).

Aspects of the process of objectification, specifically, the externalization and materialization of meaning and value, are central to understanding meanings people make from material culture (Keane 2007; D. Miller 2005; Myers 2001). Because objectifications are in part products of speakers' metapragmatic and meta-cultural rationalizations, they involve a degree of reflection, assessment, and critique. These reflexive dimensions doubly involve language in objectification: as part of the objectification process and as its object, often at the same time. Accents, lexical elements, registers, and styles of language may undergo different objectification processes than nonlinguistic objects would in order to circulate, complex processes involving abstraction of local forms as they take on meanings and values that can move across contexts. In some instances, reflexivity and performativity allow "language to 'objectify' its own praxis" (Lee and LiPuma 2002: 193). For instance, "qualisigns" – those signs that represent a particular attribute of a thing – enable objects to circulate precisely because they do not have a "representative" value in a Saussurian sense but do have an indexical one shaped by context (Manning and Meneley 2008:

287–288; see Keane 2003; Munn 1986).⁹ As objectifications circulate and are taken up in new contexts, they may transform social meanings, relationships, and values, as well as form connections between everyday contexts of talk and other types of circulation (see Shankar 2006).

Linguistic objectification can encompass entire languages but also single out particular linguistic features, such as the transformation of indexical signs into icons, or "rhematization" (Gal 2005; Irvine and Gal 2000; see Peirce 1955). As a mode of signification that depends on re- semblance between signifier and signified, icons focus attention on form. Feld et al. (2006; see Porcello 1998) enumerate iconic words such as *click, boom,* and *rumble,* which music producers use to describe the sounds they produce on a continuum from onomatopoeic to arbitrary. This is a precise metalanguage for these speakers, because not being able to line up a sound token with a particular sound puts one at a professional disadvantage. Indexes such as accents may also be transformed into icons (Cavanaugh 2005), but note that although both accents and sound tokens are indexes, accents become pragmatic icons and sound tokens become semantic icons; both rely on language ideologies that construct the indexical ground against which these sounds become meaningful and invoke the dynamics of power that underpin their semiotic transformation and enable their subsequent circulation.

The objectification of lexical elements, as well as register and genre, at the community level is often anchored within particular contexts of performance or display. For instance, Moore (1988) documents what he calls the objectualization of words – words taking on object-like qualities – among speakers of Wasco, an endangered language of the American northwest. He shows that the use of objectualized words occurs in very particular contexts of display and wealth distribution to establish their value as alienable objects suitable for bestowal. Similarly, Rosaldo (1984) shows how for the Ilongot, oratory, when it occurs in particular contexts, is "the reciprocal gift of words" (p. 144) that gives form to anger and leads eventually to an exchange of gifts for wrongs. Metapragmatic work that focuses on the form of words as much as on their meaning objectifies these linguistic forms in ways that iconize or rhematize them and allow them to gather value, articulate social relations, and potentially circulate more widely than originally intended.

Other scales of and contexts for circulation offer different possibilities for language objectification, such as the rise of print capitalism as part of nation building. Select forms of language were materialized into print form in ways that

---

9 Indexicality refers to context-based signification, specifically via contiguity or causality. Scholarship on indexicality focuses on the deployment or formation of indexes and the indexical dimensions of meaning.

unified disparate contexts into imagined communities and gave fixity to the forms of the language being printed, thus delineating higher status forms as standards and others as nonstandards (Anderson 1991; see Cody 2009; Urban 2001). Although print – language materialized in text form – is often central to these processes, it is not the only type of language objectification that occurs. Silverstein (1996) argues that the creation of a standard in the United States involved conditions under which "language acquires 'thinginess' such that the properties language takes on are continuous with those of other objects in the culture" (pp. 290–291). The circulation of this standard-language-as-thing – through print, but also via interactional activities such as, e.g., language training courses – in turn helps to demarcate the very boundaries of the nation-state.

Linguistic circulation that occurs through media has considered form in the examination of intertextual and interdiscursive links and emphasized material properties specific to a medium (Bier 2008; Spitulnik 1996). Work on "mediatization" (Agha 2011b; Bucholtz 2011) links contexts of communication and draws attention to the materiality of mediated language, as in the relationship between medical funding and training and the production and circulation of mediatized public health discourse (Briggs 2011). Eisenlohr (2004, 2010) discusses mediatized identities and authorities that form through the circulation of Islamic cassette sermon recordings. Much like the way texts may be interpreted differently as their material forms circulate (Gal 2003), the material form of recordings as well as their aural qualities index various types of religious authority and meaning as they circulate (see F. Miller 2005). Likewise, digital technologies unite form and meaning in the platform they provide for communication and signification; for instance, Gershon's (2010) "media switching" draws attention to how speakers see the choice of medium as contributing to the meaning of what is said within it.

The materialities of new media technologies have been shown to transform everyday talk. For instance, the digitized artifact introduces material communicative evidence into the structure of face-to-face conversations (Hall 2011). Moral panics about texting or the supposed loss of face-to-face sociality caused by the growth of computer-mediated social media (Thurlow 2006), such as contempt for or ridicule of sites such as Facebook, are in large part anxieties about the material forms that linguistic exchanges take, forms seen as inherently different from unmediated contexts. Innovative spellings in texting, for instance, may become icons of new types of identity and sociality among youth (Crystal 2009; Jones and Schieffelin 2009). In all these cases, processes of objectification complicate and may refashion the indexical embedding of a wide range of linguistic forms in face-to-face contexts, giving them novel meanings as they circulate into new contexts and their material forms – sounds, print tokens, and various media instantiations – become part of what these linguistic forms are and do interactionally.

# 7 Language commodification in global capitalism

Do aspects of language circulate in the same way that other commodities do? As the commodification of language takes various forms across ethnographic contexts, from Wolof nobles purchasing the verbal performances of griots in Senegal (Irvine 1989) to phone sex service operators in the Bay Area adopting particular gendered styles of speaking to please their customers (Hall 1995), this question is best addressed through ethnographic specifics. That language commodification is also always a process of transformation contributes to the construction of linguistic value and potentially transforms linguistic meaning. Whereas all commodified language is objectified, the reverse may not be true. In addition, objectified language need not circulate beyond its original context, but commodified language is always ready to move beyond local communities and societies into national and global contexts – levels at which language use can be difficult to analyze.

Differences emerge between language commoditization and circulation within national boundaries versus the ways these occur within globalized flows of capital and structures of power. Neoliberal deregulation and capitalist economic structures are characterized by increasing commodification of linguistic forms whose entry into global arenas of circulation is inflected with sociopolitical hierarchies of power (Cameron 2000; Duchêne and Heller 2012; Gal 2007; Heller 2003, 2011; Urciuoli 2008). Circuits of media, migration, consumer culture, and other vectors help form the distinctly neoliberal character of contemporary circulation, which Urban (2001) calls "meta-culture" in order to consider words in things, as well as culture passing through words. The commodification of language is indeed implicated in political economic transformations within nation-states (Heller 2003; Inoue 2006), as language may be "made the object of a brisk commerce in goods-and-services for which experts make themselves available" (Silverstein 1996: 291). For example, through the commodification of Basque, which is achieved in large part due to the application of neoliberal Total Quality Management (TQM) schemes, Urla (2012) argues that "language tends increasingly to be thing-ified, treated as a discrete, measurable and bounded entity, on this grid of discrete countable units" (p. 89). The application of TQM has also meant a professionalization of Basque language activism in ways that transform it from a political activity into an economic one.

Focusing on these processes may illuminate local, national, and global scales of linguistic circulation and how intersections of capital, built environment, and performance of linguistic register create, for instance, nearly identical conversational exchanges in chain stores in disparate global locations. The neoliberal workplace in particular is marked by distinct styles and registers acquired, valued, and performed in commodified ways. These may include how particular ways of speaking gain economic value within a job market or other economically contingent contexts (Manning 2008), such as in Cameron's (2000) research in call centers, which reports on the gendered ways in which workers are expected to perform affect and the evaluation of their success through customer feedback. Speakers involved in professions that entail the deployment of particular speech styles may develop complicated relationships to their own and other speech varieties via contradictory indexical linkages between self and speech, that is, between the perceived authentic self and the potentially inauthentic performance of job-related linguistic styles (Cowie 2007; Heller 2003). Considering the material dimensions of connections across interactional contexts allows us to scrutinize the various ways in which talk may be linked to or part of economic processes. Power is implicated here, as in Holmes's (2009) work on central banking, where bank officials create and publicly tell narratives that model economic processes with the goal of creating future expectations by iconically linking their talk to monetary value. Similarly conceptualizing interdiscursive links across spatially and temporally distant contexts, Gal (2007: 3) offers the concept of "clasp" as a way to highlight interdiscursive power dynamics between those who produce certain discourses and those who take them up or are subject to them (see Cavanaugh 2012).

Global capitalism is also characterized by contradictory, albeit intertwined, discourses that alternately value language according to "pride," anchored in indexical fields of authenticity, heritage, and communalism, or "profit," which depicts language's economic potential within the new global economy (Duchêne and Heller 2012). The discourse of profit, in particular, results in linguistic Taylorization, i.e., the direct integration of ways of speaking or writing into economic forms and structures, as in the case of Japanese handwritten "girl-graphs," which, after they fell out of fashion as a form of calligraphic resistance, continued to circulate in mass-produced versions (Miller 2011). In such contexts, "language as a marker of authenticity renders it particularly salient as a commodifiable resource" (Del Percio and Duchêne 2012: 49); this essential connection to authenticity can become problematic as speakers and interlocutors are reconfigured into linguistic producers and consumers in a global marketplace. The risk of problematic connections with speakers may be especially high for minority languages whose value is anchored in discourses of authenticity, as languages move into neoliberal realms of value that regard speakers as customers in language-planning efforts (Mac Giolla Chríost 2005).

As a process of material transformation in which particular aspects and features of a language variety are metapragmatically vetted and objectified, language commodification augers a number of outcomes, both to speakers – as their relationships to what they speak become mediated by global capitalist economic forms and practices – as well as for languages themselves. In the case of Basque discussed above, Urla maintains that the "thing-ification" of language may result in an increased focus on reported language choice as the preferred type of evidence to measure language use at the expense of more ethnographic investigations of syncretic and other mixed patterns of use. Likewise, McEwan-Fujita (2005) demonstrates how neoliberalism frames and impacts the ongoing language shift away from Gaelic toward English and shows how Gaelic language activists are involved in EU funding schemes that measure success in minority-language planning by quantifying the creation of enterprise rather than documenting Gaelic use.

What is shared across these cases is a focus on the form of language as key to its value and shifting location within economic structures and processes. The materiality of form, whether it is entextualized in authoritative texts, is aurally monitored by various types of listeners, or takes the shape of language varieties deemed authentic or inauthentic by experts, has a concrete presence in the world, distinct from the nondurable nature of most interactional language. This concrete presence, in turn, depends on the iconicity and increased fixity of linguistic form, such that only certain texts, accents, and speaking styles are transformed into commodities and become eligible to circulate.

# 8 Anticapitalism and directions for future research

In outlining the emergent scholarly field of inquiry of language materiality through studies of material culture, capitalism, and linguistic anthropology, and in demonstrating the myriad forms language objectifications take as they circulate across various contexts and scales, we have aimed to show the dynamic ways in which linguistic forms rely on and coproduce material contexts and how linguistic practices can involve processes of signification and valuation alongside objects. The significance of drawing attention to this "dynamic coexistence," to use Peirce's (1955) compelling phrase, can be found in the numerous ethnographic contexts discussed here, as well as in many that have created formative moments in our political present.

To conclude, we mention three cases that illustrate the academic purchase of a language materiality approach that integrates the linguistic and the material. First, the 2011 revolutions in the Middle East, especially the Egyptian revolution centered in Tahrir Square, relied heavily on numerous material communicative forms such as signs and banners, and burgeoned via social media sites, email, and mobile technologies, which provided running updates about locations and tactics. Second, the anticapitalist demonstrations encompassed in the Occupy Wall Street movement were marked by the materiality of microphones replaced by embodied communication in the form of the "human megaphone," repeated waves of announcements from crowd centers to peripheries, later aided by a smartphone app. In both events, the notion of protest relied on the interaction between the vocalization of dissent and the materiality of bodies, tents, and signs, as well as on the physical manipulation of public space. Their retroactive branding also created objectifications that circulated to other parts of the world as the "Arab Spring" and the "Occupy" movement. In a third case exemplifying the crisis unfolding in the European Union, Northern Italian and other small-scale heritage food producers may no longer be able to rely on national or EU-backed certifications such as DOP (Denomination of Protected Origin), which once ensured added value, and must find more global routes to lucrative markets. Their pursuits of value are linguistic as much as material, including the production of extensive documentation of quality standards as well as verbal performances of authenticity at food conferences and with consumers. In all these cases, global economic and political structures are mediated through local linguistic and material practices.

We believe that the 2011 Middle East revolutions, the Occupy movement, and the economic uncertainty in the European Union are best seen as processes built on a materiality that finds value within particular political economies. Indeed, the "99%" rallying cry against income inequality, much like the citizenry of various Middle East countries protesting the lack of economic opportunity and leadership of their complacent rulers and those outside the halls of power in Europe voicing critiques of political compromises that threaten their livelihoods, tells a story of material and linguistic inequality that helps to make this disparity visible and thus more real. The language of anticapitalism, then, is as inherently steeped in materiality as it is in neoliberalism and global capitalism, and each requires the other for the successful performance of protest or revolution. Retaining analytical divisions between language and materiality may elide the identification of such interacting processes of value formation and the production of meaning. As our social media-saturated world proceeds amid neoliberal ideologies that commodify linguistic forms, which in turn circulate in political economies far from their originary contexts, analytic and ethnographic perspectives that encompass language and materiality within their purview are acutely situated to understand, track, and analyze the attendant dynamics and complexities of identity, subjectivity, and power in everyday life.

# 9 Postscript

The human impacts of neoliberal policies with which we concluded the chapter have only accelerated; scholars have attended to these exigencies, but "language never exists outside of . . . . material conditions or apart from its moments of deployment" (Shankar and Cavanaugh 2017:13). As we write this post-script, we find ourselves again in a moment of crisis and protest, when anticapitalism, inequality, and the materiality of language are once more – or perhaps are still – central areas of inquiry and advocacy. We offer the following list of references for further reading on these matters.

**Acknowledgments:** For their critical feedback and insightful recommendations, we are very grateful to Micaela di Leonardo, Ayala Fader, Jessica Greenberg, Monica Heller, Miyako Inoue, and Jessica Winegar. We also thank Barnor Hesse, Fred Myers, Bambi Schieffelin, and our anonymous reviewers for their helpful suggestions, as well as Don Brenneis for his editorial guidance. Any errors and misinterpretations are our own.

# References

Agha, Asif. 2007. *Language and social relations*. Cambridge, UK: Cambridge University Press.
Agha, Asif. 2011a. Commodity registers. *Journal of Linguistic Anthropology* 21 (1). 22–53.
Agha, Asif. 2011b. Meet mediatization. *Language Communication* 31. 163–170.
Ahearn, Laura. 2001. *Invitations to love: Literacy, love letters, and social change in Nepal*. Ann Arbor: University of Michigan Press.
Alim, Samy, Awad Ibrahim, & Alastair Pennycook. 2008. *Global linguistic flows: Hip hop cultures, youth identities, and the politics of language*. New York: Routledge.
Anderson, Benedict. 1991 [1983]. *Imagined communities: Reflections on the origin and spread of nationalism*. London: Verso.
Appadurai, Arjun. 1986. Introduction: Commodities and the politics of value. In Arjun Appadurai (ed.), *The social life of things: Commodities in cultural perspective*, 3–63. Cambridge, UK: Cambridge University Press.
Appadurai, Arjun. 1996. *Modernity at large*. Minneapolis: University of Minnesota Press.
Bakhtin, Mikhail. 1981. *The dialogic imagination: Four essays*, ed. by Michael Holquist. Austin: University of Texas Press.
Basso, Keith. 1996. *Wisdom sits in places: Landscape and language among the Western Apache*. Albuquerque: University of New Mexico Press.
Bier, Jess. 2008. How Niqula Nasrallah became John Jacob Astor: Syrian emigrants aboard the Titanic and the materiality of language. *Journal of Linguistic Anthropology* 18 (2). 171–179.
Bourdieu, Pierre. 1977. The economics of linguistic exchange. *Social Science Information* 16 (6). 645–668.
Bourdieu, Pierre. 1984. *Distinction: A social critique of the judgment of taste*. Cambridge, MA: Harvard University Press.
Bourdieu, Pierre. 1991. *Language and symbolic power*, ed. by J. B. Thompson. Cambridge, MA: Harvard University Press.
Brenneis, Don. 1984. Grog and gossip in Bhatgaon: Style and substance in Fiji Indian conversation. *American Ethnologist* 11 (3). 487–506.

Briggs, Charles. 2011. On virtual epidemics and the mediatization of public health. *Language Communication* 31. 217–228.
Briggs, Charles & Richard Bauman. 1995. Genre, intertextuality, and social power. In B. G. Blount (ed.), *Language, culture, and society*, 567–608. Prospect Heights, IL: Waveland.
Bucholtz, Mary. 2011. Race and the re-embodied voice in Hollywood film. *Language Communication* 31. 255–265.
Cameron, Deborah. 2000. Styling the worker. *Journal of Sociolinguistics*. 4 (3). 323–347.
Carr, Summerson. 2010. Enactments of expertise. *Annual Review of Anthropology* 39. 17–32.
Cavanaugh, Jillian. 2005. Accent matters: The material consequences of sounding local in northern Italy. *Language Communication* 25. 127–148.
Cavanaugh, Jillian. 2009. *Living memory: The social aesthetics of language in a northern Italian town*. Malden, MA: Wiley-Blackwell.
Cavanaugh, Jillian. 2012. Entering into politics: Interdiscursivity, register, stance, and vernacular in northern Italy. *Language in Society* 41. 1–23.
Cavanaugh, Jillian R. & Shalini Shankar. 2014. Producing authenticity in global capitalism: Language, materiality, and value. *American Anthropologist* 116 (1). 51–64.
Cavanaugh, Jillian R. & Shalini Shankar (eds.). 2017. *Language and materiality: Ethnographic and theoretical explorations*. New York: Cambridge University Press.
Cody, Francis. 2009. Daily wires and daily blossoms: Cultivating regimes of circulation in Tamil India's newspaper revolution. *Journal of Linguistic Anthropology* 19 (2). 286–309.
Comaroff, John & Jean Comaroff. 2009. *Ethnicity, inc*. Chicago: University of Chicago Press.
Coombe, Rosemary. 1998. *The cultural life of intellectual properties: Authorship, alterity, and the law*. Durham, NC: Duke University Press.
Coupland, Nikolas. 2010. Introduction: Sociolinguistics in the global era. In N. Coupland (ed.), *Handbook of language and globalization*, 1–27. Malden, MA: Wiley-Blackwell.
Coupland, Nikolas. 2011. How frequent are numbers? *Language Communication* 31. 27–37.
Coward, Rosalind & John Ellis. 1977. *Language and materialism: Developments in semiology and the theory of the self*. Boston: Routledge & Kegan Paul.
Cowie Claire. 2007. The accents of outsourcing: The meanings of "neutral" in the Indian call centre industry. *World Englishes* 26 (3). 316–330.
Crystal, David. 2009. *Txtng: The Gr8 Db8*. New York: Oxford University Press.
Danet Brenda. 1997. Books, letters, documents: The changing aesthetics of texts in late print culture. *Journal of Material Culture* 2. 5–38.
Daniel, Valentine. 1984. *Fluid signs: Being a person the Tamil way*. Berkeley: University of California Press.
Del Percio, Alfonso & Alexandre Duchêne A. 2012. Commodification of pride and resistance to profit: language practices as terrain of struggle in a Swiss football stadium. See Duchêne & Heller 2012, pp. 43–72
Duchêne, Alexandre & Monica Heller (eds.). 2012. *Language in late capitalism: Pride and profit*. New York: Routledge.
Duranti, Alessandro & Charles Goodwin (eds.). 1992. *Rethinking context: Language as an interactive phenomenon*. Cambridge, UK: Cambridge University Press.
Eckert, Penelope. 2000. *Linguistic variation as social practice: The linguistic construction of identity in Belten High*. Malden, MA: Wiley-Blackwell.
Eisenlohr, Patrick. 2004. As Makkah is sweet and beloved, so is Madina: Islam, devotional genres, and electronic mediation in Mauritius. *American Ethnologist* 33 (2). 230–245.

Eisenlohr, Patrick. 2010. Materialities of entextualization: The domestication of sound reproduction in Mauritian Muslim devotional practices. *Journal of Linguistic Anthropology* 20 (2). 314–333.

Fader, Ayala. 2009. *Mitzvah girls: Bringing up the next generation of Hasidic Jews in Brooklyn.* Princeton, NJ: Princeton University Press.

Faudree, Paja. 2012. Music, language, and texts: Sound and semiotic ethnography. *Annual Review of Anthropology* 41. 519–536.

Feld, Steven. 1990. *Sound and sentiment: Birds, weeping, poetics, and song in Kaluli expression.* Philadelphia: University of Pennsylvania Press.

Feld, Steven. & Keith Basso (eds.). 1996. *Senses of place.* Santa Fe, NM: School of American Research Press.

Feld, Steven, Aaron Fox, Thomas Porcello & David Samuels. 2006. Vocal anthropology: From the music of language to the language of song. In Alessandro Duranti (ed.), *A companion to linguistic anthropology*, 321–45. Oxford: Blackwell.

Fox, Aaron. 2004. *Real country: Music and language in working class culture.* Durham, NC: Duke University Press.

Gal, Susan. 1989. Language and political economy. *Annual Review of Anthropology* 18. 345–367.

Gal, Susan. 1991. Between speech and silence: The problematics of research on language and gender. In M. Di Leonardo (ed.), *Gender at the crossroads of knowledge*, 175–203. Berkeley: University of California Press.

Gal, Susan. 2003. Movement of feminism: The circulation of discourses about women. In Barbara Hobson (ed.), *Recognition struggles and social movements: Contested identities, agencies and power*, 175–203. Cambridge, UK: Cambridge University Press.

Gal, Susan. 2005. Language ideologies compared. *Journal of Linguistic Anthropology* 15 (1). 23–37.

Gal, Susan. 2007. *Circulation in the "new" economy: Clasps and copies.* Presented at the Annual Meeting of the American Anthropologist Association, 106th, Washington, DC.

Gershon, Ilana. 2010. Breaking up is hard to do: Media switching and media ideologies. *Journal of Linguistic Anthropology* 20 (2). 389–405.

Geurts, Kathryn. 2002. *Culture and the senses: Bodily ways of knowing in an African community.* Berkeley: University of California Press.

Goffman, Ervin. 1979. *Gender advertisements.* New York: Harper Collins.

Gumperz, John. 1982. *Discourse strategies.* New York: Cambridge University Press.

Hall, Kira. 1995. Lip service on the fantasy lines. In Kira Hall & Mary Bucholtz (eds.), *Gender articulated: Language and the socially constructed self*, 183–216. London: Routledge.

Hall, Kira. 2011. *The new Bahan Chod.* Presented at the Annual Meeting of the American Anthropology Association, 110th, Montreal.

Harvey, David. 2005. *A brief history of neoliberalism.* Oxford: Oxford University Press.

Hebdige, Dick. 1979. *Subculture: The meaning of style.* New York: Routledge.

Heller, Monica. 2003. Globalization, the new economy, and the commodification of language and identity. *Journal of Sociolinguistics* 7 (4). 473–492.

Heller, Monica. 2011. *Paths to post-nationalism: A critical ethnography of language and identity.* New York: Oxford University Press.

Hill, Jane. 2000. "Read my article": Ideological complexity and the overdetermination of promising in American presidential politics. In P. V. Kroskrity (ed.), *Regimes of language. Ideologies, politics, and identities*, 259–292. Santa Fe, NM: School of American Research Press.

Hill, Jane. 2008. *The everyday language of white racism.* Malden, MA: Wiley-Blackwell.

Ho, Karen. 2009. *Liquidated: An ethnography of Wall Street*. Durham, NC: Duke University Press.
Hoffman, Katherine. 2008. *We share walls: Language, land, and gender in Berber Morocco*. Malden, MA: Wiley-Blackwell.
Holmes, Douglas. 2009. Economy of words. *Cultural Anthropologist* 24 (3). 381–419.
Hull, Matthew. 2003. The file: Agency, authority, and autography in an Islamabad bureaucracy. *Language Communication* 23. 287–314.
Hull, Matthew. 2012. Documents and bureaucracy. *Annual Review of Anthropology* 41. 251–267.
Inoue, Miyako. 2006. *Vicarious language: Gender and linguistic modernity in Japan*. Berkeley: University of California Press.
Inoue, Miyako. 2011. Stenography and ventriloquism in late nineteenth century Japan. *Language Communication* 31. 181–190.
Irvine, Judith. 1989. When talk isn't cheap: Language and political economy. *American Ethnologist* 16 (2). 248–267.
Irvine, Judith. 2001. "Style" as distinctiveness: The culture and ideology of linguistic differentiation. In Penelope Eckert & John Russel Rickford (eds.), *Style and sociolinguistic variation*, 21–43. Cambridge, UK: Cambridge University Press.
Irvine, Judith. 2005. Knots and tears in the interdiscursive fabric. *Journal of Linguistic Anthropology* 15 (1). 72–80.
Irvine, Judith & Susan Gal. 2000. Language ideology and linguistic differentiation. In Paul Kroskrity (ed.), *Regimes of language. Ideologies, politics, and identities*, 35–83. Santa Fe, NM: School of American Research Press.
Jaffe, Alexandra. 1999a. *Ideologies in action: Language politics in action*. Berlin: Mouton de Gruyter.
Jaffe, Alexandra. 1999b. Packaged sentiments: The social meaning of greeting cards. *Journal of Material Culture* 4 (2). 115–141.
Jakobson, Roman. 1960. Closing statement: Linguistics and poetics. In Thomas Sebeok (ed.), *Style in language*, 350–59. Cambridge, MA: MIT Press.
Jones, Graham. 2012. Magic with a message: The poetics of Christian conjuring. *Cultural Anthropologist* 27 (2). 193–214.
Jones, Graham. & Bambi Schieffelin. 2009. Talking text and talking back: "My BFF Jill" from boob tube to YouTube. *Journal of Computer-Mediated Communication* 14 (4). 1050–1079.
Keane, Webb. 2003. Semiotics and the social analysis of material things. *Language Communication* 23 (2–3). 409–425.
Keane, Webb. 2007. *Christian moderns: Freedom and fetish in the mission encounter*. Berkeley: University of California Press.
Kockelman, Paul. 2006. A semiotic ontology of the commodity. *Journal of Linguistic Anthropology* 16 (1). 76–102.
Kroskrity, Paul. (ed.). 2000. *Regimes of language. Ideologies, politics, and identities*. Santa Fe, NM: School of American Research Press.
Lee, Benjamin. 1997. *Talking heads: Language, metalanguage, and the semiotics of subjectivity*. Durham, NC: Duke University Press.
Lee, Benjamin. & Edward LiPuma. 2002. Cultures of circulation: The imaginations of modernity. *Public Culture* 14 (1). 191–213.
Mac Giolla, Chríost. 2005. Prestige planning and the Welsh language: Marketing, the consumer-citizen and language behaviour. *Current Issues in Language Planning* 6 (1). 64–72.
Malinowski, Bronislaw. 1984 [1922]. *Argonauts of the western Pacific*. Long Grove, IL: Waveland.

Manning, Paul. 2008. Barista rants about stupid customers at Starbucks: What imaginary conversations can teach us about real ones. *Language Communication* 28 (2).101–126.
Manning, Paul. 2010. The semiotics of brand. *Annual Review of Anthropology* 39. 33–49.
Manning, Paul & Anne Meneley. 2008. Material objects in cosmological worlds: An introduction. *Ethnos* 73 (3). 285–302.
McElhinny, Bonnie. (ed.). 2007. *Words, worlds, and material girls: Language, gender, globalization*. Berlin: Mouton deGruyter.
McEwan-Fujita, Emily. 2005. Neoliberalism and minority-language planning in the Highlands and Islands of Scotland. *International Journal of Sociology and Language* 171. 155–171.
McRobbie, Angela. 1991. *Feminism and youth culture*. New York: Routledge.
Mendoza-Denton, Norma. 2008. *Homegirls: Language and cultural practice among Latina youth gangs*. Malden, MA: Wiley-Blackwell.
Meneley, Anne. 2007. Like an extra-virgin. *American Anthropologist* 109 (4). 678–687.
Mertz, Elizabeth & Richard Parmentier (eds.). 1985. *Semiotic mediation: Sociocultural and psychological perspectives*. Orlando, FL: Academic.
Miller, Daniel. 1998. Why some things matter. In D. Miller (ed.), *Material cultures: Why some things matter*, 3–21. Chicago: University of Chicago Press.
Miller, Daniel. (ed.). 2005. *Materiality*. Durham, NC: Duke University Press.
Miller, Flagg. 2005. Of songs and signs: Audiocassette poetry, moral character, and the culture of circulation in Yemen. *American Ethnologist* 32 (1). 82–99.
Miller, Laura. 2011. Subversive script and novel graphs in Japanese girls' culture. *Language Communication* 31. 16–26.
Modan, Gabriella. 2007. *Turf wars: Discourse, diversity and the politics of place*. Malden, MA: Wiley-Blackwell.
Moore, Robert. 1988. Lexicalization versus lexical loss in Wasco-Wishram language obsolescence. *International Journal of American Linguistics* 54 (4). 453–468.
Moore, Robert 2003. The genericide to viral marketing: On brand. *Language Communication* 23 (3–4). 331–359.
Munn, Nancy. 1986. *The fame of Gawa: A symbolic study of value transformation in a Massim (Papua New Guinean) society*. Durham, NC: Duke University Press.
Myers, Fred. 2001. Introduction: The empire of things. In Fred Myers (ed.), *The empire of things: Regimes of value and material culture*, 3–63. Santa Fe, NM: School of American Research Press.
Parmentier, Richard. 1994. *Signs in society: Studies in semiotic anthropology*. Bloomington: Indiana University Press.
Peirce, Charles. 1955. *Philosophical writings of Peirce*, ed. by Justus Buchler. New York: Dover.
Porcello, Thomas. 1998. "Tails out": Social phenomenology and the ethnographic representation of technology in music-making. *Ethnomusicology* 42 (3). 485–510.
Rampton, Ben. 2006. *Language in late modernity*. Cambridge, UK: Cambridge University Press.
Reyes, Angela. 2007. *Language, identity, and stereotype among southeast Asian youth*. New York: Routledge.
Rosaldo, Michelle. 1984. Words that are moving: The social meanings of Ilongot verbal art. In Donald Brenneis & Fred Myers (eds.), *Dangerous words: Language and politics in the Pacific*, 131–160. New York: New York University Press.
Schieffelin, Bambi, Kathryn Woolard & Paul Kroskrity (eds.). 1998. *Language ideologies: Practice and theory*. New York: Oxford.

Schneider, J. G. 2006. Language and mediality: On the medial status of "everyday language." *Language Communication* 26. 331–342.
Shandler, Jan. 2006. *Adventures in Yiddishland: Postvernacular language and culture*. Berkeley: University California Press.
Shankar, Shalini. 2006. Metaconsumptive practices and the circulation of objectifications. *Journal of Material Culture* 11 (3). 293–317.
Shankar, Shalini. 2008. *Desi land: Teen culture, class, and success in Silicon Valley*. Durham, NC: Duke University Press.
Shankar, Shalini. 2011. Reconsidering language use and style among youth of the new immigration. *Identities* 18 (6). 646–671.
Shankar, Shalini. 2012. Creating model consumers: Producing ethnicity, race, and class in Asian American advertising. *American Ethnologist* 39 (3). 378–391.
Silverstein, Michael. 1996. Monoglot "standard" in America. In Don Brenneis & Ronald Macaulay (eds.), *The matrix of language*, 284–306. Long Grove, IL: Waveland.
Silverstein, Michael. 2003. Indexical order and the dialectics of sociolinguistic life. *Language Communication* 23 (2–3). 193–230.
Silverstein, Michael. 2005. Axes of evals: Token versus type interdiscursivity. *Journal of Linguistic Anthropology* 15 (1). 6–22.
Silverstein, Michael. 2011. The "message" in the (political) battle. *Language Communication* 31. 203–216.
Silverstein, Michael & Greg Urban (eds.). 1996. *Natural histories of discourse*. Chicago, IL: University of Chicago Press.
Spitulnik, Debra. 1996. The social circulation of media discourse and the mediation of communities. *Journal of Linguistic Anthropology* 6 (2). 161–187.
Swigart, Leigh. 2001. The limits of legitimacy: Language ideology and shift in contemporary Senegal. *Journal of Linguistic Anthropology* 10 (1). 90–130.
Taylor, Jessica. 2009. "Speaking shadows": A history of the voice in the transition from silent to sound film in the United States. *Journal of Linguistic Anthropology* 19 (1). 1–20.
Thurlow, Crispin. 2006. From statistical panic to moral panic: The metadiscursive construction and popular exaggeration of new media language in the print media. *Journal of Computer-Mediated Communication* 11. 667–701.
Urban, Greg. 2001. *Metaculture: How culture moves through the world*. Minneapolis: University of Minnesota Press.
Urciuoli, Bonnie. 2008. Skills and selves in the new workplace. *American Ethnologist* 35 (2). 211–228.
Urla, Jackie. 2012. Total quality language revival. In Alexandre Duchêne & Monica Heller (eds.). *Language in late capitalism: Pride and profit*, 73–92. New York: Routledge.
Voloshinov, Valentin. 1973. *Marxism and the philosophy of language*. Cambridge, MA: Harvard University Press.
Weidman, Amanda. 2010. Sound and the city: Mimicry and media in South India. *Journal of Linguistic Anthropology* 20 (2). 294–313.
Weiner, A. 1984. From words to objects to magic: "Hard words" and the boundaries of social interaction. In D. L. Brenneis & F. R. Myers (eds.), *Dangerous words: Language and politics in the Pacific*, 161–191. New York: New York University Press.
Weiner, Annette. 1992. *Inalienable possessions: The paradox of keeping while giving*. Berkeley: University of California Press.
Weiner, James. 1991. *The empty place: Poetry, space, and being among the Foi of Papua New Guinea*. Bloomington: Indiana University Press.

Williams, Raymond. 1977. *Marxism and literature*. Oxford: Oxford University Press.
Willis, Paul. 1981 [1977]. *Learning to labor: How working class kids get working class jobs*. New York: Columbia University Press.
Wittgenstein, Ludwig. 1991. *The blue and brown books: Preliminary studies for the "Philosophical Investigation."* Malden, MA: Wiley-Blackwell.
Woolard, Kathryn. 1985. Language variation and cultural hegemony: Toward an integration of sociolinguistic and social theory. *American Ethnologist* 12 (4). 738–748.
Woolard, Kathryn. 1998. Introduction: Language ideology as a field of inquiry. In Bambi Schieffelin, Kathryn Woolard & Paul Kroskrity (eds.), *Language ideologies: Practice and theory*, 3–47. New York: Oxford.
Woolard, Kathryn. 2008. Why dat now? Linguistic-anthropological contributions to the explanation of sociolinguistic icons and change. *Journal of Sociolinguistics* 12 (4). 432–452.
Zimman, Lal & Kira Hall. 2010. Language, embodiment and the "third sex." In Carmen Llamas & Dominic Watt (eds.), *Language and identities*, 167–178. Edinburgh: Edinburgh University Press.

# Further reading

Bonilla, Yarimar and Jonathan Rosa. 2015. "#Ferguson: Digital Protest, Hashtag Ethnography, and the Racial Politics of Social Media in the United States." American Ethnologist 42(1):4–17.
Bucholtz, Mary, and Kira Hall. 2016. Embodied Sociolinguistics. In Sociolinguistics: Theoretical Debates, edited by Nikolas Coupland, 173–197. Cambridge: Cambridge University Press.
Cavanaugh, Jillian R. 2016. Documenting Subjects: Performativity and Audit Culture in Food Production. American Ethnologist 43(4):691–703.
Chumley, Lily Hope, and Nicholas Harkness, eds. 2013. Special Issue on Qualia. Anthropological Theory 13(1–2).
Dick, Hilary. 2018. Words of Passage: National Longings and the Imagined Lives of Mexican Immigrants. Austin, TX: University of Texas Press.
Gershon, Ilana. 2017. Language and the Newness of Media. Annual Review of Anthropology 46: 15–31.
Heller, Monica and Bonnie McElhinney. 2017. Language, Capitalism, Colonialism: Toward a Critical History. University of Toronto Press.
Inoue, Miyako. 2018. Word for Word: Verbatim as Political Technologies. Annual Review of Anthropology 47: 217–32.
Novak, David, and Matt Sakakeeney. 2015. Keywords in Sound. Durham, NC: Duke University Press.
Riley, Kathleen C. and Jillian R. Cavanaugh. 2017. "Tasty Talk, Expressive Food: An Introduction to The Semiotics of Food-and-Language." Semiotic Review 5.
Shankar, Shalini 2015. Advertising Diversity: Ad Agencies and the Creation of Asian American Consumers. Durham, NC: Duke University Press.
Shankar, Shalini. 2016. "Coming in First: Sound and Embodiment in Spelling Bees." Journal of Linguistic Anthropology 26(2):119–140.
Webster, Anthony 2017 "So it's got three meanings dil dil:" Seductive ideophony and the sounds of Navajo poetry. Canadian Journal of Linguistics/Revue canadienne de linguistique. 62(2):173–195.

Carl Lounsbury
# Chapter 13
# The language of building in the southern American colonies

The story of early southern architecture can be traced in the language of its builders and users. Next to farming, the building trades were one of the largest and most important sources of employment in early America. Although much of the language used by the thousands of skilled craftsmen and laborers who plied their trades was highly technical in nature, the universality of building meant that much of the vocabulary found its way into everyday usage. The transformation of English into a distinctly American English can be discerned in the words used by America's early builders. Similarly, the emergence of regional dialects and expressions appears in the common spellings and names attached to architectural features, building types, and construction practices.

Most architectural dictionaries define a timeless, universal language of building. In contrast, a study of the architecture of the old South in the period from first settlement to the second quarter of the nineteenth century reveals a dynamic transformation in the conceptualization of design, the introduction of a host of foreign terms into the language of building, and the filtering and reshaping of traditional English building terms by a colonial population. From the fortified earthfast dwellings of John Smith's Jamestown to the intellectualized landscape of Thomas Jefferson's Monticello, southern architectural forms and landscape underwent a revolutionary metamorphosis. So too did the language of building from Smith to Jefferson. It had been founded upon the workaday grammar of English artisans but was altered by new world conditions and the slow absorption of the self-conscious, scholarly grammar of classical architecture rooted in Latin texts. This academic language of Renaissance antiquarians and gentlemen architects spread across Europe in the sixteenth and seventeenth centuries but had scarcely affected the vernacular of English builders during the early decades of American colonization. By the time of

---
**Note:** This essay is a revised version of the introduction in Carl Lounsbury. 1994. *An illustrated glossary of early southern architecture and landscape*. New York: Oxford University Press; reprint Charlottesville: University of Virginia Press, 1999.

---
**Carl Lounsbury,** Senior Architectural Historian at Colonial Williamsburg, retired, and Adjunct Associate Professor of History at William and Mary, carllounsbury@gmail.com

Jefferson's death in 1826, it had made strong inroads in the contracts, accounts, and conversations of builders and their clients. However, as late as the 1820s, the arcane grammar and rules of the classical orders had by no means displaced the less explicit but well understood language of the trades in terms of "workmanlike craftsmanship."

Because the language of building reflects the currency of certain design ideas and architectural forms at any given period, it is possible to observe fundamental shifts in the way southerners thought and wrote about building during the first two hundred years of settlement. Although immigrants to the new world in the early seventeenth century brought English tools, skills, and habits of building to their task of constructing shelters, dwellings, agricultural structures, public buildings, and fortifications, the economic, social, and environmental conditions that shaped the early colonies in the Chesapeake and the Carolinas subtly but substantially transformed their methods.

Architecturally, Britain at the time of the settlement of North America was a land marked by many strong regional contrasts. From the west country to East Anglia, in the expanding metropolis of London and the populous home counties, and stretching northward to the remote dales of Yorkshire and beyond, domestic architecture diverged widely in plan, room uses, materials, construction methods, and finishes. Regional distinctions were evident in the names given to various rooms and parts of the house. The principal, all-purpose room known as the "hall" in the south of England and the "house" throughout much of the north was also called "forehouse," "fireroom," and "housebody" in many subregions. In the north of England and in Scotland, a gable was called a "gavel," while in the southwest the French word "pignon" was widely used (Salzman 1952). Variations also appeared in the terms given framing members. A "teazle post" was a principal post in Yorkshire, while a "span piece" was a Devonshire term for a roof collar (Bagenal 1970: 16). Many builders referred to small upright timbers set between posts as "studs," but "punch" or "puncheon" was widely in circulation. In the seventeenth century, the term "quarter" began to supersede puncheon on the building site (Salzman 1952: 205–206). The latter term survived a transatlantic crossing and occasionally appeared in colonial contractual agreements.

In the century prior to North American settlement, the English increasingly erected solidly constructed dwellings, replacing impermanent structures. Many people improved older houses by the insertion of floors over rooms once open to the roof. The construction of masonry chimney stacks in place of wooden ones or hearths open to the roof provided more efficient heating and the introduction of window glass, paneling, and decorative plasterwork lightened, brightened, warmed, and enhanced many interiors. New terms such as "wainscot" and "casement" entered into the vocabulary to describe certain features associated with these housing improvements.[1] More houses acquired service rooms for food preparation, storage, and domestic manufacturing. Dairies, bakehouses, and butteries emerged as essential spaces in many dwellings. This transformation of domestic life from the old communal patterns of the open hall of a medieval household into a more comfortable, private, and specialized house did not occur evenly across Britain. In some of the prosperous areas such as the southeast in counties like Kent and Sussex, such developments had occurred some 50 to 100 years before the settlement of Jamestown in 1607. Elsewhere, such as the pastoral highlands of the north, age-old patterns continued with few signs of change.

Layered over this body of indigenous architecture and regional building vocabulary was a new interest in foreign forms and ways of thinking about building. At the top level of society in country houses owned by the aristocracy, on the burgage plots of rich London merchants, and in the buildings constructed by the cognoscenti associated with the royal court as well as the planned developments in the city of Westminster, the Renaissance rediscovery of the form and language of classical architecture of antiquity began to influence ideas about design. Although books explaining the rules and forms of this architectural grammar would be an important transmitter of this language to America in the late colonial and early republican eras, the first signs of the impact of Renaissance classicism on English vernacular practices and thus on early American building appeared much earlier. These ideas grew slowly but steadily through the seventeenth century, influencing everything from the overall form of buildings and placement of apertures to the pattern of interior finishes and the shape of molding profiles. Misapplication of this language also made its way into use. Although the Italian name for an open square was "piazza," the English applied the term to describe the ground-floor arcade that surrounded the squares at Covent Garden and the Royal Exchange in London. In this sense, the term was appropriated in the late seventeenth century by Chesapeake colonists to refer to the arcaded space of public buildings such as the college building at William and Mary and the capitol at the other end of the Duke of Gloucester Street in Williamsburg (Lounsbury 2011: 204, 207, 223).

The geographical diversity of Britain, combined with the dynamic trends in its architecture, provided the first settlers of the Chesapeake with a rich mixture

---

**1** Joined paneling known as "wainscot," consisting of boards or panels held in place by narrow wooden strips of horizontal rails and vertical stiles, came into fashion in England in the late sixteenth century. For about a hundred years, it was considered like textile hangings, which it replaced, as moveable furniture that could be taken apart, transferred, and installed in another room or house. Gradually in the seventeenth century it became seen as an integral fixed part of a building. (For a discussion of its earlier connotation, see Cook 1984.)

of alternatives in construction technologies, building types, and words used to describe domestic and public spaces. The emergence of a plantation society in Virginia and Maryland by the middle of the seventeenth century and the consequent formation of a creole culture fostered the growth of distinctive vernacular building practices based mainly on new materials and new construction technologies, including impermanent building practices. The expansion of British settlement to the Carolina lowcountry in the late seventeenth century led to the emergence of tabby as a wall material. It was composed of sand, lime, oyster shells, and water, which were mixed together and poured in layers into plank formwork and allowed to settle and harden for a number of days. As early as the 1650s, colonists in the Chesapeake adapted log building methods, a central and north European form of construction unknown in Britain, from the Scandinavian settlers in the Swedish colony in the Delaware Valley. The Swedes stacked round, hewn, and sawn logs or poles on top of one another so that they were notched or lapped over one another at the corners. The methodology gave rise to the use of terms such as "skinned," "barked," and "scalped" to refer to how the timbers were shaped, and the individual logs that formed the walls were sometimes distinguished as a "round" (Lounsbury 2010: 77–82).

Although buildings such as Bacon's Castle (1665) in Surry County, Virginia, and Arlington (1675), the home of the Custis family on the Eastern Shore of the colony, resembled in plan, construction, and scale some of the buildings erected by the minor gentry and prosperous farmers in many parts of England, most farmhouses and public structures erected by this dispersed agricultural society varied significantly from standard English patterns. By the middle of the seventeenth century, immigrants to the southern colonies acknowledged this difference between well-framed "English houses," with beaded and chamfered beams fastened with strong joints, and a cheaper and more prevalent form of riven clapboard carpentry. Early contracts often described buildings as a system of repetitive units fabricated of so many lengths of boards applied to a rudimentary framing system. The signature feature of this construction form was the covering of four- or five-foot-long riven or cleaved clapboards, which provided the structural rigidity necessary to secure the wall framing members and roof trusses. The lower part of this hewn and riven frame was secured into posts or sills that sat in or on the ground rather than a masonry foundation. To further reduce the amount of skilled craftsmanship needed to erect these kinds of structures, artisans developed ways to separate the complicated joinery that anchored roof frames to walls. A new framing member, the "false plate," sat on top of ceiling joists that jetted or extended out beyond the plane of the wall. On top of the joists at their ends, carpenters secured the false plate, which allowed them to set the feet of the common rafters so that the roof framing no longer needed to be tied into wall posts with complicated blind dovetail joints. The colonists rarely considered these buildings – known as earthfast construction by modern scholars and as "Virginia houses" by contemporaries – as anything more than inferior but necessary structures. In this earthfast system, the placement of apertures and fabrication of other major elements, which later craftsmen and builders would carefully design and provide decorative finishes, were left to the discretion of workmen known as "clapboard carpenters." Rarely did building agreements specify finish details. The paucity of skilled joiners in the records before the late seventeenth century testifies to the pervasiveness of rude quality of construction and finish. Most earthfast houses seldom lasted more than a decade without the need of substantial repairs caused by rot and termites exacerbated by the humid climate.

The use of simplified construction techniques should not mask the radical restructuring that was taking place in the arrangement and function of rooms and the increasing specialization of spaces in domestic and public architecture. For most of the seventeenth century, southern colonists experimented with many English house types, juggling elements to fit the demands of a plantation culture that was becoming highly dependent on servant and slave labor needed to cultivate the tobacco fields that brought wealth to a few planters. The archaeological evidence from scores of early Chesapeake sites reveals a tremendous range of house forms and construction methods. (For a summary of early housing, see Carson and Lounsbury 2013.) Featuring a central chimney with flanking rooms, lobby-entry houses, common in many parts of England and long associated with the early New England landscape, were erected in the Chesapeake in the middle of the seventeenth century but gradually tailed off in popularity. Dozens of house types characteristic of the English inheritance gradually were pared down to a few well-considered options. By the beginning of the eighteenth century, southerners had completely rethought the configuration of the English house, consigning many service spaces such as the kitchen, pantry, and buttery to detached structures called "outhouses." The documentary record does not initially give full voice to this reorientation of domestic spaces. Only by the careful reading of contractual agreements and estate inventories can the movement of functions out of the main living space be detected.

The emergence of new building types and names such as "smokehouse" and the disappearance of room names such as "buttery" make explicit this transformation of the English house in the new world. A smokehouse was a building in which meat, especially pork and fish, were cured by concentrated exposure to enveloping smoke. The term first appears at the beginning of the eighteenth century to define a distinctive form, usually square with no apertures except a door and an open hearth on the floor with poles and collars used to hang the hams and other meats. Other new domestic outbuildings appear around the same time, including the "wash house" or "laundry" and the "milk house" or "dairy." As with many new building types that developed to serve a particular function in these dispersed rural colonies, the names they were called varied from region to region or over time. Evolving as a place for the storage of cheese, butter, and milk on shelves with a pyramid roof with deep eaves and ventilated openings with s-shaped struts or strigils just below, the term "dairy" replaced "milk house" as the name for such structures in Virginia and parts of the lower South, while in the northern Chesapeake the older term remained predominant. A building in which clothes, linens, and other items were cleaned, wash houses first appeared in South Carolina in the early eighteenth century, and by the time of the Revolution they were being used in parts of Maryland and occasionally Virginia, where the synonymous term "laundry" was more common.

The names given to other emerging building types were sometimes peculiar to one region while others could be found across the South but with variant nomenclature. In the tobacco colonies of the Chesapeake, new structures for the storage and packing of the region's chief staple appeared as early as the second quarter of the seventeenth century, as documents from that time are filled with "tobacco houses," "rolling houses," and "prize houses." As enslaved Africans replaced white indentured servants as the principal laborers on these plantations, planters moved their black slaves who once lodged in their houses into separate houses that began to be described as "quarters," in the English sense of lodgings or barracks for military or domestic staff. South of the Chesapeake, the term "Negro houses" was most common, and eventually by the end of the colonial period "slave houses" had become current throughout the region. In the Chesapeake, the term "ordinary" became the most common way to describe an alehouse, though "tavern" was also in vogue for better public houses of refreshment and accommodation. By the late seventeenth century, planters were moving maize or Indian corn that had previously been stored in lofts of dwellings outside to "corn houses" and "corncribs," where they provided shelter for corn that was shelled and intended for human consumption, or on the cob and provender for livestock, in which case the latter was well ventilated with slatted openings.

A small structure housing a latrine with an enclosed seat on a raised platform produced perhaps the most variants, including many euphemisms that had short-lived currency. "Necessary house," which is the most common term given to this building type, appears from the mid-seventeenth century onwards. "House of office," and less frequently "office house," and "house of ease" also appear in records from the late seventeenth century, but were less commonly used in many areas of the South. Except in South Carolina and, perhaps, Georgia, the term "privy" appears infrequently before the Revolution. Only in the mid-nineteenth century does it begin to be used with any regularity throughout the region. Finally, the colonial records are sprinkled with a few terms such as "cloacina temple," "little house," and "water closet." Competing with this structure for having the greatest variety of terms assigned to it is a small structure sometimes located nearby. Built as a place for chickens and other fowl to roost and nest, and to be protected from predators, "henhouse" was the most pervasive term for such buildings throughout most of the South. The term was used to the exclusion of all others in Virginia, whereas "chicken house," "poultry house," and "fowl house" could be found throughout the South, especially the latter two in South Carolina, where no one ever saw a fox in a henhouse.

The language of building changed dramatically in the last decades of the seventeenth century and the first two or three of the next century. The growing influence of Renaissance ideas on early American building appears in new words and phrases in contracts and accounts. Fashionable words such as "architecture," "modillion," "architrave," and "fretwork" embellish the descriptions of new dwellings and the specifications for churches and courthouses. These words reflect a new desire to conceal the structural frame of a building beneath applied decorative elements. Exposed framing members, carefully finished with carved moldings, beads, and chamfers, the hallmark of traditional English carpentry work, disappeared, replaced by smooth planar surfaces and works of the joiners' art. The juncture of rafters, wall plates, and joists at the eaves were enclosed by "cornices." Doorposts received decorative "frontispieces." Interior walls were sheathed with wainscoting or plaster and corner posts were encased or "guttered" to hide their presence. Complex and sometimes intricately carved chimney pieces replaced chamfered structural beams called "manteltrees." Contracts grew longer as colonists made specific choices of a greater variety of finish treatments and new items, such as sash windows, which replaced casements, and paneled wainscoting.

Specifications that contained terms such as "out to out," "in the clear," and "pitch" (meaning height of a wall rather than the angle of a roof) indicated that buildings began to be thought of in three dimensions with a concern for overall appearance. Design drawings first made their appearance in the southern colonies in the very late seventeenth century. A "draft," or more commonly "draught," designated a sketch of a building or its parts and was used almost synonymously with "plat" to denote a graphic representation of a design. It was supplanted by the term "plan" by the 1730s, which defined the position and relationship of apertures, chimney, partition walls, staircases, and other elements. Additional drawings of elevations, sections, and specific details such as moldings, chimney pieces, and windows began to appear at this time, but were by no means standard drawings for another century; they were visual devices for conveying abstract architectural principles of proportion and symmetry, hallmarks of the new conceptual models of a style that modern architectural historians have variously denominated classical, academic, or Georgian.

By the middle of the eighteenth century, booksellers in Annapolis, Williamsburg, Charleston, and other places had begun to import an ever-growing number of English architectural books that provided builders and some clients with the images and the precepts of classical design. Many expensive folios had copper-plate engravings of plans, elevations, sections, and details of large aristocratic palaces, smaller country houses, public buildings, churches, follies, and other buildings as well as many details of chimney pieces, frontispieces, fences, bridges, and other features. These seldom provided examples that American colonists could use given their scale and expense, which was unsuitable for even the wealthiest merchants, professionals, and planters. However, smaller and cheaper publications with illustrations of details of the new classical design vocabulary as well as detailed illustrations of the five orders of classical architecture and essays on mensuration and the layout of construction details such as brick arches and staircases provided much more useful information for colonial craftsmen. In addition, a large number of these pocket editions introduced the terminology of this new language of building. English publications such as William Salmon's *Palladio Londinensis, or the London Art of Building*, which circulated widely in the American colonies in the mid-eighteenth century, offered a glossary that spoke to this overlay of terminology: "Cima-Recta, or Cymaise, from the Greek Kymation, a Wave, called by English Workmen Ogee, which is of two Kinds, viz. Cima Recta, and Cima-Reversa, or the back Ogee, whose Beauty consists in having its Height and Projecture equal to each other" (for more, see "The builder's dictionary," an appendix to Salmon 1738).

Books may have been one way of introducing this new language associated with this style of building, but perhaps far more influential were the thousands of British-trained craftsmen who continued to emigrate to the new world colonies in search of greater opportunities to ply their trades, or as convicts who were often found guilty of petty crimes and transported to the Chesapeake colonies for their transgressions. However they arrived, many brought with them fully developed skills and knowledge of this classical language of architecture, with its accompanying set of rules governing the shape, proportioning, and combination of elements. Cognizant of its growing cachet and the desire among the wealthiest colonists to emulate cosmopolitan tastes, joiners, cabinetmakers, and bricklayers made the self-conscious language and knowledge of Georgian architecture an essential element of their workshops and practice. In 1769, Ezra Waite, "Civil Architect, House-builder in general, and Carver, from London," proclaimed in the newspaper his ability to provide such expertise. He offered proof of his talents and understanding of the intricacies of this system in the tabernacle frames, cornices, architraves, and other enriched or carved woodwork he fabricated for Miles Brewton's house, the costliest and most ornate house erected in Charleston in the years preceding the Revolution. He appealed to men of good taste that "if on inspection of the above mentioned work, and twenty-seven years of experience, both in theory and practice, in noblemen and gentlemen's seats, be sufficient to recommend, he flatters himself to give satisfaction to any gentleman, either by plans, sections, elevations, or executions" (Waite 1769).

However, this wave of fashion, which Waite exemplified and rode full crest, did not wash away the older language and practice of traditional building. Classical cyma and ovolo moldings remained ogees and quarter rounds to the builders who worked on the best churches in Charleston as well as backwoods farmhouses in North Carolina and Delaware. Acknowledging the forms of classical design, the language of building nonetheless remained distinctly vernacular among carpenters and bricklayers in these regions. The precepts of classical design and the terminology in which it was expressed made inroad among cabinetmakers, some joiners, and a few craftsmen like Waite and John Hawks, the architect of Tryon's Palace in New Bern, for whom high fashion created choices of finishes and details that dictated the calling out of explicit design features.

Although the history of design in the southern colonies centers on the introduction and adaptation of academic ideas, the course of that transformation was charted on the construction site and at the workbench. The authority of the drawing board had not trumped practical experience on the building site. Provincial architecture was not a diminished image of metropolitan design ideas, diluted or distorted by rude or ill-trained artisans unable to comprehend the sophistication and complexity of original forms. Rather, southern architecture was selective in nature. Colonists carefully chose those aspects of the metropolitan and academic corpus that suited their own peculiar needs and desires (Upton 1982). Academic design did not displace the local vernacular but became intricately woven into the native building practices, creating distinctive regional forms. Many features of this eighteenth-century academic architecture – rubbed brickwork, hipped roofs, and oval windows – merged with local elements from the previous century so that the great houses, courthouses, and churches constructed in the late colonial period were blends of Anglo-Georgian ideals and creole building customs. Colonial merchants and planters built "double-pile" dwellings but arranged and used their rooms in a manner that diverged from English ways. In Virginia, county courthouses incorporated features borrowed from English public buildings, such as the arcade and cupola, but employed them in such a manner as to devise a unique regional building type (Lounsbury 2005).

Colonial Charleston, Annapolis, Williamsburg, and New Bern were not merely smaller and less lavish reflections of Georgian London. Among other features, open porches or "piazzas," wood shingles, and beaded weatherboards set them apart. Social conditions, levels of wealth, access to materials, technological capabilities, crafts skills, climate, street arrangements, lot sizes, and topography shaped each town's response to building forms. Unlike the production of some domestic goods such as ceramics, fabrics, silver, and even furniture, which served simple functions and were made by one or only a handful of individuals in a few operations, the process of designing, building, and furnishing a house was a complex one involving the participation of dozens of people in various and ever-changing combinations and circumstances. Individual elements such as a window architrave or even more complex pieces such as a manel or a paneled door may show few variations from examples illustrated in imported builders' books, but their execution, treatment, and mixture with other features almost invariably reveal local or regional patterns, which English architectural historians in the late nineteenth century, picking up from its linguistic origins, denominated as "vernacular" in contrast to academic of metropolitan models of classical design (see, e.g., Addy 1898; Johnson 2010). Architectural moldings, balusters, paneled dados, and other Georgian details might attest to the superficial resemblances of dwellings in eighteenth-century Bristol and Charleston, but differences in materials, construction, scale, plans, and the arrangement of buildings in the streetscape made the architectural character of the two ports as distinct as the accents of their inhabitants.

Regional variations remained firmly entrenched in the building process because much of the design and fabrication of buildings was left in the hands of skilled craftsmen. The thousand and one decisions about any building – the finish of a piece of material, the arrangement of the jack arch over an aperture, or the detailing of a staircase – continued to be resolved by joiners, carpenters, and bricklayers on the job site. Although building specifications grew in their list of particulars as clients indicated their choices of treatments and details, many fundamental as well as minor elements were left to the traditional rules governing the execution of workmanlike craftsmanship (see Bishir 1991; Carson and Lounsbury 2013). Contracts may have required good, well-fired bricks and hard lime mortar, but rarely did they specify types of bonding, mortar joint width and finishes, or range of brick colors. It was understood by longstanding experience what was expected and any variation from time-honored practices of a particular city or region required explicit explanation. Thus, the uniformity in color of the brickwork in Charleston in the late colonial period distinguishes it from the characteristic penchant for variegated surfaces in the Chesapeake. Each region had evolved its own standards of practice. While the dimensioning of framing members was frequently included in specifications, less was said about the spacing of studs, posts, joists, and rafters or the types of joints used to secure these elements together. What was not spelled out was left to custom, so that tradition continued to shape the form and finish of most buildings erected in the colonial period.

A hallmark of eighteenth-century southern architecture was the growth in the specialization of building types and room uses. At the beginning of the century, there were a few distinguishing features that differentiated the exterior of a store from a dwelling or a courthouse from a stable. The hull of the same wooden frame could have been used for any of them and the similarity of size, scale, and finish treatment belied any functional differences. Rearrangement of the furniture or moving a partition wall could turn a dwelling into a courthouse or a store into a stable. Gradually, the growth of highly specialized functions requiring specific furniture, spatial arrangements, light, finishes, and details transformed people's perceptions of the nature and form of public, commercial, agricultural, religious, and domestic structures. Courthouses acquired large-scale openings, arcades, and cupolas on their exteriors and specialized fittings for officials on the inside. Store owners constructed buildings with larger apertures or bow windows on the front of the shop but few or no openings alongside walls, which were lined with shelves. Large trade signs hung from shop fronts and long sales counters inside provided additional space for merchants to display their wares to customers. Many fashionable taverns shed their domestic appearance by the construction of an enclosed bar, and their plans accommodated large public entertaining rooms that sometimes rivaled the best merchant houses with their marble chimney pieces and other genteel decorations and furnishings. Churches grew in scale and acquired cupolas and steeples. The architecture of city and countryside became more diversified as specialized functions shaped the form, finish, and materials of many warehouses, schools, exchange, smokehouses, dairies, and kitchens became recognizable building types.

Domestic architecture shared in this growing specialization of spaces as southerners reordered the manner in which they worked, slept, dined, and socialized in their dwellings. In the century before the Revolution, room configurations and uses underwent profound alterations driven by needs for personal privacy and functional segregation. Throughout the seventeenth century and much of the next, most individuals occupied multipurpose, communal living spaces where household activities – entertaining, cooking, eating, sleeping and working – occurred within one or two rooms. The communal nature of these rooms was evident in the nonspecialized goods and furnishings that filled them. Benches, chairs, and tables served many purposes. Owing to the growth of genteel refinement that redefined the rules of personal and public behavior, the advent of a consumer revolution that resulted in the importation or manufacture of thousands of household and personal goods, and changes in the dynamics of familial behavior, there was a growing tendency to rearrange and segregate domestic activity into discrete locations. A new emphasis on entertaining guests away from the daily chores of household work led to the setting aside of rooms for the reception of visitors. Such rooms contained specialized implements and fittings for their entertainment such as new forms of seating furniture, tea sets, and fashionable dining equipage (Carson 2017). To underscore the social importance of the new entertaining spaces, "dining rooms," "drawing rooms," and "saloons" received the best architectural finishes, such as carved chimney pieces, paneled wainscoting, paperhangings, or built-in buffets or "bowfats" in which to display costly china and glass. Mop boards or washboards protected the lower part of plaster walls from damage from the vigorous cleaning of the floors. Other specialized rooms and spaces appeared to contain separate activities such as a library or nursery, or to segregate visitors and servants from members of the family such as the passage and servants' hall. With the growing concern for individual space, the number of bedchambers in large houses began to increase (Wenger 1986, 1989). As in other spheres, these changes in the dynamics of domestic life spawned a wealth of new terms and names for rooms. Although English terminology often provided the precedent, southerners appropriated them to describe their own peculiar circumstances. In Delaware and parts of Maryland in the eighteenth and nineteenth centuries, a building or a room where food was prepared was sometimes referred to as a "cookhouse" or "cook room." The term seems to have gained currency when kitchens became detached from the main dwelling house. In the late seventeenth century onward, a "cuddy" in Virginia and perhaps elsewhere referred to a small closet or a cupboard for the storage of miscellaneous goods.

In the decades following the Revolution, bookish men such as Thomas Jefferson and a rising generation of professional architects led by Benjamin Henry Latrobe, Robert Mills, and William Nichols attempted to move building to a level of self-conscious complexity and refinement that required a degree of specificity previously unseen. These men saw buildings as exemplars of taste and in their view the South along with the rest of the new nation had few monuments worthy of its political and cultural aspirations. What they saw as ill-proportioned public buildings and unassuming dwellings exposed a wide gulf between the ideals and the traditional. Jefferson was a harsh judge of the older forms. In *Notes on the state of Virginia* (1785), his criticism of the second capitol in Williamsburg (1752–53) expressed this dissatisfaction. The two-story building was "a light and airy structure, with a portico in front of two orders, the lower of which, being Doric, is tolerably just in its proportions and ornaments, save only that the intercolumnations are too large. The upper Ionic is much too small for that on which it is mounted, its ornaments not proper to the order, nor proportioned within themselves. It is crowned with a pediment, which is too large for its span. Yet on the whole, it is the most pleasing piece of architecture we have" (Jefferson 1955[1785]). The harmony was in the details, and anything that failed to measure up to such rigorous standards was repudiated as naïve at best and barbaric at worst.

In his travels throughout the upper South, Latrobe observed numerous examples of the misapplication of classical detailing and took time to sketch an improperly designed Tuscan entablature on the Loudoun County courthouse in Leesburg, Virginia. A few builders and carpenters recognized and understood these new rules of classical scholarship, but the accompanying grammar was scarcely evident in their designs or in the contractual language that described their work. Although terms such as "caulicole," "gutta," "intercolumniation," "list," "module," "parastata," "peripteral," and "socle" had been used and illustrated in English architectural books that had been imported into the English colonies since the second quarter of the eighteenth century, few builders, besides the English émigré John Hawks in New Bern in his design of Governor William Tryon's palace, tried to apply the rules and employ the terms of classical architecture to the world of building design. Jefferson was one of the first native designers to grasp the nuances of proportioning and detailing inherent in this system and tried to impose order on the orders in the South. A self-taught pedant, he maintained that his source of architectural guidance was Andrea Palladio's (1570) *Four books of architecture*, going so far as to declare to one contemporary who sought his advice about building, that it "was the Bible. You should get it & stick close to it" (Jefferson 2012). His understanding of this arcane knowledge was embodied and expressed in his use of this specialized language.

Older vernacular ways of conveying information no longer suited these heralds of sophisticated international design. In the state capitol in Richmond and in the nation's capitol in Washington, Jefferson, and Latrobe invoked design sources that stood well beyond the local or even regional building tradition. Professional architects left little to chance as contracts called for builders and craftsmen to follow the specific designs and detailed working drawings (Bishir et al. 1990; Carson and Lounsbury 2013). Through their efforts, the architect's drawing was beginning to dislodge the job site methods of the carpenter's rule as the arbiter of form. Relaxed attitudes toward classical proportioning had no place in the world where capitals and entablatures were based on specific classical examples that had been measured and drawn in painstaking detail. Latrobe and the growing coterie of professional architects soon expanded the southern architectural vocabulary. However, in so doing, these practitioners built on a vast sub-structure of traditional terms that reflected a solidly rooted vernacular building process, one that would flourish well into the nineteenth century.

## References

Addy, S. O. 1898. *The evolution of the English house*. London: Swan Sonneschein.
Bagenal, Hope. Collection of Local Building Terms. *Vernacular Architecture*. 1970. 1 (16).
Bishir, Catherine. 1991. Good and sufficient building. In Thomas Carter & Bernard Herman (eds.), *Perspectives in vernacular architecture, IV*, 44–52. Columbia: University of Missouri Press.
Bishir, Catherine W., Charlotte V. Brown, Carl R. Lounsbury & Ernest H. Wood III. 1990. *Architects and builders in North Carolina: A history of the practice of building*. Chapel Hill: University of North Carolina Press.
Carson, Cary. 2017. *Face value: The consumer revolution and the colonizing of America*. Charlottesville: University of Virginia Press.
Carson, Cary & Carl Lounsbury (eds.). 2013. *The Chesapeake House: Architectural investigation by Colonial Williamsburg*. Chapel Hill: University of North Carolina Press.
Cook, John (ed.). 1984. *The wainscot book: The houses of Winchester Cathedral Close and their interior decoration, 1660–1800*. Winchester: Hampshire County Council.
Jefferson, Thomas. 1955[1785]. *Notes on the state of Virginia*, ed. by W. Peden. Chapel Hill: University of North Carolina Press.
Jefferson, Thomas. 2012. *The Papers of Thomas Jefferson, September 1815 to April 1816*. Ed. by J. Jefferson Looney. Princeton: Princeton University Press.
Johnson, Matthew. 2010. *English houses 1300–1800: Vernacular architecture, social life*. Essex, UK: Pearson Education Limited.
Lounsbury, Carl. 1999 [1994]. *An illustrated glossary of early southern architecture and landscape*. New York: Oxford University Press; reprint Charlottesville: University of Virginia Press.
Lounsbury, Carl. 2005. *The courthouses of early Virginia: An architectural history*. Charlottesville: University of Virginia Press, 2005.
Lounsbury, Carl. 2010. Log building in the Chesapeake. *Vernacular Architecture* 41. 77–82.
Lounsbury, Carl. 2011. *Essays in early American architectural history: A view from the Chesapeake*. Charlottesville: University of Virginia Press.
Salmon, William. 1738. *Palladio Londinensis, or the London Art of Building*, 2nd edn. London: A. Ward.
Salzman, L. F. 1952. *Buildings in England down to 1540: A documentary history*. Oxford: Clarendon Press.
Upton, Dell. 1982. Vernacular domestic architecture in eighteenth-century Virginia. *Winterthur Portfolio* 17. 95–119. *Vernacular Architecture*. 1970. 1 (16).

Waite, Ezra. 1769. *South Carolina Gazette and Country Journal*, August 22.
Wenger, Mark R. 1986. The central passage in Virginia: Evolution of an eighteenth-century living space. In Camille Wells (ed.), *Perspectives in vernacular architecture, II*, 137–149. Columbia: University of Missouri Press.
Wenger, Mark R. 1989. The dining room in early Virginia. In Thomas Carter & Bernard Herman (eds.), *Perspectives in vernacular architecture, III*, 149–159. Columbia: University of Missouri Press.

Mark Richard Lauersdorf
# Chapter 14
# Historical sociolinguistics and the necessity of interdisciplinary collaboration

## 1 Introduction

This chapter presents a broad foundational notion of interdisciplinarity in historical sociolinguistics and an argument for increased implementation of true interdisciplinary collaboration in the field in order to achieve a greater level of insight and a more profound understanding of the data and its contexts. It is also proposed that we must continue to pursue this broader interdisciplinary collaboration as a regular part of the baseline conversations and training, and as a standard feature in the general practice of the discipline of historical sociolinguistics in order to bring the field forward.

## 2 Some background for the discussion

Before laying out the arguments for considering a broader scope of disciplines and increased interdisciplinary collaboration in historical sociolinguistics, it is necessary to review the notion of historical sociolinguistics as a multidisciplinary field of investigation and establish a definition of interdisciplinary research as background information for the ensuing discussion.

### 2.1 Historical sociolinguistics as a multidisciplinary field

The field of historical sociolinguistics and its research objectives have been defined variously:

> to investigate and provide an account of the forms and uses in which variation may manifest itself in a given speech community over time, and how particular functions, uses and kinds of variation develop within particular languages, speech communities, social groups, networks and individuals; (Romaine 1988: 1453)

---

**Mark Richard Lauersdorf,** University of Kentucky, lauersdorf@uky.edu

https://doi.org/10.1515/9781501514371-014

> a broader definition of historical sociolinguistics as "the reconstruction of the history of a given language in its socio-cultural context" is, in its simplicity, far more inclusive;
> (Conde-Silvestre and Hernández-Campoy 2012: 1)

> historical sociolinguistics *par excellence* aims to study [historical] language use, as produced by individual language users, embedded in the social context in which these language users operate, and understood not only from a communicative angle but also as conscious or unconscious acts of identity and social distinction; (Auer et al. 2015: 9)

> the application/development of sociolinguistic theories, models, and methods for the study of historical language variation and change over time, or more broadly, the study of the interaction of language and society in historical periods and from historical perspectives. (North American Research Network in Historical Sociolinguistics [NARNiHS] http://narnihs.org/?page_id=226 – accessed 28 August 2020)

For their differences, what is common across all of these definitions is the inclusion of three principal elements: the linguistic, the historical, and the social; and here, already, we see one part of the intent behind the title of this chapter – historical sociolinguistics *inherently* involves multiple fields of inquiry as an area of linguistic investigation.

Discussions of the multidisciplinary nature of the field of historical sociolinguistics are mostly found in general overview articles and chapters describing in broad terms the scope, emphasis, and goals of the field. Thus, such descriptions of multidisciplinarity in historical sociolinguistics have tended to focus primarily on the interconnections between the linguistic subfields that are immediately illustrated in its name – historical linguistics and sociolinguistics (in their various permutations) – in addition to the obvious connections to the field of history, specifically social history. This focus on a set of primary fields is usually supplemented by a brief account of additional linguistic fields variously connected to historical sociolinguistics and some examples of additional non-linguistic fields that inform historical sociolinguistic research:

> a variety of perspectives are needed to enrich our understanding of the past, and relevant innovative models and methods are also being developed in other, non-history disciplines. [. . .] Figure 2.1[1] connects historical sociolinguistics with its neighboring fields in more specific terms. These associated fields range from humanities and social science

---

1 The "Figure 2.1" in question places the field of historical sociolinguistics in the center of a circular array of the "neighboring fields" of (listed here in clockwise order from the top of the circular array): sociolinguistics, dialectology, sociopragmatics, discourse studies, philology, corpus linguistics, histories of individual languages, historical linguistics, and social history, with each of these "neighboring fields" annotated with examples of areas of investigation within the field, e.g., sociolinguistics: language sociology, social dialectology, interactional sociolinguistics; or

disciplines to methodological specializations such as corpus linguistics. [. . .] Other sub-disciplines could also have been included, such as cognitive linguistics, while some exert their influence through several fields listed. Sociology, for example, informs not only sociolinguistics and sociopragmatics but also, to the extent that they are always distinguishable, social history and historical sociology;

(Nevalainen and Raumolin-Brunberg 2012: 26–27)

it is clear that historical sociolinguistics is by its very nature a multidisciplinary endeavor, drawing heavily on advances in social and cultural history, philology and paleography, corpus linguistics and modern day sociolinguistics, as well as sociology and social psychology – even more so than in more traditional approaches to historical linguistics. The collaboration with historians sharing a similar interest in the social and identificatory functions of language holds particular potential; (Auer et al. 2015: 8)

This implies combining "methods from the rich philological tradition of textual interpretation with recent work within the field of quantitative sociolinguistics and the study of literacy, discourse and pragmatics" (Romaine 2005: 1697), as well as adopting a variety of paradigms and research orientations which renders historical sociolinguistics an inherently inter- and cross-disciplinary field, which according to Bergs (2005: 8–9) is hybrid in nature and lies at the intersection of linguistics, social sciences, and history. The numerous (sub-)disciplines from which historical sociolinguists can draw constructive inspiration and helpful analytical tools would then include philology, paleography, discourse and genre studies, literacy studies, social history and cultural history, corpus linguistics, modern sociolinguistics, sociology and social psychology. (Russi 2016: 6)

Within this same genre of overviews of the field, Bergs (2005, chapter 2), presents perhaps the most extensive discussion of the inherent multidisciplinarity of the field and the implications of that multidisciplinarity for how historical sociolinguistic research is performed. He considers that "historical sociolinguistics (J. Milroy 1992a) or socio-historical linguistics (Romaine 1982b) is to be found at the intersection not of two, but of three different fields: *history*, *social sciences*, and *linguistics*" (2005: 12); where "*social sciences* is to be understood as a short-hand form that subsumes an open list of different disciplines such as anthropology, psychology, sociology, gender studies, cultural studies, economics, geography, and politics" (2005: 8). In his extended discussion (2005: 8–21), Bergs explores the ramifications of working at that intersection of three different fields, coming to the conclusion that "as such, [historical sociolinguistics] not only has to incorporate theories, practices, and paradigms from all three fields, but it also has to struggle with and in conflicts that originate in all three areas" (2005: 12). As might be anticipated by the nature of the genre,

---

social history: demographic and economic history, family history, gender relations, cultural history (Nevalainen and Raumolin-Brunberg 2012: 27).

such overview treatments generally do not go more broadly or deeply into these issues except to illustrate specific points of argument, or in application to specific aspects of individual case studies or investigations. What is generally missing in all of this, and what this chapter seeks to undertake, is a more thorough discussion of the inherent multidisciplinarity of historical sociolinguistics, focusing on a fuller scope of that multidisciplinarity, and on how creating an enhanced ethos of broad interdisciplinary collaboration among practitioners of historical sociolinguistics has the potential to maximize future outcomes of research in the field.

## 2.2 Disciplinary borrowing, multidisciplinary research, interdisciplinary research

I have thus far been using the term *(inherently) multidisciplinary* to describe the field of historical sociolinguistics. The intended sense of that term, in that usage in this chapter, is simply the general idea that there are multiple fields that come together in historical sociolinguistics that can be identified as established individual academic disciplines/fields unto themselves – at a minimum: historical linguistics, sociolinguistics, and (social) history (and, as will be discussed below, ideally many more). However, the term multidisciplinary, when discussed in the context of research practice (i.e., *multidisciplinary research*) has a specific meaning, especially when contrasted with the term *interdisciplinary research*. In this context, it is also necessary to discuss the related notion of *disciplinary borrowing*.

For the remainder of this chapter, we will operate with the definitions/concepts of *disciplinary borrowing, multidisciplinary research*, and *interdisciplinary research* as put forth in the report *Facilitating interdisciplinary research* (Institute of Medicine 2005):[2]

> *[b]orrowing* describes the use of one discipline's methods, skills, or theories in a different discipline. A borrowed technique may be assimilated so completely that it is no longer considered foreign, and it may transform practice without being considered interdisciplinary. An example of borrowing is the use of physical-science methods in biologic research, such as electron microscopy, x-ray crystallography, and spectroscopy. Such borrowing may be so extensive that the origin of the technique is obscured; (p. 27)[3]

---

[2] For further discussion of these terminological and conceptual differences in the broader context of the full field of linguistics, see Childs (this volume).
[3] In giving this definition, the report references: Klein (2000); Holton, Chang, and Jurkowitz (1996).

*multidisciplinary research* is taken to mean research that involves more than a single discipline in which each discipline makes a separate contribution. Investigators may share facilities and research approaches while working separately on distinct aspects of a problem. For example, an archaeological program might require the participation of a geologist in a role that is primarily supportive. Multidisciplinary research often refers to efforts that are additive but not necessarily integrative; (pp. 27, 29)[4]

Interdisciplinary research (IDR) is a mode of research by teams or individuals that integrates information, data, techniques, tools, perspectives, concepts, and/or theories from two or more disciplines or bodies of specialized knowledge to advance fundamental understanding or to solve problems whose solutions are beyond the scope of a single discipline or field of research practice. Research is truly interdisciplinary when it is not just pasting two disciplines together to create one product but rather is an integration and synthesis of ideas and methods. An example is the current exploration of string theory by theoretical physicists and mathematicians, in which the questions posed have brought fundamental new insights both to mathematicians and to physicists. (pp. 26–27)

Emphasizing the coming together of disciplines in a synthetic fashion in interdisciplinary versus multidisciplinary research, the report further states (as annotations to a graphic illustration visually demonstrating the differences):
- "Multidisciplinary: Join together to work on common problem, split apart unchanged when work is done" (p. 29).
- "Interdisciplinary: Join together to work on common question or problem. Interaction may forge a new research field or discipline" (p. 29).

Put yet another way that further emphasizes the synthesizing, integrative nature of interdisciplinary research versus the combinatory, additive nature of multidisciplinary research:

Whereas, multidisciplinary research combines two or more disciplinary perspectives, the cooperating experts speak as separate voices each from within their own specialism. [. . .] interdisciplinary collaboration is considered to integrate approaches, methods and theories from different scientific disciplines to solve complex scientific problems, which may over time lead to the creation of new scientific fields, such as biochemistry, neuroscience or environmental humanities.[5] (Budtz Pedersen 2016: 5)

---

**4** In giving this definition, the report references: Friedman and Friedman (1985); Porter and Rossini (1986); Klein (1990).
**5** Budtz Pedersen cites Klein (2010), Stokols et al. (2003), and Wagner et al. (2011) as sources for these distinctions.

## 3 Disciplinary borrowing, multidisciplinary research, interdisciplinary research, and historical sociolinguistics

Given the discussion above concerning the inherent multidisciplinarity of historical sociolinguistics and the three different ways of incorporating input from multiple disciplines in cross-disciplinary research, a closer look is warranted at the way in which historical sociolinguistics draws on its multiple disciplinary sources and implements them in its research paradigms.

### 3.1 Disciplinary borrowing, multidisciplinary research, and historical sociolinguistics

In the implementation of theories, models, methods, tools, data, and information from other disciplines, work in the field of historical sociolinguistics has, in the past, exhibited primarily two of the three types of cross-disciplinary work defined above: *disciplinary borrowing* and *multidisciplinary research*. As examples of disciplinary borrowing in the realm of theory/model/method, one might consider the use of uniformitarianism (from geology),[6] or the founder principle/founder effect (from biology),[7] or social network analysis (from sociology)[8] in historical sociolinguistic work, each of these borrowings having been "assimilated" to a large degree into historical sociolinguistic practice and hence "no longer considered foreign."[9] As illustrations of multidisciplinary research by historical sociolinguists engaged with scholars of other disciplines in the pursuit of common questions/problems and the generation of tools, data, and information, one might look to the project that resulted in the *Records of the Salem witch-hunt* (Rosenthal et al. 2009), involving linguists, historians, and archivists in a full and rich accounting of the textual evidence behind the

---

6 For an exhaustive treatment of the concept and its deployment in historical linguistics, see Janda and Joseph (2003: 23–37). See Bergs (2012) for a discussion of the uniformitarian principle in historical sociolinguistic research.
7 For an initial application of the founder principle to creole genesis, see Mufwene (1996).
8 See Milroy (1980) and Milroy and Milroy (1985) for early explicit adoption of the principles of social network structures in linguistics. For an in-depth discussion of the use of social network analysis in historical sociolinguistic investigation, see Bergs (2005).
9 Though textbooks (and some other treatments) will still often discuss the disciplinary origins of these concepts.

historical period in question, or the digital history project, *The Old Bailey proceedings online* (Hitchcock et al. 2012), and its linguistic derivative, the *Old Bailey corpus* (Huber, Nissel, and Puga 2016), now considered "one of the largest diachronic collections of spoken English with detailed utterance-level sociolinguistic annotation" and thus a major resource "for fine-tuned, multivariate studies, including historical sociolinguistic approaches" (https://fedora.clarin-d.uni-saarland.de/oldbailey/ – accessed 28 August 2020).

In the examples provided (meant to be illustrative and by no means exhaustive), we can clearly see the basic characteristics of disciplinary borrowing as described in 1.2 above: "[a] borrowed technique may be assimilated so completely that it is no longer considered foreign, and it may transform practice without being considered interdisciplinary. [. . .] Such borrowing may be so extensive that the origin of the technique is obscured"; and we can recognize the core traits of multidisciplinary research: "research that involves more than a single discipline in which each discipline makes a separate contribution"; "working separately on distinct aspects of a problem"; undertaking "efforts that are additive but not necessarily integrative." Interestingly, the commonness in linguistics of specifically multidisciplinary research practice has been investigated and substantiated empirically (at least within a specific community of linguists) with the finding that:

> Researchers belonging to a well-established discipline with a strong consensus on basic principles, traditions and career structures (such as *linguistics*, classics and historiography) engage mostly in *multidisciplinary collaboration* in which they cooperate with researchers from other established disciplines. Here, collaboration is structured around a division of cognitive labour, with different disciplines taking responsibility over different steps and components in the research process.
>
> (Budtz Pedersen 2016: 5, emphasis mine)[10]

All of this is not to say, however, that *all* cross-disciplinary work in historical sociolinguistics is built on disciplinary borrowing and multidisciplinary research, and that synthesizing, integrative *interdisciplinary* research is not to be found in the field.

---

**10** Budtz Pedersen provides the following description of the investigation that arrived at the quoted conclusion: "To gain more insight into the nature of interdisciplinary collaboration, the Humanomics Research Centre in Copenhagen has carried out a survey of attitudes towards interdisciplinary research among 1100 Danish humanities scholars. We looked at different strategies for engaging in interdisciplinary research, as well as different modes of interdisciplinary research to identify barriers and possibilities for collaboration (Budtz Pedersen and Stjernfelt 2016)" (2016: 5).

## 3.2 *Internal* interdisciplinary research and historical sociolinguistics

Taking a specific reading of our definition of interdisciplinary research as "a mode of research by [. . .] *individuals* that integrates information, data, techniques, tools, perspectives, concepts, and/or theories from two or more [. . .] *bodies of specialized knowledge* to advance fundamental understanding or to solve problems whose solutions are beyond the scope of a single [. . .] *field* of research practice" (Institute of Medicine 2005: 26, emphasis mine), we could say that any individual scholar who has undergone sufficient training in two or more of the linguistic fields commonly associated with historical sociolinguistics (section 1.1) is equipped to perform interdisciplinary research. Put another way, it can be argued that *individual* historical sociolinguists, by the very nature of their training in historical linguistics and sociolinguistics (and perhaps other linguistic areas), and their research practice employing their training in those multiple linguistic areas, are automatically always engaged in interdisciplinary research.

Indeed, the report *Facilitating interdisciplinary research* includes the additional factor of "mode of participation" in its consideration of interdisciplinary research (IDR), and this includes the "mode" of the "individual participant":

> IDR can also be described in terms of *modes* of participation. In one mode an *individual* investigator masters and integrates several fields. The investigator may conceive a new problem or method or may venture far enough from his or her original discipline to create a new field. For example, Albert Einstein ventured from his field of physics into Riemann geometry to describe his new General Theory of Relativity.
>
> (Institute of Medicine 2005: 29, emphasis mine)

But this is where the present discussion aspires to go beyond the already established[11] notion of the internal interdisciplinarity of historical sociolinguistics (i.e., that historical sociolinguistics is interdisciplinary in drawing on multiple areas in linguistics), and beyond the types of cross-disciplinary work seen in disciplinary borrowing and multidisciplinary research, and also (and especially) beyond the notion of the individual historical sociolinguist as inherently practicing interdisciplinary research as an individual researcher.

---

11 See the treatment of the multidisciplinarity of historical sociolinguistics in the overview articles mentioned in section 1.1.

# 4 The necessity of interdisciplinary *collaboration* in historical sociolinguistics

The quote presented above concerning "modes" of interdisciplinary research continues as follows:

> In a second mode, a *group of investigators, each with mastery in one field*, learn to communicate and *collaborate* on a single problem. In some cases, such groups may be quite large, as in high-energy physics and genomics research.
> (Institute of Medicine 2005: 29, emphasis mine)

It is this mode of interdisciplinary *collaboration*, involving *teams* of individual experts, that will be emphasized in the remainder of this chapter as a desideratum for advancing research in the field of historical sociolinguistics in the future.

## 4.1 Use all the data! – the necessity of the *team*

I have made the case elsewhere for an overarching *modus operandi* in historical sociolinguistic research that is based on a call to "use all the data!" (Lauersdorf 2018a, b). This stance involves the following principles (2018b: 211–212):[12]

(1) Identify all possible sources of language data – data may be "hiding" where you don't expect it, in unexplored physical locations and in unexplored textual locations.
(2) Consult the entirety of the language data available to you – avoid selective sampling (inclusion or exclusion) of language data on the basis of *a priori* notions of what kind of data you need, how much data you need, where it should come from, etc.
(3) Language data isn't the only data – use all the socio-historical data!
   (a) Identify and use all possible sources of socio-historical data (again being on the lookout for socio-historical data "hidden" in unexpected

---

[12] Compare with Janda and Joseph's "informational maximalism": "To a great extent, then, what we should really strive for, in diachronic pursuits such as historical linguistics, is what could be called 'informational maximalism' – that is, the utilization of all reasonable means to extend our knowledge of what might have been going on in the past, even though it is not directly observable. Normally, this will involve a heavy concentration on the immediate present, but it is in fact more realistic just to say that we wish to gain a maximum of information from a maximum of potential sources: different times and different places – and, in the case of language, also different regional and social dialects, different contexts, different styles, different topics, and so on and so forth" (2003: 37).

places and using the entirety of the socio-historical data available to you).
(b) We only have the language data that history leaves us (what has "survived" through time), so wrap the language data in all possible socio-historical datasets to help complete the picture.

These principles also include a set of corollaries, formulated originally in regard to data visualization (Lauersdorf 2018a: 112), but proposed here as necessary for all data analysis in historical sociolinguistics in general:

Corollary 1: If you use all the data, *view* all the data.
    (a) If you view all the data, view all the *combinations*.
    (b) If you view all the data, view all the *angles*.
    (c) If you view all the data, use all the *techniques*.

This call to "use all the data!" in historical sociolinguistic investigation derives, in part, from the so-called "bad data problem", noted by Labov in his statement that "[h]istorical linguistics can [. . .] be thought of as the art of making the best use of bad data" (1994: 11), and now often re-cast as a problem of "imperfect" data (Janda and Joseph 2003: 14), or "making the best use of the data available" (Nevalainen and Raumolin-Brunberg 2017: 26). Given that the available data for historical sociolinguistics is "imperfect" (i.e., limited, fragmentary, or incomplete), it is imperative to gather as much of it as possible for a given investigation, from all interrelated sources, linguistic and socio-historical. Additionally, the calls to "use all the data!" and "view all the data!" also derive from the conviction that using a selective sample and/or selective methods of analysis of the available data (based on *a priori* assumptions about the features and categories that one should expect to find in the data) limits what one is actually able to find, given that portions of the data are not being considered and that only certain analytical viewpoints are being entertained.[13]

If one subscribes to the principles and corollaries of the investigative frame of "use all the data!", this has direct implications for the conception of interdisciplinary research in historical sociolinguistics. It takes interdisciplinary research beyond individual scholars and linguistics-internal interdisciplinarity, increasing the need for a true *collaborative interdisciplinary team* from an increasingly

---

[13] If this sounds to the reader like a call for more *data-driven* work in historical sociolinguistics, that would be an accurate interpretation, and while the scope of this chapter does not allow for further elaboration in that direction, I have issued just such a call elsewhere (see Lauersdorf 2018b).

large number of fields to effectively implement the work, as no "individual investigator" can fully and effectively "master and integrate several fields" (Institute of Medicine 2005: 29) when the task is to find and consider all the data, both linguistic and socio-historical, in all its combinations and angles, using a full range of techniques/methods.

## 4.2 Broadening the conversation – the necessity of *more positions* on the team

Taking it as a given that historical sociolinguistics has linguistic-internal ties in at least all of the previously mentioned directions: sociolinguistics, dialectology, socio-pragmatics, discourse studies, philology, corpus linguistics, histories of individual languages, historical linguistics, paleography, cognitive linguistics,[14] the discussion turns here to *non*-linguistic collaboration. With the understanding that the field of historical sociolinguistics involves, at a required minimum, *historical* linguistics and *socio*linguistics, it is easy to see how the non-linguistic collaborative team has traditionally included, at the very least, *social/cultural historians*; indeed, this has been the most utilized point of non-linguistic collaboration in work done in the recent decades of expansion of the field. As stated by Auer et al.:

> Aiming to move beyond a socially informed historical linguistics or a historically informed sociolinguistics, the goal of many historical sociolinguists has always been to contribute to a *social history* of language (cf. Burke 2004, Burke 2005). As such, the field has a lot to gain from *interactions with colleagues in social or cultural history*, as can be seen from a number of multidisciplinary conferences, workshops and publications over the past years (e.g. Langer et al. 2012). (2015: 9, emphasis mine)[15]

---

[14] Clearly this list is not exhaustive of the full range of linguistic-internal connections that can and should be made, depending on the historical sociolinguistic research questions being posed. As examples of possible additions, one can consider anthropological linguistics, sociophonetics, or, indeed, any part of the formal core of linguistics, from phonetics through semantics, that can provide theoretical and descriptive insights on the structural variation and change observed historically.

[15] I would contend, though, that many of these "multidisciplinary conferences, workshops and publications" have been in the realm of multidisciplinary research "in which each discipline makes a separate contribution" and where "[i]nvestigators [. . .] [are] working separately on distinct aspects of a problem" (Institute of Medicine 2005: 27), rather than being examples of interdisciplinary research where "it is not just pasting two disciplines together to create one product but rather is an integration and synthesis of ideas and methods" (Institute of Medicine 2005: 27).

And that has been a fruitful and productive starting point. But, if one considers the social factors that are customarily cited as influential in language variation and that are studied in both present-day and historical contexts – age, ethnicity, gender, region, and social status – it then becomes necessary to also consider adding a place on the historical sociolinguistics research team for cultural/social anthropologists, ethnologists, gender-studies specialists, cultural/social/human geographers, sociologists, and political scientists, in all cases both theoretically and historically oriented.[16]

At this point it is highly likely that, while it is perhaps enlightening for colleagues from other linguistic fields or from outside of linguistics, much of the foregoing discussion of interdisciplinary connections is probably not notionally new for most researchers in the field of historical sociolinguistics. But I would like to turn now to the "use all the data!" principles cited in section 3.1 as the stimulus for further, potentially less-common considerations of necessary team members for historical sociolinguistic research, beginning with the first principle: "Identify all possible sources of language data". In the search for "data [that] may be 'hiding' where you don't expect it, in unexplored physical locations and in unexplored textual locations", it is indispensable to enlist the collaborative assistance of special collections librarians, museum curators, and archivists. Not only do they have a strong overview of their document collections and can thus readily supply us with the historical textual data that we are looking for, but, given the intimate specialist knowledge that they bring from their positions and their collections, they are also often aware of documents and text types, both directly and indirectly related to the parameters of our research questions, that are not even on our source lists and that we have possibly never even considered. And, perhaps even more importantly, special collections librarians, museum curators, and archivists are the ones who wrap the socio-historical meta-data around the textual and other elements that they curate, which speaks directly to principles 3a) "Identify and use all possible sources of socio-historical data" and 3b) "wrap the language data in all possible socio-historical datasets": because of the interconnectedness of socio-historical meta-data throughout library and museum collections, these library and museum specialists are strategically positioned to collaborate on the discovery and

---

[16] At the risk of sounding repetitive, it bears mentioning, once again, that this is not intended to be an exhaustive list. A given research question in historical sociolinguistics may further benefit from collaboration with (socio)economists, social psychologists, researchers in the history of science, law, and education, religious studies specialists, and any of an entire range of disciplinary expertises that would help interpret specific aspects of human social interaction in the past.

incorporation of additional "socio-historical data 'hidden' in unexpected places" (principle 3a), such as the information that is extractable from materials with little or no running text but with a wealth of correlatable socio-historical content, e.g., government records (census, immigration, judicial, surveyor), church records (baptism, marriage, death), photographic or other pictorial representations, and many other items that, once again, we may not even be aware of.[17] Of course, as the collection of materials gathered (both linguistic and socio-historical) increases in diversity, it is necessary to keep in mind several more points of collaboration that have long been utilized in historical sociolinguistics by adding members to the team from genre studies and literacy studies (mentioned by Russi 2016: 6 above), as well as experts in public records.

Using all the data and viewing all the data (in "all the combinations" and "all the angles" using "all the techniques" – corollaries 1a-c), also brings into sharp focus the need to consider questions of computational processing, and statistical and visualization methods of data analysis. It has become commonplace in historical sociolinguistics to work with digital corpora of source texts, and there is also a growing awareness of the need for digital preparation of the socio-historical data in a way that it can be analyzed interactively with the textual corpora. As these digital datasets, both linguistic and socio-historical, grow in size and sophistication, the computational complexity involved in using and viewing "all the data" increases; and thus the need also increases for collaborators on the historical sociolinguistic team who can address the specific challenges involved in "big data" analysis.[18] For this, we call on colleagues in information science, computer science, informatics, statistics, i.e., the specialists in data modelling, algorithms, text mining, quantitative analysis, statistical measures, and data visualization, not to mention computing architecture, to handle the tasks of using and viewing all the data at a "big data" scale.

As we close this discussion on increasing the scope of the team in order to broaden our interdisciplinary conversations, it bears repeating that we are discussing this in the frame of true interdisciplinary collaboration. The important notion to take away from this section is that, as we strive to build on the current

---

**17** As examples of work in historical sociolinguistics that takes into account the types of records described here, where there is little-to-no running text but nevertheless a wealth of correlatable socio-historical information, consider Wilkerson and Salmons (2008); Bousquette and Ehresmann (2010); Wilkerson and Salmons (2012).
**18** Detailed discussion of the complexities of undertaking analysis of "big data" exceeds the scope of this chapter. Among the many early baseline discussions of the problems and potential in big data analytics see, for example, Keim et al. (2012); Zhang et al. (2012); Fan, Han, and Liu (2014); Gandomi and Haider (2015); Tsai et al. (2015).

interdisciplinary successes of the field, we can increase and enhance the potential for innovation and new discoveries if the additional members that we add to the historical sociolinguistics research team are incorporated as true collaborators, engaging with us in interdisciplinary research that "integrates information, data, techniques, tools, perspectives, concepts, and/or theories from two or more disciplines or bodies of specialized knowledge to advance fundamental understanding or to solve problems whose solutions are beyond the scope of a single discipline or field of research practice" (Institute of Medicine 2005: 26). Such synthesizing, integrative work seeks to overcome "the fact that different disciplines work with different theoretical languages that incorporate different epistemic goals and strategies" (Budtz Pedersen 2016: 4) and attempts to create shared conceptual spaces, forging common theoretical frameworks, research strategies, and goals. But that would be hard, wouldn't it?

## 4.3 Collaboration is hard

As the scientific trend toward larger-scale interdisciplinary research collaboration progresses from the bench sciences to the social sciences and humanities, an increasingly large number of studies are appearing regarding the mechanisms, processes, practices, and limitations of true interdisciplinary collaboration in the humanities and social sciences, investigating the factors in effective collaboration, from individual predisposition and training, to research cultures in individual disciplines, to institutional infrastructures, to funding mechanisms.[19] Given that the success of interdisciplinary collaboration, and the identification of its problems and its benefits, ultimately has implications for both institutional and funding policies and infrastructures, much of the research into facilitating true interdisciplinary collaboration has come from the fields of policy studies and education management/administration. Regardless of the impetus behind the studies, in the end, the conclusion regarding interdisciplinary collaborative research, especially in the humanities and social sciences, is that true interdisciplinary collaboration, while desirable, is hard:

> [Interdisciplinarity is] a process that does not work automatically or only through its structure. Interdisciplinarity must be acquired, it does not arise magically, even if the term is often used today as a magic word. Inter- and transdisciplinary processes and

---

**19** See, for example, Jeffrey (2003); van Rijnsoever and Hessels (2011); Lewis, Ross, and Holden (2012); Bozeman et al. (2016); Lewis, Letina, and Woelert (2016); Green et al. (2017); Iglič et al. (2017); Lewis (2017); as well as the many references cited in each of these.

structures must be constantly scrutinized, specifically with regard to the friction losses that are inevitable in translating between disciplines, languages, and cultures. Just as two particles dissolved in water first have to change, strip off, and rebuild their protective hydration shells in order to interact with one another, administrative structures, academic practices, and personal prejudices often interfere in interdisciplinary processes before the principle actors even come into play. (Folkers 2010: 33, translation mine)[20]

Indeed, some argue that the (infra)structures and practices that have developed historically, specifically in the humanities, might prove to be a thicker "protective shell" that is more difficult to "change, strip off, and rebuild" than in other disciplines:

> Where the sciences often rely on research laboratories where students and other collaborators work together, the "laboratory" of the humanist scholar has usually been the physical or digital library or archive (Barrett 2005; Goodrich-Jones 1995;[21] Stone 1982; Wiberley & Jones 1989). Thus, the work of humanists tends to be solitary, consisting primarily of reading and writing (Stone 1982). Although humanists, like other scholars, meet at conferences and frequently exchange information and ideas about their work with colleagues (Ross, Terras, Warwick, & Welsh 2011), they are usually less inclined to engage in close collaborations. That is, most publishing, data analysis, and grant writing in the humanities is still single- or dual-authored (Larivière, Gingras, & Archambault 2006). Although there has been much optimism about how the collaborative model could be applied to the humanities to increase information flow, co-publishing, and innovation, few studies have actually observed the extent to which such networks are successful in practice (Chuk, Hoetzlein, Kim, & Panko 2012; McGrath 2011). (Quan-Haase, Suarez, & Brown 2015: 566)

However, it is not just the disciplinary area of the humanities that is potentially disadvantaged in its pursuit of interdisciplinary collaboration. Evidence suggests that the overall setting of academia exacerbates the constraints already in place on interdisciplinary collaboration regardless of the discipline:

> Interdisciplinarity has long been accepted and familiar in many industrial and government laboratories and other nonacademic settings; such settings traditionally emphasize teams and problem-driven research, and they permit researchers to move easily between laboratories, to share their skills, and to acquire new ones. In academe, however, such

---

**20** Recall also the comments from Bergs (2005): "Historical sociolinguistics (J. Milroy 1992a) or socio-historical linguistics (Romaine 1982b) is to be found at the intersection not of two, but of three different fields: history, social sciences, and linguistics. As such, it not only has to incorporate theories, practices, and paradigms from all three fields, *but it also has to struggle with and in conflicts that originate in all three areas*" (12, emphasis mine).
**21** The author's name, William Goodrich Jones, has been misinterpreted as "Goodrich-Jones" in this quotation. It has been correctly listed in the references at the end of this chapter under Jones (1995).

> collaboration is often impeded by administrative, funding, and cultural barriers between departments, by which most research and teaching activities are organized.
>
> (Institute of Medicine 2005: xi)

It is important to note, however, that the tide is slowly turning also in the academic world, driven in part on the very pragmatic level of competitive research funding and the slow but steady push by both public and private funding agencies and organizations toward interdisciplinary research models. Certain trends and tendencies seem to indicate that future research funding, also in the humanities and social sciences, will increasingly be tied to notions of interdisciplinary collaboration, rewarding researchers that present their work as necessarily building on the expertise of multiple disciplines, and that reflect strong interdisciplinarity in the profile of the team they wish to assemble to perform the research.

In the summary of its findings, the report on *Facilitating interdisciplinary research* described the "current situation" of interdisciplinary research (in 2005) in part as:

> Interdisciplinary thinking is rapidly becoming an integral feature of research as a result of four powerful "drivers": the inherent complexity of nature and society, the desire to explore problems and questions that are not confined to a single discipline, the need to solve societal problems, and the power of new technologies.
>
> (Institute of Medicine 2005: 2)

The fact that these identified "drivers" are largely present in the work of historical sociolinguistics might account, in part, for the observable trend that the field is thinking and working in the direction of ever greater interdisciplinary collaboration, despite the aforementioned constraints. A likely additional factor contributing to the progress of historical sociolinguistics toward ever greater interdisciplinary collaboration is the increased visibility of the field among the larger scientific public. One of the recommendations of the *Facilitating interdisciplinary research* document is that "Professional societies should seek opportunities to facilitate IDR at regular society meetings and through their publications and special initiatives" (Institute of Medicine 2005: 6), and this is exactly what has happened in recent years in the field of historical sociolinguistics, starting with the creation of the Historical Sociolinguistics Network (HiSoN) in 2005, followed by formation of the North American Research Network in Historical Sociolinguistics (NARNiHS) in 2016,[22] both dedicated to serving as focal points (through conferences, projects, publications, and outreach) for bringing together scholars from across the disciplines interested in pursuing the inherently interdisciplinary task of studying "the

---

[22] HiSoN = https://hison.sbg.ac.at/; NARNiHS = http://narnihs.org/ – both accessed 28 August 2020.

interaction of language and society in historical periods and from historical perspectives." (North American Research Network in Historical Sociolinguistics [NARNiHS] http://narnihs.org/?page_id=226 – accessed 28 August 2020).

It is important at this juncture to note that, even with the desire to engage in interdisciplinary collaborative research, and an increasingly welcoming and active context in which to do it, the process is not only hard, but also, very often, long; and the length of the process is a cumulative result of the individual, disciplinary, institutional, and financial factors discussed:

> Many of the challenges associated with interdisciplinary research increase with the cognitive distance between disciplines including, among other things, the development of a common theory language and methodology. [. . .] The example of environmental studies illustrates how long time [sic] it takes to establish an integrated knowledge field.[23] In this case it took more than half a century before interdisciplinary research centres, research careers and interdisciplinary journals were established. Overcoming barriers to interdisciplinary collaboration, such as the cognitive distance between expert fields, or the difficulty of choosing a clear publication strategy[24] requires significant investment of time and resources on the part of researchers, as well as careful attention to the different incentive structures of the collaborating disciplines. (Budtz Pedersen 2016: 4)

So, the "bad news" is that creating a fully embedded culture of true interdisciplinarity in a given area of research may take a very long time; however, the "good news" is that the field of historical sociolinguistics has already started the process and is steadily moving it forward.

---

**23** The inserted ellipsis in this quote stands in for Budtz Pedersen's recounting of the decades-long history of the progression from "climate science [. . .] as a synthesis of different disciplines within the natural sciences" to the "integrat[ion of] S[ocial] S[cience] [and] H[umanities] expertise into the field of climate science – leading to the establishment of environmental humanities" (Budtz Pedersen 2016: 4).

**24** Creating a "clear publication strategy" for interdisciplinary linguistic work is exactly the goal of the new book series, "Interdisciplinary Linguistics", in which the present volume is appearing as the first publication. As stated in the book series overview statement: "The *Interdisciplinary Linguistics* series is a cohesive collection for linguistic research that falls outside the traditional bounds of sociolinguistics and applied linguistics. With the understanding that theoretical stances and ideas about human behavior can and do cross over disciplinary boundaries, the volumes in this series take full advantage of the fact that linguistics sits at the intersection of humanities and the social sciences. The series aims to present new connections and fresh viewpoints in order to contribute to the interdisciplinary inquiry into the nature of human language" (https://www.degruyter.com/view/serial/INTLING-B?language=en – accessed 28 August 2020).

## 5 Interdisciplinary collaboration and the future of historical sociolinguistics

It is encouraging that the recommendations for pursuing true interdisciplinary collaboration that are laid out in this chapter are already being implemented to varying degrees by individual scholars and research groups in historical sociolinguistics in projects that represent initial forays into the type of integrative interdisciplinary collaboration described here. Indeed, a sample of what true interdisciplinary collaboration could bring to the field is provided in the recent collection of studies *Exploring future paths for historical sociolinguistics* (Säily et al. 2017). Stated in the words of the editors in their introductory chapter: "The volume showcases the wide range as well as the complexity of the field of historical sociolinguistics and re-emphasises the need to reach out to other disciplinary fields, *often in the form of actual collaborations between scholars from different disciplines.* This will in turn have an impact on the methods applied, the discovery and choice of data and the advancements of theories" (p. 2, emphasis mine), and "multidisciplinarity is essential to all of the studies [in the collection], to an even greater extent than has been customary before in the inherently multidisciplinary field of historical sociolinguistics" (p. 7). That such a collection of work can now be readily assembled, that it contains a rich variety of examples of true interdisciplinary collaborative work, and that it is sufficient to fill a volume of 331 pages is a testament to the distance that the field has come in recent years in adding true interdisciplinary collaboration to its disciplinary borrowing and multidisciplinary research paradigms.

In that light, this chapter ends with a call to continue this progress and with a plaidoyer to the field – historical sociolinguistics will certainly benefit if true interdisciplinary collaboration that "move[s] beyond single disciplines to address research topics from new perspectives, theories, concepts and methodologies that together form a body of knowledge beyond the traditional disciplinary boundaries" (Budtz Pedersen 2016: 4) becomes one of the hallmarks of work in the field. The potential for innovation and new discoveries will certainly increase if we work intently and intentionally to create a research context for historical sociolinguistics where:

1) true interdisciplinary collaboration is a part of the training that we provide in the field. Undergraduate and graduate classrooms and seminars, professional summer schools and workshops, grant-funded research opportunities – every setting in which researchers gain educational exposure to the work we do and how we do it – should bring together and harmonize a wealth of voices, from across the disciplinary areas of expertise, to be involved in the training provided in those settings;

2) true interdisciplinary collaboration is a part of the ethos of our research community and its practice, welcoming researchers from myriad disciplines into our brainstorming, our grant writing, our laboratories, and our research centers. If we create research settings that are truly interdisciplinary, they have the potential to become self-perpetuating, automatically drawing in scholars from across the disciplines who are looking for the stimulation and inspiration provided by vibrant interdisciplinary environments, communities, and experiences;
3) true interdisciplinary collaboration is on full display in our public-facing venues: in our presentations, in our publications, in our public scholarship, in our professional societies and conferences. We need to provide identifiable points of contact for colleagues from other disciplines to discover and join us in our interdisciplinary endeavors in historical sociolinguistics. The display window must be lit, and the "welcome" sign must be on, signaling that historical sociolinguistics is open for interdisciplinary business.[25]

Two quotes, both of which also figure in *Facilitating interdisciplinary research* (Institute of Medicine 2005), serve nicely here as concluding, summary statements for the foregoing thoughts on historical sociolinguistics and the necessity of interdisciplinary collaboration:

> We are not students of some subject matter, but students of problems. And problems may cut right across the borders of any subject matter or discipline. (Popper 1963: 88)

> The time is upon us to recognize that the new frontier is the interface, wherever it remains unexplored. [. . .] In the years to come, innovators will need to jettison the security of familiar tools, ideas, and specialties as they forge new partnerships.
> (Kafatos and Eisner 2004: 1257)

---

[25] Säily et al. (2017) also make suggestions in similar directions in the summary statement of their introduction to their volume: "Although increasing multidisciplinarity and technological advancements undoubtedly take the field forward, they may also lead us to some directions that are more difficult to foresee. For one thing, historical sociolinguists who want to pursue the suggested directions will need to possess a broader set of skills and learn to work in multidisciplinary – and multilinguistic – teams in "labs", sharing resources, ideas and tasks. Such cross-fertilisation will bring anticipated insights and solutions into the problems of bad data, for example, but it will most likely also bring forth new ideas altogether. In terms of undergraduate education this often means a change of mindset on the part of teachers and students alike. Ideally, multidisciplinary and multilinguistic cooperation will increase general awareness of the kind of knowledge that historical sociolinguists produce and make it even more influential outside its own circles" (p. 15).

# References

Auer, Anita, Catharina Peersman, Simon Pickl, Gijsbert Rutten & Rik Vosters. 2015. Historical sociolinguistics: The field and its future. *Journal of Historical Sociolinguistics* 1 (1). 1–12.
Barrett, Andy. 2005. The information-seeking habits of graduate student researchers in the humanities. *Journal of Academic Librarianship* 31 (4). 324–331.
Bergs, Alexander. 2005. *Social networks and historical sociolinguistics: Studies in morphosyntactic variation in the Paston letters (1421–1503)*. Berlin & New York: Mouton de Gruyter.
Bergs, Alexander. 2012. The uniformitarian principle and the risk of anachronisms in language and social history. In Juan Manuel Hernández-Campoy & Juan Camilo Conde-Silvestre (eds.), *The handbook of historical sociolinguistics*, 80–98. Chichester, West Sussex: Wiley-Blackwell.
Bousquette, Joshua & Todd Ehresmann. 2010. West Frisian in Wisconsin: A historical profile of immigrant language use in Randolph Township. *It Beaken* 72 (3/4). 241–270.
Bozeman, Barry, Monica Gaughan, Jan Youtie, Catherine P. Slade & Heather Rimes. 2016. Research collaboration experiences, good and bad: Dispatches from the front lines. *Science and Public Policy* 43 (2). 226–244.
Budtz Pedersen, David. 2016. Integrating social sciences and humanities in interdisciplinary research. *Palgrave Communications* 2: 16036. 1–7. https://doi.org/10.1057/palcomms.2016.36 (accessed 28 August 2020).
Budtz Pedersen, Daniel & Frederik Stjernfelt (eds.). 2016. *Kortlægning af dansk humanistisk forskning* [mapping of Danish humanities research]. Copenhagen: Hans Reitzels Forlag.
Burke, Peter. 2004. *Languages and communities in Early Modern Europe*. Cambridge: Cambridge University Press.
Burke, Peter. 2005. *Towards a social history of Early Modern Dutch*. Amsterdam: Amsterdam University Press.
Childs, Becky. 2021. The value of interdisciplinary and transdisciplinary linguistic research. This volume.
Chuk, Eric, Rama Hoetzlein, David Kim & Julia Panko. 2012. Creating socially networked knowledge through interdisciplinary collaboration. *Arts and Humanities in Higher Education* 11 (1–2). 93–108.
Conde-Silvestre, Juan Camilo & Juan Manuel Hernández-Campoy. 2012. Introduction. In Juan Manuel Hernández-Campoy & Juan Camilo Conde-Silvestre (eds.), *The handbook of historical sociolinguistics*, 1–8. Chichester, West Sussex: Wiley-Blackwell.
Fan, Jianqing, Fang Han & Han Liu. 2014. Challenges of big data analysis. *National Science Review* 1 (2). 293–314.
Friedman, R. S. & R. C. Friedman. 1985. Organized research units of academe revisited. In Brian W. Mar, William T. Newell & Börje O. Saxberg (eds.), *Managing high technology: An interdisciplinary perspective*, 75–91. Amsterdam: North Holland-Elsevier.
Folkers, Gerd. 2010. Interdisziplinär forschen, aber wie? [research interdisciplinarily, but how?]. *Horizonte – Das Schweizer Forschungsmagazin* [horizons – the Swiss research magazine]. 84 (March 2010). 33. http://www.snf.ch/SiteCollectionDocuments/horizonte/Horizonte_gesamt/Horizonte_84_D.pdf (accessed 28 August 2020).
Gandomi, Amir & Murtaza Haider. 2015. Beyond the hype: Big data concepts, methods, and analytics. *International Journal of Information Management* 35 (2). 137–144.

Green, Harriett, Angela Courtney, Megan Senseney & Maria Bonn. 2017. Humanities collaborations and research practices: Investigating new modes of collaborative humanities scholarship. In Dawn M. Mueller (ed.), *At the helm: Leading transformation (The Proceedings of the ACRL 2017 Conference, March 22–25, 2017, Baltimore, Maryland)*, 292–304. Chicago: Association of College and Research Libraries. http://www.ala.org/acrl/sites/ala.org.acrl/files/content/conferences/confsandpreconfs/2017/HumanitiesCollaborationsandResearchPractices.pdf (accessed 28 August 2020).

Hitchcock, Tim, Robert Shoemaker, Clive Emsley, Sharon Howard, Jamie McLaughlin, et al. 2012. *The Old Bailey proceedings online, 1674–1913*. Version 7.0. https://www.oldbaileyonline.org (accessed 28 August 2020).

Holton, Gerald, Hasok Chang & Edward Jurkowitz. 1996. How a scientific discovery is made: A case history. *American Scientist* 84 (4) (July-August). 364–375.

Huber, Magnus, Magnus Nissel & Karin Puga. 2016. *Old Bailey corpus 2.0*. hdl:11858/00-246C-0000-0023-8CFB-2. https://fedora.clarin-d.uni-saarland.de/oldbailey/ (accessed 28 August 2020).

Iglič, Hajdeja, Patrick Doreian, Luka Kronegger & Anuška Ferligoj. 2017. With whom do researchers collaborate and why? *Scientometrics* 112. 153–174. https://link.springer.com/article/10.1007/s11192-017-2386-y (accessed 28 August 2020).

Institute of Medicine. 2005. *Facilitating interdisciplinary research*. Washington, DC: The National Academies Press. https://doi.org/10.17226/11153 (accessed 28 August 2020).

Janda, Richard D. & Brian D. Joseph. 2003. On language, change, and language change – Or, of history, linguistics, and historical linguistics. In Brian D. Joseph & Richard D. Janda (eds.), *The handbook of historical linguistics*, 3–180. Oxford: Blackwell Publishing.

Jeffrey, Paul. 2003. Smoothing the waters: Observations on the process of cross-disciplinary research collaboration. *Social Studies of Science* 33 (4). 539–562.

Jones, William Goodrich. 1995. The disappearance of the library: Issues in the adoption of information technology by humanists. *New Directions for Higher Education* 90. 33–41.

Kafatos, Fotis C. & Thomas Eisner. 2004. Unification in the century of biology. *Science* 303 (February 27). 1257.

Keim, Daniel, Leishi Zhang, Miloš Krstajić & Svenja Simon. 2012. Solving problems with visual analytics: Challenges and applications. *Journal of Multimedia Processing and Technologies* 3 (1). 1–11.

Klein, Julie Thompson. 1990. *Interdisciplinarity: History, theory, and practice*. Detroit: Wayne State University Press.

Klein, Julie Thompson. 2000. A conceptual vocabulary of interdisciplinary science. In Peter Weingart & Nico Stehr (eds.), *Practising interdisciplinarity*, 3–24. Toronto: University of Toronto Press.

Klein, Julie Thompson. 2010. *Creating interdisciplinary campus cultures: A model for strength and sustainability*. San Francisco: Jossey Bass & Association of American Colleges and Universities.

Labov, William. 1994. *Principles of linguistic change. Volume 1: Internal factors*. Oxford: Blackwell Publishing.

Langer, Nils, Steffan Davies & Wim Vandenbussche (eds.). 2012. *Language and history, linguistics and historiography. Interdisciplinary approaches*. Oxford: Peter Lang.

Larivière, Vincent, Yves Gingras & Éric Archambault. 2006. Canadian collaboration networks: A comparative analysis of the natural sciences, social sciences and the humanities.

*Scientometrics* 68 (3). 519–533. https://link.springer.com/article/10.1007/s11192-006-0127-8 (accessed 28 August 2020).

Lauersdorf, Mark Richard. 2018a. Linguistic visualizations as *objets d'art*? In Noah Bubenhofer & Marc Kupietz (eds.), *Visualisierung sprachlicher Daten* [visualization of linguistic data], 91–122. Heidelberg: Heidelberg University Publishing.

Lauersdorf, Mark Richard. 2018b. Historical (standard) language development and the writing of historical identities: A plaidoyer for a data-driven approach to the investigation of the sociolinguistic history of (not only) Slovak. In Stephen M. Dickey & Mark Richard Lauersdorf (eds.), *V zeleni drželi zeleni breg: Studies in honor of Marc L. Greenberg*, 199–218. Bloomington, Indiana: Slavica Publishers (appeared 2019).

Lewis, Jenny M. 2017. Barriers to research collaboration: Are social scientists constrained by their desire for autonomy? https://blogs.lse.ac.uk/impactofsocialsciences/2017/10/17/barriers-to-research-collaboration-are-social-scientists-constrained-by-their-desire-for-autonomy/ (accessed 28 August 2020).

Lewis, Jenny M., Srebrenka Letina & Peter Woelert. 2016. *Research collaboration: Understanding disciplinary differences in structures and effects*. Melbourne: Melbourne School of Government Working Paper, University of Melbourne. https://minerva-access.unimelb.edu.au/bitstream/handle/11343/129582/2016+Woelert+-+Research+Collaboration+-+Understanding+disciplinary+differences+in+structures+and+effects.pdf;jsessionid=2A9A1157D2B9B413D46E18C68C9D968D?sequence=1 (accessed 28 August 2020).

Lewis, Jenny M., Sandy Ross & Thomas Holden. 2012. The how and why of academic collaboration: disciplinary differences and policy implications. *Higher Education* 64. 693–708.

McGrath, Laura (ed.). 2011. *Collaborative approaches to the digital in English studies*. Logan, UT: Computers and Composition Digital Press.

Milroy, Lesley. 1980. *Language and social networks*. Oxford: Basil Blackwell.

Milroy, James. 1992. *Linguistic variation and change: On the historical sociolinguistics of English*. Oxford: Blackwell.

Milroy, James & Lesley Milroy. 1985. Linguistic change, social network, and speaker innovation. *Journal of Linguistics* 21: 339–384.

Mufwene, Salikoko S. 1996. The founder principle in creole genesis. *Diachronica* 13 (1). 83–134.

Nevalainen, Terttu & Helena Raumolin-Brunberg. 2012. Historical sociolinguistics: origins, motivations, and paradigms. In Juan Manuel Hernández-Campoy & Juan Camilo Conde-Silvestre (eds.), *The handbook of historical sociolinguistics*, 22–40. Chichester, West Sussex: Wiley-Blackwell.

Nevalainen, Terttu & Helena Raumolin-Brunberg. 2017. *Historical sociolinguistics: Language change in Tudor and Stuart England*, 2nd edn. London: Routledge.

Popper, Karl R. 1963. *Conjectures and refutations: The growth of scientific knowledge*. New York: Routledge and Kegan Paul.

Porter, Alan L. & Frederick A. Rossini. 1986. Multiskill research. *Knowledge: Creation, diffusion, utilization* 7 (3) (March). 219–246.

Quan-Haase, Anabel, Juan Luis Suarez & David M. Brown. 2015. Collaborating, connecting, and clustering in the humanities: A case study of networked scholarship in an interdisciplinary, dispersed team. *American Behavioral Scientist* 59 (5). 565–581.

Romaine, Suzanne. 1982. *Socio-historical linguistics: Its status and methodology*. Cambridge: Cambridge University Press.

Romaine, Suzanne. 1988. Historical sociolinguistics: problems and methodology. In Ulrich Ammon, Norbert Dittmar & Klaus J. Mattheier (eds.), *Sociolinguistics: An international handbook of the science of language and society*, Vol. 2, 1452–1469. Berlin: Walter de Gruyter.

Romaine, Suzanne. 2005. Historical sociolinguistics/Historische soziolinguistik. In Ulrich Ammon, Norbert Dittmar, Klaus J. Mattheier & Peter Trudgill (eds.), *Sociolinguistics/ Soziolinguistik: An international handbook of the science of language and society/Ein internationales Handbuch zur Wissenschaft von Sprache und Gesellschaft*, Vol. 2, 2nd edn., 1696–1703. Berlin & New York: De Gruyter.

Rosenthal, Bernard, Gretchen A. Adams, Margo Burns, Peter Grund, Risto Hiltunen, Leena Kahlas-Tarkka, Merja Kytö, Matti Peikola, Benjamin C. Ray, Matti Rissanen, Marilynne K. Roach & Richard B. Trask (eds.). 2009. *Records of the Salem witch-hunt*. Cambridge: Cambridge University Press.

Ross, C., M. Terras, C. Warwick & A. Welsh. 2011. Enabled backchannel: Conference Twitter use by digital humanists. *Journal of Documentation* 67: 214–237.

Russi, Cinzia. 2016. Introduction. In Cinzia Russi (ed.), *Current trends in historical sociolinguistics*, 1–18. Berlin: Walter de Gruyter – De Gruyter Open: https://doi.org/ 10.1515/9783110488401 (accessed 28 August 2020).

Säily, Tanja, Arja Nurmi, Minna Palander-Collin & Anita Auer. 2017. The future of historical sociolinguistics? In Tanja Säily, Arja Nurmi, Minna Palander-Collin & Anita Auer (eds.), *Exploring future paths for historical sociolinguistics*, 1–19. Amsterdam: John Benjamins.

Stokols, Daniel, Juliana Fuqua, Jennifer Gress, Richard Harvey, Kimari Phillips, Lourdes Baezconde-Garbanati, Jennifer Unger, Paula Palmer, Melissa A. Clark, Suzanne M. Colby, Glen Morgan & William Trochim. 2003. Evaluating transdisciplinary science. *Nicotine & Tobacco Research* 5 (Supplement 1). 21–39.

Stone, Sue. 1982. Humanities scholars: Information needs and uses. *Journal of Documentation* 38 (4). 292–313.

Tsai, Chun-Wei, Chin-Feng Lai, Han-Chieh Chao & Athanasios V. Vasilakos. 2015. Big data analytics: A survey. *Journal of Big Data* 2, article 21. 1–32. https://doi.org/10.1186/ s40537-015-0030-3 (accessed 28 August 2020).

van Rijnsoever, Frank J. & Laurens K. Hessels. 2011. Factors associated with disciplinary and interdisciplinary research collaboration. *Research Policy* 40: 463–472.

Wagner, Caroline S., J. David Roessner, Kamau Bobba, Julie Thompson Klein, Kevin W. Boyack, Joann Keyton, Ismael Rafolse & Katy Börner. 2011. Approaches to understanding and measuring interdisciplinary scientific research (IDR): A review of the literature. *Journal of Informetrics* 5 (1). 14–26.

Wiberley, Stephen E., Jr. & William G. Jones. 1989. Patterns of information seeking in the humanities. *College & Research Libraries* 50. 638–645.

Wilkerson, Miranda E. & Joseph Salmons. 2008. "Good old immigrants of yesteryear" who didn't learn English: Germans in Wisconsin. *American Speech* 83 (3). 259–283.

Wilkerson, Miranda E. & Joseph Salmons. 2012. Linguistic marginalities: Becoming American without learning English. *Journal of Transnational American Studies* 4 (2). 1–28. https:// escholarship.org/uc/item/5vn092kk (accessed 28 August 2020).

Zhang, Leishi, Andreas Stoffel, Michael Behrisch, Sebastian Mittelstädt, Tobias Schreck, René Pompl, Stefan Weber, Holger Last & Daniel Keim. 2012. Visual analytics for the big data era – A comparative review of state-of-the-art commercial systems. *2012 IEEE Conference on visual analytics science and technology (VAST 2012)*, 173–182. New York: IEEE. http://doi.ieeecomputersociety.org/10.1109/VAST.2012.6400554 and https://ieeexplore.ieee.org/document/6400554/ (both accessed 28 August 2020). Retrieved from: https://scibib.dbvis.de/uploadedFiles/zhang.pdf (accessed 28 August 2020).

Jiyoon Lee, Matthew Schreibeis
# Chapter 15
# Comprehensive review of the effect of using music in second language learning

## 1 Introduction

The present chapter reviews the application of music to teaching and learning a second language (L2). Conversations about the potential effect of music on brain function have widely circulated among the general public since Rauscher, Robinson, and Jens' (1998) study examining the impact of Mozart's music on listeners' spatial reasoning, finding that those who listened to ten minutes of a piece for two pianos performed better on a shape-predicting task than in situations where they listened to a relaxation tape or worked in silence. Although their study had a small number of participants (n=36), and the music's positive effect on participants' spatial reasoning lasted only 10–15 minutes after the treatment, an oversimplification of the experiment results led people to believe that classical works by Bach or Mozart could help listeners enhance their memory and boost brain functions in the areas of mathematical analysis, analytical reasoning, or spatial reasoning.

Language teachers also share anecdotes in which they play classical music to relax their learners or use target cultures' folk songs, lullabies, or children's songs to teach L2 vocabulary, grammar, or pronunciation. Their positive perception of using music in L2 classrooms was well documented in Medina (2002). L2 teachers believed that repetition in song lyrics helps L2 learning by increasing learners' memory and that song lyrics could provide authentic input to learners (Medina 2002). Surveys also showed that learners also generally appreciate music in language classrooms (Chou 2014; Dolean 2016). Chou (2014) and Dolean (2016) reported survey results showing that learners felt that music provided them with an enjoyable L2 learning experience, principally because of a reduction in learners' anxiety.

A small number of empirical research studies have examined the effect of music on L2 learning and reported the characteristics of music as a treatment or

---

**Jiyoon Lee,** University of Maryland, Baltimore County, jiyoon@umbc.edu
**Matthew Schreibeis,** Hong Kong Baptist University, mschreib@hkbu.edu.hk

https://doi.org/10.1515/9781501514371-015

an instructional tool in detail (Lee and Schreibeis 2012). The dearth of information on which L2 teachers can confidently rely leads them to anecdotal or indiscriminate selection of music (Lems 2005; Lee and Schreibeis 2012). This chapter aims to provide informative pedagogical suggestions by critically reviewing intervention studies that incorporate music in L2 learning. The first section of the chapter provides background information on the relationship between music and language teaching by reviewing (1) the commonalities between language and music, and (2) pedagogical reasons to include music in language education in relation to learners' affects (e.g., motivation, anxiety). The second section provides an overview of intervention studies using music in language teaching and reviews the validity of the studies with a focus on characteristics of music as a treatment. The chapter concludes with suggestions for increased collaboration among language teachers, language acquisition researchers, music researchers, and composers to develop language teaching materials that reflect a more comprehensive understanding about the relationship between language and music.

## 2 Background information

### 2.1 Commonalities between language and music

Language and music have several commonalities, including perceptive and cognitive attributes. Describing the similarities between language and music, Patel (2008) argued that music and oral language share representation mechanisms, including phonological, prosodic, lexical, semantic, syntactic, rhythmic, melodic, and harmonic features. Chobert and Besson (2013) also explained that pitch and duration, two distinct features of sound production, dictate the melodic and rhythmic features of both language and music. Heffner and Slevec (2015) considered pitch constraints in music and vowel harmony in language to be examples of prosodic constraints found in both domains. For example, they suggested that the seven-note pitch collection of the G major scale (G, A, B, C, D, E, and F-sharp) are compatible to Turkish vowel harmony in relation to lip rounding and tongue position (Heffner and Slevec 2015: para. 23). Patel (2008) argued that the relationship between oral language and music is also reflected in regional variation of note lengths in music and syllable lengths in language.

Syntactically, as Asano and Boeckx (2015) pointed out, there are hierarchical structures in language and music. While music is frequently structured through temporal features (e.g., form, phrase, meter, and rhythm) and pitch features, including harmonic structures, oral language is similarly structured with phonemes, stress, and intonations. In addition, both music and language share rising and falling pitches, which can be conceived of through melodic contour in music and lexical tones in language (Arbib 2013).

Cognitive scientists – brain researchers, in particular – often focus on the location of language and music processing in the brain. That is, music is processed in Broca's area and the right-hemisphere homologue, the same locations where syntactic analysis happens when comprehending oral language (Patel 2008). This may suggest that humans perceive linguistic and musical data in a similar manner. Schön et al. (2008) provided empirical evidence that the brain processes musical and linguistic input in the same areas. They compared language learning based on speech sequences to language learning in relation to sung sequences. Manipulating musical properties (e.g., pitch and contour), their study provided convincing evidence for the connections between language and music processing. Through their findings, they argued sung melodic structures are helpful when people segment new words, especially in the early stages of learning a language.

Another interesting research area in language-music studies in cognitive science concerns the role of music in information recall (e.g., de Groot 2006; Purnell-Webb and Speelman 2008; Salcedo 2010). de Groot (2006) investigated the impact of background music on participants' ability to recall foreign language vocabulary. While his control group learned target vocabulary in silence, his treatment group learned the same vocabulary while an excerpt of Bach's Brandenburg Concerto No. 4 was played. Engaging in six treatment sessions and four vocabulary tests, the participants in the experimental group outperformed the control group. His study revealed that background music may have a positive impact on learners' ability to recall foreign language vocabulary. He also reported that while the positive effect of background music was small in the first test, it gradually increased, and that the effect was greater for infrequent words than frequent words. The findings were also confirmed in later studies using songs. For instance, Salcedo (2010) examined the effect of songs on recalling texts in a Spanish classroom in an American college. She divided participants into three groups: a music treatment group that listened to the songs; a text-treatment group that listened to the lyrics of the songs read by a native speaker of Spanish; and a control group. Her findings showed that the music treatment group outperformed both the text-treatment and control groups when recalling texts in the immediate post-test and the delayed post-test.

## 2.2 Affect, music, and language learning

Some of the arguments for introducing music in L2 teaching have focused on learners' affective states, including motivation and anxiety. In particular, recent interest in music in L2 teaching contexts is closely related to the expansion of research on motivation. Studies have shown that motivation is multifaceted and may potentially have many subconstructs. Motivation may also impact the relative ease of learning L2, as well as the amount of effort learners make in learning a new language (Arnold and Herrick 2017; Chou 2014; King 2010; Lee and Shin 2019). Those who support the use of music in L2 classrooms argue that song, in particular, can be a vehicle to motivate learners by providing authentic input and introducing target culture (Abbott 2002; Richards 1969; Shin 2017). Furthermore, presenting a theory of multiple intelligences, which attempted to explain learners' internal factors related to motivation, Gardner (2011) suggested that musical intelligence is one of eight intelligences, which also include spatial, logical-mathematical, linguistic, kinesthetic, interpersonal, intrapersonal, and naturalist. He also argued that everyone possesses all eight intelligence at varying degrees and suggests that teachers should be encouraged to develop lessons that can accommodate learners' multiple intelligences. He also maintained that musical intelligence develops during the same period in early life as linguistic intelligence.

Along with enhancing learners' motivation, the concerns of learners' anxiety in L2 classrooms also direct language teachers' and researchers' attention to introducing music in L2 classrooms. In the 1980s, Suggestopedia advocates supported using background music to create a conducive environment for language learning. For instance, Lozanov and Gateva (1988) suggested that when the target learning material was read aloud, teachers could play a selection of works they considered an "active concert", such as Beethoven's Violin Concerto or Haydn's Symphony No. 67 in F Major. Conversely, playing works like Handel's *Water Music* and Bach's Fantasy in G major, which they termed a "passive concert", could help learners transfer learned information to long-term memory; they believed this would lower learners' psychological barriers and promoted unconscious learning (Engh 2013). Similar discussions are also found in Krashen's affective filter hypothesis (Krashen 1985), where Krashen argued that it is critical to lower learners' affective filter for them to fully engage in language learning. Several studies were conducted to examine whether music could play a role in lowering the affective filter (Schön et al. 2008; Dolean 2016). Dolean (2016) examined the influence of using songs to teach French to 8th graders. He reported that his participants enjoyed learning through songs, and that his participants reported that they felt less anxious when learning French using music.

# 3 Intervention studies

While the previously discussed studies suggest a positive effect in using music to teach L2, not all of them employed an intervention approach to systematically collect evidence in support of their claims. Therefore, the authors decided to review only the empirical studies that used music as a treatment. Using databases that included ERIC, PsycINFO, and LLBA, limiting the publication date from 2001 to 2019, and including only those studies appearing in peer-reviewed journals, the authors identified a good number of publications showing the positive effect of music on L2 learning. However, the majority of these studies lacked empirical evidence. Instead, they argued generally for the use of music in language classrooms, provided resources, or described activities for using music as teaching methods (e.g., Abbott 2002). While these works could certainly prove helpful for language teachers, the goal of this chapter is to evaluate reliable evidence to support or reject the claims that music facilitates language learning. Hence, the authors reviewed only intervention studies that employed quasi-experimental or experimental designs, incorporated pre- and post-tests to investigate the gain in learners' linguistic abilities, and described the music that they employed as a treatment. Out of 34 studies, 10 met these criteria. A summary of the studies the authors reviewed is provided in the appendix.

The 10 intervention studies retained for analysis in the current study adopted a general design of pre-test, treatment(s), and post-test. Some studies include a delayed-post-test to measure the long-term effect of treatments or control groups. A control group is a group of participants who participate in the study in the exact same ways as experimental groups except for the treatment; they take both pre- and post-tests and, ideally, spend similar time receiving input but not the treatment (Mackey and Gass 2005). Research designs that include control groups may provide more reliable evidence and support stronger arguments than experiments that rely solely on a post-test to assess treatment. However, not all of the selected studies employed control groups.

## 3.1 Participants

The age ranges of participants in the selected research studies vary. Some of the participants were as young as four years old; other studies observed learners at middle schools or adult learners. Regardless of participants' ages, the studies show music making a generally positive impact in participants' post-test performance.

The number of participants in the reviewed studies was relatively small for a conventional intervention design. The largest number of participants was 64 in Davis and Fan (2016). They provided 15 lessons, each 40 minutes long, using English songs to teach English vocabulary to 64 kindergarten children in China. The participants were not divided into treatment or control groups; instead, they selected control or experimental vocabulary items. Depending on the sequence of treatments, each group of participants received different experimental vocabulary items. The second largest number of participants was 63, in Fonseca-Mora, Jara-Jiménez, and Gómez-Domínguez (2015); they were divided into two treatment groups (i.e., musical and non-musical treatment) and a control group. The number of participants who received phonological awareness instruction through music was 18. This number of participants is typical for most of the intervention studies the authors reviewed for the chapter.

## 3.2 Analysis methods

Descriptive statistics and the percentage calculation of gains from pre-tests to post-tests were frequently used in the selected studies. These analytic methods help readers understand general trends of the treatment impact; however, rigorous statistical analyses, including parametric analyses and inferential statistics (e.g., ANOVA, MANOVA, regression analysis), would strengthen the studies' arguments. Finally, unless a study is a true experimental study, with a control group, it is a challenge to make a causality conclusion or strong claims that the experimental groups' better performance directly relates to the incorporation of music.

When using inferential statistics, the reviewed studies often used non-parametric analysis. It is assumed that due to the small number of participants and the fact that the studies did not employ random assignments of participants, the researchers employed non-parametric analysis. For instance, Coyle and Gomez Gracia (2014) and Fonseca-Mora et al. (2015) use non-parametric analyses including Friedman tests and Wilcoxon signed-rank tests. When the studies used parametric analyses including $t$-tests or analysis of variance (ANOVA), only a couple of studies reported normality reports before reporting mean differences analyses. In particular, Ludke and her colleagues (2014) implemented an experimental design and randomly assigned the participants into three treatment groups: speaking, rhythmic speaking, or singing conditions. Investigating the respective effect of the three conditions on L2 phrase learning, they provided a 15-minute Hungarian lesson to 60 adult speakers of English. In the pre- and post-tests, the participants were asked to recall and produce learned Hungarian expressions. They reported the test of homogeneity before they compared the means among the participant groups. Based on the positive homogeneity test results, they conducted both ANOVA and multivariate analysis of variance (MANOVA). Their results showed that the singing group outperformed the other two groups. Their research findings are convincing, as they adopted an experimental design with random assignment as well as relatively rigorous statistical analyses.

Employing an experimental design or a quasi-experimental design is critical to increasing the trustworthiness of the research findings. An experimental design will help researchers safely rule out potentially interfering individual factors. Among the individual factors that can impact the results of the studies are learners' personality and musical aptitude. For instance, Furnham and Allass (1999) reported that extroverts performed better with treatments using music than introverts did. Musical aptitude is another factor that plays an important role in determining the effect of music in language learning. For example, research generally shows that those who have higher musical aptitude perform better in learning L2 pronunciation (Milovanov et al. 2008; Li and Dekeyser 2017). A true experimental design may rule out any unexpected effects of individual factors; however, none of the studies reviewed fell into that category.

## 3.3 Characteristics of music in the studies

The intervention studies the authors reviewed used vocal music rather than instrumental music as their treatments. In some studies, participants sang songs (e.g., Legg 2009; Coyle and Gomez Gracia 2014; Ludke et al. 2014; Good, Russo, and Sullivan 2015; Alissari and Heikkola 2016; Davis and Fan 2016; Ludke 2018), while in others, participants listened to the songs (e.g., de Groot and Smedinga 2014; Moradi and Shahrokhi 2014; Fonseca-Mora et al. 2015). Believing that songs helped learners understand culture as well as practice language, researchers of the reviewed studies focused on nursery rhymes and folk songs. Nursery rhymes were often used, as they have a high degree of repetition in lyrics, and folk songs were used because they convey significant cultural knowledge. They believed that these song types could provide cultural understanding for those who did not grow up in the target language culture as well as opportunities for practicing pronunciation.

Coyle and Gomez Gracia (2014) used children's songs to teach English vocabulary to preschool children in Spain. They measured the participants' receptive and productive vocabulary knowledge prior to and after three 30-minute lessons using songs. In the lesson, participants sang the song *The wheels on the bus*, in which the target vocabulary of instruction is included in the lyrics. The song's lyrics emphasize vocabulary repetition including "round", "beep", "open", "shut", and "ding". For example, the second stanza of the song goes:

> The horn on the bus goes
> "Beep, beep, beep
> Beep, beep, beep
> Beep, beep, beep"
> The horn on the bus goes
> "Beep, beep, beep"
> All through the town.

Musically, the work is in a moderate tempo simple quadruple meter (4/4) and consists of a single 8-bar phrase, which is repeated for each stanza. The major key melody is mostly built on triads that outline tonic and dominant harmonies. Many arrangements of the song exist, and while Coyle and Gomez Gracia did not specify the version they used, they reported statistically significant gains in receptive vocabulary knowledge. The participants' productive vocabulary knowledge, however, did not improve much.

Good, Russo, and Sullivan (2015) also used a song, *Functions of the face* by The Short and Curlies (2009), to investigate the impact of singing songs on pronunciation, text recall, and translation of L2. Randomly assigning Spanish-speaking children into a group that sang the song and a group that read the lyrics, Good and colleagues taught "Functions of face" for 20 minutes, four times over two weeks. The contemporary rock style of this children's song includes guitars and drums. With an upbeat tempo in simple quadruple meter (4/4), the major mode melody is mostly stepwise. The lyrics pose questions that orient the listener to the parts of the face:

> Why does a table look like a table?
> And why do my daddy's feet smell gross?
> Why does lasagna taste so delicious?
> And why can I hear the piano playing notes?

In the post-tests on English pronunciation, lyric recall, and lyric translation, those who received lessons by singing songs outperformed the group who read lyrics.

While most previous studies used preexisting songs, two studies used songs that were newly composed to teach specific target linguistic features. Teaching vocabulary and improving the ability to recall texts, Legg (2009) composed a song in a blues style, which he felt was suitable due to its relative simplicity and accessibility. Using the song, he taught French vocabulary to middle school students. The experimental group outperformed the control group in translating French sentences. However, as the author acknowledged, more rigorous research methodology should be used to confirm the effect of music. In particular, because the pre- and post-tests were not standardized or validated, it is not straightforward to confirm his results.

Ludke et al. (2014) composed a series of target phrases in Hungarian, in which the rhythm and melodic contour reflect the natural prosody of the text within a pitch framework consistent with patterns found in Hungarian folk songs. Rather than categorize this as a song, it is simply a sung setting of specific foreign language phrases. This presents an interesting and easy-to-adapt model for other vocabulary or longer phrases.

Compared to the studies by Moradi and Shahrokhi (2014) and Fonseca-Mora et al. (2015), where the participants actively listened to music to learn target language used in the songs, de Groot and Smedinga (2014) examined the influence of passive exposure to background music on learning L2 vocabulary. Specifically, they played pop songs in a language with which the participants had no prior exposure (i.e., Greek) and pop songs in languages with which the participants were familiar (Dutch and English).

As the songs played in the background, participants were shown target vocabulary items on the computer screen with their L1 translation and learned vocabulary. One group worked while pop songs in Greek played, another in Dutch, and a third group in English. Everyone worked in silence before they were grouped into three different conditions. They found that those who learned vocabulary while pop songs in a familiar language played in the background performed poorly on vocabulary recall tests compared to those who learned with background pop songs in an unfamiliar language or when they learned in silence. However, all groups performed similarly in a delayed vocabulary post-test given one week later, suggesting the adverse effect of background music in a familiar language was temporary.

Although published in the Video and Media Interest section of the *TESOL Newsletter*, it is worth mentioning Lee and Schreibeis (2012) for its methodology. We conducted an experimental study using songs and lyrics composed especially for the study in order to test the effect of specific melodic types as tools for learning synforms, which are vocabulary items with the same roots but different affixes (e.g., tasteful, tasty; sensitive, sensible; credible, credulous). Participants were divided into four groups, the first three of which received musical instruction, and a fourth group that did not. Among the musical groups, all three used identical lyrics with the same rhythm, through which the target vocabulary was delivered; no separate instruction was given. The first two groups sang songs with identical chord progressions but different melodies: while the first group gradually ascended an octave, outlining a major scale (Figure 15.1), the second group's range was restricted to the first three notes of the major scale (Figure 15.2). The third group spoke the lyrics rhythmically with a repeated drum pattern as accompaniment. Prior to and after the treatments, the participants took tests on noticing the target vocabulary (i.e., circle words that were recognized), comprehending the target vocabulary (i.e., select the meaning of target vocabulary from multiple choices), and producing the target vocabulary (i.e., fill in the blanks).

**Figure 15.1:** Experimental group 1.

The post-test showed that those who received instruction with the first musical selection, which exhibited ascending melodic structure, outperformed the other three groups. Because all other musical factors were controlled, this experiment represents a more convincing example of the efficacy of a particular musical structure, that is, ascending melodic structure, for teaching vocabulary through music.

**Figure 15.2:** Experimental group 2.

# 4 Implications and future directions

Research has suggested that language and music share several perceptive and cognitive commonalities. Even with the limited information available, it is possible to argue that music has great potential as a valuable subject for cognitive, emotional, and language development. Music can be used to teach unfamiliar vocabulary, pronunciation, or prosody in both first and second language. While the studies discussed present a clear positive potential for using music as part of L2 teaching, we need to be cautious about their future applications due to a number of underlying issues. The most fundamental of these is a lack of specificity about music that is used. While there is no doubt merit in the idea of using music generally as part L2 teaching, the lack of specificity about the chosen repertoire belies the complexity of identifying useful musical selections for teaching among the infinite music available to educators. The scope of this repertoire is staggering and includes folk, sacred, classical, and popular styles, among others, from every corner of the globe. Adding to the complexity is the fact that even if considering a well-known traditional or popular song, for example, there may be numerous arrangements with varied accompaniments or even in differing styles. The enormous range of repertoire raises issues about the complexity of the music used; the level of performance difficulty if the selection is, for example, a song to be sung; the musical background of the participants; and the familiarity of a given musical style or particular selection to a group of learners. This familiarity could be based on individual experience, cultural familiarity, or both, and may be especially relevant in more culturally diverse teaching environments.

It is important to remember that the function of including music in L2 is to enhance learning and not, for example, as part of a singing lesson. Because of this, instructors must be able to practically incorporate whatever music they choose. The music itself, regardless of style, must be sophisticated enough for learners to engage with, whether through singing, listening, or some other activity, but not so complex, difficult to produce or perform, or unfamiliar as to distract or in any other way negatively impact the learning experience. Further, the musical selection must be geared toward specific task(s), e.g., pronunciation, vocabulary, or cultural awareness. This is a distinct goal from simply having an enjoyable experience by singing or listening to music in class or from promoting a generally positive or relaxing classroom environment.

The music used in the reviewed studies has many features that language teachers could manipulate and use for their own instructional purposes; however, without even basic musical training, the task would be a challenge. Therefore, we recommend that teacher education courses include basic information about music to help language teachers make more informed decisions when choosing musical selections. We further suggest collaboration among language researchers, music researchers, and composers in developing language teaching materials that build off existing and future research findings.

Further research must be done to isolate specific musical parameters along the lines of Lee and Schreibeis (2012). This could include additional studies on the effects of specific melodic patterns, as well as harmonic, rhythmic, timbral and other musical parameters. The goal of these studies would be to determine which precise musical structures can be used to highlight particular linguistic features. Ultimately, this work must lead to the creation of lesson-specific teaching materials that incorporate music specifically composed for a particular task or target linguistic feature. This could include individual exercises, which, ideally, could be flexible enough to apply to multiple situations or vocabulary items or an entire L2 method using music as a key component. The key to future use of music as an effective component of L2 learning, regardless of how it is used, lies in those with expertise in language and music working together to achieve the same teaching and curricular goals.

## Note

The first author of the chapter is an applied linguist and teacher educator, and the second author is a music composer and music educator. The chapter was a product of the two authors' collaboration across two disciplines. Over the course of writing this chapter together, the two authors developed a further understanding of each other's fields, which will provide an opportunity for future collaboration of a more rigorous and informed nature on music and L2 learning.

## References

Abbott, Marilyn. 2002. Using music to promote L2 learning among adult learners. *TESOL Journal* 11 (1). 10–17.

Alissari, Jenni & Leena Maria. Heikkola. 2016. Increasing fluency in L2 writing with singing. *Studies in Second Language Learning and Teaching* 6 (2). 271–292.

Arbib, Michael. 2013. *Language, music, and the brain: A mysterious relationship.* Cambridge, MA: The MIT Press.

Arnold, Jean & Emily Herrick (eds.). 2017. *New ways in teaching with music.* Alexandria, VA: TESOL.

Asano, Rie & Cedric Boeckx. 2015. Syntax in language and music: What is the right level of comparison? *Frontiers in Psychology* 6. 942.

Chobert, Julie & Mireille Besson. 2013. Musical expertise and second language learning. *Brain Sciences* 3. 923–940.

Chou, Mu-Hsuan. 2014. Assessing English vocabulary and enhancing young English as a foreign language (EFL) learners' motivation through games, songs, and stories. *Education 3-13* (42/3). 284–297.

Coyle, Yvette & Remei Gomez Gracia. 2014. Using songs to enhance L2 vocabulary acquisition in preschool children. *ELT Journal* 68 (3), 276–285.

Davis, Glenn & Wenfang Fan. 2016. English vocabulary acquisition through songs in Chinese kindergarten students. *Chinese Journal of Applied Linguistics* 39 (1). 59–71.

de Groot, Annette. 2006. Effects of stimulus characteristics and background music on foreign language vocabulary learning and forgetting. *Language Learning* 56 (3). 463–506.

de Groot, Annette & Hilde Smedinga. 2014. Let the music play! A short-term but no long-term detrimental effect of vocal background music with familiar-language lyrics on foreign language vocabulary learning. *Studies in Second Language Acquisition* 36. 681–707.

Dolean, Dacian. 2016. The effects of teaching songs during foreign language classes on students' foreign language anxiety. *Language Teaching Research* 20 (5). 638–653.

Engh, Dwayne. 2013. Why use music in English language learning? A survey of the literature. *English Language Teaching* 6 (2). 113–127.

Fonseca-Mora, Carmen, Pilar Jara-Jiménez & Maria Gómez-Domínguez. 2015. Musical plus phonological input for young foreign language readers. *Frontiers in Psychology* 6 https://doi.org/10.3389/fpsyg.2015.00286.

Furnham, Adrian & Kathryn Allass. 1999. The influence of musical distraction of varying complexity on the cognitive performance of extroverts and introverts. *European Journal of Personality* 13 (1). 27–38.
Gardner, Howard. 2011. *Frames of mind: The theory of multiple intelligences*. New York: Basic Books.
Good, Arla, Frank Russo, & Jennifer Sullivan. 2015. The efficacy of singing in foreign-language learning. *Psychology of Music* 43 (5). 627–640.
Heffner, Christopher & Robert Slevc. 2015. Prosodic structure as a parallel to musical structure. *Frontiers in Psychology* 6. n.p.
King, Roberta. 2010. Music and storytelling in the EFL classroom. *Humanising Language Teaching* 12 (2). n.p.
Krashen, Stephen. 1985. *The input hypothesis: Issues and implications*. London: Longman.
Lee, Jiyoon & Matthew Schreibeis. 2012. The influence of different melodic structure on second language vocabulary acquisition. *TESOL Video News*. Retrieved from http://newsmanager.commpartners.com/tesolvdmis/issues/2012-08-10/7.html.
Lee, Jiyoon & Hye Won Shin. 2019. Associations between perceived self-efficacy, perceived value, and academic achievement: Exploring a gender difference within English-Medium Instruction. *Modern English Education* 20 (3). 46–56.
Legg, Robert. 2009. Using music to accelerate language learning: An experimental study. *Research in Education* 82 (1). 1–12.
Lems, Kristin. 2005. Music works: music for adult English language learners. *New Direction for Adult and Continuing Education* 107. 13–21.
Li, Man & Robert DeKeyser. 2017. Perception practice, production practice, and musical ability in L2 Mandarin tone-word learning. *Studies in Second Language Acquisition* 39 (4). 593–620.
Lozanov, Georgi & Evalina Gateva. 1988. *The foreign language teacher's Suggestopedic manual*. Amsterdam, Netherlands: Gordon and Breach.
Ludke, Karen. 2018. Singing and arts activities in support of foreign language learning: An exploratory study. *Innovation in Language Learning and Teaching* 12 (4). 371–386.
Ludke, Karen, Fernanda Ferreira & Katie Overy. 2014. Singing can facilitate foreign language learning. *Memory & Cognition* 42 (1). 41–52.
Mackey, Alison & Susan Gass. 2005. *Second language research: Methodology and design*. Mahwah, NJ: Lawrence Erlbaum Associates.
Marlin, Lene. 1999. Playing my game [CD]. Europe: Virgin.
Marlin, Lene. 2003. Another day [CD]. Norway: EMI Music.
Medina, Suzanne. 1993. The effect of music on second language vocabulary acquisition. *National Network for Early Language Learning* 6 (3).
Medina, Suzanne. (2002). Using Music to Enhance Second Language Acquisition: From Theory to Practice. In Lalais, J and Lee, S. (2002). Language, Literacy and Academic Development for English Language Learners. Pearson Educational Publishing.
Milovanov, Riia, Minna Huotilainen, Vesa Välimäki, Paulo Esquef & Mari Tervaniemi. 2008. Musical aptitude and second language pronunciation skills in school-aged children: Neural and behavioral evidence. *Brain Research* 1194: 81–89.
Moradi, Fereshteh & Mohsen Shahrokhi. 2014. The effect of listening to music on Iranian children's segmental and suprasegmental pronunciation. *English Language Teaching*, 7 (6). 128–142.

Patel, Aniruddh. 2008. *Music, language and the brain*. Oxford, England: Oxford University Press.
Pausini, Laura. 2002. *From the inside* [CD]. Europe: Atlantic.
Purnell-Webb, Patricia & Craig Speelman. 2008. Effects of music on memory for text. *Perceptual and Motor Skills* 106 (3). 927–957.
Rauscher, Frances, K. D. Robinson & J. J. Jens. 1998. Improved maze learning through early music exposure in rats. Neurol. Res. *National Center for Biotechnology Information* 20 (5). 427–432.
Richards, Jack. 1969. Songs in language learning. *TESOL Quarterly* 3 (2). 161–174.
Salcedo, Claudia. 2010. The effects of songs in the foreign language classroom on text recall, delayed text recall and involuntary mental rehearsal. *Journal of College Teaching and Learning* 7 (6). 19–30.
Schön, Daniele, Maud Boyer, Sylvian Moreno, Mireille Besson, Isabelle Peretz & Regine Kolinsky. 2008. Songs as an aid for language acquisition. *Cognition* 106 (2). 975–983.
Shin, Joan Kang. 2017. Get up and sing! Get up and move! Using songs and movement with young learners of English. *English Teaching Forum* 55 (2). 14–25.
Tamta. 2006. *Tamta* [CD]. Greece: Minos EMI.
The Short & Curlies. 2009. Functions of the face. On Sharing [CD]. Toronto, Canada: Studio 8.

# Appendix Intervention research studies

| Study | N of participants | Participants' age | Target forms/features | Characteristics of music as a treatment |
|---|---|---|---|---|
| Alissari & Heikkola 2016 | 51 (Experimental n = 11) | 18–33 | Writing fluency in Finnish | 11 Finnish children's songs and 7 pop songs |
| Coyle & Garcia 2014 | 25 | 5 years old | English vocabulary | Three 30-minute song lessons. The wheels on the bus – repetition |
| Davis & Fan 2016 | 64 | 4–5 years old | English vocabulary | All songs consisted of new texts set to familiar melodies including *Twinkle Twinkle Little Star* and *The More We Get Together*, or very simple and repetitive melodies. |

(continued)

| Study | N of participants | Participants' age | Target forms/ features | Characteristics of music as a treatment |
| --- | --- | --- | --- | --- |
| de Groot & Smedinga 2014 | 41 | College students | English vocabulary | Pop songs by Tamta (2006), tracks 2, 6, 8, 10, and 11; Pausini (2002), track 1; Marlin (1999) tracks 3 and 8; Marlin (2003) tracks 1 and 3 |
| Fonseca-Mora et al 2015 | 63 (Experimental n = 18) | 7–8 years old | English vocabulary | Songs with lyrics. The musical experimental group was taught through video-clips that included musical elements such as songs with lyrics. |
| Good et al 2015 | 38 (Experimental n = 16) | 9–13 years old | English pronunciation, lyric recall, comprehension | Functions of the face |
| Legg 2009 | 56 (Experimental n = 27) | Year 8 | French vocabulary | Blues style, primary chords, quadruple time, diatonic, modest range in D minor |
| Ludke et al 2014 | 60 (Experimental n = 20) | 18–29 years old | Hungarian vocabulary | Stimuli that modeled after Hungarian folk song |
| Ludke 2018 | 45 (Experimental n = 23) | 12–13 years old | French Beginning vocabulary and pronunciation, sentence structures | Songs with target vocabulary and chanting, rap songs, students' musical composition using target vocabulary, pronunciation, and grammatical structures. |
| Moradi & Shahrokhi 2014 | 30 (Experimental group n = 15) | 9–12 years old | English pronunciation | Listening to 7 songs for 20 minutes each time during 25 lessons |

K. Jason Coker
# Chapter 16
# Trashing the Bible

"It may not be too much to claim that the future of our world will depend on how we deal with identity and difference." Miroslav Volf wrote this over 20 years ago in his now classic *Exclusion and embrace* (1996: 20). We are slowly coming to terms with how prophetic this simple sentence was and is. Even aside from the global politics of identity, the racial injustices in the United States that have only been highlighted by the public murders of young, unarmed African American men press the intellectual community to take action. By bringing the fields of Critical White Studies and Biblical Studies into dialogue, I hope this essay is a small step in that direction.

Several years ago, my friend was working as a school social worker at a high school for "at-risk" teenagers. Demographically, the school was primarily Hispanic and African American. In a job training workshop for the students, the workshop leaders explained to the students how to interview for a job. Importance was placed on how the students dressed and spoke during an interview. Particular attention was given to young men wearing their pants around their waist and using a belt to keep them there. Young women were told to wear appropriate clothing that was not too revealing. All of them were told to clean up their language and use correct grammar and pronunciation. What struck me about this job training workshop was that young Hispanic and African American students were implicitly being told that the only way they would ever get a job is if they became white. The culture of the economy is white. To participate in the economic culture, one must perform whiteness. This is implicit, yet systemic, racism that defines *appropriate* clothing and *correct* grammar and pronunciation based on the cultural norms of whiteness with little exception.[1]

---

[1] On two different occasions, one in Starkville, Mississippi, and one in New Orleans, Louisiana, I was challenged by school teachers who said that this was not racial but economic in nature. They argued that teaching minority teenagers to dress and speak "right" was not racial but based on "middle class" culture. In other words, the advice to dress and speak "right" had nothing to do with race, but with class. I still resist this logic, but will concede that this is the exact intersection of race and class in the US. The sociological impact on minority teens, however, still enforces the notion that their identities/cultures are inadequate to participate in the US economy.

---

**K. Jason Coker,** National Director, Together for Hope: A Rural Development Coalition, jason@cbfms.org

Whiteness, however, is more slippery than its ideology purports. While skin color is *a* defining characteristic in racial discourse, performativity is also crucial. Performance was the most crucial aspect in the job training workshop I just described, and this type of racial performance also stratifies whiteness from within. William Aal calls this racial performance of whiteness "wonderbreading" (2001: 299). He argues that "In order to make it into the category of 'white' and receive its privileges, people were forced to give up their loyalty to their own traditions, language, community, and principles" (Aal 2001: 299). While Aal speaks specifically of non-white's "wonderbreading," it is clear that this also applies to all people. Even whites who cannot or do not perform whiteness are marked – whiteness of a different kind: almost the same but not quite, or not quite white. I will call this *white hybridity*. By this, I do not mean biracial identity; rather, I mean white people who fail to perform whiteness. Performance, then, determines the difference between pure whiteness and white hybridity. Exploring the purity/hybridity divide within whiteness will help make whiteness more visible. By making whiteness visible, I hope to show the dehumanizing effects of whiteness within white culture.

At the same time, I will analyze the conflict between Paul and James within the New Testament to use the biblical text as an interdisciplinary dialogue partner in the purity/hybridity conversation. James, as I will show below, represents a nativist/purist identity within the emerging Jesus-following movement, while Paul represents a more hybrid negotiation of identity within the same movement at the same time. I argue that the conflict between James and Paul is one of purity/hybridity based on performance, so it may provide a productive theoretical space to explore as I attempt to bring Biblical Studies into dialogue with Critical Race Theory in general, and Critical White Studies in particular.

In another manuscript, I reinterpreted the interaction between James and Paul in terms of postcolonial theory (Coker 2015). This framework provided newer vocabulary to describe how James and Paul engaged each other and negotiated Judean identity in relation to Roman imperialism. Whether the Letter of James is authentic or not, the content of the letter is summarized best as a concentrated focus on purity and perfection that definitively separates Judean identity from Roman identity. James does this in the context of the early Jesus movement as he accesses the Hebrew Scriptures through Jesus tradition (2:1–13, specifically) while mentioning Jesus's name twice (1:1; 2:1). James's focus on purity and perfection is constantly repeated throughout the letter, and is found in what most scholars consider the theme verse for the entire letter: "Piety that is pure and undefiled before God, the Father, is this: to care for orphans and widows in their distress, and to keep oneself unstained by the world" (1:27). Piety, which some translate as religion, is not simply having the right belief, that is, faith. Piety requires action (or performance) that separates pure from impure, undefiled from defiled, unstained from stained, and God from world. James essentializes identity in a nativist fashion that clearly identifies the performance necessary to distinguish Judean, Jesus movement identity from Roman cultural norms like the patronage system (2:1–13), friendship (4:1–12), and landownership (5:1–6). James defines true identity in terms of actions (2:14–24), language (3:1–12), thought (3:13–18), friendship (4:1–12), and business (4:13–17). Purity and perfection are the overarching characteristics related to each of these categories, which rhetorically separates James's audience from "the world." This is most pronounced in James 4:4, where he writes, "Whores! Do you not know that friendship with the world is enmity with God? Therefore whoever wishes to be a friend of the world becomes an enemy of God." Any transgression of this cultural boundary or mixing with the world is understood as infidelity (whores), hypocrisy (two-faced or double-minded), and sin. This is analogous to the "wonderbreading" in whiteness.

If James calls for an ancient form of wonderbreading, Paul represents his antithetical other. In his brief analysis of benefaction in "Pauline associations," Zeba A. Crook (2017: 201) convincingly argues that there are at least three areas where wealthier benefactors within the Pauline community contributed to Paul's ministries in Corinth: space, travel, and service. Whether it was actual physical space to meet; the cost of traveling for Paul, his associates, or letter delivery to and from Paul; or official service rendered to Paul's associations, e.g. as a treasurer for the collection Paul was delivering; these three areas show how ingrained Paul was in the patronage system of the Roman world – the same patronage system James so clearly opposes in James 2:1–13, where he utterly turns the patronage system on its head: "Has God not chosen the poor . . . " (2:5). Paul's assimilation with Roman culture as a diasporic Jew within the Jesus-following movement embodied a hybridity James would reject as "friendship with the world" (4:4). Paul's hybridity was an affront to James's purity.

Purity is an important trope within whiteness, as George Yancy makes clear: "As a racial and spatial signifier, whiteness maintains its 'purity' through processes of insularity, that is, through processes of avoidance and of maintaining distances from those (nonwhites) defined as different/deviant. To traverse this racial distance, to become 'unclean,' is to challenge the meaning of who constitutes one's neighbor, etymologically, 'to dwell near'" (2012: 6). Purity, both in James and in whiteness, separates clean and unclean, acceptable and unacceptable. In this way, the race line between white and nonwhite is the line between privilege and oppression or access and no access or good and bad. In *Learning to be white: Money, race, and God in America*, Thandeka (2002: 4–5) asks a blistering, but important, question: "When did you learn to be White?" The nature of the question assumes whiteness to be socially constructed and performative. Failing to perform whiteness has terrible consequences, as Thandeka's story of Sarah shows:

> At age sixteen, Sarah brought her *best friend* home with her from high school. After the *friend* left, Sarah's mother told her not to invite her *friend* home again. 'Why?' Sarah asked, astonished and confused. 'Because she's colored,' her mother responded. 'That was not an answer,' Sarah thought to herself. It was obvious that her *friend* was colored, but what kind of reason was that for not inviting her to Sarah's house? So Sarah persisted, insisting that her mother tell her the real reason for her action. None was forthcoming. The indignant look on her mother's face, however, made Sarah realize that if she persisted, she would jeopardize her mother's affection toward her. This awareness startled Sarah because she and her mother were the *best of friends*. Nothing – Sarah had always believed until that moment – could jeopardize their closeness. But now, she had glimpsed the unimaginable, the unspeakable – the unthinkable. Her relationship with her mother was not absolutely secure. It could crumble. Horrified by what she had just glimpsed, Sarah severed her *friendship* with the girl. (Thandeka 2002: 1–2)

This is only one story that Thandeka tells of how white people "learn" to be white. I emphasize the idea of friendship in Sarah's story because of the obvious connection to James 4:4 regarding correct friendship as a boundary marker for identity. In both cases there is a definitive choice: God or the world for James and mother or friend for Sarah. Both cases effectively draw a line based on identity, but clearly show that these identities are based on choice/performance rather than some natural phenomena, as Aal (2001: 296) makes clear: "the structures of injustice are not natural phenomena ('the way the world has and will always be') but were created by humans in specific historical contexts and therefore *can be changed*." For James, to cross this border is infidelity (whore – 4:4); for Sarah, to cross this border is another kind of betrayal.

While these two different negotiations of identity have some parallels, there are also marked differences. Negotiating Judean identity within the early Jesus movement in relation to Roman imperialism and negotiating white identity within whiteness in modern America are fundamentally different based – at least – on power. The concentration on purity and perfection in the Letter of James creates an essentialist/nativist identity that confronts and resists Roman power. In this way, the cultural negotiation in the Letter of James is a nativism from the margins or nativism from below. While Paul's identity negotiation in his epistles contradicts the way in which James is constructing identity, he is also building an anti-Roman identity, while using the tools of empire. In other words, both James and Paul, while they are confronting each other, are doing so in the margins – subaltern sidelines. Learning to be white is a cultural negotiation that does not resist power. Learning to be white and performing whiteness – wonderbreading – is the attempt to access power rather than resist it. While these negotiations are different, I use the constructed nature of both specifically to critique the idea that "whiteness functions as a transcendental norm, as that which defines nonwhite bodies as different and deviant . . . ." (Yancy 2012: 7). I, then, bring this critique into interdisciplinary dialogue with the James-Paul debate where identity construction is the central point to the letter.

Contrary to James's concentration on purity and perfection, Paul's letters evidence a fundamentally different way to negotiate Judean identity within the Jesus movement. This is, in part, due to the fact that Paul was a Diaspora Jew living most of his live traveling through the Roman Empire. His ideological negotiations regarding his identity varied greatly based on where he was and what he was doing. At times, Paul seems to acquiesce to Roman authority, and at other times he seems to resist it. A clear instance of accepting the status quo of Roman imperialism is famously captured in Romans 13:1: "Every one should be subject to the governing authorities; for there is no authority except from God, and those authorities that exist have been instituted by God." This passage suggests a high level of assimilation to Roman culture and law on behalf of Paul. Biblical scholars who suggest Paul is an anti-imperial and/or anti-Roman agent of God work hard to create a hermeneutic that navigates around this passage (cf. Elliott 2008; Brett 2008).[2] Ernest Käseman (1980: 354) argues that this section is so foreign to most of Paul's writings that he calls Romans 13: 1–7 "an alien body in Paul's exhortation." Neil Elliott agrees and argues that "The language of submission and fear that appears here is a *startling exception* to the rhetoric of the rest of the letter . . . ." (2008: 153; emphasis mine) However, other biblical scholars take the passage at face value and argue that Paul is acquiescing to Roman power.[3]

In another place, however, Paul argues that his disciple's true citizenship is not in this world – the Roman world – but in the one to come: "But our citizenship is in heaven, and it is from there that we are expecting a Savior, the Lord Jesus Christ" (Phil. 3:20). This is more than simple dual-citizenship. Paul clearly prefers his identity "in Christ" to any of his other "nested identities," including his possible Roman citizenship (see Acts 22:28). (For more on Paul's

---

[2] See also Coker (2015) for an extended argument about the relationship between James and Paul with specific attention given to Paul's cultural hybridity.

[3] See Dunn (1988) and Moxnes (1995) for just two of the many scholars who espouse this view.

"nested identities," see Hodge 2005: 272.) Already there is an ambivalence in Paul's negotiated identity with regard to Roman imperialism. In some places, he acquiesces (Rom. 13:1–7); in other places, he resists (Phil. 3:20); still yet, in other places, he will do whatever he needs to do (1 Cor. 9:20–23). This strategic assimilation positions Paul as one who resists any fixed identity and places him squarely among other Diaspora Jews who negotiated a fluid identity within the Roman Empire. Time does not allow us in this essay to thoroughly detail all the Pauline scholarship that focuses on Paul's complex relationship with Roman imperialism, but "Paul's reception among modern scholars as either an anti-imperial agent or Roman replica adds strength to the argument that Paul is a hybrid" (Coker 2015: 180).

Paul's hybridity comes from his status as a Diaspora Jew and puts him in conflict with James's sense of purity – an essentialized purity deeply connected to the center of Jewishness in Jerusalem. In his analysis of Paul's diaspora hybridity, Ronald Charles (2014: 112) shows that "Diaspora describes nonessentialist and plural identities that are in process, even when these multiple sites of identities might be construed as untouched." Charles's focus on Paul's diasporic/hybrid identity helps position Paul in the larger Roman world, but also within the emerging Jesus movement, which was still mainly Jewish. Charles's work on Paul's diaspora/hybrid identity is informed by Sze-Kar Wan's Asian-American reading of Paul. Wan (2000: 122) informatively argues that Paul's identity is "a diaspora identity that turns out to be not an erasure of their Jewish or Hellenistic identity but a hybridization of both." Wan (2000: 126) goes on to say that, at least in his Letter to the Galatians, Paul "implies a new identity for the Galatian community that is a combination of *both* Jewish *and* Hellenistic traits." The quintessential passage from Paul's letters, however, that speaks to his capacity to morph and change depending on the context, is 1 Corinthians 9:20–23:

> To the Jews I became as a Jew, in order to win Jews. To those under the law I became as one under the law (though I myself am not under the law) so that I might win those under the law. To those outside the law I became as one outside the law (thought I am not free from God's law but am under Christ's law) so that I might win those outside the law. To the weak I became weak, so that I might win the weak. I have become all things to all people, that I might by all means save some. I do it all for the sake of the gospel, so that I may share in its blessings.

Paul as chameleon stands in stark contrast to any form of "pure and undefiled piety" (James 1:27). Paul's hybridity in a diasporic context transgresses the essentialist identity supported and encouraged in the Letter of James. Wan – following Paul – critiques such essentialized identity like that in James as "An originally anti-imperialistic strategy to protect minority rights by sealing off all possibilities of intercultural and cross-cultural exchanges has ironically given fuel to political chauvinism" (Wan 2000: 109). Due to his location outside of Judea and his proximity to non-Judean culture, Paul's mixing and hybridization made him a Judean of a different kind.

White hybridity, as I described briefly above, better known as Poor White Trash, also unravels and stands in contrast to the essentialist identity built into whiteness. Poor and trash indicate oppression and marginality, while white glows with privilege. The paradox of Poor White Trash is to be kind of white, but never quite white – whiteness of a different kind. If someone is poor *and* white, they can only be trash – a breed apart. Poverty does not perform as white because the culture of the economy *is* white. Poor White Trash suffers from a white ethnic identity crisis because they are what Thandeka (2002: 41) calls "facsimile whites." This crisis of white hybridity does psychological damage to Poor White Trash. Laurel Johnson Black (1997: 389) captures this psychological pain in an autobiographical essay:

> Working poor, we were alternately afraid and ashamed and bold and angry. We prayed to nothing in particular that no one would notice our clothes or that the police wouldn't notice the car didn't have a valid inspection sticker. My mother had to decide between a tank of gas and an insurance payment. She had to decide whether or not we really needed a doctor. We shopped as a group so that if my new dress for the year cost two dollars less than we had thought it would, my sister could get one that cost two dollars more. We didn't say such things out loud, though we thought them all the time. If I ate seconds, maybe I was eating my sister's dress. If Susan was really sick, then maybe I couldn't get new shoes. But if anyone ever said those things, it would all come crashing in. All of it – the idea that working hard would get you some place better, that we were just as good as anyone else – would crash to the floor like some heirloom dish that would never be the same again, even if we could find all the shards.

Thandeka (2002: 53) further delineates the result of this pain as, "Having shifted focus from class issues to racial feelings, the common white man, in effect, had been robbed by his own racial 'brothers.' Such racial assaults by those who ostensibly love one most can produce feelings of white shame, masked as white pride." Both Thandeka and Black show how a sense of pride and boldness arises out of this white racial hybridity. The contradiction between low class (trash) and racial privilege (white) creates a psychological trauma where the only place of pride is in white skin, so that space is double-downed and championed. In fact, many Poor White Trash have a tremendous amount of disdain for white elite culture. Instead of performing whiteness, they perform trashiness. Poor White Trash have accepted the shame that American elite culture has projected onto them. Poor White Trash self-representation is exactly the same as the pejorative representations that exist in American stereotypes, but they have transformed the meanings of these representations. Two representations of Poor White Trash that come from American elite culture exemplify the pejorative nature of these representations. William Alexander Percy's scathing statement about Poor White Trash is one example of the extent to which the white elite ridicule Poor White Trash. Percy, the son of one of the richest farm owners in the history of the Mississippi Delta, describes "white" people without privilege as,

> The poor whites of the South: a nice study in heredity and environment. Who can trace their origin, estimate their qualities, do them justice? Not I. This much, however, it is safe to assert: they were not blest with worldly goods or mental attainments. If it (this breed of poor whites) was ever good, the virus of poverty, malnutrition, and interbreeding has done its degenerative work: the present breed is probably the most unprepossessing on the broad face of the ill-populated earth. I can forgive them as the Lord God forgives, but admire them, trust them, love them – never. Intellectually and spiritually they are inferior to the Negro, whom they hate. (Percy 1941: 19–20)

It is clear from Percy's description that he considers poor whites as something completely other and altogether different from the kind of white person he is. Although many readers shutter at Percy's racism, most would not totally disagree with what he says about Poor White Trash. In fact, Percy's comments have become paradigmatic in jokes about Poor White Trash. Erskine Caldwell is another author who wrote about Poor White Trash in his novel *Tobacco Road* (1932). Although Caldwell's representations of Poor White Trash are fictional, they bear the full weight of Poor White Trash stereotypes. This passage from *Tobacco Road* shows how shameful Caldwell's representations are:

> "Dude's sixteen years old now," Jeter said. "That makes him two years younger than Ellie May. Well, pretty soon he'll be getting him a wife, I reckon. All my other male children married early in life, just like the gals done. When Dude gets married, I won't have none of my children left with me, except Ellie May. And I don't reckon she'll ever find a man to marry her. It's all on account of that mouth she's got. I been thinking I'd take her up to Augusta and get a doctor to sew up her lip. She'd marry quick enough then, because she's got a powerful way with her, woman-like. Ain't nothing wrong with her, excepting that slit in her lip. If it wasn't for that, she'd been married quick as Pearl was. Men here around Fuller all want to marry gals about eleven or twelve years old, like Pearl was. Ada, there, was just turning twelve when I married her." (Caldwell 1932: 52)

Jeter Lester is the patriarch of a Poor White Trash family in *Tobacco Road* that encapsulates Caldwell's notions of Poor White Trash, that is, sexual deviance, birth defects, ugliness, etc. These characteristics are eerily similar to the "scientific" evidence that eugenic theory developed about Poor White Trash only a few decades before Caldwell's *Tobacco Road* was published. This confluence between "science" and literature amounted to an all-out assault on Poor White Trash. Caldwell and Percy's representations of Poor White Trash are characterized by shame and disgust. These representations have become typical and/or stereotypical of Poor White Trash in modern America while Caldwell and Percy have been praised as literary artists. Indeed, James C. Cobb, who falls victim to Percy's writing skills, says of Percy,

> Only after the war, however, did observers begin to recognize that, despite the poverty, illiteracy, and rural isolation which afforded ready-made excuses for cultural aridity, the Delta was also a flourishing center for literature and the arts. By the end of the 1940s, the region could claim not only William Alexander Percy and David L. Cohn but Pulitzer Prize-winning journalist Hodding Carter. (Cobb 1992: 306)

Poor White Trash, however, have taken these representations and transformed what they mean. They have transformed the meaning of shame. What is a matter of scorn for American elite culture is a matter of honor among Poor White Trash. Jim Goad personifies this subversion in his *Redneck Manifesto* (1998). In his work, he fully accepts and embraces his shameful self. By taking so much pride in his "shameful" self-representation, Goad transforms and redefines shame. Goad nearly restates Caldwell and Percy's representation of Poor White Trash when he says,

> I'm equal parts city slime and country vermin. My mother was urban Philly garbage; my father was rural Vermont scum. Together they fled to a concrete Dogpatch five miles outside the City of Brotherly Love to live the half-baked consumerist dreams of post-World War II suburban trash. I am the direct product of miscegenated, cross-pollinated trash.
> (Goad 1998: 24)

Goad's self-representation seemingly puts him in complete agreement with Caldwell and Percy's representation of Poor White Trash. His self-understanding, however, reveals how dangerous of a hybrid he is. Goad claims his own identity in such a way that he gains the power to project his own self-representation. While fully embracing the representations of Poor White Trash in American society, Goad simultaneously and paradoxically transforms this shameful self-understanding to a *not so shameful self*. Goad captures the pejorative objectification of Poor White Trash and completely subverts it. In the words of bell hooks, "White trash were different because they flaunted their poverty, reveled in it, and were not ashamed. White trash saw themselves as above the law and as a consequence they were dangerous. White trash were folks who, as our neighbors were fond of saying, 'did not give a good goddamn'" (2000: 112). Referring to this epistemological gap between the American elite and Poor White Trash, Constance Penley (1997: 90) emphatically states:

> A Southern white child is required to learn that white trash folks are the lowest of the low because socially and economically they have sunk so far that they might as well be black. As such, they are seen to have lost all self-respect. So it is particularly unseemly when they appear to shamelessly flaunt their trashiness, which, after all, is nothing but an aggressively in-your-face reminder of stark class difference, a fierce fuck-you to anyone trying to maintain a belief in an America whose only class demarcations are the seemingly obvious ones of race.

What these citations reveal is an obvious contradiction in representation. American elite culture's representation of Poor White Trash is a representation of pure shame – again, a whiteness of a different kind. Poor White Trash, contrarily, constructs a subjectivity of self-representation that acknowledges its marked whiteness and hybrid and subverts shame into pride.

This hybridity is the paradox that causes white elite culture problems. Poor White Trash is needed in order to show how nice "real whites" are, but at the same time, Poor White Trash needs to be hidden from the public sphere because it is proof that white superiority does not guarantee economic upward mobility or power, which disrupts white racist ideology. In his book *The Color of Class: Poor Whites and the Paradox of Privilege*, Kirby Moss (2003: 3) is informative on this point:

> I argue that while mainstream society loosely embraces its lower-class members, at the same time it locks poor Whites discursively away and out of sight for a number of ideological reasons . . . . Narratives and prevailing images of poor Whites are conveniently missing from the middle-class ideological portrait of itself because to acknowledge poverty and banality within its own ranks erodes the eminent, constructed image of Whiteness.

By embracing an identity of oppression and marginality, Poor White Trash begins to unravel whiteness in particular and race in general. The hybrid nature of Poor White Trash challenges the conception of whiteness as essentially superior and ontologically privileged. Due to this disruptive significance, Poor White Trash must be silenced in order for the wealthy elite to maintain their position of control. There are striking parallels to James 3:1–12, where James attempts to silence the hybrid tongue. bell hooks also deals with the harsh class lines that are maintained by the white elite in order to keep Poor White Trash silent and separate:

> It was in high school that I first began to understand class separation between whites. Poor white kids kept to themselves. And many of their well-to-do white peers would rather be seen talking to a black person than speaking to the white poor, or worse, to white trash. There was no danger that the black person they were talking to would want

> to come and hang out at their home or go to a movie. Racial lines were not crossed outside school. There could be no expectation of a reciprocal friendship. A privileged white person might confuse the issue if they showed attention to an underprivileged white peer. Class boundaries had to remain intact so that no one got the wrong idea. Between black and white there was no chance of a wrong idea: the two simply did not meet or mix. (hooks 2000: 113)

Poor White Trash identity, then, paradoxically maintains and destabilizes white identity proper. As long as Poor White Trash do not fully embrace their identity as Poor White Trash, but simply as White, then there is no threat to white ideology, because they will always feel ashamed of being white and poor. This shame will keep them in their place–a place that is all too often violent for racial Others. Within the Pauline letters, this parallel is evidenced in Paul's continual need to legitimize his authority. Whenever this shame is disregarded and Poor White Trash identity is fully embraced in the public sphere, whiteness begins to deconstruct. White elites, therefore, must keep Poor White Trash silent and separate, while at the same time using Poor White Trash as an example of racism in order to deflect the racism that is implicit in their own culture.

Whether a successful interaction between Critical White Studies and Biblical Studies or not, this essay attempts to make visible the devastating power dynamics within whiteness using the category of Poor White Trash and using the James/Paul debate as a loose parallel in ancient identity negotiation. While the inter-white racial and class friction can function as an example to understand an ancient identity negotiation in Judaism/early Christianity, my greatest hope is that this interdisciplinary work might encourage other white biblical scholars to use their academic acumen and privilege to engage in anti-racist biblical studies. This is a modest attempt to follow the urging of Rev. Otis Moss III (2015: 33):

> America is in need of anti-racism activists, preachers, and thinkers who are not people of color. America desires voices with a moral center that dare speak truth to power and walk humbly with our God. These yet-to-be United States wait patiently for your voice, song, poem, essay, sermon, and action to join the cadre of women and men who seek to dismantle and repent from this original sin called racism.

# References

Aal, William. 2001. Moving from guilt to action: Antiracist organizing and the concept of "whiteness" for activism and the academy. In Birgit Brander Rasmussen, Eric Klinenberg, Irene J. Nexica & Matt Wray (eds.), *The making and unmaking of whiteness*, 294–310. Durham, NC, and London: Duke University Press.

Black, Laurel Johnson. 1997. Stupid rich bastards. In Richard Delgado & Jean Stefancic (eds.), *Critical white studies: Looking beyond the mirror*, 387–394. Philadelphia: Temple University Press.
Brett, Mark G. 2008. *Decolonizing God: The Bible in the tides of empire*. The Bible in the Modern World 16. Sheffield: Sheffield Phoenix Press.
Caldwell, Erskine. 1932. *Tobacco road*. Athens and London: University of Georgia Press.
Charles, Ronald. 2014. *Paul and the politics of diaspora*. Minneapolis: Fortress Press.
Cobb, James C. 1992. *The most southern place on Earth: The Mississippi Delta and the roots of regional identity*. New York and Oxford: Oxford University Press.
Coker, K. Jason. 2015. *James in postcolonial perspective: The letter as nativist discourse*. Minneapolis: Fortress Press.
Crook, Zeba A. 2017. Economic location of benefactors in Pauline communities. In Thomas R. Blanton, IV & Raymond Pickett (eds.), *Paul and economics: A handbook*, 183–204. Minneapolis: Fortress Press.
Dunn, James D. G. 1988. *Romans 9–16*. Word Bible Commentary, 38B; Dallas: Word Books.
Elliott, Neil. 2008. *The arrogance of nations: Reading Romans in the shadow of empire*. Minneapolis: Fortress Press.
Goad, Jim. 1998. *Redneck manifesto: How hillbillies, hicks, and white trash became America's scapegoats*. New York: Simon & Schuster.
Hodge, Caroline Johnson. 2005. Apostle to the Gentiles: Constructions of Paul's identity. *Biblical Interpretation* 13 (3). 270–288.
hooks, bell. 2000. *Where we stand: Class matters*. New York & London: Routledge.
Käsemann, Ernest. 1980. *Commentary on Romans*. Geoffrey W. Bromiley (trans. and ed.). Grand Rapids, MI: William B. Eerdmans Publishing Company.
Moss, Kirby. 2003. *The color of class: Poor whites and the paradox of privilege*. Philadelphia: University of Pennsylvania Press.
Moss, Otis. 2015. Facing America's original sin. *Reflections: A magazine of theological and ethical inquiry* (Fall). 33.
Moxnes, Halvor. 1995. The quest for honor and the unity of the community in Romans 12 and in the orations of Dio Chrysostom. In Troels Engberg-Pedersen (ed.), *Paul in his Hellenistic context*, 203–230. Minneapolis: Fortress Press, 1995.
Penley, Constance. 1997. Crackers and whackers: The white trashing of porn. In Matt Wray & Annalee Newitz (eds.), *White trash: Race and class in America*, 89–112. New York and London: Routledge.
Percy, William Alexander. 1941. *Lanterns on the levee: Recollections of a planter's son*. Baton Rouge: Louisiana State University Press.
Thandeka. 2002. *Learning to be white: Race money, race, and God in America*. New York and London: Continuum.
Volf, Miroslav. 1996. *Exclusion and embrace: A theological exploration of identity, otherness, and reconciliation*. Nashville: Abingdon Press.
Wan, Sze-Kan. 2000. Does diaspora identity imply some sort of universality? An Asian-American reading of Galatians. In Fernando F. Segovia (ed.), *Interpreting beyond borders*, 107–131. The Bible and Postcolonialism 3. Sheffield: Sheffield Academic Press.
Yancy, George. 2012. Introduction: Framing the problem. In George Yancy (ed.), *Christology and whiteness: What would Jesus do?*, 1–18. London and New York: Routledge.

Jason M. Thomas
# Chapter 17
# Towards a post-structuralist economics

## 1 Introduction

During the first decade of the twenty-first century, Americans became increasingly fixated on homeownership as a foundational element of sound personal finances. To rent was to "throw money away," a senseless decision embraced only by the ignorant or stupid. Homeownership rates rose to record levels, undoubtedly due, in part, to all of the first-time buyers impelled by harangues from family, friends and colleagues to vacate perfectly suitable rental units.

Homeownership was never the panacea touted by its advocates. Unless a prospective homebuyer possesses sufficient liquidity to buy a home outright – i.e. they're rich and have no need for impromptu seminars on financial responsibility – they must borrow the requisite sum through a home mortgage. In this new arrangement, the "homeowner" remains a renter, but instead of renting the residence directly from a landlord now rents the capital in a mortgage market. For first-time buyers, that means trading a very simple and typically short-term rental contract for a long-term financial obligation that is far more complex and onerous. Money previously "thrown away" on rent is not buried in a backyard treasure trove, but instead sent to a bank or mortgage servicer to cover the interest on the mortgage loan, property taxes and insurance, and (typically) some portion of the outstanding principal balance.

Whether it is preferable to rent the capital or the home itself depends on a number of factors, including the expected length of stay, the prevailing rates of interest, taxation, and depreciation, and – most importantly – the trajectory of house prices. When house prices rise, it is generally better to rent the capital; the principal balance owed on the mortgage is fixed in advance so any appreciation in the market value of the home increases its owner's net worth on a dollar-for-dollar basis. When house prices decline, it would be better to rent the residence itself so as to avoid the commensurate dollar-for-dollar drop in home equity.

---

The views expressed herein are those of the author and do not necessarily reflect those of The Carlyle Group.

---

**Jason M. Thomas,** Head of Global Research, The Carlyle Group, Washington, D.C. Jason. thomas@carlyle.com

https://doi.org/10.1515/9781501514371-017

Between April 1998 and July 2006, average house prices in the U.S. rose at an annualized rate in excess of 9%.[1] The typical homeowner who purchased a $200,000 home with an $180,000 mortgage at the start of this period would have seen their home equity rise more than twelve-fold by its end (from $20,000 to $256,225). While financial windfalls of this magnitude can turn people into true believers in the merits of "buying" rather than "renting," these fortuitous capital gains have nothing to do with "homeownership," as commonly understood, but instead reflect the financial payoff from a 10-to-1 leveraged position in an appreciating asset.

Discourses surrounding homeownership seemed to obscure the speculative nature of these returns. Mortgage finance companies like Fannie Mae synonymized homeownership with the "American dream" and touted housing as Americans' most reliable "store of wealth."[2] Marketing campaigns narrativized home ownership as the surest path to financial success and affluent neighborhoods, themes also trumpeted by elected officials in Congressional hearings on the fruits of federal housing policy. Such accounts implanted associations between homeownership and wealth in the minds of observers that provided the perfect narrative frame to (mis)interpret the nearly $9 trillion increase in housing-related net worth observed between 1998 and 2006.

The pervasiveness of such narratives spurred demand for property at precisely the time when the rental market should have looked most attractive to marginal households. By 2006, house prices had risen so far, so fast that the relative cost of renting fell to just 58% of the cost of "buying" an equivalent residence, on average, across the U.S.[3] For "hot" markets, like Miami, San Diego and Las Vegas, "buying" became twice as expensive as renting. Such a meteoric rise in prices created "affordability" issues as the median house price rose as a multiple of median income. To overcome this obstacle, mortgage finance companies devised more complex and speculative products to allow a larger number of households to qualify for the larger mortgage principal balances necessary to overpay for the same shelter services they could obtain in the rental market at half the price.

Narrative necessity could not trump physical reality in perpetuity. Once house prices stopped rising, they had to fall. In the absence of the "wealth creation" spurred by debt-financed speculation – and the consumption funded by "cash-out" refinancings, home equity loans and lines of credit – there was no

---

[1] Federal Reserve Bank of St. Louis. Accessed July 2020.
[2] Cf. https://adage.com/article/news/fannie-mae-sells-american-dream-foundation-plans-commercials-fall-tv/61692
[3] As measured relative to 2000 levels. Bureau of Labor Statics, Owners' Equivalent Rent, measured against the Case-Shiller National House Price Index.

reason to overpay for housing services, and existing price levels could not be maintained. House prices swiftly collapsed, returning to levels consistent with equivalent rents in less than three years' time. Housing-related net worth plunged by more than $7 trillion, and default rates on mortgages rose to never-before-seen levels, triggering a financial crisis unlike any observed in an advanced economy since the 1930s.

The scale of the fallout seems proportionate to the strength of the narrative frame. This was not history's first asset price "bubble," but the role that homeownership narratives played in its inflation allows one to appreciate how certain messages can inure investors and households to accumulating risks. By contextualizing the rapid improvement in household financial positions as intrinsic to homeownership, prevailing narratives diminished the natural suspicion that parabolic price increases and yawning price-to-rent imbalances might have otherwise aroused. The "throwing money away" rhetoric both disguised the market's fragility and lured new entrants by demeaning the entirely sensible decision to rent. Bubbles, it seems, depend on some narrative construct, specific to that time and place, to allay the anxieties and analyses that would otherwise prevent them from forming in the first place.

## 2 Rhetoric and economic outcomes

It should come as no surprise that discourses influence economic outcomes. Global advertising spending exceeded $560 billion in 2019,[4] with hundreds of billions of dollars more spent on in-house media relations and communications professionals and public affairs firms. Corporations engage consumers through "brand identification," a complex discursive process that creates emotional or psychological bonds to products, services or the businesses themselves (Tuškej, Golob, and Podnar 2013). Language and related imagery also intermediate the relationships of businesses with capital market participants. A corporation's identity, values, strategy and performance do not arise organically in the minds of stock and bond investors, but reflect the verisimilitude achieved by coordinated investor relations campaigns. Corporations also construct specialized narratives that define the firm (or industry) and its objectives in terms aligned with the socioeconomic concerns and political goals of elected officials and regulators.

The sheer amount of time, attention and money devoted to corporate communications strategies strongly suggests that discursive practices could meaningfully

---

[4] Statistica, Nov 12, 2019.

explain fluctuations in spending patterns, asset prices, and policy outcomes. While this contention may seem uncontroversial to practitioners, or researchers in other social sciences where language is understood to precede or intermediate thought, economists are trained to look skeptically at such explanations. As a discipline, economics fetishizes the identification of "structural relationships." It is not enough to observe that two variables move together over extended periods; such co-movement must be consistent with theory-based restrictions and remain invariant over time. As such, covariation between quantities only becomes economically meaningful to the extent that it corresponds with a preordained conception of human behavior premised on self-interest, rational decision-making, and the sequential updating of beliefs in response to new information.

Canonical asset pricing models, for example, assume the existence of a "representative agent" who rationally consumes, saves and constructs investment portfolios so as to maximize lifetime utility (Merton 1973). Implicit to these models is the idea that the prices of stocks, bonds, real estate and other assets are "forward-looking," a contention shared by virtually all practitioners. The price of stocks today does not depend on current "fundamentals" (i.e. economic variables like GDP, dividends, corporate earnings and interest rates), but investors' collective expectations for how those variables are likely to evolve over time. This schema endows asset prices with an oracular quality; fluctuations in the stock market become revelatory because they manifest from new expectations about the future.

What do stock market gyrations tell us about the future? This is perhaps the central question of financial economics. Standard theory assumes that asset prices reflect *all* available information, a condition known as "informational efficiency." If the price of an asset failed to include some piece of information relevant to its future value or cash flows, investors would have a financial incentive to buy or sell the asset in whatever quantities necessary to bring the price into the proper alignment. A perspicacious corporate communications strategy that "artificially" boosts investor demand for company stock would simply create profit opportunities for arbitrageurs able to "see through" the rhetoric. Observed stock market fluctuations are therefore thought to reflect these corrective trades as well as investors' probabilistic reassessments of future cash flows.

The assumed rationality of all economic agents creates a paradox. Corporate managers would not rationally spend hundreds of billions of dollars to develop and disseminate messages if these communications strategies bore no fruit; either business managers are irrational or markets are not informationally efficient. This is similar to the celebrated critique of Grossman and Stiglitz (1980): if markets were informationally efficient, there would be no financial incentive for investors to expend the time and money necessary to estimate the "true" distribution of future cash flows. The very process through which investors are assumed to bid prices back to efficient levels *necessarily* requires a persistent state of informational *inefficiency* to remunerate investors for the costs of accessing, processing and ultimately incorporating all relevant information into asset prices. This persistent state of uncertainty and flux also generates returns to communications strategies able to shape the perceptions of market participants, resulting in a dialogic interplay between the messages of businesses and investors in their securities.

Information is not just costly to access, but also difficult to interpret. Celebrated papers in behavioral, experimental and information economics demonstrate how cognitive biases and limitations in humans' information processing capacity can generate outcomes that depart from those predicted by models that assume rational expectations, infinite horizons and perfect information (Thaler 2017). Such research is often presented as helpful correctives that identify factors that impede investors from correctly intuiting the "correct" value of an asset. But these findings also help businesses refine their messages in ways that boost sales and demand for their securities. Nadler and McGuigan (2017) show how digital marketers appropriate behavioral economics' insights to identify cognitive and affective biases and target resulting vulnerabilities.

While the behavioral and experimental economics literature identifies the channels through which discourse and corporate narrativization could influence economic outcomes, most of it continues to privilege the canonical model as the baseline from which "mispricing" should be measured. Informational frictions and cognitive biases tend to be presented as obstacles to achieving a "true" knowledge of the world, with laboratory experiments designed to explain why market prices could persistently deviate from "equilibrium" levels. In other words, the research challenges the empirical validity of structural models, not their theoretical content. Many behavioral economists use their findings to solicit practitioners under the guise of avoiding common "mistakes," thereby turning unconscious biases into expensive baggage that investment firms should be willing to pay top dollar to shed through seminars and related training.

The notion that asset prices could be "wrong" due to humans' incompetence at grasping "reality" seems horribly out of step with trends in other social sciences where knowledge is always situated and expectations contingent on experiences. Perhaps this is due to the pretentions of many economists, who are often inclined to view their discipline as a close relative of the physical sciences, with underlying structural relationships that await discovery and precise mathematical specification. Rather than contribute to "mispricing," the dynamic interplay between the discourses of businesses, households and investors seems integral to price formation itself. Orienting thought around a preexisting, idealized price seems more likely to obscure rather than reveal the temporal factors driving the observed price variation, even in cases, like housing, where prices reach levels unlikely to prove sustainable over the longer term.

## 3 Advent of narrative economics

In his 2017 Presidential Address to the annual meeting of the American Economic Association, Robert Shiller lamented the hermeneutical gap that had opened between economics and other social sciences. It had come time, in his view, for economists to "grapple with issues that have troubled literary theorists," especially the narrative construction of economic perceptions, the manner in which these narratives are transmitted and received by economic agents and their role in shaping economic outcomes.

A narrative approach to financial economics takes no issue with the standard assumption that asset prices reflect investors' conditional expectations for their future payoffs, formed on the basis of all information available at that moment in time. But rather than a mathematical abstraction, or throwaway assumption, the specific nature of the information – the language and symbolic systems used to express it, the vantage point from which it proceeds, and the recurring patterns observed in the manner in which it is presented – becomes central to the analysis. Just as the literary theorist understands all thought to be intermediated by language, so too is all market-relevant information.

There's an adage among stock market investors that if it's in the news, it's in the price. The message is two-fold: if an investor is going to gain an edge relative to the competition, it will come from proprietary information and analysis, not widely-consumed media accounts. But it also suggests that the news provides a snapshot of the conventional wisdom or collective understanding that is essential for interpreting market dynamics. Asset prices are underpinned by popular narratives articulated through observable textual formulations, and it is unwise to take a position in the former without a full understanding of the latter.

Asset prices and investor expectations tend to react differently to the same information depending on macroeconomic context (Frydman, Mangee, and Stillwagon 2020). The monthly U.S. employment report is perhaps the most market-sensitive package of macroeconomic data released to the public, providing a snapshot of labor demand, wages and output. While the report generates a predictable spike in trading volumes and volatility, its impact on stock prices varies depending on the prevailing market narrative (cf. Mitchell and Mulherin 1994; Clare and Courtenay 2001; Petralias and Dellaportas 2015). While a strong report typically signals a robust economy likely to boost corporate earnings and stock prices, surprisingly weak employment reports were associated with *positive* stock returns between 2010 and 2018 (Kurov and Stan 2018). Ask any market participant from this era to explain why "bad news" for the economy might have been "good news" for stocks, and they would dutifully explain that unexpected economic weakness increased the odds that the Federal Reserve would ease monetary policy in response. Fed policymakers used oral and textual communications to implant expectations in the minds of investors and members of the financial news media that inverted the normal relationships between asset prices and economic data.

The primary function of the financial news media is to construct narratives to "explain" fluctuations in asset prices, often through reference to broader trends in the economy, policy and society as well as "technical" factors like trading positions and fund flows. This discourse tends to be self-referential – phenomena used to explain prior fluctuations tend to serve as the preferred basis for interpreting current movements – and diachronic: "today, we learned something about tomorrow that we didn't know yesterday." As but one recent example: financial journalists cited the U.S.-China trade dispute over 10,000 times over the course of 2019 to explain stock market fluctuations. Stocks would decline on "renewed trade fears"[5] and then rise when market participants became more confident that a "trade deal" would be reached.[6]

An observer of both the stock market and the news media's coverage of it recognizes the existence and interplay of two related but ultimately distinct time series: (1) the daily closing prices of individual stocks and stock indexes like the S&P 500; and (2) the text from news services like Bloomberg, Reuters and Dow Jones that assign meaning to those prices. Historically, financial economists have tended to focus obsessively on the first and largely ignore the second. Now that increases in computational power and storage capacity allow researchers to treat text as data this has begun to reverse. The text now draws as much or more attention than the numbers themselves (Gentzkow, Kelly, and Taddy 2019).

---

5 https://www.cnbc.com/2019/08/09/stock-market-china-us-trade-relations-in-focus-once-again.html
6 https://www.wsj.com/articles/global-stocks-rise-as-investors-peg-hopes-on-trade-deal-11575456078

## 4 Narrative research programs: Text-mining, linguistic formalism and narrativization

Textual research in economics can be grouped into three broad categories. The first, text-mining, accounts for the bulk of published papers in the field. This form of narrative, or textual, research involves the close reading of central banks' policy statements, companies' earnings releases, macroeconomic data announcements and, most importantly, the news coverage of all three. The language used to describe newly-released macroeconomic data, both in the text of the government agency's release as well as that of the accompanying news coverage, often influences asset prices more than the numbers themselves (Shapiro, Sudhof, and Wilson 2020). In the 2010–2018 period, bad employment reports would generate optimistic news stories that focused on the increased likelihood for Fed stimulus rather than the weakening real economy.[7] The same dynamics are evident for individual stocks, where news coverage of company earnings releases could choose to compare the newly-released metrics to past performance, company guidance or analysts' expectations, each of which could yield different discourses and stock price reactions. Company earnings releases are accompanied by language and graphics inviting readers to adopt a certain interpretive framework for precisely this reason.

In virtually all cases, this close "reading" of releases and associated news stories is computer-assisted, with algorithms used to assess the "sentiment" of the text based on past returns data or surveys. Systematic analysis of texts determine whether the use of certain words or combinations of words contextualize the data or shape attitudes in ways that predict returns or otherwise anticipate shifts in economic performance (Ke, Kelly, and Xiu 2019). The natural language processing or computational linguistics field of machine learning allows large volumes of text to be evaluated relative to past returns data to determine what precise textual formulations generate the most predictable market responses.

Textual analysis has also become especially popular among policymakers, who have begun to evaluate how markets respond to the use of certain words and phrases in their policy pronouncements. Textual analysis conducted by Shapiro and Wilson (2019) of the Federal Reserve Bank of San Francisco reveals that the verbal communications of policymakers often respond to incoming data in ways that depart meaningfully from their stated objectives. Specifically, they find that policymakers were less tolerant of inflation and reacted more

---

7 https://blogs.wsj.com/moneybeat/2014/02/07/with-weak-jobs-report-investors-still-eyeing-fed-help/

forcefully to declines in the stock market than would be expected based on their past commitments and policy framework. Not surprisingly, market-based measures of inflation expectations have tended to more closely track the inflation target revealed by the text (1.5%) rather than the Fed's official 2% target. Likewise, market participants have come to expect the Fed to ease policy in response to sharp declines in stock market indexes (the so-called "Fed Put") even as stock market declines are only supposed to factor into decisions to the extent they contribute directly to rising unemployment (Cieslak and Vissing-Jorgensen 2020).

The second main category of textual research in economics takes an explicitly linguistic approach, measuring how the grammatical and syntactic structure of languages influences economic fluctuations and decision-making. Chen (2013) finds that differences in the way languages encode time correspond to cross-sectional differences in savings rates and other intertemporal decisions. Languages like English, for example, require its speakers to encode a distinction between the present and future in ways that languages like German do not.

Chen finds that the more salient the grammatical separation between present and future, the more dissociated the future becomes from the present among speakers of that language. As a result, speakers of strong future-time-reference languages, like English, tend to spend more of their current income (i.e. save less) than speakers of weak future-time-reference (FTR) languages, like German and especially Chinese, whose speakers can express an event in the future exactly as in the present or the past. Among advanced economies, Chen finds that countries with weak FTR languages save 6% more of their national income each year than countries with strong FTR languages. These results are largely replicated by Guinn (2017), which relies on data from Switzerland to show how financial decisions differ across similarly situated households living in different language regions of the country. Low-to-middle income households in the German-speaking region of the country are 11% more likely to save than the same households in the French-speaking region.

Kim, Kim and Zhou (2017) find that grammatical structure also influences financial reporting behavior. Corporate managers that speak weak FTR languages are found to be less likely to engage in accrual earnings management, likely because they perceive the potential negative future consequences to be more imminent. These results provide a potential causal channel through which "culture" could influence economic outcomes, a hypothesis that the economics establishment has thus far been unwilling to accept given the way it conflicts with representative agent theory. (The contention is that "culture" proxies for some other unobserved heterogeneity across populations that leads to differences in risk aversion or expected income growth that explain the differences in savings rates).

The third and final broad group of textual research seeks to explain economic fluctuations in terms of the emerging storylines or popular narratives identified through systematic analysis of news stories, company earnings releases and related forms of discourse. The idea that "reality" could be narratively constructed has a long history in the social sciences (Bruner 1991) but, as Shiller notes, this type of textual analysis is likely to prove the most controversial among mainstream economists. Identifying the direction of causality can seem insurmountable; does discourse really drive economic trends or merely describe them? In many ways, this criticism echoes that of "framing bias" or "salience theory": Does some phenomenon receive attention because it is important in its own right or because of the meaning assigned to it by the editorial decisions of media companies and privileged discourses of elite social networks (Baresch, Hsu, and Reese 2020)?

In many social sciences, suspicion of "objective" standards of value makes it easier to conclude that discourses have no underlying meaning beyond those assigned by gatekeepers. This is a harder sell among financial economists because of the difficulty delineating *precisely* between reality and rhetoric's impact on asset prices. For example, were the U.S.-China trade negotiations really so consequential to corporate "fundamentals" to warrant the concomitant fluctuations in stock prices observed over the course of 2019? Or did asset prices become *unduly* sensitized to the profit implications of the trade dispute because of the massive amount of news coverage it garnered? If it was the later, asset prices were not responding to observed changes in the "objective" probabilities of future cash flows, but only the portion of the payoff that was most "salient" in the minds of investors (Bordalo, Gennaioli, and Shleifer 2013).

## 5 Narrative construction of economic reality

Climate change provides fertile ground for research into the economic impact of prevailing narratives. The past two years have witnessed a sharp rise in the use of the phrase "climate crisis" in lieu of "climate change," "climate risk" or "global warming" to describe the nature of the threat facing the planet from the emissions of carbon dioxide and other greenhouse gases (Thomas and Starr 2020). Such usage conveys a sense of urgency about the nature of the threat that has been increasingly reflected in asset prices. As use of "climate crisis" transitioned from a relative novelty to the primary phrase employed to describe unfolding climatic phenomenon (Figures 17.1 and 17.2), the market value of integrated oil and gas companies declined sharply relative to their earnings.

By early 2020, these businesses traded at a 50% discount relative to comparable companies in other sectors of the economy, on average.[8] At the same time, the valuations assigned to companies inside of the energy sector became increasingly dispersed, with renewable energy companies and electric vehicle and battery manufacturers trading at huge premiums to integrated oil and gas companies (Figure 17.3). By the end of 2019, when the phrase "climate crisis" appeared once every 250 words in a representative sample of articles, every 10% increase in the share of an energy company's revenues attributable to renewable sources translated to a 25% increase in its valuation.

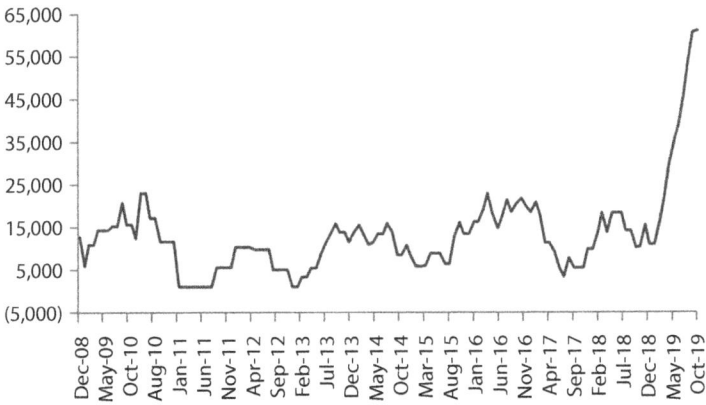

**Figure 17.1:** New mentions of "climate crisis" by month.

To many observers, these price adjustments look entirely rational, as the revenues and profits of companies engaged in the extraction, refining and transportation of fossil fuels would be expected to atrophy in the years ahead, as energy production shifts to renewable sources and a larger share of surface transportation vehicles become electrified. Many observers would also argue that "climate crisis" is less a narrative innovation than an apt description of our current ecological circumstances. The "rhetoric" in this case may simply be catching up with the underlying reality. While that may indeed be the case, there is no evidence to suggest that the science or probabilistic assessments of climate scenarios changed in a manner commensurate with the shift in rhetoric. Moreover, there can be little doubt that the phase "climate crisis" conveys a very different message to lay observers than the more benign "climate change," and it is far

---

[8] S&P Capital IQ Data, Accessed February 2020.

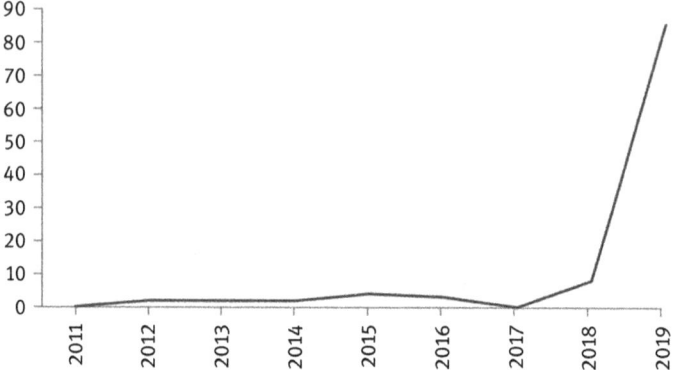

**Figure 17.2:** Investment research reports including "climate crisis" by year.

more likely to lead investors to divest oil and gas assets, reduce carbon footprints and redirect capital towards green energy and related storage technology – precisely the shifts observed in markets over a period contemporaneous with the shift in phraseology.

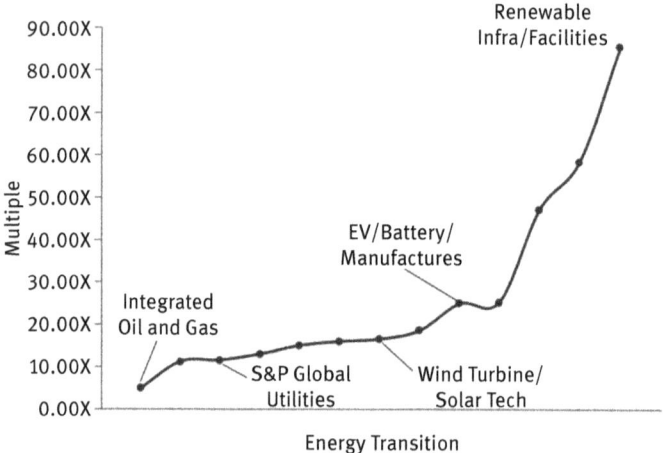

**Figure 17.3:** Valuation multiples have adjusted to energy transistion risk in advance of changes in fundamentals.

Important narrative innovations occur outside of the news media and often involve the sudden appearance and mimetic repetition of certain phrases or textual characterizations in all aspects of economic life. Economically meaningful rhetorical shifts are especially evident in corporate financial disclosures and related communications. Each quarter, corporate management teams release a battery of statistics regarding the financial health of the business accompanied by text and graphics describing management's assessment of macroeconomic and industry conditions, corporate strategy, risks and other topics of potential relevance to investors, such as environmental, social and governance practices. Unless badly managed, such communications tend to have an internal coherence such that the description of corporate strategy tends to dovetail with management's expectations for the near-term evolution of the industry and broader economy. As a result, one can gain insights regarding the likely direction of business spending, mergers and acquisitions activity, and staffing needs based on the stories management teams tell their investors (and themselves) about the likely direction of the economy.

At the end of 2018, computational analysis of the text of these communications (both regulatory filings and conference call transcripts) revealed a dramatic increase in the use of "late cycle" to describe the economic environment (Figure 17.4). Certainly, the expansion had grown long in the tooth; by July 2018, the uninterrupted period of growth following the Global Financial Crisis had become the second longest on record. But, as the saying goes, expansions don't die of old age. Time, in this case, is a confounding variable; the onset of recession is not a function of the length of time since the last recession, but the scale of imbalances that had accumulated, over time, due to excessive investment, imprudent borrowing and reckless businesses expansion. Those excesses can build up over relatively short periods, as between 2002 to 2007, or take a while to manifest themselves, as in the case of the United Kingdom's economy, which avoided sequential quarters of contraction between 1992 and 2008. At the end of 2018, there were few signs that the U.S. economy was at imminent risk of falling into recession, and no central bank or professional forecaster anticipated one.

By engaging in such discourse, business managers risked talking themselves into a recession. Management teams employed "late cycle" as a narrative predicate to justify conservatism in their business strategy. Because it was "late cycle," management reasoned to investors, the business would be less aggressive in its expansion plans, hold more liquidity on its balance sheet, and take a more circumspect approach to additional hiring. As the share of businesses citing "late cycle" concerns rose exponentially at the end of 2018 and into 2019, business investment slowed materially and finished the year in negative territory (Figure 17.5). While the aforementioned U.S.-China trade war contributed to the drop, the initial turndown corresponded exactly to the sudden increase in businesses' invocation of late-cycle concerns and preceded the trade war's intensification.

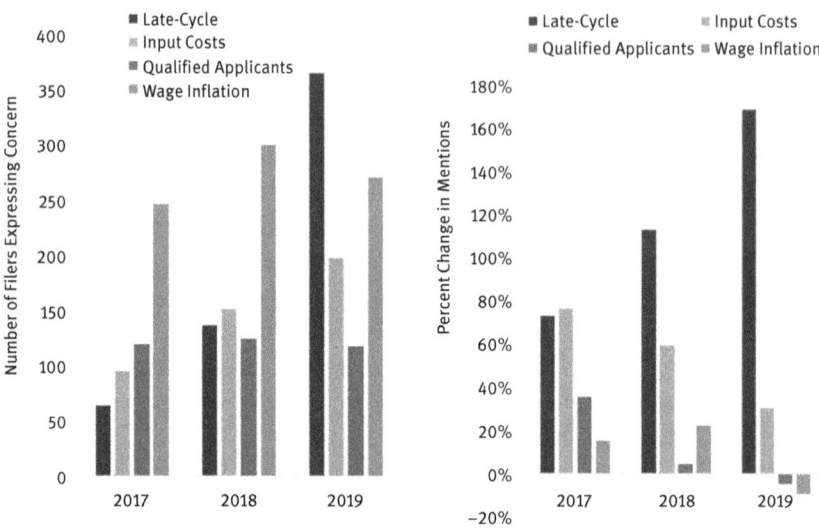

**Figure 17.4:** Late-cycle fears have quickly emerged as the key concern among management teams; inflationary pressures fading in significance.

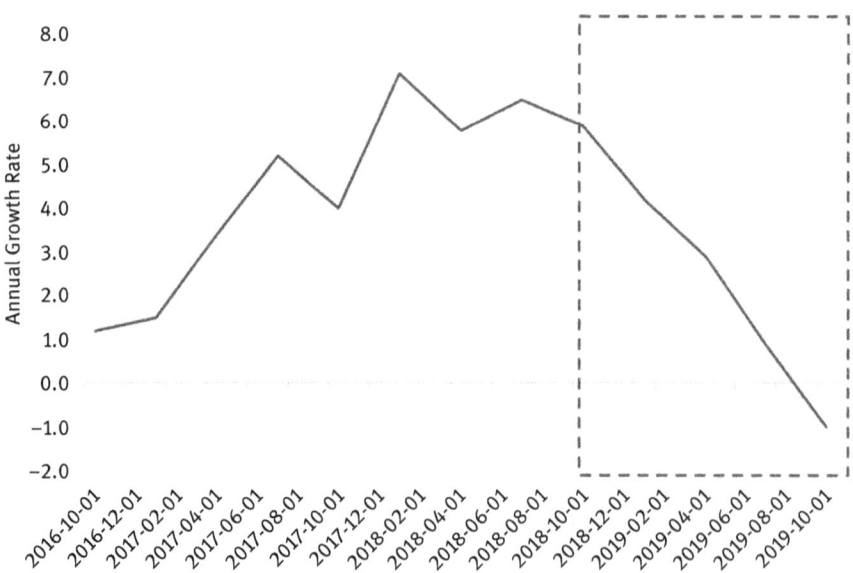

**Figure 17.5:** Real business investment slows dramatically in response to increased invocations of "late cycle" fears.

The process by which these narratives spread across businesses is not well understood, but it seems to involve a degree of mimicry, as businesses incorporate others' themes and ideas into their own presentations and thinking. (Businesses are known to analyze their peers' financial disclosures and earnings transcripts for competitive intelligence assessments, often employing natural language processing techniques). Financial analysts and news journalists may also play a role in the propagation of narratives, as the questions they ask business managers often stem from issues raised on prior conference calls or interviews. Shiller (2017) suggests epidemiological models could be employed to analyze the spread of these narratives.

## 6 Conclusion

The turn towards textual or narrative analysis in economics reflects the combined effects of new technology and the softening of old prejudices and pretensions. As a large and growing share of human communication gets recorded and stored as digital text, new doors have been opened for quantitative researchers looking to enrich existing models of asset prices and macroeconomic dynamics. And as "behavioral" approaches to economic analysis became more widespread, economists became better acquainted with the psychological literature and epistemological trends in other social sciences that look suspiciously at some of the assumptions at the heart of canonical economic models. But whereas most behavioral economics research presents itself as a helpful corrective that identifies "real world" impediments to a "true" understanding of the world, the narrative approach takes a step further, arguing that discourses not only capture but also constitute economic reality. Narratives are capable of changing behavior and influencing economic outcomes in ways that heighten verisimilitude, reinforce convictions and gain new adherents. Appreciation for this reflexive character changes one's conception of the origin of economic phenomena and casts doubt on the predictive value of models that fail to account for it.

## References

Baresch, Brian, Shih-Hsien Hsu & Stephen Reese. 2020. The power of framing: New challenges for researching the structure of meaning in the news. *Journalism's Futures*, University of Texas in Allan, S. (2010). The Routledge companion to news and journalism. London: Routledge. p. 637–647.

Bordalo, Pedro, Nicola Gennaioli & Andrei Shleifer. 2013. Salience and asset prices. *American Economic Review: Papers & Proceedings* 103 (3). 623–628.
Bruner, Jerome. 1991. The narrative construction of reality. *Critical Inquiry* 18. 1–21.
Chen, Keith. 2013. The effect of language on economic behavior: Evidence from savings rates, health behaviors, and retirement assets. *American Economic Review* 103 (2). 690–731.
Cieslak, Anna & Annette Vissing-Jorgensen. 2020. The economics of the Fed Put. *NBER Working Papers* 26894. National Bureau of Economic Research.
Clare, Andrew and Roger Courtenay. 2001. Assessing the Impact of Macroeconomic News Announcements on Securities Prices. Bank of England Working Paper No. 125. Bank of England.
Frydman, Roman, Nicholas Mangee & Josh Stillwagon. 2020. How market sentiment drives forecasts of stock returns. *Institute for New Economic Thinking Working Paper Series* (115). Institute for New Economic Thinking.
Gentzkow, Matthew, Bryan Kelly & Matt Taddy. 2019. Text as data. *Journal of Economic Literature* 57 (3). 535–574.
Grossman, Sanford & Jospeh Stiglitz. 1980. On the impossibility of informationally efficient markets. *American Economic Review* 70 (3) 393–408.
Guinn, Benjamin. 2017. Culture and household saving. *ECB Working Papers* 2069. European Central Bank. Frankfurt.
Ke, Zheng Tracy, Brian Kelly & Dacheng Xiu. 2019. Predicting returns with text data. *NBER Working Papers* 26186. National Bureau of Economic Research. Cambridge, MA.
Kim, Jaehyeon, Yongtae Kim & Jian Zhou. 2017. Languages and earnings management. *Journal of Accounting and Economics* 63 (2). 288–306.
Kurov, Alexander & Stan Raluca. 2018. Monetary policy uncertainty and the market reaction to macroeconomic news. *Journal of Banking & Finance* 86 (C). 127–142.
Merton, Robert. 1973. An intertemporal capital asset pricing model. *Econometrica* 41 (5). 867–887.
Mitchell, Mark & Harold Mulherin. 1994. The impact of public information on the stock market. *Journal of Finance* 49 (3). 923–50.
Nadler, Anthony & Lee McGuigan. 2017. An impulse to exploit: The behavioral turn in data-driven marketing. *Critical Studies in Media Communication* 35. 151–165.
Petralias, Athanassios & Petros Dellaportas. 2015. Volatility prediction based on scheduled macroeconomic announcements. *Canadian Journal of Statistics* 43. 199–223.
Shapiro, Adam Hale, Moritz Sudhof & Daniel Wilson. 2020. Measuring news sentiment. Working Paper Series. Federal Reserve Bank of San Francisco. San Francisco.
Shapiro, Adam Hale & Daniel Wilson. 2019. Taking the Fed at its word: A new approach to estimating Central Bank objectives using text analysis. Working Paper Series. Federal Reserve Bank of San Francisco. San Francisco.
Shiller. Robert. 2017. Narrative economics. *American Economic Review* 107 (4). 967–1004.
Thaler, Richard. 2017. Behavioral economics: Past, present, and future. *American Economic Review* 106 (7). 1577–1600.
Thomas, Jason & Megan Starr. 2020. From impact investing to investing for impact. The Carlyle Group. Washington, DC.
Tuškej, Urška, Ursa Golob & Klement Podnar. 2013. The role of consumer-brand identification in building brand relationships. *Journal of Business Research* 66. 53–59.

Heidi E. Hamilton
# Chapter 18
# Life as a linguist among clinicians: Learnings from interdisciplinary collaborations on language and health

> Collaboration across qualitative and quantitative ways of knowing can be viewed akin to the ethnographic process of bridging cultures, and as such it should concentrate on including all perspectives and discovering common ground for understanding.
>
> Robins et al. (2008: 5)

## 1 Introduction

Whether describing symptoms, reporting results of medical testing, assessing one's health risk, or considering next steps in a treatment plan, language is at the center of many health care encounters. The language used by health professionals as well as by individuals who have paused in their life to focus on health (their own or that of others) allows us to glimpse what they are thinking: It sheds light on their medical reasoning, their health-related memories, their experiences of health in the here-and-now, their mental projections into possible health futures.

Over the past four decades or so, linguists have been applying their insights in efforts to understand some of the myriad ways in which language intersects with the dynamic and critically important domains of health. As these undertakings have become more expansive, collaboration across disciplines and between research and practice has also become increasingly common. The intricacies of the mutual effects between language and human health – how language use affects health as well as how health affects language – have encouraged linguists to reach across disciplinary boundaries in their examinations of public and private dimensions of health communication. Given this large and multi-faceted landscape, most of these investigators have carved out specific areas on which to focus, e.g., patient-provider interactions (Ainsworth-Vaughn 1998; Heritage and Maynard 2006; Roberts 1999); mental health and counseling (Capps and Ochs 1995; Ferrara 1994; Peräkylä 1995; Ribeiro 1994); discourse of disability (Al Zidjaly 2015); narrative as related to cognition and

---
**Heidi E. Hamilton,** Georgetown University, hamilthe@georgetown.edu

https://doi.org/10.1515/9781501514371-018

experience of illness (Hunter 1991; Mattingly 1998); the discourse of public health (Higgins and Norton 2009); and health and risk communication (Sarangi and Clarke 2002; Jones 2013), to name just a few. In order to learn about these areas, researchers have examined language evidence from a wide variety of sources: recorded and transcribed clinical encounters, interviews, focus groups and other naturally-occurring spoken discourses; written online communication, medication package inserts, and other authentic written texts; personal experience narratives; linguistic corpora and survey databases; and ethnographic research field notes.

These linguists are sometimes members of interdisciplinary health care teams whose sustained work exemplifies the kind of "joint problematization" celebrated by Sarangi and Candlin (2003), some of them translating what they know about communication into educational and training materials to be implemented within health care institutions. Others remain within their home academic departments, analyzing selected audio- and video-recordings and transcripts in an effort to illuminate patterns within specific health care settings (and, in so doing, learning about discourse more generally), perhaps accepting occasional invitations to collaborate or consult on a case-by-case basis with the aim of identifying solutions to specific health communication challenges. Still others attempt (as have I) to live in both worlds, shuttling between linguistics conferences and health and medical conferences; these individuals are eager to cross-pollinate ideas, sequentially learning and teaching with an eye toward systematically translating one set of disciplinary assumptions and frameworks into another.

But within all the valuable publications resulting from such interdisciplinary engagement, only a very few pages have been devoted to the types of intriguing challenges that typically arise during the actual design and execution of such research – and, importantly, how these are negotiated and resolved. Coupland (1997: 33) describes a typical problem at an early stage of such teamwork as "bolting one methodology onto another and one analytical perspective onto another, without fully achieving integration." At a much later stage in the teamwork – when the results of empirical study are written up – Roberts (1997: 68) claims that "the process of intellectual negotiation between practitioners and researchers seems to evaporate" along with associated key insights from which interested readers of the publications could learn.

It is these kinds of challenges related to the attunement of disciplinary paradigms that have invigorated me over the past 30 years in my work as a linguist among clinicians in interdisciplinary projects surrounding a variety of health concerns, including head injuries; inter-professional hospital communication; genetic counseling discourse; the impact of the chief complaint on the shape of physician-patient discourse; sociocultural barriers to mental health treatment; health literacy and adherence in chronic disease management; genetic risk assessment in hereditary breast cancer; and the lived experiences of children of parents with mental illness.

In this work, I view health issues from the perspective of an interactional sociolinguist[1] who thrives on communicating the power and relevance of this approach to students as well as to professionals outside the field of linguistics. And, although some of my resulting interactions with professionals representing other disciplines have been limited to one-time meetings or workshops, the most gratifying interactions have been centered within very close sustained collaborations over an extended period of time within carefully constructed interdisciplinary teams that have sought solutions to "real world" problems.

Over these many years, I have learned a great deal through interactions with a wide variety of professionals, including medical specialists, nurses, genetic counselors, speech and language pathologists, social workers, attorneys, and communication scientists. Sometimes these experiences have been uplifting and energizing, and I have come away feeling that I have represented linguistics well and that the insights from our discipline have been extraordinarily helpful; at other times, I have been left with a sinking feeling that I was unable to communicate across the disciplinary boundaries in the sound bite format that is frequently expected.

Regardless of the degree of perceived success, each such interaction has taught me incrementally more about the challenges related to interdisciplinary research that may surface at virtually every phase of a study. Different disciplinary paradigms influence decisions regarding what kinds of research questions are thought to be both answerable and useful or important. They also influence what participants and settings can be included in a study, what kinds of language data can be collected and how, what types of theoretical frameworks and analytical units can be brought to the research, as well as what

---

[1] Although I am arguably best known within linguistics for my work examining naturally-occurring interactional language use by and with individuals with Alzheimer's disease (e.g., Hamilton 1994, 2019), the vast majority of my work in that domain has been carried out individually as an interactional sociolinguist outside of sustained involvement in interdisciplinary projects. In this chapter, then, I focus on interdisciplinary projects that represent my work in other areas of health. In recent years I have increased my engagement with dementia researchers representing other disciplines (e.g., in exciting initiatives at the University of Southern Denmark [SDU] on "Creativity and Dementia") and look forward to continuing this important work across disciplines within SDU's anticipated research center on "Living with Dementia" (In Danish: Det at leve med demens [LIDEM]), which aims to involve the humanities, social sciences, health sciences, and engineering sciences.

counts as research findings, and how these findings should be reported (see Hamilton and Hamaguchi [2015] for additional information).

With the firm conviction that the positives of such experiences (far) outweigh the negatives, in what follows I share some of my insights and experiences. It is my hope that these shared learnings may encourage and assist linguists who are interested in entering into interdisciplinary collaborations within health care. Such preparation regarding the kinds of differences that can exist when undertaking interdisciplinary research – along with suggestions regarding how to make the most of one's role in such research – may make the crucial difference between a linguist leaving a project in frustration or being able to contribute to lasting changes (see also Hamilton and Chou 2014: 1–12 and Alatis, Hamilton, and Tan 2002: 251–265).

# 2 Interdisciplinary projects in which I have participated

Since 1990, I have been fortunate to participate in a variety of interdisciplinary health projects, eight of which are briefly described in Table 18.1. Due to space constraints, only four of these (*Defense Head Injury Project*, *Hospitalk*, *Genetic Counseling as Discourse*, and *Managing the Dialogue*) are more fully characterized in sections 2.1–2.4 below.

## 2.1 Linguistic consultant, *Defense Head Injury Project*

The Defense Head Injury Project was launched at Walter Reed Army Medical Center (now called Walter Reed National Military Medical Center) to evaluate active duty military persons who had suffered a traumatic brain injury by, for example, parachuting into a grove of trees, followed by a period of more than 24 hours of amnesia. During early pilot tests leading up to the design of the patient evaluation protocol, the speech and language pathologists involved in the project realized that the language and communication problems of their patients were different from those with whom these clinicians had been trained to work, i.e., the more "classic" aphasias. After turning to studies within the area of pragmatics in the speech and language pathology literature (Ehrlich and Sipes 1985; Prutting and Kirchner 1987), the clinicians decided they could benefit from a linguistic perspective. As I was teaching a course in pragmatics that semester at Georgetown University (just across town from Walter Reed), they reached out to me. And since

**Table 18.1:** Selected interdisciplinary projects in which the author has participated (Projects in bold are characterized in Sections 2.1–2.4).

| Interdisciplinary project | My role |
|---|---|
| **Defense Head Injury Project** (Walter Reed Army Medical Center, Washington, DC) | Consulting discourse analyst over approximately three years (weekly to monthly meetings with two speech-language pathologists). Graduate students were involved through a seminar on Language in Clinical Populations. |
| **Hospitalk** (Georgetown University Medical Center) | Consulting discourse analyst over approximately two years (regular meetings with Dean of the School of Nursing; Chair of the Department of Medicine, and Associate Director of Nursing Administration at the Medical Center). Graduate students were involved as ethnographic fieldworkers in the hospital, recorded selected interactions, carried out interviews with staff members, and were involved in research team meetings. |
| **Genetic Counseling as Discourse** (Georgetown University Medical Center) | Consulting discourse analyst over approximately two years (regular meetings with two genetic counselors). Graduate students were involved as research assistants, sat in on and recorded counseling sessions, and were involved in research team meetings. Genetic counselors also participated fully in two semester-long graduate linguistics courses (Sociolinguistic Field Methods and Health Discourse) to familiarize themselves with discourse theories and methods. |
| **Managing the Dialogue: Physician-Patient Talk** (Health Communication Company) | Consulting discourse analyst over approximately ten years (meetings with a variety of medical researchers, physicians, nurses, and patient advocates on thought leadership teams according to the goals of each project). |
| Sociocultural Barriers to Mental Health Treatment (Georgetown University Medical Center) | Consulting discourse analyst over approximately two years (regular meetings with two psychiatrists). Psychiatrists also participated fully in one semester-long graduate linguistic course (Health Discourse) to familiarize themselves with discourse theories and methods. |

**Table 18.1** (continued)

| Interdisciplinary project | My role |
| --- | --- |
| *Health Literacy and Medical Adherence* (Indiana University Purdue University Indianapolis) | Consulting discourse analyst over approximately two years (meetings with interdisciplinary team members including an endocrinologist, a pharmacist, an attorney, communication scientists and linguists). |
| *Testing a Culturally Adapted Telephone Genetic Counseling Intervention to Enhance Genetic Risk Assessment in Underserved Latinas at Risk of Hereditary Breast Cancer* (Georgetown University Medical Center) | Mentor and faculty advisor for a social psychologist within the university's Department of Oncology (monthly meetings with team members representing oncology, genetic counseling, and health communication) |
| *Children of Parents with Mental Illness* (Research Group of the Ludwig Boltzmann Gesellschaft, Vienna, Austria) | Advisor for Principal Investigator Dr. Jean Paul, Medical University of Innsbruck, Innsbruck, Austria (meetings with team members representing psychiatry, mental health services, behavioral neuroscience, genetic counseling, information technology, and patient advocacy) |

I had recently completed a nearly five-year longitudinal interactional sociolinguistic study of conversations I had had with one individual with Alzheimer's disease (Hamilton 1994) and had been consulting on an informal basis on discourse-level phenomena with the Language in the Aging Brain project at the Boston Veterans Administration Hospital (see Albert and Knoefel 2011; Obler and Gjerlow 1999), I was pleased to have an opportunity to be involved in an active way with an ongoing project of this type. Over nearly three years,[2] I met approximately once a month – at times as frequently as once a week – with clinicians at the hospital. In order to introduce Georgetown University linguistics graduate students to some of these compelling issues, I offered a medical discourse seminar in which students were able to analyze audio-recordings of therapist-patient interviews and narratives written by the first six patients in the study. These students' seminar papers were then shared with the Walter Reed clinicians who found them to be highly informative and thought-provoking.

---

[2] My involvement in this project ended with the onset of my university leave to take care of my son, who underwent bone marrow transplantation five months after birth.

Over the course of my time at Walter Reed, I was primarily involved in four kinds of activities: 1) designing tasks as part of a test battery that would elicit extended periods of naturally-occurring conversational discourse and elicited personal experience narratives; 2) examining recorded interactions in which the test battery was administered with an eye toward identifying ways in which the language used by the interviewer influenced language produced by the patient (and vice versa) – to provide counter-evidence to the clinicians' initial assumption that neither the test situation nor the interviewer would significantly influence the language produced by the patient; 3) devising appropriate categories and descriptions of a range of appropriate and inappropriate behaviors as part of the construction of the rating scale (e.g., to evaluate the patients' performance on the test battery); and 4) consulting with the clinicians as they completed the performance scale based on their engagement with recordings of patients undergoing the test battery; it was in this activity that I was able to teach the clinicians to approach their data as linguists, so that they had experience on which they could build from session to session. Through these encounters (usually sparked by a clinician's observation: "Something strange is going on here, but I can't quite put my finger on it"), our discussions became increasingly sophisticated over time, and the division of labor involved in such analysis shifted from the linguist to the clinician. At the same time, I became more familiar and comfortable with the work of speech and language pathologists and was able to predict much more effectively which aspects of linguistics would likely be of interest to them.

## 2.2 Co-organizer and faculty facilitator of *Hospitalk*

Approximately two years after I had concluded my involvement at Walter Reed, I was approached by three individuals then associated with the Georgetown University Medical Center: Dr. John Eisenberg, Chairman of the Department of Medicine; Dr. Elaine Larson, Dean of the School of Nursing; and Ms. Kathleen Mitchell, RN, Associate Director of Nursing Administration. They were interested in involving linguists in the evaluation and assessment of possible changes in communication patterns between physicians and nurses as the result of impending staffing and scheduling changes at the Medical Center. The resulting project, which I termed "Hospitalk," started off with a group of eight student research assistants paid by the Medical Center and several volunteers. Students carried out systematic ethnographic observations on several hospital units, interviewed individual nurses and physicians, and audio-recorded inter-professional interactions on the hospital floors, including weekly interdisciplinary discharge rounds.

Very soon after we began our study, financial constraints at the hospital forced one of the hospital units (importantly, the unit that was the center of our experimental control group) in our study to close; shortly thereafter, both Eisenberg and Larson notified me that they would be leaving the university for positions elsewhere. As one of the final tasks of their time at Georgetown, Larson, Eisenberg, and Mitchell worked with me on an article for publication in a clinical performance journal (Larson et al. 1998). At that point, my participation in this project was further complicated by a major health crisis in my immediate family, as my then four-year-old son had to undergo his second bone marrow transplantation. When I returned to Georgetown after caring for my son, my attention was directed toward other research projects. Several student team members and I presented our findings on the discourse in hospital rounds in a conference symposium, and research on the *Hospitalk* data continued to be carried out by one of the original graduate students on the research team who, in the meantime, had become a tenure-track faculty member at another university (Graham 2009). And so, although this project began with a great sense of excitement and energy on the part of the entire team, it was ultimately not as successful as the other projects characterized in this chapter. Our weekly team meetings lacked the two-way mutually informative nature related to clinical *and* linguistic insights, as they were most frequently carried out without the participation of the clinical team members, who had too many competing professional responsibilities. As linguists, we were collecting data and carrying out analyses, but not learning from or teaching our clinical team members in a systematic and sustained way.

## 2.3 Collaborator, *Genetic Counseling as Discourse: A Sociolinguistic Analysis*

During the height of my engagement in the Hospitalk project, two genetic counselors at Georgetown University Medical Center, Judith L. Benkendorf and Michele Prince, invited me to join them in writing a proposal to study the discourse of genetic counseling encounters; they were especially interested in discovering how their profession's principles and code of ethics were being put into practice in their sessions with patients. I was intrigued by the prospect of studying this specific kind of health care visit, since my son's bone marrow transplants were necessitated by a genetic disorder of the immune system (Wiskott-Aldrich Syndrome). Having lost two brothers and two male first cousins to the consequences of this syndrome, I had grown up well aware of the difficult decision-making that accompanies such family challenges. Although I was already busy with *Hospitalk*, I agreed to take on this project.[3] Our proposal to the National Society of Genetic Counselors was successful. The first year of our project was supported by a fellowship that allowed us to audio-record and transcribe 43 (primarily prenatal) genetic counseling sessions. Graduate students in sociolinguistics joined the team as transcribers and analysts; our weekly interdisciplinary meetings at the medical center contained some of the most illuminating and exciting discussions of my academic career. In contrast to the projects characterized above, the two genetic counselors participated in each team meeting; additionally, the counselors participated fully in semester-long graduate classes on sociolinguistic field methods and medical discourse.

Symposia and workshops with my colleagues Benkendorf and Prince, along with graduate student research assistants, were held at an annual education conference of the National Society of Genetic Counselors, a genetic counseling training program of the Johns Hopkins University/National Genome Research Institute at the National Institutes of Health (NIH), and two linguistics conferences (American Association for Applied Linguistics and the Georgetown University Round Table on Languages and Linguistics). In the sessions for health care providers, our emphasis was on teaching basic concepts and frameworks of discourse analysis and raising the awareness of these medical professionals regarding the power of their language choices and interactional strategies; in the sessions for linguists, our emphasis was on the shaping influences of the genetic counseling principles of non-directiveness and patient-centeredness (see Benkendorf et al. 2001; Gordon et al. 2002).

## 2.4 Co-founder and study designer, *Managing the Dialogue: Physician-Patient Talk*, MBS/Vox (a Commonhealth Company)

Approximately one year after the Hospitalk project came to an end, I received an invitation from Joseph Gattuso of CommonHealth, a health communications company, to design a methodology that would enable multiple relatively small-scale (sample size of 30–40 patients) interactional sociolinguistic studies that could be used to investigate physician-patient interactions that center on a wide range of medical concerns. As I had not yet systematically studied the discourse

---

[3] In retrospect, my decision to agree to this project despite being very involved in Hospitalk was a good one; as noted above, the Hospitalk project ended prematurely due to factors outside our control, and the Genetic Counseling as Discourse project turned out to be mutually engaging for several years.

of physician-patient interactions that are so central to published sociolinguistic research on medical discourse, I eagerly accepted this new challenge. We based our studies on John Gumperz' (1982, 1999) seminal work on "crosstalk" to include video-recording of the physician-patient interaction, in addition to separate post-interviews with the physician and patient(s). This design was an important departure from the vast majority of investigations of physician-patient communication that tend either to be based on post-interviews and questionnaires alone (not on the actual visit between the physician and the patient) or only on the visit (with no post-interview to highlight differences and similarities in perceptions, comprehension, meaning making processes, etc.).

Over the subsequent 10 years, I participated in more than 40 studies of this type centered on problems related to a wide range of diseases and health conditions, including ADHD, allergy, Alzheimer's disease, anticoagulation/antiplatelet therapy, arthritis, metastatic breast cancer, chemotherapy-induced anemia, contraception, chronic occlusive pulmonary disease, dementia, depression, diabetes, gingivitis, hepatitis C, high cholesterol, hormone replacement therapy, hypertension, irritable bowel syndrome, lung cancer, lymphoma migraine, melanoma, migraine, mild cognitive impairment, onychomycosis, osteoporosis, muscular pain management, and rheumatoid arthritis. During this time, I served on national advisory boards for Hepatitis C, chemotherapy-induced anemia, and migraine, and taught health communication units as part of Continuing Medical Education (CME) with the University of Illinois and The Johns Hopkins University (see Hamilton 2003, 2004; Hamilton, Nelson, and Gordon 2006a; Hamilton et al. 2006b; Davidson et al. 2007; Nelson and Hamilton 2007; Hamilton et al. 2008).

# 3 What I've learned from cross-disciplinary collaborations

The most casual reader will have noticed in the project characterizations in sections 2.1–2.4 that these studies were all initiated by health care professionals who reached out to me as a linguist. Even though they did not consider themselves experts in linguistics, they knew enough about the discipline to anticipate that a linguist might provide an intriguing (or even critical) perspective in their understanding of an important heath care issue. In my experience this is how things frequently proceed in the world, where one opportunity can lead to another. That said, there is no reason for interested linguists to sit back and wait for health professionals to come calling. Readers can certainly take the proverbial bull by the horns and reach out to professionals in any area of health care that interests them. Why am I confident that this kind of engagement may be welcomed?

A glance at the shifting landscape in health care over the past decade or two leads me to be optimistic about increasing opportunities for health care collaboration. Space constraints limit full characterization of these, but a quick listing may suffice:

- **The National Institutes of Health (NIH) place value on innovative interdisciplinary investigations as characterized by mixed methods research** defined as "the collection, analysis, and integration of both quantitative data (e.g., RCT[4] outcome) and qualitative data (e.g., observations, semi-structured interviews) to provide a more comprehensive understanding of a research problem than might be obtained through quantitative or qualitative research alone" (Cresswell and Plano Clark 2017; Guetterman et al. 2019). This situation means that medical researchers who typically rely on quantitative methods may be eager to include more qualitative perspectives typical of discourse analysis if a case can be made that this inclusion may result in a fuller understanding of mechanisms and contexts not previously understood.
- **The United States Medical Licensing Exam (USMLE), a three-step examination for medical licensure in the United States, added an assessment of clinical skills (Step 2 Clinical Skills)** as demonstrated through video-recorded in-person interactions with standardized patients in 2004, so that standards to practice medicine safely would include "not only clinical competence but also the ability to communicate effectively with patients and colleagues"[5] (Cuddy and Peitzman 2015). The resulting redesign of medical school curricular materials to focus more intentionally on what has been traditionally characterized as "bedside manner," so as to better prepare medical students for success in this aspect of the licensing exam, has opened up

---

4 This acronym refers to "randomized controlled trial," the gold standard in medical research. In this type of investigation "subjects are randomly assigned to one of two groups: one (the experimental group) receiving the intervention that is being tested, and the other (the comparison group or control) receiving an alternative (conventional) treatment. The two groups are then followed up to see if there are any differences between them in outcome. The results and subsequent analysis of the trial are used to assess the effectiveness of the intervention, which is the extent to which a treatment, procedure, or service does patients more good than harm. RCTs are the most stringent way of determining whether a cause effect relation exists between the intervention and the outcome" (Kendall 2003).

5 See the website of the United States Medical Licensing Examination for more detailed information regarding the clinical skills examination: https://www.usmle.org/frequently-asked-questions/#step2cs

collaborative opportunities for discourse analysts (see Chou et al. 2011; Charon 2014; Blatt, Spinazzi, and Greenberg 2014; Tsai, Lu, and Frankel 2014).

- **Recent advances in genomic medicine (see Manolio et al. 2019) and increased importance of shared decision making (SDM) in clinical practice** (Barry and Edgman-Levitan 2012; Shay and Lafata 2015) both lead to a heightened focus on the quality of communication in patient-provider interactions. In the case of genomic medicine, a patient's genetic information, lifestyle, and environment enter into discussions of "tailored" treatment plans to address an individual's health concern. In the case of shared decision-making, patients and clinicians jointly consider options that will help patients enact their own informed preferences for health care (Lamb, Wang, and Lyytinen 2019: 1103). And as scientific information becomes more central to health care decision-making, patients' health literacy (Rubin 2014) and numeracy (Zarcadoolas and Vaughon 2014) become increasingly important. In all these situations, discourse analysts are particularly well suited to investigate the linguistically nuanced ways in which patients and clinicians demonstrate their degree of attunement (Hamilton 2004) across these many dimensions of talk.

- **The increasing incorporation of new technologies into health care** (see Hamilton and Chou 2014: 8–9; Jones 2015: 850–852) over the past 10–15 years has shaped interactions between clinicians and their patients, interactions among medical professionals as they manage patient care, and even patients' interactions with each other as they seek out and provide information and support. Qualitative researchers have carried out work in the areas of telemedicine (Turner 1996; Robinson, Turner, and Wood 2015), text-messaging in the area of disease management (Turner et al. 2013), computers in the in-office clinical encounter (Crampton, Reis, and Shachak 2016), and online health support groups (Hamilton 1998; Stommel 2009). Discourse analysts with expertise in the areas of computer-mediated communication (Herring and Androutsopoulos 2015) and multimodality (Kress 2010), especially with a focus on the role of objects (in this case, laptops or other screens) in the environment to shape unfolding interaction (Goodwin 2013; Nevile et al. 2014), may find themselves particularly drawn to and prepared for particularly insightful work in this area.

But despite this optimistic perspective regarding possible opportunities for linguists on interdisciplinary teams, joining forces with health care researchers as a linguist who uses primarily qualitative methods is not necessarily straightforward. Robins et al. (2008: 3) characterize the challenge this way: "Researchers have long recognized the fact that qualitative and quantitative research methods are based on different philosophies of knowledge, but little attention has been paid to how these differences can bring about real-world dilemmas for a mixed-methods research team." It is in this spirit that I now recommend some ways to address (or, even in some cases, to avoid) such dilemmas.

## 3.1 The real world's calling: Are you ready?

Before you put yourself forward as a collaborating linguist within an interdisciplinary team project (no matter whether you or a clinical researcher has initiated the contact), it is important to take time for a period of self-reflection: Consider what you could offer the team based on your professional expertise and/or your professional or personal experiences.[6] Identify what real world issues you find intriguing that may be related to the project. Once you have taken the time to consider how you might contribute, do your research: Visit websites, read relevant articles in disciplinary journals, conduct informational interviews with professionals to whom you may have access through friends or colleagues. Based on this work, identify goals and challenges that seem to be central to this area and consider how, if at all, language is implicated in these goals and challenges. Pay special attention to assumptions related to language and communication, especially in relation to theories or methods that are central to the studies. Predict areas of possible match or mismatch between your approach to linguistic analysis and what appears to be the case in other disciplines that are central to the project – and be ready to address these issues.

## 3.2 Getting your foot in the door

Once you have prepared yourself and have been invited to a meeting (whether face-to-face or virtual), aim to communicate in a confident, prepared, professional, open, and engaging manner – in the words of Shuy (2002: 73), you should be able

---

[6] As a useful first step in this process, I recommend reading Goodwin (1994) on the notion of "professional vision" as a backdrop on which to consider how you have learned to "see" in specific ways through your study of linguistics. Following this reflection, move on to consider aspects of your life outside of linguistics (including personal experiences, interests, and other professional training) that have contributed to the way you have come to view the world. In my case, for example, my vision of health care was fundamentally shaped by my own life's journey as a carrier of the Wiskott-Aldrich Syndrome gene and the subsequent bone marrow transplantations that my son (and daughter as his donor) underwent. This period of deep reflection will help you begin to realize the relationship between your own distinctive ways of seeing and your potential to impact the health care world in positive ways.

to navigate the "paradox of being expert, yet understandable" (that is, steer away from using too much jargon – and if you think you must, provide clear and concise definitions). Be prepared to characterize your understanding of linguistics, comparing and contrasting your approach with other ways of investigating language use with which your interlocutor may be familiar. Find out what your conversation partner thinks linguistics[7] is and what it might be able to offer. Taking time at this stage to attune these understandings may fend off possible problems associated with a mismatch regarding thinking about your areas of expertise.

Throughout the interaction, one of your primary goals should be to identify some of the ways in which linguistics might be brought to bear on any of a range of "real world" challenges that are highlighted by your partner. Position yourself as an active learner; ask questions about the goals and challenges you're discerning from the interaction; listen to the responses to these questions with your linguist's "antennae" up; and respond with relevant linguistic approaches coupled with concise relevant illustrations from previous work you have done or with which you are familiar. I have found that placing myself in the position of a learner seems to open up the conversation; it allows me to display genuine happy surprise when I make a link between a framework, strategy, or feature in my linguistic toolbox that would seem to be effective for the job at hand.

### 3.3 Once you're in (AKA "sink or swim")

Once you have made it onto the research team, your work as a linguist negotiating life outside your comfort zone is not done – in fact, it has only just begun. Any future success that the team enjoys will depend to a great extent on all participants – including you – taking the time to make a sustained effort toward the establishment and maintenance of a healthy and respectful working relationship. Based on experiences of my own, as well as those I have witnessed, I offer the following common-sense guidelines.

---

[7] In my experience, many health care professionals who have little or no relationship to the field of linguistics assume linguistics will be most obviously helpful in connection to issues of foreign language use by patients and/or a need for language interpreters in their practices. Additionally, they may consider you to be a "language expert" (in the sense of a prescriptivist) and find themselves "on guard" regarding their own language use in your early interactions with them. To the extent that you are prepared for these possible mindsets, you will be able to address them briefly and move on to discuss other ways in which you may be useful to the team.

1. **Be aware of underlying assumptions, encourage them to come to the surface, and discuss them in detail**: Early in the interdisciplinary relationship, exchange basic publications from your respective fields as they relate to the project at hand. Discuss this literature and elaborate upon it by avoiding jargon and using real-life examples. Identify the assumptions in the studies about the nature of language, interaction, methodology, and whatever else you think might be relevant. Discuss the notions underlying these assumptions, identifying related apparent assumptions on the part of the clinicians and being careful to point out similarities and differences between what you assume and what they assume. Try not to be judgmental; at this point, both sides are learning. If something seems strange or just plain wrong, find out more about it by probing in a relatively neutral way. Robins et al. (2008: 5) advise that "fundamental philosophical differences may not be resolved but workable solutions can be found if the challenges are viewed as philosophical rather than personal."

2. **Continue to build up mutual frames of reference and shared knowledge**: Both sides should begin in the early meetings by defining terms and concepts in as simple a way as possible without, of course, being misleading. Consider thoughtfully at the outset of the project the ways in which language is defined, considered, and characterized within your own and your collaborators' disciplines – and engage in explicit discussions centered on authentic language data with these fellow researchers. Build on these simple definitions in subsequent meetings, bringing in more and more sophistication as the data and discussion warrant it. The time spent bringing underlying assumptions to the surface and working through resulting differences will help to reduce subsequent confusion and frustration. In my experience, this persistence (if done in a low-key way) does eventually pay off. Approximately two years after my first meeting with the Defense Head Injury Project speech and language pathologists, and after relentless emphasis about the importance of context in the analysis of patients' language use in the diagnostic interview, the clinicians eventually decided to initiate a small qualitative study to investigate the ecological validity[8] of the assessment of patients' communicative abilities during the diagnostic interview. In this new study, ratings made by the diagnosing clinician were to be compared with those made independently in more informal settings during the first week of treatment by the therapist. It seemed that my point about the importance of context had finally been accepted as potentially relevant for the clinicians' work.

---

[8] That is the extent to which the patients' test performance predicts behaviors in real world settings.

3. **Respectfully offer assistance in any area of the project that involves language**: Be alert to any opportunity to get in your linguistic "two-cents-worth." Such opportunities may occur at virtually any level: selecting or creating a test battery, performance scale, or interview question; discussions as to how to administer a test, conduct an interview, or carry out other type of institutional interaction; and, importantly, the analysis (at a range of levels of linguistic specificity) of the resulting discourse. Be ready to act as a guinea pig in pilot tests of specific tasks and, importantly, do not be reluctant to discuss the pros and cons of the tasks you just undertook. If you would like your involvement to extend beyond on-site advice, discussion, and analysis to subsequent microanalysis of the data for your own research purposes, discuss this early in your engagement with the clinicians so that they can begin to work out agreements with research staff regarding access to data, necessary permission by the patients in connection with Institutional Review Board (IRB) regulations, and eventual authorship concerns (see also section 3.4 below). All this said, be open to the idea that non-linguist colleagues may not "see" language as being as centrally important to a particular issue as you do (see Hamilton and Chou [2014: 4–5] for more extensive discussion of this notion). No matter how exciting or compelling you may think a particular linguistic finding is, sometimes your colleagues may label it a "fun fact" and question whether it is actually relevant to an important issue within the health care world.

4. **Suggest ways in which your students may become involved in the project**: Setting up a course or series of workshops within which students can work with the data in the ongoing project has the potential to benefit all involved (assuming, of course, that the IRB allows for this kind of engagement). In this way, students will have opportunities to apply what they have been learning about language to a real-life project and to discuss the ups and downs of working in an interdisciplinary endeavor without having individually to seek access to such a project. As the link between the students and the clinicians, you will have opportunities to discuss relevant issues and concerns with other linguists. And, finally, the clinicians will have opportunities to gain new perspectives and insights, including some valuable constructive criticism, regarding their project.

5. **Keep an open mind and be patient**: By keeping an open mind and listening critically to what your team members say, you will learn a great deal about why their assumptions and methodologies are as they are. Real world considerations that enter the discussion may necessitate revision of a task or instrument, or demand a compromise in order to allow the project to proceed. Insisting that things be carried out in the most linguistically informed way may

actually result in your influence being cut off entirely or at least greatly reduced. In my view, if we are indeed trying to use our linguistic knowledge to shape health care in a positive way, keeping communication and influence lines open within the team, even in the face of having to make some concessions, is the prudent choice to make. And finally, be patient: changing assumptions and learning new definitions and methodologies takes time. Do not expect others to be convinced immediately that your approach is the one that should be adopted. A full two years after I had become involved in the Defense Head Injury Project, one of my speech and language pathologist collaborators remarked: "This is all very complex. You've been telling us this and we're finally beginning to understand it." Importantly, if you have been deeply engaged and learning along the trajectory of the project, your own ideas regarding what is relevant and important will be shifting – and you will find yourself having reached a place where you can authentically participate in the "joint problematization" (Sarangi and Candlin 2003) that is the hallmark of successful interdisciplinary efforts.

6. **Retain your outsider status/perspective**: Of course, it is important to attempt to learn as much as you can about the assumptions and methodologies ascribed to by team members with whom you are working. But experience has led me to believe that you will continue to be most beneficial to the professional relationship if you keep your linguist identity firmly intact. Your knowledge about the other discipline will help you design more convincing arguments and fend off additional potential criticism (e.g., frequently in the areas of sample size and the relative value of small studies); it will also help you focus in on the most crucial areas of application. But it is only by continuing to provide information as yet unknown to your team members and by continuing to play devil's advocate that you can help move the project in the direction in which you anticipate it would be most successful. This will usually be welcomed within a healthy interdisciplinary team. To illustrate, during a team meeting after I had offered yet another piece of constructive criticism followed by an apologetic remark ("That's just from my perspective, of course"), one of my colleagues commented, "That's okay, Heidi. We need you to be different!"

## 3.4 What's next?

As a given interdisciplinary team project nears its completion, you will undoubtedly be involved in the process of creating products meant to disseminate key research outcomes. These may take the interactional form of conference presentations or professional training sessions or webinars (including those that may count toward professionals' continuing medical education) or the written form of co-authored publications. And, although this phase of your involvement may well be the most gratifying in terms of your work reaching a wider audience, it may also be an area in which you may be caught off guard. In my experience, disciplinary differences between linguistics and team science related to co-authorship practices occasionally ruffle the feathers of team members who up until that point have enjoyed a healthy working relationship. Frank conversations at several points along a given research project trajectory with reference to published guidelines about co-authorship (see Fontanarosa, Bauchner, and Flanagin 2017; Hundley, van Teijlingen, and Simkhada 2013; Robins et al. 2008: 6)[9] may help to bring these differences to the surface and to facilitate subsequent decisions in this potentially fraught area.

Before moving on to your next project, take time to reflect on what you have gained during your time as an interdisciplinary team member. What aspects of linguistics were particularly well received by others? When did you receive pushback and did your given response at the time appear to be convincing? Were any of the findings you enthusiastically brought to team meetings met with withering responses? Were you stretched to the point of feeling uncomfortable as key nuances in your discussion or analysis were swept away in the service of a quicker, less detailed one? Tuck these insights away to be used in your next project; by recognizing the importance of this iterative process, you will keep learning. You will begin your next participation at a more informed level and will continue to grow in your overall abilities and importance to the team.

## 4 In closing

Interdisciplinary encounters that come along with the application of linguistics to health care concerns can range from the highly frustrating to the highly gratifying. As noted throughout this chapter, sometimes frustrations enter when "real life" intervenes; in my case, a hospital wing unexpectedly closed due to financial constraints early in our data collection, colleagues moved on to new professional positions, and my young son needed to undergo two bone marrow transplantations. These kinds of issues cannot be controlled.

---

**9** See also advice from the Office of Research Integrity of the United States Department of Health and Human Services: https://ori.hhs.gov/authorship-issues-and-conflicts-interest

More typically, whether you find yourself batting your head against the wall of indifference to linguists' perspectives on language or you find yourself in a nurturing learning environment has very much to do with a sense of common purpose among all concerned and an open-mindedness regarding the inevitable divergent – and sometimes opposing – viewpoints. Similar to the work that goes into becoming fluent enough in world languages to be able to translate in a highly nuanced way between them, "[r]esearchers who inhabit both academic and applied worlds not only need to become fluent in the codes of each context, they also need to develop the ability to translate each world's logic to the other one" (Wasson 2004: 122).

And of all these possible differences, the way in which representatives of various disciplines view language is arguably the most critical. While running the risk of overgeneralization, researchers trained in fields outside what Bucholtz and Hall (2005) call "sociocultural linguistics"[10] tend to consider language in a more static way than do scholars who were trained within this sociocultural approach to language. And since many health research teams comprise individuals who have disciplinary backgrounds in medicine, nursing, public health, psychology, and social work, it is likely that a linguist's perspective on language will be in the minority. Illustrations of this non-linguistic understanding of language include the identification of stable lexical meanings that are understood to reflect the world directly; the connection of single functions to individual grammatical structures; and a focus on standard language use (sometimes in a prescriptivist way, although not always) to the exclusion of regional, social, and stylistic variation. These practices are in stark contrast to sociocultural language scholars' dynamic notions of lexical and utterance meaning with the accompanying theoretical interest in socially meaningful variation and the conceptualization of discourse as being interactively co-constructed. In the dynamic view, language does not merely reflect the world but works to create it as well, along with its myriad meanings, social dynamics, relationships, and institutions.

These contrasting understandings of language, not surprisingly, are associated with different research paradigms. One finds, for example, that the more static understanding of language works most expediently with quantitative and positivist approaches to research, whereas the dynamic understanding of language is more philosophically aligned with qualitative research methods.

---

10 "By sociocultural linguistics, we mean the broad interdisciplinary field concerned with the intersection of language, culture, and society. This term encompasses the disciplinary subfields of sociolinguistics, linguistic anthropology, socially oriented forms of discourse analysis (such as conversation analysis and critical discourse analysis), and linguistically oriented social psychology, among others" (Bucholtz and Hall 2005: 586).

Specifically, in hypothesis-driven scientific endeavors, replicability as well as internal and external validity characterize methodological rigor; in studies of this type, it is preferable to work with an understanding of language that has less "wiggle room" in its definitions, so that language data can be coded and counted with a high degree of inter-rater reliability. Given the tighter operational definitions, such approaches can handle vastly larger datasets much more efficiently (see Chou et al. 2011).

The dynamic understanding of language, on the other hand, tends to work more smoothly with qualitative studies that seek to understand situated interpretation; i.e., how "hearers infer speakers' underlying strategies and intentions by interpreting the linguistic cues which contextualize their messages" (Schiffrin 1987: 21). Because such researchers seek to understand "joint efforts from interactants to integrate knowing, meaning, speaking, and doing" (Schiffrin 1987: 29) in interactional discourse, the datasets tend to be much smaller (to allow for such fine-grained and nuanced analyses) with ecological validity a primary aim.

These differences can be mind-boggling and highly challenging at times. But, as argued above, a significant investment in time and effort to discuss relative values of each type of approach can lead to the desired outcome of moving beyond differences in assumptions toward a joint solution. It is in this important way that interested and engaged linguists can find themselves to be critically important parts of valuable interdisciplinary team efforts focused centrally on the work of improving health communication and associated health-related issues.

# References

Ainsworth-Vaughn, Nancy. 1998. *Claiming power in doctor-patient talk*. Oxford: Oxford University Press.

Al Zidjaly, Najma. 2015. *Disability, discourse and technology: Agency and inclusion in (inter)action*. London: Palgrave Macmillan.

Alatis, James E., Heidi E. Hamilton & Ai-hui Tan (eds). 2002. *Language, linguistics, and the professions: Education, journalism, law, medicine, and technology (GURT 2000)*. Washington, DC: Georgetown University Press.

Albert, Martin L. & Janice E. Knoefel (eds.). 2011. *Clinical neurology of aging*, 3rd edn. Oxford: Oxford University Press.

Barry, Michael J. & Susan Edgman-Levitan. 2012. Shared decision-making: Pinnacle of patient-centered care. *New England Journal of Medicine* 366 (9). 780–781.

Benkendorf, Judith, Michele Prince, Heidi E. Hamilton, Mary Rose & Anna DeFina. 2001. Does indirect speech promote nondirective genetic counseling? *American Journal of Medical Genetics* 106. 199–207.

Blatt, Benjamin, Noemi Alice Spinazzi & Larrie Greenberg. 2014. Communication skills training for resident physicians: a physician-educator perspective. In Heidi E. Hamilton & Wen-

ying Sylvia Chou (eds.), *The Routledge handbook of language and health communication*, 294–326. New York: Routledge.
Bucholtz, Mary & Kira Hall. 2005. Identity and interaction: A sociocultural approach. *Discourse Studies* 7 (4–5). 585–614.
Capps, Lisa & Elinor Ochs. 1995. *Constructing panic: The discourse of agoraphobia*. Cambridge: Harvard University Press.
Charon, Rita. 2014. Why read and write in the clinic? The contributions of narrative medicine to health care. In Heidi E. Hamilton & Wen-ying Sylvia Chou (eds.), *The Routledge handbook of language and health communication*, 245–258. New York: Routledge.
Chou, Wen-Ying Sylvia, Paul Han, Alison Pilsner, Kisha Coa, Larrie Greenberg & Benjamin Blatt. 2011. Interdisciplinary research on patient-provider communication: A cross-method comparison. *Communication & Medicine* 8. 29–40.
Coupland, Nikolas. 1997. Language, ageing and ageism: a project for applied linguistics? *International Journal of Applied Linguistics* 7 (1). 26–48.
Crampton, Noah H., Shmuel Reis & Aviv Shachak. 2016. Computers in the clinical encounter: a scoping review and thematic analysis. *Journal of the American Medical Informatics Association* 23. 654–665.
Cresswell, John W. & Vicki L. Plano Clark. 2017. *Designing and conducting mixed methods research*, 2nd edn. Thousand Oaks: Sage.
Cuddy, Monica M. & Steven J. Peitzman. 2015. Performance in physical examination on the USMLE Step 2 Clinical Skills Examination. *Academic Medicine* 90 (2). 209–213.
Davidson, Bradley, Diane Blum, David Cella, Heidi E. Hamilton, Lillian Nail & Roger Waltzman. 2007. Communicating about chemotherapy-induced anemia and related fatigue: Recommendations from an observational linguistic study. *Journal of Supportive Oncology* 5. 36–40, 46.
Ehrlich, Jonathan S. & Amy Sipes. 1985. Group treatment of communication skills for head trauma patients. *Cognitive Rehabilitation* 3 (1). 32–37.
Ferrara, Kathleen. 1994. *Therapeutic ways with words*. Oxford: Oxford University Press.
Fontanarosa, Phil, Howard Bauchner & Annette Flanagin. 2017. Authorship and team science. *JAMA (Journal of the American Medical Association)* 318 (24). 2433–2437.
Goodwin, Charles. 1994. Professional vision. *American Anthropologist* 96 (3). 606–633.
Goodwin, Charles. 2013. The cooperative transformative organization of human action and knowledge. *Journal of Pragmatics* 46 (1). 8–23.
Gordon, Cynthia, Michele Prince, Judith Benkendorf & Heidi E. Hamilton. 2002. "People say it's a little uncomfortable": Prenatal genetic counselors' use of constructed dialogue to reference procedural pain. *Journal of Genetic Counseling* 11. 245–263.
Graham, Sage. 2009. Hospitalk: Politeness and hierarchical structures in interdisciplinary discharge rounds. *Journal of Politeness Research* 5. 11–31.
Guetterman, Timothy C, Rae V. Sakakibara, Vicki L. Plano Clark, Mark Luborsky, Sarah M. Murray, Felipe González Castro, John W. Creswell, Charles Deutsch & Joseph J. Gallo. 2019. Mixed methods grant applications in the health sciences: An analysis of reviewer comments. *PLoS ONE* 14 (11). e0225308.
Gumperz, John. 1982. *Discourse strategies*. Cambridge: Cambridge University Press.
Gumperz, John. 1999. On interactional sociolinguistic method. In Srikant Sarangi & Cecilia Roberts (eds.), *Talk, work and institutional order*, 453–471. Berlin: Mouton.
Hamilton, Heidi E. 1994. *Conversations with an Alzheimer's patient: An interactional sociolinguistic study*. Cambridge: Cambridge University Press.

Hamilton, Heidi E. 1998. Reported speech and survivor identity in on-line bone marrow transplantation narratives. *Journal of Sociolinguistics* 2 (1). 53–67.

Hamilton, Heidi E. 2003. Patients' voices in the medical world: An exploration of accounts of noncompliance. In Deborah Tannen & James E. Alatis (eds.), *Linguistics, language, and the real world: Discourse and beyond*, 147–165. Washington, DC: Georgetown University Press.

Hamilton, Heidi E. 2004. Symptoms and signs in particular: The influence of the medical condition on the shape of physician-patient talk. *Communication & Medicine* 1. 59–70.

Hamilton, Heidi E. 2019. *Language, dementia and meaning making: Navigating challenges of cognition and face in everyday life*. Cham: Palgrave Macmillan.

Hamilton, Heidi E., Meaghan Nelson & Cynthia Gordon. 2006a. Physicians, nurses and patients communicating in Hepatitis C: An in-office sociolinguistic study. *Gastroenterology Nursing* 29 (5). 364–370.

Hamilton, Heidi E., Meaghan Nelson, Paul Martin & Scott Cotler. 2006b. Communication and comprehension of response in Hepatitis C. *Clinical Gastroenterology and Hepatology* 4 (4). 507–513.

Hamilton, Heidi E., Cynthia Gordon, Meaghan Nelson, Paul Martin & Scott Cotler. 2008. "'We're talking about cure": How physicians describe outcomes to HCV therapy. *Journal of Clinical Gastroenterology* 42. 419–424.

Hamilton, Heidi E. & Wen-Ying Sylvia Chou. 2014. Introduction: Health communication as applied linguistics. In Heidi E. Hamilton & Wen-ying Sylvia Chou (eds.), *The Routledge handbook of language and health communication*, 1–12. New York: Routledge.

Hamilton, Heidi E. & Toshiko Hamaguchi. 2015. Discourse and aging. In Deborah Tannen, Heidi E. Hamilton & Deborah Schiffrin (eds.), *The handbook of discourse analysis*, 705–727. Oxford: Wiley Blackwell.

Heritage, John & Douglas Maynard. 2006. *Communication in medical care: Interaction between primary care physicians and patients*. Cambridge: Cambridge University Press.

Herring, Susan & Jannis Androutsopoulos. 2015. Computer-mediated discourse 2.0. In Deborah Tannen, Heidi E. Hamilton & Deborah Schiffrin (eds.), *The handbook of discourse analysis*, 127–151. Oxford: Wiley Blackwell.

Higgins, Christina & Bonnie Norton (eds). 2009. *Language and HIV/AIDS*. Bristol: Multilingual Matters.

Hundley, Vanora, Edwin van Teijlingen & Padam Simkhada, P. 2013. Academic authorship: Who, why and in what order? *Health Renaissance* 11 (2). 98–101.

Hunter, Kathryn Montgomery. 1991. *Doctors' stories: The narrative structure of medical knowledge*. Princeton: Princeton University Press.

Jones, Rodney. 2013. *Health and risk communication: An applied linguistic perspective*. New York: Routledge.

Jones, Rodney. 2015. Discourse and health communication. In Deborah Tannen, Heidi E. Hamilton & Deborah Schiffrin (eds.), *The handbook of discourse analysis*, 841–857. Oxford: Wiley Blackwell.

Kendall, Jason. 2003. Designing an research project: Randomized controlled trials and their principles. *Emergency Medicine Journal* 20 (2). 164–168.

Kress, Gunther. 2010. *Multimodality: A social semiotic approach to contemporary communication*. New York: Routledge.

Lamb, Christopher C., Yunmei Wang & Kalle Lyytinen. 2019. Share decision making: Does a physician's decision-making style affect patient participation in treatment choices for primary immunodeficiency? *Journal of Evaluation in Clinical Practice* 25. 1102–1110.

Larson, Elaine, Heidi E. Hamilton, Kathleen Mitchell & John Eisenberg. 1998. Hospitalk: An exploratory study to assess what is said and what is done between physicians and nurses. *Clinical Performance and Quality Health Care* 6. 183–189.

Manolio, Teri A., Carol J. Bult, Rex L. Chisholm, Patricia A. Deverka, Geoffrey S. Ginsburg, Gail P. Jarvik, Howard L. McLeod, George A. Mensah, Mary V. Relling, Dan M. Roden, Robb Rowley, Cecelia Tamburro, Marc S. Williams & Eric D. Green. 2019. Genomic medicine year in review: 2019. *American Journal of Human Genetics* 105 (6). P1072–1075.

Mattingly, Cheryl. 1998. *Healing dramas and clinical plots: The narrative structure of experience*. Cambridge: Cambridge University Press.

Nelson, Meaghan & Heidi E. Hamilton. 2007. Improving in-office discussion of chronic obstructive pulmonary disease: Results and recommendations from an in-office linguistic study in COPD. *The American Journal of Medicine* 120 (8A). S28–S32.

Nevile, Maurice, Pentti Haddington, Trine Heinemann & Mirka Rauniomaa. 2014. On the interactional ecology of objects. In Maurice Nevile, Pentti Haddington, Trine Heinemann & Mirka Rauniomaa (eds.), *Interacting with objects: Language, materiality, and social activity*, 3–26. Amsterdam & Philadelphia: John Benjamins Publishing Company.

Obler, Loraine K. & Kris Gjerlow. 1999. *Language and the brain*. Cambridge: Cambridge University Press.

Peräkylä, Anssi. 1995. *AIDS counselling: Institutional discourse and clinical practice*. Cambridge: Cambridge University Press.

Prutting, Carol A. & Diane M. Kirchner. 1987. A clinical appraisal of the pragmatic aspects of language. *Journal of Speech and Hearing Disorders* 52. 105–119.

Ribeiro, Branca. 1994. *Coherence in psychotic discourse*. Oxford: Oxford University Press.

Roberts, Celia. 1997. There's nothing so practical as some good theories. *International Journal of Applied Linguistics* 7 (1). 66–78.

Roberts, Felicia. 1999. *Talking about treatment: Recommendations for breast cancer adjuvant therapy*. Oxford: Oxford University Press.

Robins, Cynthia, Norma Ware, Susan Dosreis, Cathleen Willging, Joyce Chung & Roberto Lewis-Fernández. 2008. Dialogues on mixed-methods and mental health services research: Anticipating challenges, building solutions. *Psychiatric Services* 59. 727–731.

Robinson, James D., Jeanine W. Turner & Kelly S. Wood. 2015. Patient perceptions of acute care telemedicine: A pilot investigation. *Health Communication* 30 (12). 1269–1276.

Rubin, Donald. 2014. Applied linguistics as a resource for understanding and advancing health literacy. In Heidi E. Hamilton & Wen-Ying Sylvia Chou (eds.), *The Routledge handbook of language and health communication*, 153–167. New York: Routledge.

Sarangi, Srikant & Christopher Candlin. 2003. Trading between reflexivity and relevance: New challenges for applied linguistics. *Applied Linguistics* 24 (3). 271–285.

Sarangi, Srikant & Angus Clarke. 2002. Zones of expertise and the management of uncertainty in genetics risk communication. *Research on Language and Social Interaction* 35. 139–171.

Schiffrin, Deborah. 1987. *Discourse markers*. Cambridge: Cambridge University Press.

Shay, L. Aubree & Jennifer Elston Lafata. 2015. Where is the evidence? A systematic review of shared decision making and patient outcomes. *Medical Decision Making* 35 (1). 114–131.

Shuy, Roger. 2002. Breaking into language and law: The trials of the insider-linguist. In James E. Alatis, Heidi E. Hamilton & Ai-hui Tan (eds.), *Language, linguistics, and the professions: Education, journalism, law, medicine, and technology (GURT 2000)*, 67–80. Washington, DC: Georgetown University Press.

Stommel, Wyke. 2009. *Entering an online support group on eating disorders: A discourse analysis*. Amsterdam: Rodopi.

Tsai, Mei-hui, Feng-hwa Lu & Richard M. Frankel. 2014. Teaching medical students to become discourse analysts: From conversational transcripts to clinical applications. In Heidi E. Hamilton & Wen-ying Sylvia Chou (eds.), *The Routledge handbook of language and health communication*, 327–343. New York: Routledge.

Turner, Jeanine. 1996. *Communicative implications of implementing telemedicine technology: A framework of telecompetence*. Columbus: The Ohio State University dissertation.

Turner, Jeanine, James D. Robinson, Yan Tian, Alan Neustadtl, Pam Angelus, Marie Russell, Seong K. Mun & Betty Levine. 2013. Can messages make a difference? The association between E-mail messages and health outcomes in diabetes patients. *Human Communication Research* 39 (2). 252–268.

Wasson, Christina. 2004. Review of James E. Alatis, Heidi E. Hamilton & Ai-Hui Tan (eds.). 2002. *Linguistics, language and the professions: Education, journalism, law, medicine, and technology*. Washington, DC: Georgetown University Press. *Language in Society* 33. 121–124.

Zarcadoolas, Christina & Wendy Vaughon. 2014. If numbers could speak: Numeracy and the digital revolution. In Heidi E. Hamilton & Wen-Ying Sylvia Chou (eds.), *The Routledge handbook of language and health communication*, 61–74. New York: Routledge.

# Index

academic language socialization  89, 93, 97
Actor-Network theory  131
African American Language  14–15, 41–42, 45–54
American English  101, 191
architecture  191–204
assemblage  4, 75–76, 99–104, 107–109, 111–117, 123–124, 129–138, 134n4, 147, 152, 158, 163, 175

Biblical Studies  247
Biblical texts and interpretation  93
big data  219
brand identification  261

ceramic objects  143
chronotope  175
Classification  119, 143, 145–147, 149, 152, 156–159
Community of practice  1, 13, 54
corpora  10, 219, 276
creaky voice  63–64, 67–68
creole culture  194, 199
Creole languages  47, 52, 62
critical applied linguistics  100, 118–119
Critical Discourse Analysis  73
critical race theory  16, 41–42, 44, 47, 53–54, 89
Critical White Studies  247
crosstalk  284

dialect atlases. *See* Linguistic Atlas Project
dialectology  10, 53, 217
digital humanities  10, 103
disciplinary borrowing  210–214, 224
distributive agency  116
domestic life  193, 202

economics  1, 4–5, 59, 74, 79–81, 83, 85, 89, 209, 262–264, 266–267, 273
ecosophy  78–79, 81, 84
embodied language  176
embodiment  2, 116, 173, 175–176
enregisterment  116, 176

entextualization  177, 182
epistemes  111, 122–124
Ethnography  12–13, 49, 89–94, 96–97, 134–135, 145, 170–172, 175, 180, 182–183, 276, 279, 281
ethnography of communication  92, 97

Gaelic  62, 182
Gender  17, 24, 43, 47, 49, 51, 59–60, 63, 65, 67–68, 89, 122, 132, 172, 176, 209, 218
gossip  65–67, 171
Grammatical gender  60–61
group, archaeological  147

health communication  275
historical sociolinguistics  207–210, 212–220, 216n13, 222–225
homeownership  259–261

indigenous languages  62–63, 120
intersectionality theory  23–24, 43–44, 49–50, 52, 54

L2 teaching  234, 241
language commoditization  180
language contact  129–130, 134, 136
language ideological assemblage  129–130, 132–137, 139
language ideology  27, 48, 59, 120–121, 130–133, 136–138, 170–172, 178
language materiality  170
language revitalization  121, 134, 136, 138
lazy reason  121
learning communities  32
Linguistic Atlas Project  10, 99, 101–102
linguistic imperialism  72

materiality  2–3, 5, 99, 116, 169–173, 175–176, 179, 182–184
mediatization  172, 179
metaphor  1–2, 3, 73–74, 76, 120, 129
mock Spanish  174
multilingualism  120, 133, 137

narrative  8, 54, 73, 94, 107, 181, 256, 260–261, 264–266, 268–271, 273, 275–276, 280–281
natural gender  60–61

perceptual dialectology  10
performativity  1, 177, 248
Positive Discourse Analysis  82
posthumanist applied linguistics  122
practice theory  1, 54

qualisigns  177

raciolinguistics  50
regional dialects  191

self-avowed authority syndrome  59
semiotic assemblage  111, 114–115, 117, 123
semiotic ecosystem  117

Social Network Theory (SNT)  1, 212
Spanish  51, 54, 61–62, 67, 238
Spanglish  51
standard language ideology  50
style shifting  46–47, 49
symbolic revalorization  67

third wave studies  13, 44
translanguaging  134
type, archaeological  147
type-variety method  147
typology  5, 149–150, 153, 156

variety, archaeological  147
voice  175

white hybridity  248, 253
wonderbreading  248–249, 251

www.ingramcontent.com/pod-product-compliance
Lightning Source LLC
Chambersburg PA
CBHW031422150426
43191CB00006B/360